D1609897

The Selected Works of
Cyril Connolly

Volume Two: The Two Natures

The Selected Works of Cyril Connolly

Volume Two:
The Two Natures

CYRIL CONNOLLY

*Edited and with an Introduction
by Matthew Connolly*

PICADOR

First published 2002 by Picador
an imprint of Pan Macmillan Ltd
Pan Macmillan, 20 New Wharf Road, London N1 9RR
Basingstoke and Oxford
Associated companies throughout the world
www.panmacmillan.com

ISBN 0 330 48600 4

1 3 5 7 9 8 6 4 2

A CIP catalogue record for this book is available
from the British Library.

Typeset by SX Composing DTP, Rayleigh, Essex
Printed and bound in Great Britain by
Mackays of Chatham plc, Chatham, Kent

For my family

Contents

Acknowledgements

Thanks to my mother for encouraging this project; Peter Straus for his enthusiasm; everyone at Picador, especially Pete Ouvry for his consistent care; William Boyd for the foreword; Deborah Rogers, my father's agent; Jeremy Lewis, ahead of me at every turn; the London Library, for having lots of books; Colindale for long, happy days of microfilm; Bella for lending her flat; Mary for the quote; and anybody interested enough to read this.

Matthew Connolly

Additional Poems and *Last Poems* by A. E. Housman. Extracts reprinted by permission of the Society of Authors as the Literary Representative of the Estate of A. E. Housman.

Modern Symposium by Goldsworthy Lowes Dickinson. Extract reprinted by kind permission of the Provost and Scholars of King's College, Cambridge.

'On a Political Prisoner' from *Michael Robartes and the Dancer* by W. B. Yeats. Extract reprinted by permission of A. P. Watt Ltd on behalf of Michael B. Yeats.

Extract from Siren Land by Norman Douglas reprinted by permission of The Society of Authors as the Literary Representative of the Estate of Norman Douglas.

Introduction

The title of Volume One, *The Modern Movement*, is, I hope, self-explanatory. This second volume, which contains works of a more personal character, had no obvious title waiting. But in the introduction to his 1973 collection *The Evening Colonnade* (a phrase from Pope) Cyril Connolly lists several other quotations that he had considered as a source of possible titles, including these lines of Wordsworth from the concluding book of *The Prelude*:

> In wholesome separation the two natures
> The one that feels, the other that observes

He felt that this could be applied to his love of nature and of books; but it seems especially appropriate to this collection, with its mix of passions and parodies.

He went on to note that these two natures were within him by inheritance, from his mother and father respectively; and that their separation was far from wholesome. This is not referred to, however, in the first piece in this volume, 'A Georgian Boyhood', which 'deliberately leaves out all those episodes in my life which do not further the growth of those literary speculations on which the first part [of *Enemies of Promise*, to be found in Volume One of this selection] is based'. Indeed, the inner conflict in his psychological makeup 'all but froze me in a permanent block', and so has no place in this 'autobiography of ideas'. The other strand linking this section of *Enemies of Promise* to its predecessors is style: the language is intended to combine "the rapidity of the colloquial with an elasticity permitting incursions into the

Mandarin of prose poetry'. Without endangering this style, I have taken the opportunity to make some minor corrections to family details; one that would require more drastic revision, however, is the sentence mentioning how his mother's family acquired their Dublin home, where he amalgamates two brothers who were on opposing sides in the Civil War. The castle is now a luxurious hotel; it would be nice to imagine Connolly devotees checking in, clutching celluloid seals, before undergoing mock beheadings in the car park with Brian Boru's (apocryphal) sword.

'An Edwardian Boyhood' concentrates on schooldays; the name 'St Wulfric's' masks the real life St Cyprian's, later savaged by Orwell in his essay 'Such, Such Were the Joys' (written at Connolly's suggestion but too inflammatory to be published at the time). It is to be regretted that the account is terminated before Connolly arrives 'up' at Oxford, and an impression of his time there has to be pieced together from other sources. I have included one such brief reference in 'A London Diary', a column written the year before *Enemies of Promise*; those interested in 'what happened next' are directed to the books recommended by William Boyd in his foreword to Volume One.

The other lengthy work in this volume is *The Unquiet Grave*, here chronologically cushioned by two pairs of meditations on the natural and observable worlds. *The Unquiet Grave* was published under the pseudonym 'Palinurus', and later editions were able to proclaim 'with an introduction by Cyril Connolly' (included here), although its authorship was never any great mystery. For many people this book is itself the masterpiece alluded to in the first sentence, but it has always been frowned upon by more puritan elements. It is essentially an outpost of romanticism, taking as its themes nature, art, nostalgia, melancholy, love, death, the restructuring of society and a search for enlightened spirituality that Connolly was to characterize elsewhere as 'Christian Humanism': 'even if Jesus did exist we shall still have to invent Him'. By the use of quotation he expands the Romantic tradition backwards and outwards; and also extends it forwards through inheritors such as Baudelaire and the Surrealists – with whom, though never a surrealist himself, he was however a sympathizer, writing the movement's post-war obituary and describing surrealism as 'essentially romantic, ego-centric and satirical'.

Is Fat a Romanticist Issue? *The Unquiet Grave* also contains Connolly's often-quoted and misquoted fat man/thin man aphorism. It has spawned many variants – I particularly like the one where the fat person claims to have several thin people inside him. Orwell writes in *Coming up for Air* that 'there's a thin man inside every fat man, just as they say there's a statue inside every block of stone'. This is a clever metaphor, but the similarity of the two quotes belies the fact that they have different meanings; Orwell makes the observation from his position as a gaunt novelist, Connolly really is signalling from the inside. It is not just a throwaway line, it is a plea for clemency. His 'new-year resolution', 'lose a stone, then all the rest will follow' he later amended to 'lose a stone and it will find its own way back'.

Of his worldly pleasures, house-hunting is included as an example here (book collecting appears in Volume One). A postscript to this piece is that a house in 'Folksbourne' – that is, Eastbourne – was indeed to be his first owned home and his final address, and he is now to be honoured by a blue plaque commemorating his residency there.

Next we edge into fiction, albeit well informed by fact. When asked to contribute an essay on sloth to a series on the seven deadly sins, Connolly instead produced a short story on the subject of covetousness, 'The Downfall of Jonathan Edax'. His two most celebrated parodies follow: 'Told in Gath' (its title derived from the same biblical verse as Huxley's *Eyeless in Gaza*), and a satire on his contemporary Brian Howard (Waugh's Ambrose Silk and a half of his Anthony Blanche), 'Where Engels Fears to Tread'. 'Write your lethal parody when you are young,' he wrote a quarter of a century later, or else 'tolerance, compassion, appreciation will do their fell work'. Huxley had been his modern literary hero; this represented a 'spiritual kicking away of a ladder'.

Following a visit to the Nazis' infamous 'Degenerate [i.e. modern] Art' display in Munich, Connolly wrote 'Year Nine'. While it failed to

stop Hitler, this satire may nevertheless possess an enduring significance: Michael Shelden, Orwell's biographer, argued that it may well
have been an inspiration for *Nineteen Eighty-Four*. Just as Evelyn
Waugh seemed to be the spectre at the feast in Volume One, so this
volume seems to involve a curious game of leapfrog between Connolly
and his formative friend, Orwell.

'Bond Strikes Camp' represents another symbiotic friendship, this
time with Ian Fleming: Connolly provided Fleming with authentic
details for the Bond stories, and Fleming was pleased to act as fact-
checker for Connolly's subversion of his famous creation. It is a
precursor, though probably not an inspiration, to a whole genre of
underground writing, 'slash lit' (from the slash between the protagonists' names, e.g. Holmes/Watson), that chronicles the gay lives of
fictional characters.*

Fiction tends back towards autobiography in the penultimate piece,
'Happy Deathbeds'. This is a long fragment exhumed and edited by my
father's biographer Jeremy Lewis, whose extremely enjoyable book has
been invaluable to my own researches. The piece was probably written
in 1948 or 1949 and received its first publication in 1996 in America.
It has since appeared in France as a *livre de poche* (as have the Bond and
Edax stories – Connolly's deep appreciation of France is reciprocated),
but this is its first publication in its entirety in Britain. It is set at the end
of the Horizon period, and anybody with an interest in those times will
have no problem in identifying those protagonists scantily veiled by
pseudonyms. Connolly's alter ego, 'Brinkley', is a name plucked from
his own ancestry and is mentioned in that context in the opening piece
in this volume.† Others are not veiled at all, such as Dick (Wyndham),
a remarkable character who was wounded in the Great War and
awarded the MC but later became a writer, painter and photographer.
He was killed while reporting in Palestine in 1948 and the piece
includes a sustained elegy for him. His millhouse at Tickerage in Sussex

*Mainly written by women. See an essay on the subject in *Inappropriate Behaviour*
(Serpent's Tail).
†A later and shorter Brinkley adventure, also unearthed by Jeremy Lewis, appeared in the
London Magazine October/November 1997 issue.

was earlier described in *The Unquiet Grave* (see p.134). There is also a cameo appearance by the fictive Goldprick, an early incarnation of Fleming's Goldfinger – a relationship now further enlivened by yet another Bond spoof, as Austin Powers squares up to Goldmember on screen.

The collection ends with the essay on poetry that he wrote in hospital and which proved to be his final article, published after his death in 1974. In setting forth his favourite poets Connolly looks back over his life and touches on themes that serve to draw together these two volumes; naturally he includes *The Prelude*. His first words to be published in a book were verse, under the nom de plume of Presto alongside Desmond MacCarthy, including the lines:

> And so I add a rhyme or two;
> they are not good, they are not true

which seem to echo his final words to his audience:
> But it is there, it will do.

Matthew Connolly
May 2002

Enemies of Promise
(1938)

Part Three: A Georgian Boyhood

Yet hark how through the peopled air
   The busy murmur glows,
The insect youth are on the wing
Eager to taste the bonied spring
   And float amid the liquid noon.
Some lightly o'er the current swim
Some shew their gayly gilded trim
   Quick-glancing to the sun.

GRAY

'What sort of thing is Tydeus?'
'Tydeus rose and set at Eton: he is only
Known here to be a scholar of Kings.'

[West to Walpole: Walpole to West,
        October, 1735]

Altro dirti non vo'; ma la tua festa
Ch'anco tardi a venire non ti sia grave.

LEOPARDI

17 *Credentials*

Up to this point the function of this work has been entirely critical and performed with those privileges of the critic which allow him to assume equality with those whom he criticizes and to take their books to pieces as if he were their equal in stature. But this equality is a fiction, just as it is a fiction that a juryman is superior to the temptations and stupidities of the prisoner he judges or qualified to convict a company director on a point of corporation law. A critic is a product of his time who may affect impartiality but who, while claiming authority over the reader, projects his doubt and aspiration. Every critic writes as if he were infallible, and pretends that he is the embodiment of impartial intellectual sanity, a reasonable though omniscient pontiff. But without his surplice the preacher of the loftiest sermon is only human or sub-human, and now is the moment to step down from the pulpit, to disrobe in the vestry. The autobiography which follows is intended to be such a disrobing; it is meant to be an analysis of the grounding in life and art which the critic received, of the ideas which formed him in youth; the education, the ideals, the disappointments from which are drawn his experience, the fashions he may unwittingly follow and the flaws he may conceal.

A critic is an instrument which registers certain observations; before the reader can judge of their value he must know sufficient of the accuracy of the instrument to allow for the margin of error. We grow up among theories and illusions common to our class, our race, our time. We absorb them unawares and their effect is incalculable. What are they? In this case, I am trying to find out, hoping that all I discover, however personal, may prove of use. To do so I have to refer to something which I find intolerable, the early aura of large houses, fallen fortunes and country families common to so many English autobiographers. If the reader can stomach this, I will try to make it up to him.

18 *The Branching Ogham*

I have always disliked myself at any given moment; the total of such moments is my life.

The first occurred on the morning of the 10th of September 1903 when I was born at Coventry where my father had gone to look after a body referred to as 'The Volunteers'. My father was in the regular army. His father, Admiral Connolly, son of a General Connolly and nephew to various other veterans of the wars with France, belonged to a naval family long resident in Bath where he had married late in life the eldest daughter of the then Rector of Bath, Charles Kemble, who had restored the Abbey in the Victorian taste and who inhabited what is now the Spa Hotel. The Kembles of Overtown near Swindon were West Country squires who in the eighteenth century had gravitated to London and Bray and made a fortune in the tea trade. Charles Kemble had inherited the wealth of these nabobs and from his mother, Miss Brooke, the estate of Cowbridge House, Malmesbury, which he had rebuilt in the baroque style with Italian workmen from the Great Exhibition. The vigorous, dominating, millionaire Rector of Bath was said to be too Broad-Church in his views to be made a Bishop, for from Wadham he had joined the Clapham Sect. The Connollys, however, were a frugal, blue-eyed, long-lived, quiet, tidy, obstinate race of soldiers and sailors; the Admiral's uncle, Captain Matthew Connolly, had been a kind of arbiter of Bath elegance in the reign of George IV. There was something eighteenth-century about the Connollys, while the Kembles were eminently Victorian. My grandfather, the Admiral, was born in 1816 and had done much of his sailing in the Mediterranean and the Pacific on wooden ships of which he was a great defender against the 'ironclad'. He was older than my grandmother, older than the Rector, his father-in-law, and died in 1901 at his house in Marlborough Buildings, Bath, with a great reputation for good looks of the genial, bearded, crusty, open sort, charm, gallantry, temper, and bad language.

Meanwhile the Rector's fortune had vanished among his eleven children, his rectory had become a public school, his country houses all been sold. He left a book called *Memorials of a Closed Ministry* and a Victorian gothic church he had built at Stockwell. The fifty thousand pounds he had contributed to the restoration of the Abbey was a bitter memory to his grandchild, whose frequent complaints about it to my mother afforded me at an early age a grudge against society. I never had a chance! Both my great-grandfather the Rector and my great-great uncle Mathew Connolly have their monuments in the Abbey and windows commemorate my great-uncle Brooke Kemble who was drowned off Tunis as a midshipman, and other members of the family. That quiet corner where are grouped in such incongruous harmony the Roman Bath, the Gothic Abbey and the eighteenth-century Colonnade is not the less sultry for enclosing my roots.

In 1900 when my father's regiment was on a visit to Ireland he met and married my mother, the daughter of Colonel Edward Vernon, D.L., J.P., of Clontarf Castle, outside Dublin. The Vernons of Clontarf were a branch of the Vernons of Haddon Hall and Tong who had come over to Ireland with the Duke of Ormond in the reign of Charles II by whom John Vernon, Paymaster-General of the Royal Army, had been given Clontarf, then a castle of the Templars. They were a fiery race, proud of their Anglo-Norman descent, their sixty-three quarterings, and their position among the sporting Church-of-England 'Ascendancy', the landlords of the Pale.

My earliest memory is of a chemist's shop in Bath with coloured bottles in the window and a circular air-cushion with a hole in the middle. This mysterious rubber object excited me beyond words. What was it for? I never knew except that it must be for something quite unimaginably disgusting and horrible. I knew it and It knew it, and It knew that I knew it. It was vice made visible. And It was for Me!

Then my father's regiment was sent to South Africa, and all my memories became exotic; arum lilies, loquats, eucalyptus, freesias, are the smells which seem to me divine essences, balms of Eden remembered from another life. The freesias grew wild in the grass and those long thin stems with their wayward creamy blossom, and their fragrance, so strangely fresh and yet sophisticated, were my first clue to the vast riches of the universe. I remember also Cape Point, the walk to the sea through clumps of rushes and over white sand feathered with the tracks of lizard and all around me an indescribable irradiation of sun and wind and space and salt. And at Montagu there was an island in the mountain river on to which I used to be hoisted, clutching a stinking meercat's skin, lord of a rock on which a bird deposited the shells of crayfish, an Ithaca twelve feet long.

We lived at Wynberg; there were chameleons in the garden and squashed apricots; on Sundays the Regiment had church parades and there were smells of pine and eucalyptus paint blisters and hot tar. I had already grown accustomed to being an only child and enjoyed playing by myself. I had a dog called Wups, a cat called One-Eye and a crowd of other animals, some real and many imaginary. I derived enormous pleasure from animals and something approaching ecstasy from the smells of flowers and fruit and from the arid subtropical scenery.

Already my life was a chain of ecstatic moments; I invented happy families of tops and fir-cones or made overtures to the sacred personages whom I learnt about from *Line upon Line*: Isaac on his way up the mountain to be sacrificed, the infant Samuel, the other children David and Benjamin. But my deepest concern was the apprehension of visual beauty. To stand among arum lilies, faintly scented, thick in texture and to break off their leaves, or among the brittle lines of sweet pea, or with my watering-can by the rose-beds smelling of wet earth and to pour out the spraying water – these were experiences, like climbing a willow tree near the stables where the green and edible willow branches hung down like the reed curtains in Spanish doorways, by which my existence was transformed! In vain Captain Scott shook hands with me on his last voyage to the South Pole, in vain I was shown the giant tortoises and the fleet at Simonstown or saw the Regiment parade on Minden Day – my relations, sadistic with One-Eye and Wups, aesthetic with pale cones of silver fir and the gummy blue cups of eucalyptus, were all that concerned me.

I twice visited South Africa; at the age of five, and six. In between we went to Ireland and stayed at Clontarf, and then at Mitchelstown Castle in Cork which left a deep impression. This castle was an enormous eighteenth-century Gothic affair, which belonged with some thirty thousand acres to my great-aunt Anna, Countess of Kingston, who had once been besieged there by the Fenians; there was a lake in the grounds, and a wishing well. Now, alas, not a stone remains. It was winter and there were icicles along the lake. I wore brown gloves on week-days and white ones on Sundays and held an icicle (the first I had seen) with its mysterious purposeful pointed whiteness, in my white glove. Of the rest of the visit I remember little. Lord Kingston, descendant of Milton's Lycidas, had long been dead, but my grandfather was there, terrifying. 'Where is Grandpapa?' I asked my nurse one morning. 'He's busy.' 'What's he doing?' 'He's doing his duty.' This answer, which would have covered the activities of all Irish landlords at that date, I took to mean that he was in the lavatory (Have you done your duty today?), and was more frightened of him than ever except when he would come in with his gun and a huge stiff dead grasshopper two feet long in his hand, waving it at me and saying 'snipe, snipe'.

This was my first visit to Ireland since babyhood and, besides the love of the beautiful, it awoke in me a new passion. I became a snob. The discovery that I was an earl's great-nephew was important to me; I soon made another. My mother's favourite sister had married a rich man. Aunt Mab was very beautiful but she also had special smells, smells of furs and Edwardian luxe. Uncle Walter gave me a steam train and a watch for Christmas. Wherever he went with Aunt Mab there were presents and large houses and the appeal her wealth made to an imaginative child was irresistible. Bishopscourt, Loughananna, Rochestown, Marlay, the names of her houses (for she moved every six months) held a poetry for me. They went with security and romance, fires and potato cakes, footmen, horses, and soft aquatinted Irish winter.

Cold grew the foggy morn, the day was brief,
Loose on the cherry hung the crimson leaf;
All green was vanished save of pine and yew
That still display'd their melancholy hue;
Save the green holly with its berries red
And the green moss upon the gravel spread.

∽

In 1910 I was sent home from Africa for good. My parents stayed on
while I went with my nurse to join my father's mother and sister in
Corsica where they had a villa. By now I was an aesthete. I adored my
mother, but lived otherwise in a world of my own. Sunsets were my preoccupation. I saw all words, people, numbers, and proper names in
colours or notes of music and there was a different colour for every day
of the week which I tried to paint but failed. I remember being often ill
with fever, and the taste of the orange-leaf tea I was given to bring my
temperature down. I added the flavour of this infusion to my ecstasies,
with walks in the 'maquis' and sessions by the garden tank where I
sailed my prickly pear leaves in the evening.

Then there was the sea itself, though, like Petronius, I cared only for
the sea-shore, for the beach by 'Les Îles Sanguinaires' where transparent
'Venus' slippers' were thrown up by the sea. One evening I was taken
out in a boat to see the French destroyers fire their torpedoes. The lurid
Mediterranean sunset, the ships, the noise, the rolling, were not to my
liking. I cried louder as each torpedo went off and from that evening
I date a horror of battleships, bands playing, noises, displays of arms,
and all official functions.

I also discovered friendship in Corsica and fell in love with a child
called Zenon, a Pole, three years older than myself. He had dark eyes,
a fringe of brown hair and adored fighting. He made cardboard
swords and shields for us on which he used to paint our coats of arms
and we would hack at each other till our escutcheons were broken.
From that moment I have seldom been heart-free and life without love
for me has always seemed like an operation without an anaesthetic.

I have been inclined to regard that condition as the justification of existence and one that takes priority over all other ideologies.

> Love the most generous passion of the mind,
> That cordial drop heaven in our cup has thrown
> To make the nauseous draught of life go down.

From Corsica we moved on to Tangier, where I was infatuated again, this time with a handsome bearded Moorish guide called Salem. We showered presents on each other and I still have a beautiful drum he gave me. Then we returned to Bath, where aged six I was sent to school as a day boy. It was the hot summer of 1910 and we wore dark blue cockades for the general election, except the dentist's son, who was a liberal. He seemed to me to smell quite different from the other boys. Oily.

I was now nearly seven and from this moment my character began to deteriorate. My grandmother spoilt me. I have since observed that it is a pleasure of grandparents to spoil their grandchildren. They revenge themselves in that way on their children for the insults they have suffered from them. My grandmother, lonely, religious, and unselfish, was only playing her biological role. The tragedy was that I found it out and recognized my victim.

I remember being spoilt as an actual sensation, waking up early on Christmas morning and seeing the thrilling contours of my presents taking shape, the stocking bulging in the dark, afterwards unpacking the toy soldiers and setting them up in the new fort, going to church in my Eton jacket and suddenly, about three o'clock, being afflicted with a sensation of utter satiety and aggressive boredom. It was like eating – having been delicate and often feverish my appetite was most stimulated by invalid foods – the egg, the grape, the pat of butter, the cutlet, the tangerine, they were my highspots. In the winter afternoon I would play by the fire with mines of matchboxes fired by trains or torn paper in the grate, for I hated to leave the fire for a moment, then tea would be brought in, my grandmother would cut the buttered toast into fingers, ready to dip into the boiled eggs. Which tastes best? The first or the second? The first finger of toast or the last little triangle dug out from the bottom with a spoon? I don't know – but I do know one should never have a third egg, and I remember the unwilling sensation of not wanting to eat it yet hating to let it go and finally forcing myself to dispose of it, and then rounding on my grandmother – a vicious little golden-haired Caligula.

To this period I trace my worst faults. Indecision, for I found that by hesitating for a long time over two toys in a shop I would be given both and so was tempted to make two alternatives seem equally attractive; Ingratitude, for I grew so used to having what I wanted that I assumed it as a right; Laziness, for sloth is the especial vice of tyrants; the Impatience with boredom which is generated by devotion; the Cruelty which comes from a knowledge of power and the Giving way to moods for I learnt that sulking, crying, moping, and malingering were bluffs that paid.

The people I had been in love with before, my mother, my nurse Betty, Wups, One-Eye, Zenon, and Salem or Selim (the spelling varied) were people who loved me, but we loved as equals, conscious of each other's rights. Sufficiently provoked One-Eye would scratch, my mother rebuke, Betty spank, Zenon, Wups, and Salem slink away. Now for the first time I learnt of unequal love. I was not in love with my grandmother, she was in love with me, or perhaps so ignorant and help-less with children as to seem in love, and I took advantage. *Sic ego perire coepi.*

At school I was popular for I had embarked on the career which was to occupy me for the next ten years of 'trying to be funny'. I was neither good nor bad at games; my favourite exercise was to take a short piece of pointed wood in my hand and meander for hours through the long summer grasses round the playing fields, calling at imaginary ports, tunnelling through the hay, chewing sorrel, and following my faint tracks in the silver grass as a liner follows a trade route. Inside my desk a cardboard shoebox perforated with holes supported a brood of cater-pillars. Who can forget that smell of caterpillars, the smell of wet card-board, drying leaves and insect excrement, the odour of northern childhood? It was on one of these long summer cruises, in a patch of cow-parsley, that I realized my own identity; in a flash it came to me that my name and myself were something apart, something that none of the other boys were or could be, Cyril Vernon Connolly, a kind of divine 'I am that I am' which I should carry all through life and at last deposit on my grave, like a retriever with a bit of stick.

I was still in love, as I had been since I first saw in *Little Arthur's History of England* the picture of the Princes in the Tower – those two royal princes, so sweetly embracing, so soon to be smothered – what only child could look at them without a disturbance or read of Prince Arthur himself, walking trustfully beside the gaoler on his way to have his eyes put out? Indeed, like many children, I had fixations on the early Plantagenets. With their remote grandeur and their drooping black moustaches these sad bad Kings seemed like my great-uncles, huge brooding stylized figures who awoke a sense of guilt.

My great friend was a boy called Hubert Fitzroy Foley. I remember leaning out of the dormitory window with him to watch the fireworks on a summer night, while the rockets went off and we heard the inevitable Gilbert and Sullivan from the distant military band. That summer I seemed to be initiated into the secrets of preparatory school life. I came to know the smell of the classrooms, of slates, chalk, and escaping gas, and to fear the green baize door which separated the headmaster's part of the house from the boys'. On the one side, silence, authority, the smell of savouries; on the other, noise and freedom.

At night we made 'tabernacles' by stretching the sheets up over the tops of the beds and I would lie in the evening sunshine playing flicking matches between the fingers of my right hand and my left or arching my hands into swan-like shapes that swooped up and down above my head. When I was ill there were cracks in the ceiling to map and explore and patterns in the wall-paper. I learnt the rhythm of the seasons: summer, which is the time for overdoing things, the recoil of creative autumn, the vibrant coma of winter and the lowering spring. I began to enjoy my work and to win prizes. I acted in a play and wrote facetious little Leacockian sketches. I declared a rebellion against the masters and returned a prize to one of them saying none of us would ever speak to them again. This was part of insensitive teasing, but he took it seriously and looked hurt. I was so spoilt that I felt bored and disappointed with myself and I tried to take it out on whom I dared. Otherwise I was a typical schoolboy, with a red cap, a belt with a snake (which I slept with under my pillow), a cricket bat, a knowledge of the tracks made by wapiti, skunk, racoon and wolverine, and a happy bitchiness which endeared me, as it was intended to, to my superiors. I went in brakes to watch matches and come home summertipsy in the dusk; I adored sausages and Sunday breakfasts, said my prayers, bickered with other boys on walks, cried 'quis' and 'ego', and was conceited and bright in the way in which so many small boys are, and which, alas, proves such a false dawn of intelligence.

I can never remember not being able to read and was already deep in 'Natural History'. I could reel off the habits of aardvarks, aye-ayes, and Tasmanian Devils, and I knew (from *The World of Wonders*) about the great Tun of Heidelberg, the deadly Upas Tree, and the Pitch Lake of Trinidad. I collected stamps, pressed flowers in blotters and adored chess. For lighter reading there were fairy stories and nonsense books. I enjoyed Burnand, Mark Twain, and Stephen Leacock, but wept at the humiliations of *Vice Versa* or the sufferings of the Yonghi Bonghi Bo. My thrill of the week was to visit a little shop on Lansdowne Hill in the early dusk of winter afternoon and receive a rolled-up bundle of 'Comic Papers'; *Chips* and *Comic Cuts*, the *Rainbow*, the *Gem* and the *Magnet* – I hold them, as I did with everything, to my nose, the smell is excruciating – damp paper, newsprint; I feel I shall burst. Ahead of me stretches the evening with my grandmother; the gas lit, the fire burning, the papers unrolled and untied, the peace and security of the literary life though even then I am depressed by the knowledge that nothing I shall find inside will come up to the sensation of opening them. As with Leopardi's peasants, the eve of the Festival will always bring me more happiness than the Feast itself.

There was one other lesson I learnt, living with my grandmother. Hitherto I had been in exotic African surroundings or in Ireland. But my grandmother was poor and we lived in 'rooms'; sometimes they were by the seaside in the isle of Purbeck, where balls bounced on the porphyry pavement, and a horse-drawn tumbril dragged the long-robed bathers far out into the string-coloured sea; sometimes they were in London, sometimes in Bath – but they were always middle class. While listening to tales of the Admiral's splendid dinner parties or of her childhood: the Rector's fine horses galloping the twenty-four miles from his country house at Malmesbury to his Palladian villa at Bath with its fourteen gardeners, the opulent safe Victorian saga, I yet was coming to know the world of the realist novel, those fuggy rooms with plush sofas and antimacassars, gas mantles, kettles on the hob, and their landladies, overfamiliar women with common voices and ripe bosoms sprayed with jet. I came into contact with the lower classes too, for we used to visit one or two old servants to whom my grandmother had made pensions. One, Old Sally, who lived in an alcoholic bed-ridden fug, distressed me particularly. Here were horrible things: illness, poverty, old age, and I felt I must make every effort to avoid coming into further contact with them.

I now made the comparison, as many a small boy would:

England = Grannie, Lodgings, School, Poverty, Middle Class.

Ireland = Aunt Mab, Castles, Holidays, Riches, Upper Class.

Ireland, therefore, became desirable and England sordid. This division, however unreal it may seem, had importance for me, it conditioned my homeless insecure lonely childhood, and made me a social hybrid. I could not consider myself entirely upper class; yet I was not altogether upper middle. I had fallen between two standards of living. With the upper class I felt awkward, dowdy, introspective and a physical coward. With the middle class I felt critical, impatient, and sparkling. This class distinction, the line between Kensington and Belgravia, is a source of anguish. To consider oneself born into one and yet be slowly conditioned to the other was as uncomfortable as having one shoulder too low.

Meanwhile my mother returned and tried to repair the damages to my character. She disapproved of the school in Bath where I was always ill. I had whooped my way through the coronation summer, I had come out in measles and german measles and chicken pox, and, after a recurrence of malaria, I was removed. My mother came down to see me while I was ill and I brought a trunk of toys, all the composition animals whom I adored in the holidays, with their house of parliament and the cricket elevens. I was ashamed of them and refused to play, for already my solitary only-child world seemed disgraceful to my social school-world, even my mother's presence in it seemed incorrect. She took me away to Ireland and so Bath – that beautiful relaxing town where the Abbey chimes played *The Harp that once through Tara's Halls* with morbid sweetness as we watched the county cricket matches, knew me no more.

Clontarf was a paradise for up in the musicians' gallery of its gothic hall was a pitch for the kind of cricket I played, bowling a marble with my left hand to my right hand which held a toy animal as bat. A book standing up was the wicket. When an animal was out another took its place. Animals that were solid like the elephant or streamlined like the seal made the best bats; animals like the giraffe, whose legs broke when they hit out, were less successful. Books were filled with their batting averages and my celluloid seal, besides being the best cricketer, was also a potent voice in my animals' parliament, and taken every night to bed with me.

My grandfather tried to give me real fielding practice on the lawn but I was frightened. There is a two-handed sword in the castle, reputed to have been used by Brian Boru in his battle there against the Danes, with which my grandfather and my great-uncle Granville Vernon would pretend to chop off my head. Their sombre jesting accentuated my cowardice, but I became interested in Brian Boru, and so was led to cultivate my 'Irish' side. I wanted to learn Gaelic and I read history books from the nationalist stand-point. Shane O'Neill, Owen Roe O'Neill, Wolfe Tone, Lord Edward Fitzgerald were my heroes and I learnt to sing the Shan Van Vocht. The last intellectual to stay at Clontarf had been Handel, whose bedroom was my nursery, and I began to be considered 'Queer'. The introduction – 'This is cousin Cyril [my nephew Cyril]. (*p*) He's supposed to be very clever. (*pp*) His grand-mother's spoilt him,' depressed me. I responded as usual by showing off and 'trying to be funny'.

I went on 'trying to be funny' till I was seventeen. This grisly process was my defence mechanism. It was the shell I was secreting as a protection from the outside world: by making people laugh I became popular, and I ultimately became feared as well. 'Go on, be funny!' some boy would command, and I would clown away or recite my poems and parodies, with their echoes of Mark Twain and Stephen Leacock. 'Connolly's being funny,' the word would go round and soon I would have collected a crowd. I revelled in this and would grow funnier and funnier till I passed quite naturally into tears. 'Connolly's not funny now. He's gone too far,' and the group would break up and leave me, except for some true friend who remained to puzzle over the psychology of the manic-depressive. 'But you were being quite funny a moment ago.' 'Oh, Boo-Hoo-Hoo. I wish I was dead.' 'Oh, shut up, Connolly.' 'Oh, go away. I hate you.' Then a master would come by and comfort me. I would be handed, still hysterical, to the matron, and the inevitable case-history would be gone over. '(*p*) It's his grandmother. (*pp*) She spoils him.'

But I could not be so funny in Ireland. My wit was the opposite of the native sense of humour, my jokes, a combination of puns and personal remarks interlarded with the wisecracks of the day ('Oh, go and eat soap' was a favourite), were beyond the Anglo-Irish, who saw only the humour of situations, and could not appreciate a *calembour*. They began to tease me about being English, which I gathered meant possessing a combina-tion of snobbery, stupidity, and lack of humour and was a deadly insult. There were many stories of social triumphs at the expense of parvenu England – especially against unpopular viceroys, like Lord Aberdeen. The Anglo-Irish were a superior people. Better born, but less snobbish; cle-verer than the English and fonder of horses; they were poorer no doubt but with a poverty that brought into relief their natural aristocracy. And, above all, they were loved (for 'being Irish' meant belonging to the Protestant Landed Gentry) by about four million devoted bog-trotters, who served them as grooms, comic footmen, gardeners, and huntsmen.

And the real Irish – what had happened to them? They were my first lost cause, and I worshipped them with passion, reciting the 'Dead at Clonmacnois' to myself in a riot of grief.

> In a quiet watered land, a land of roses,
> Stands Saint Kieran's city fair
> And the warriors of Erin in their famous generations
> Slumber there.

> There beneath the dewy hillside sleep the noblest
> Of the Clan of Conn,
> Each below his stone with name in branching Ogham
> And the sacred knot thereon.

> Many and many a son of Conn the Hundred Fighter
> In the red earth lies at rest;
> Many a blue eye of Clan Colman the turf covers,
> Many a swan-white breast.

Even today such verses typify Ireland, the soft constipating weather, the unreality of that green cul-de-sac turned away from Europe where the revolutions lead backwards and the Present is invariably the victim of the Past.

In the meanwhile what of Clan Colman? Great-Uncle Granville obligingly made a list of chieftains for me. They were not all extinct; behind the Anglo-Norman families of the Pale, the Fitzgeralds, de Burghs, Tristrams, Talbots, Vernons, and Plunkets, lurked the remnant of an older race – the O'Grady of Killyballyowen, the O'Gorman, the O'Connor Don, the Magillicuddy of the Reeks, the O'Reilly and the Fox! These were the legitimate rulers, downtrodden heirs of Shane and Owen Roe. I begged Uncle Granville to point them out to me. To serve the O'Gorman! To speak Gaelic, wear a saffron Irish kilt, and sing the Shan Van Vocht!

> In the curragh of Kildare
> And the boys will all be there

with the O'Connor Don! The parliament of animals became supporters of the movement and the great seal himself, a fine cricketer and a generous statesman, added the letters D.A.I. (Dublin and Irish) after his name. I planned a restoration of the monarchy and pestered my Uncle Granville about the claims of various families. Who should be considered the rightful king of Ireland, the successor of Brian Boru? Naturally all Connollys, O'Connors, and O'Connells, through Conn, the King of Connaught. That pointed to Edward Connolly of Castletown. But his family had taken the name Connolly and were really Pakenhams. Besides, his Gaelic . . .? The O'Briens were Uncle Granville's candidates for the vacant throne. They had a Gaelic motto and were descended from Brian Boru himself through the kings of Thomond. Lord Inchiquin had the best right to the crown of Tara. For my own part I had no personal ambition, nothing to hope for from the Restoration.

> It was friends to die for
> That I would seek and find

and my day-dreams ended in my being sacrificed for the new king, like little Arthur.

This Irish nationalism may seem an extraordinary phase but it must be remembered that there are still several million who believe in it. Gaelic is now compulsory in Ireland, and I believe Lord Cullen of Ashbourne even wore a saffron kilt in Richmond Park. Monarchy has lost ground there since 1912, but at that time the revolutionary movement was unknown to me. My own feelings were romantic and literary, in fact English.* Ireland represented glamour and luxury, and I tried to make a religion out of them. Of course, I was a failure with the Irish. I never could learn the Gaelic Alphabet, nor for that matter could I talk with an Irish brogue and the only Irish people I knew were the housekeeper at Clontarf and her husband.

*The surnames of my eight great-grandparents were Connolly, Hewitt, Kemble, Cattley, Vernon, Bowles, Brinkley and Graves. The Vernons had no Irish blood, the Connollys, at any rate since the early eighteenth century, had never been there and now despite my early infatuation nothing infuriates me more than to be treated as an Irishman.

All my cousins were healthy, destructive, normal children. I was lonely, romantic, and affected and already the friction between extrovert and introvert was set up. I was extremely shy, for the effort to accommodate my inner life to my outer one was proving harder and harder. I was sentimental at night and facetious in the morning. Between morning and evening my personality would swing from one mood to the other as I watched my wisecracking morning self with its defiant battle-cry 'Oh, go and eat soap,' turn by degrees into the tearful Celtic dreamer who believed in ghosts and at night would go into a trance over a line of poetry. My appetite for Gaelic and ghosts waxed and waned with my craving for titles. There were evenings when I wanted to kill myself because I was not the O'Grady of Killballyowen. Why had not my father got a title? Why was I not the heir to Castletown? It was heartless, anguishing – why be born, why live at all if I could not have one? Nobody understood me. Nobody cared, and I would scream and scream with real tears and screams that grew more and more artificial as I had to raise my voice to carry to the dining room. Nobody loved me, nobody understood me, nobody would give me what I wanted, there was an Elemental under the bed. I could die for all they cared. Wur! Wur! Wur! till at last my mother appeared in evening dress and would sit with me and stroke my head smelling of chocolates.

The fever I got from time to time was a recurrence of African malaria, and was just enough to cause anxiety – the anxiety enough to procure me privileges. And in the morning, when my night fears had been discussed and I would come down to an atmosphere of sympathy, it was 'Oh, go and eat soap', or 'Stick him with a fork'.

Such were these early excesses that today I cannot listen to any discussion of titles or open a peerage without feeling sick, as from the smell of rubber steps and stale whisky on the stairway of a Channel boat. I shall never be able to breathe till they are abolished. Nor has 'being understood' proved reassuring.

In the end I compromised on the brogue. I pretended that I had got rid of it except in moments of great excitement and I would even affect to lose my temper so as to try out a few phrases, though I was careful to do this when no Irish boys were in the room. My new history books taught me to abominate England for I read *Tales of a Grandfather* at the same time and it never occurred to me that the England I hated, the oppressor of the Celt and the Gael, the executioner of Fitzgerald, Emmet, and Wolfe Tone, was made manifest in my grandfather, who owned a thousand acres of suburban Dublin, and a shoot in Kerry; that the Anglo-Irish were themselves a possessor class whose resentment against England was based on the fear that she might not always allow them to go on possessing.

19 *White Samite*

The new school my parents chose for me was on the coast. At first I was miserable there and cried night after night. My mother cried too at sending me and I have often wondered if that incubator of persecution mania, the English private school, is worth the money that is spent on it or the tears its pupils shed. At an early stage small boys are subjected to brutal partings and long separations which undermine their love for their parents before the natural period of conflict and are encouraged to look down on them without knowing why. To owners of private schools they are a business like any other, to masters a refuge for incompetence, in fact a private school has all the faults of a public school without any of its compensations, without tradition, freedom, historical beauty, good teaching, or communication between pupil and teacher. It is one of the few tortures confined to the ruling classes and from which the workers are still free. I have never met anybody yet who could say he had been happy there. It can only be that our parents are determined to get rid of us!

Yet St Wulfric's where I now went was a well run and vigorous example which did me a world of good. We called the headmistress Flip and the headmaster Sambo. Flip, around whom the whole system revolved, was able, ambitious, temperamental and energetic. She wanted her venture to be a success, to have more boys, to attract the sons of peers and to send them all to Eton. She was an able instructress in French and History and we learnt with her as fast as fear could teach us. Sambo seemed a cold, business-like, and dutiful consort. The morale of the school was high and every year it won a shooting trophy and the Harrow History Prize from all the other preparatory schools. Inside the chapel was a chaplain, inside the gym a drill-sergeant and there were a virid swimming-pool, a cadet corps, carpenter's shop, and riding class.

The school was typical of England before the last war; it was worldly and worshipped success, political and social; though Spartan, the death-rate was low, for it was well run and based on that stoicism which characterized the English governing class and which has since been under-estimated. 'Character, character, character,' was the message which emerged when we rattled the radiators or the fence round the playing fields and it reverberated from the rifles in the armoury, the bullets on the miniature range, the saw in the carpenter's shop, and the hoofs of the ponies on their trot to the Downs.

> Not once or twice in our rough island's story
> The path of duty was the way to glory

was the lesson we had to learn and there were other sacred messages from the poets of private schools: Kipling or Newbolt.

Muscle-bound with character the alumni of St Wulfric's would pass on to the best public schools, cleaning up all houses with a doubtful tone, reporting their best friends for homosexuality and seeing them expelled, winning athletic distinctions – for the house rather than themselves, for the school rather than the house, and prizes and scholarships and shooting competitions as well – and then find their vocation in India, Burma, Nigeria, and the Sudan, administering with Roman justice those natives for whom the final profligate overflow of Wulfrician character was all the time predestined.

After I had spent one or two terms at St Wulfric's, blue with cold, haunting the radiators and the lavatories and waking up every morning with the accumulated misery of the mornings before, the war broke out.

My parents had taken a house in London in Brompton Square and the holidays had become an oasis after St Wulfric's austerity. In the big room at the top of the house with my grandfather's sea chest and the animal books by Ernest Thompson Seton, a fire and the view of the sea-green limes of the Brompton Oratory, or in the drawing-room with its vine-clad balcony and rose-wood furniture from Cowbridge I could be happy. The square abounded with looper caterpillars, tight in the shallow earth wriggled the pupae of the privet moth (in those that did not wriggle the ichneumon was at work). On Sundays people made jokes about not going to church but went and the churches disgorged their top-hatted congregations into the Park from whence they strolled back, myself in top hat and Eton jacket moving in an Anglo-Irish phalanx and imagining I was Charles Hawtrey, through gates and squares and crescents aromatic with Sunday luncheons, the roast beef, the boredom, the security of 1913. At night my fear of the dark was still acute. I had to have night-lights and I had a terror of anything 'going out' – I could not bear a dying fire or a guttering candle, or even a clock to run down – it seemed a kind of death-agony.

The rest of my time at St Wulfric's was spent on a war-time basis. The school throve; its *raison d'être* apparent in the lengthening Roll of Honour. Old boys came down in uniform and retired generals lectured to the corps while the boys stuck flags into maps, gave Woodbines to the wounded soldiers, and learned to knit; doing without more and more, as Flip's organizing genius found its expression.

The master who first took me in hand was Mr Ellis. He was gruff and peppery with an egg-shaped bald head. He and Mr Potter, the high-priest of the shooting trophies, were professional teachers, the rest makeshifts thrown up by the war. Ellis was pro-German; the Germans deserved to win the war, he thought, because of their superior efficiency. The boys respected his point of view; to them, a German victory would have seemed natural, a chastisement on England for neglecting duty and discipline, and not listening to 'Lest we forget'. He made me enthusiastic over algebra and as my enthusiasm grew I became good at it.

From that moment Daddy Ellis befriended me. He called me Tim

Connolly and built up a personality for me as the Irish Rebel, treating me as an intelligent and humorous person, an opponent to respect. When the Germans conquered our decadent country through their discipline and the superiority of their general staff I should be one of the first elements to be shot.

My new personality appealed to me. I changed my handwriting and way of doing my hair, jumped first instead of last into the fetid plunge-bath, played football better, and became an exhibit: the gay, generous, rebellious Irishman, with a whiff of Kipling's McTurk. Flip also admired the transformation and began to introduce me to parents as 'our dangerous Irishman', 'our little rebel'. At that time I used to keep a favour chart in which, week by week, I would graph my position at her court. I remember my joy as the upward curve continued, and I began to make friends, win prizes, enjoy riding, and succeed again at trying to be funny. The favour charts I kept for several terms; one's favour began at the top and then went downwards as term wore on and tempers.

When angry, Flip would slap our faces in front of the school or pull the hair behind our ears, till we cried. She would make satirical remarks at meals that pierced like a rapier and then put us through interviews in which we bellowed with repentance – 'It wasn't very straight of you, was it, Tim? Don't you *want* to do me credit – don't you *want* to have character – or do you simply not care what I think of you as long as you can get a few cheap laughs from your friends and shirk all responsibility?' The example of brothers or cousins now in the trenches was then produced to shame us. On all the boys who went through this Elizabeth and Essex relationship she had a remarkable effect, hotting them up like Alfa-Romeos for the Brooklands of life.

The one thing that would bring our favour back (for, woman-like, Flip treated the very being-out-of-favour as a crime in itself, punishing us for the timid looks and underdog manner by which we showed it) was a visit from our parents and many a letter was sent off begging for their aid. I was restored, after a low period during which I had been compared before the whole school to the tribe of Reuben because 'unstable as water thou shalt not excel', by an inquiry for me from Lord Meath, the founder of Empire Day. Sometimes we could get back by clinging to friends who were still 'in favour'. It might drag them down or it might bring us up and the unhappiness of these little boys forced to choose between dropping a friend in his disgrace or risking disgrace themselves was most affecting.

I had two friends whose 'favour' was as uncertain as my own, George Orwell and Cecil Beaton. I was a stage rebel, Orwell a true one. Tall, pale, with his flaccid cheeks, large spatulate fingers, and supercilious voice, he was one of those boys who seem born old. He was incapable of courtship and when his favour went it sank for ever. He saw through St Wulfric's, despised Sambo and hated Flip but was invaluable to them as scholarship fodder. We often walked together over the downs in our green jerseys and corduroy breeches discussing literature, and we both won, in consecutive years, the inevitable 'Harrow History Prize'. There was another prize for having the 'best list' of books taken out of the library during the term, the kind which might have been invented only to create intellectual snobs and to satiate boys with the world's culture at a time when they were too young to understand it. The books were given out in the evening by Flip herself and a way by which it was sometimes possible to get back into 'favour' was by taking out or returning one which caught her eye. Old boys who came down promptly inquired, 'What sort of favour are *you* in?' and letters to those who had gone on always ended up, 'I am (touch wood) still in good favour' – 'I shall have to do something, I'm losing favour' – or 'I am in the most awful favour'; unjust at the time as this feminine tyranny seemed it was a valuable foretaste of the world outside; even the nickname Flip suggested some primitive goddess of fortune. Thus, although I won the prize through heading my list with 'Carlyle's *French Revolution*' – and Orwell won it next, we were both caught at last with two volumes of *Sinister Street* and our favour sank to zero.

We both wrote poetry. At sunset or late at night in the dark, I would be visited by the Muse. In an ecstasy of flushing and shivering, the tears welling up as I wrote, I would put down some lines to the Night Wind.

The next morning they would be copied out. Although the process of composition always seemed an authentic visitation, the result was an imitation of Stevenson or Longfellow or my favourite, Robert W. Service. I would compare them with Orwell's and be critical of his, while he was polite about mine, then we would separate feeling ashamed of each other.

The remarkable thing about Orwell was that alone among the boys he was an intellectual and not a parrot for he thought for himself, read Shaw and Samuel Butler and rejected not only St Wulfric's, but the war, the Empire, Kipling, Sussex, and Character. I remember a moment under a fig-tree in one of the inland boulevards of the seaside town, Orwell striding beside me and saying in his flat, ageless voice: 'You know, Connolly, there's only one remedy for all diseases.' I felt the usual guilty tremor when sex was mentioned and hazarded, 'You mean going to the lavatory?' 'No – I mean Death!' He was not a romantic, he had neither use for the blandishments of the drill-sergeant who made us feel character was identical with boxing nor for the threats of the chaplain with his grizzled cheektufts and his gospel of a Jesus of character who detested immorality and swearing as much as he loved the Allies. 'Of course, you realize, Connolly,' said Orwell, 'that, whoever wins this war, we shall emerge a second-rate nation.'

Orwell proved to me that there existed an alternative to character, Intelligence. Beaton showed me another, Sensibility. He had a charming, dreamy face, enormous blue eyes with long lashes and wore his hair in a fringe. His voice was slow, affected and creamy. He was not good at games or work but he escaped persecution through good manners, and a baffling independence. We used to mow the lawn together behind an old pony, sit eating the gooseberries in the kitchen garden, or pretend to polish brass in the chapel; from Orwell I learnt about literature, from Cecil I learnt about art. He occupied his spare time drawing and painting and his holidays in going to the theatre.

On Saturday nights, when the school was entertained in the big schoolroom by such talent as the place could offer, when Mr Potter had shown lantern slides of *Scrooge* or Mr Smedley, dressed up like a pirate at a P. & O. gala, had mouthed out what he called 'Poethry' – there would be a hush, and Cecil would step forward and sing, 'If you were the only girl in the World and I was the only boy.' His voice was small but true, and when he sang these sentimental songs, imitating Violet Loraine or Beatrice Lillie, the eighty-odd Wulfricians felt there could be no other boy in the world for them, the beetling chaplain forgot hell-fire and masturbation, the Irish drill-sergeant his bayonet practice, the staff refrained from disapproving, and for a moment the whole structure of character and duty tottered and even the principles of hanging on, muddling through, and building empires were called into question.

On other Saturday nights gramophone records were played; when we came to 'I have a song to sing O, sing me your song O' I would open a book which I had bought in the Charing Cross Road, at the prepared place, and read:

> Far out at sea when the evening's dusk is falling you may often observe a dark-coloured bird with white under-plumage flit by just above the waves – another and another make their appearance, and you soon find out that a party of Manx Shearwaters have paid your vessel a passing call. They are nocturnal birds for the most part, spending the hours of daylight in their burrows, and coming out in the gloom to speed across the frowning waters in quest of food. There is something very exciting about the appearance of this singular bird. The noisy gulls which have been playing about all day drop slowly astern as the sun nears the west; the parties of Razorbills and Guillemots and Puffins have sped away to their distant breeding colonies; and the wide waste of waters seems unusually destitute and dreary as the night approaches, and the evening breeze fluttering in the sails, and through the rigging, is the only sound that breaks the oppressive stillness. But the hour of the Manx Shearwater's ghostly revelry has come, he holds high carnival over the waste of gray waters, flitting about in most erratic manner in his wild impetuous course, following the curve of every wave, dipping down into the hollows, where he is almost invisible, and then mounting the foamy crests, where you catch a brief glimpse of his hurried movements.

The combination of the music with this passage was intoxicating. The two blended into an experience of isolation and flight which induced the sacred shiver. The classroom disappeared, I was alone on the dark seas, there was a hush, a religious moment of suspense, and then the visitation – the Manx shearwaters appeared, held their high carnival, etc., and vanished. At length the schoolroom where each boy sat by his desk, his few possessions inside, his chartered ink channels on top, returned to focus. This experience, which I repeated every Saturday, like a drug, was typical of the period. For those were the days when literature meant the romantic escape, the purple patch; when none of our teachers would have questioned the absolute beauty of such a line as 'clothed in white Samite, mystic, wonderful!' We were still in the full Tennysonian afterglow and our beliefs, if the muse of St Wulfric's could have voiced them, would have been somewhat as follows.

'There is a natural tradition in English poetry, my dear Tim. Chaucer begat Spenser, Spenser begat Shakespeare, Shakespeare begat Milton, Milton begat Keats, Coleridge, Shelley, Wordsworth, and they begat Tennyson who begat Longfellow, Stevenson, Kipling, Quiller-Couch, and Sir Henry Newbolt. There are a few bad boys we do not speak about – Donne, Dryden, Pope, Blake, Byron, Browning, Fitzgerald, who wrote *The Rubá'iyá of Omar Khayyám*, and Oscar Wilde who was a criminal degenerate. Chaucer is medieval but coarse, Spenser is the poet's poet, Shakespeare you will remember from your performance as the witch ('aroint thee, witch, the rumfed runion cried her husbands to Aleppo gone the master of the tiger, but in a sieve I'll thither sail and like a rat without a tail I'll do I'll do and I'll do'). Precisely. Milton was a great poet, he wrote *L'Allegro, Il Penseroso*, and *Paradise Lost*; Keats wrote *The Ode to a Nightingale*; and Tennyson wrote *The Lady of Shalott* – and what else? *Morte d'Arthur, Locksley Hall, In Memoriam, Break, Break, Break*, and *Crossing the Bar*. Longfellow wrote *Hiawatha*, Stevenson *Under the Wide and Starry Sky*, Kipling *Sussex* and *If* and *Gunga Din*, Quiller-Couch is a Good Influence and *Drake's Drum* and *Lyra Heroica* are by Sir Henry Newbolt.

'There are other good poems, *Chevy Chase, John Gilpin, The*

Armada, The Ancient Mariner, Gray's *Elegy.* A poem is good either because it is funny (Ingoldsby Legends, Bab Ballads) or because it makes you want to cry. Some funny poems make you want to cry (the Jumblies, the Dong with a Luminous Nose); that is because you are not a healthy little boy. You need more Character. The best poems have the most beautiful lines in them; these lines can be detached, they are purple patches and are Useful in Examinations. Gray's *Elegy* is almost all Purple Patch and so is the *Ode to a Nightingale,* especially

> Magic casements, opening on the foam
> Of perilous seas, in faëry lands forlorn.

When you come to a purple patch you can tell it by an alarm clock going off, you feel a cold shiver, a lump in the throat, your eyes fill with tears, and your hair stands on end. You can get these sensations for yourself when you write poems like your *Ode on the Death of Lord Kitchener* or *To the Night Wind.*

'Nobody wrote so many purple patches as Tennyson, and he had character too (*Bury the Great Duke, Charge of the Light Brigade, The Revenge*). Kipling is the only great poet alive today. Poetry is romantic, purple – a help in time of trouble – or else it is clever and funny, like Calverley – or has Character. (Life is real, Life is earnest, And the grave is NOT its goal.) It is also something to be ashamed of, like sex, and (except with the chaplain) religion.'

My experience with the Manx shearwater fulfilled these conditions. It was prose, so could not become poetry and truly purple, till heightened by music. It was romantic; something out of the ordinary, remote, and false, for in real life I should hate tossing about the Hebrides in a small boat – and escapist, since I imagined myself away from my present surroundings, alone on the northern waters, and yet not alone, a Manx shearwater, playing with others of my kind. The twilight was 'my' time of day (the time I felt most the poetic thrill), the waste of grey waters was my weepy Celtic spiritual home. Because poetry was associated with emotional excess, night, and unhappiness, I felt disgusted with it by day as by a friend in whom when drunk one has unwisely confided and I never exhibited the Manx shearwater even to Orwell.

It will be seen that the thread running through this autobiography is an analysis of romanticism, that romanticism in decline under whose shadow we grew up. Romanticism I would call the refusal to face certain truths about the world and ourselves, and the consequences of that refusal. It is a refusal which can be both splendid and necessary, this pretence that truth is beauty and beauty truth, that love is stronger than death, the soul immortal and the body divine – but in the hundred years that have elapsed since the romantic revival we have had too much of it. By the twentieth century the best work has been done and those of us who thought we were angels or devils have had a long struggle to free ourselves from such ideology. We have been the dupe of words and ideas, we have been unable to know when we are well off, we have expected too much from life, too many treats and we have precipitated crises to satisfy the appetite for sensation acquired in childhood; the womb world of the hot bath and the celluloid duck has been too near us. The romantic's artillery is always bracketing over the target of reality, falling short into cynicism or overreaching it into sentimental optimism so that, whatever the achievements of romanticism in the past, to be a romantic today, knowing what we know about the nature of man and his place in the universe, is the mark of a wilful astigmatism, a confession of cowardice and immaturity.

If but some of us lived in the world of romantic poetry, we all lived in the world of romantic love; there was no sentiment in *Maud* or *In Memoriam* that to us seemed exaggerated, we accepted 'being half in love with easeful death' as a matter of course, like the psychology of the *Belle Dame Sans Merci*. Love was a recurrent ecstasy which drove us to make sacrifices for an object which might or might not be aware of them. Reciprocation killed love faster than anything, then came Ridicule; it was only Ignorance in the Beloved that could permit the emotion to last. The prosaic Sambo seemed to have a flair for detecting our romances and he would try to expel the Cyprian by taps on the head from his heavy silver pencil.

Always I long to creep
Into some still cavern deep,
There to weep and weep, and weep
My whole soul out to Thee.

Such was my ideal, and if it met with any opposition I would reply in
the romantic's way with a spiteful poem.

The boy whom I loved for the last three years I was at St Wulfric's
was called Tony Watson. He was small, brown, wiry, good at games,
untidy and silent, with a low brow, green eyes, and a fringe of rough
short hair. I describe him because he is a type that has recurred through
my life and which gets me into trouble. It is that faunlike, extrovert
creature with a streak of madness and cruelty, not clever, but nar-
cissistic and quick to adapt itself to clever people. In appearance it is
between colours with a small mouth, slanting eyes, and lemon-yellow
skin.

By the time I was twelve all four types to which I am susceptible had
appeared. I do not know whether it is glands, numerology, the stars or
mere environment which dispose one to these fierce sympathies, inherited as if from another life, but by now I recognize my kindred forms
with some familiarity; the Faun, the Redhead, the Extreme Blonde, and
the Dark Friend.

The Fauns well know their fatal power which a series of conquests
have made obvious and they derive a pleasure that I mistake for reciprocation, from the spectacle of its workings. Age is often unkind to
these charmers and the world is apt to turn against them. With the other
types my relations are happier. I supply them with vitality and intensive
cultivation, they provide me with affection, balance, loyalty, good taste.
The Extreme Blondes are quiet, intelligent, humorous, receptive; they
have an impressive reserve against which I roll, like the Atlantic Ocean
on the Cornish cliffs, confident that they will be able to withstand me.
The Dark Friends are the most sympathetic, they have brown eyes and
oval faces; they like my jokes and look after me when I am ill, but it is
one of the hardships of romantic love that rarely is it bestowed on

people like ourselves and the Dark Friends end by being Consolers. The Redheads have some of the quieting effect of the Extreme Blondes but they may suddenly become as deleterious as the Faun. They are a special type, not the dreamy, brown-eyed, long-faced auburn, nor the aggressive albino, but the gay, thin, dashing green-eyed variety.

Being an only child I romanticized sisterhood, I wanted an Electra and longed for a relationship with sister types of the same age. I liked health and equality in women, an implicit friendship. I desired the same for my imaginary brothers. The Dark Friends and the Extreme Blondes supplied this, the Redheads added an excitement which raised it to perfection. And then the exotic Faun would reappear and all peace of mind would vanish. As with other only children my desire for a brother or sister was so strong that I came to see existence in terms of the couple; in whatever group I found myself I would inevitably end by sharing my life with one other, driven by an inner selection through a course of trial and error till after forming one of a group of four or five and then of a trio, I achieved my destiny as one half of a pair.

I christened this search for the '*dimidium animae meae*' the Pair System, and I was fascinated, when later I read the Symposium of Plato, to come across his theory that human beings had once been double and were for ever seeking the counterpart from whom they had been so rudely forced. We were all one half of a Siamese Twin.

> The brothered one, the not alone
> The brothered and the hated.

But it is a romantic theory and it is part of the romantic's misfortune that in the search for his affinity he is not guided by a community of interests but by those intimations which are the appeal of a mouth or an eye, an appeal which is not even private, so that the spectacle is presented of half a dozen Platonic half-men trying to unite with the same indifferent alter ego. Love at first sight – and the first sight is the supreme consummation for romantics – is an intuition bred by habit of the person who can do us harm.

Yet Tony Watson let me down lightly. He was a wild little boy with plenty of character but not of the right kind. He taught me to smoke (which I hated); to rag in the corridors at night, fighting among the coats hanging from their pegs, and to take part on the downs in gang warfare, which I adored. He moved in a fast set of hard-smoking and hard-swearing cronies from whom he protected me. Our unlikeness made us over-polite. He accepted my devotion, even to a poem beginning, 'Watson, the silent, Watson, the dauntless' and showed me, in return, an extraordinary drawing, a Parthenon Frieze on sheets of paper stuck together that unfolded like a concertina, to reveal a long procession of soldiers – cavalry, infantry, artillery, wounded and dying, doctors, nurses, gurkhas, staff-officers, and engineers on their way to the war.

For most of us the war was skin-deep. The *Titanic* had gone down, the passengers all singing, 'Nearer my God to Thee' – that was terrible – and now the war: pins stuck in maps, the Kaiser dying of cancer of the throat, Kitchener drowned, ration cards, Business as Usual, a day when we were told of the Battle of Jutland and another when we heard that a terrible thing had happened, a revolution in Russia with a monster called Kerensky now in power. None of us, except perhaps Orwell, believed that England could lose the war or that we would grow up to fight in it nor were we old enough to understand the peril of our elder cousins or the tragedy when, like Uncle Granville's only son, they were killed on the first day of the Gallipoli slaughter. And meanwhile Watson's exact and bloodthirsty pageant grew fuller, a page at a time, till it stretched, by 1917, the whole length of the schoolroom.

Tony shared my love of animals and drew for me pictures of foxes in lonely postures barking to the moon. I had several excruciating moments with him. Once we vowed blood-brotherhood in the Albanian fashion. Tony cut a cross on each left hand and we held the bleeding scratches together. Another time, left in the bathroom alone, he came up to me, wrapped in his bath towel, and pursed his lips for a kiss. My spinster modesty made me flinch. He turned away and never did it again while for weeks I lay awake angry and miserable. He slept in a dormitory called the Red Room; I was in a two-bedded one across the passage with the Dark Friend, his cousin, Frankie Wright. Tony would come over in the morning after a night of pillow fighting, gang reprisals, and smoking on the roof, and get into my bed where my innocence hung round my neck like an albatross. Then the eight o'clock bell would ring and we would troop down to the ghastly plunge-bath. There was a smell of gooseflesh and slimy water. One by one, under the cold eye of Sambo and to the accompaniment of such comments as 'Go on Marsden, you stink like a polecat', we dived or jumped in until it was the turn of the group of water-funks who shrank down the steps, groaning wer-wer-wer, while the sergeant-major waited to haul them out from the stagnant depths by a rope attached to a pole. When the last had been towed it was time to dress and go on the asphalt for 'gym'.

Year by year, the air, the discipline, the teaching, the association with other boys and the driving will of Flip took effect on me. I grew strong and healthy and appeared to be normal for I became a good mixer, a gay little bit who was quick to spot whom to make up to in a group and how to do it. I knew how far to go in teasing and responding to teasing and became famous for my 'repartee'. I had a theory that there was one repartee effective for every situation and spent weeks in elaborating it. At that time the magic phrase seemed, 'Dear me, how very uninteresting!' If I had to choose one now it would be 'This is a very bad moment for both of us.' I kept a Funny Book which contained satirical poems and character sketches. I became good at history, that is to say I learnt dates easily, knew which battle was fought in the snow and who was 'the little gentleman in black velvet'. I read Dickens, Thackeray, Carlyle, and Scott and got marks for them, and for pleasure John Buchan. It was time for me to go up for a scholarship. I had crammed Watson energetically for the common entrance which he just managed to pass and when I saw him again in the holidays he was a dapper public schoolboy with his hair brushed back, a felt hat and a cane and we had nothing to say to each other.

My first attempt at a scholarship was at Wellington with Orwell. I hated every moment: the blue-suited prefects bustling about the dismal brick and slate, the Wellingtonias and rhododendrons, infertile flora of the Bagshot sand. It was winter and an old four-wheeler bore me from the examinations to my great-aunts with whom I was staying. The musical groaning of the wheels and springs in the winter stillness had a profound effect and I felt like Childe Roland, mystical and Celtic. Pines and heather, the whortle-bearing ridges, seemed to have a message for me, to be the background for some great event as I trundled over them after the afternoon paper. Orwell got a scholarship which he did not take. I failed but the experience was considered good practice.

A year later I went up for Eton, which was very different. Sambo took charge of us; he knew many people there and we had tea with old Wulfrician boys and masters. I had a moment on Windsor Bridge; it was summer, and, after the coast, the greenness of the lush Thames Valley was enervating and oppressive; everything seemed splendid and decadent, the huge stale elms, the boys in their many-coloured caps and blazers, the top hats, the strawberries and cream, the smell of wisteria. I looked over the bridge as a boy in an outrigger came gliding past, like a waterboatman. Two Etonians were standing on the bridge and I heard one remark, 'Really that man Wilkinson's not at all a bad oar.' The foppish drawl, the two boys with their hats on the back of their heads, the graceful sculler underneath, seemed the incarnation of elegance and maturity.

There was no doubt that this was the place for me, for all of it was, from the St Wulfric's point of view, utterly and absorbingly evil. I got in twelfth on History and English as Orwell, after Wellington, had done the year before. In case there was no vacancy I went up for one more scholarship, this time at Charterhouse where we did the examination in a cellar during an air raid.

My last year at St Wulfric's was rosy. I was in sixth form which had its own sitting-room, with Ned Northcote, the captain of the school (Extreme Blonde), Frankie Wright (Dark Friend), and Nigel Kirk-patrick (Faunlike). We were about as civilized as little boys can grow to be. We were polite and we hardly ever caned anyone. We wrote to each other in the holidays, we got on with each other's parents, we went to theatres together and took tea at Rumpelmayer's. Ned was captain of the eleven and Nigel of the football team. I was head of the sixth.

My lack of character was now a permanent feature. I was *unreliable*. For that reason I was head of the sixth but not captain of the school; I occupied already the position I was so often to maintain in after life, that of the intellectual who is never given the job because he is 'brilliant but unsound'. I was also a physical coward, though I learnt how to conceal it, a natural captain of second elevens, and a moral coward by compensation, since, in an English community, moral cowardice is an asset.

Already I had accepted the theory that (1) Character is more important than intellect. (2) Intellect is usually found without character (Oscar Wilde). (3) Intellect, when found with character, is called Nous. (Intellect plus character = Nous plus gumption.) Character is desirable because it makes for success at school (winning colours and reporting best friend for homosexuality), prepares boys for the university, and is the foundation of success in business, politics, the army, the navy, the Indian and Egyptian civil services, and the African Police. But my analysis of success had disclosed another quality which seemed, in school life at any rate, to go as far. It might be called Prettiness. In the matriarchy of St Wulfric's, it was not Character, but Character plus Prettiness that succeeded; Colin and Nigel Kirkpatrick in their green kilts, even the outlawed Tony Watson or Roy Brown with his fine treble voice; they were the favoured of fortune, petted when others were scolded, permitted to wait on parents and old boys at Sunday night supper in their blue suits, introduced to the guests when they brought the food into the room and in a position to stuff their pockets with potato salad when they took it out.

Prettiness alone (Cecil) was suspect like intellect alone (Orwell) but prettiness that was good at games meant 'Character' and was safe. Since I was not pretty I worked hard to be charming and the four of us grew so civilized that we became inseparable. We were a little clique at the head of the school, a kind of 'Souls' of St Wulfric's, gay, powerful, introspective, and absorbed in each other's impressions. We took to visiting in our cubicles at night. One evening, after lights out, Ned

Northcote and Frankie Wright were talking in mine when we heard the matron pass along.

> Stalk and sneak, stalk and sneak,
> Maud of the rubbery shoes.
> Sneak sneak every week,
> Maud of the rubbery shoes.
> Over the cubicle wings you go
> Hearing the Red Room whispering low . . .

I had once written to please Tony, and now it was my turn to be caught.

Maud went into Northcote's cubicle. No sign of him. She called out in a terrible voice, 'Where's Northcote?' I answered from my cubicle, 'I think he went to the lavatory.' We heard her go along to open the door and lost our heads, like rabbits chased by a ferret. Ned bolted the latch of my cubicle with a toothbrush, and started to climb over the partition into his own. But Maud came and rattled it. 'Why is this door locked? Open it this instant.' I was afraid to. Silence. At last, with white face, Frankie opened it and she burst in. There was an eternity of waiting while our crime was reported, and then the three of us were taken down and caned by Sambo in our pyjamas. The locked door was evidence which our being a trio instead of the usual compromised pair could not palliate. It was Oscar Wilde over again.

The caning was only the beginning; next day our sergeant's stripes were removed, we were turned out of sixth form and a period of miserable disfavour started from which there seemed no hope of escape. But my scholarship was needed, like Ned's bowling, for propaganda; gradually we were forgiven, and our disgrace forgotten except by ourselves. For we never felt quite the same, we grasped that since we were all completely innocent there must be a pitch of civilization which, once reached, brought down a Nemesis. Character was safest: we had seen the writing on the wall.

Before I went to Eton I had spent the Christmas of 1917 in Ireland, in my aunt's house at Rathfarnham. The Easter Rebellion had taken place since I was last there and to be pro-Irish, pro-Celt, pro-Gaelic was no longer a harmless eccentricity. I used to go riding with a groom over the Wicklow mountains and for the first time the Sinn Feiner of St Wulfric's met his equal. Frank the groom was supposed to command a company of the Irish republican army whom he drilled in the glens of Kilmashogue and up by the Hell Fire Club. I afterwards pretended that I had been present at these parades but never met anyone with him except an old hermit. We went to the Abbey Theatre and saw Synge acted and heard 'God Save the King' hissed, and to Clontarf for a pink-coated Christmas dinner at which everyone told hunting stories in the brogue. I felt dowdy, awkward, and English again.

Otherwise my holidays had been uneventful. My great moment at home had been the purchase of a bicycle with three speeds which I called the Green Dragon. I rode it over to where we lived at Crondall and a few days later was allowed to go away for a night by myself. My mother and my favourite Great-uncle Granville saw me off. I bicycled that day from Farnham to Winchester, stayed at the George and went over the school and the Cathedral. The hotel people thought I had run away from somewhere and were suspicious, for the sight of a tourist of thirteen booking a room and dining by himself with a guidebook propped up was unusual. It was the first welling up of the passion for travel that was to dominate my spare time for the next twenty years.

I was still ignorant of anything which I had not read in a book but just before I went to Eton a concerted attack was made on my modesty. My father struggled to explain the facts of life and the chaplain at St Wulfric's gave the boys who were leaving a seedy exhortation. Sambo was more precise. We were going into a world full of temptations, he said, especially the Etonians; we must report any boy at once who tried to get into our bed, never go for a walk with a boy from another house, never make friends with anyone more than a year and a half older (eventually it would be younger), and above all, not 'play with ourselves'. There was an old boy from St Wulfric's who became so self-intoxicated that when he got to Oxford he had put, in a fit of remorse, his head under a train. That miserable youth, I afterwards learnt, had attended all the private schools in England.

Sambo gave a few examples of Wulfricians who had made good and mentioned cases where those who were doing well and were now heads of their houses, had been able to lend a helping hand to those floundering amid the sexual difficulties due to lack of character. The other boys leaving looked at me curiously, for I was warned to be careful, my literary temperament rendering me especially prone to 'all that kind of poisonous nonsense' and I was told that the boy with 'character' in my election at Eton who would, although not an old Wulfrician, keep an eye on me, was called Meynell. The Easter term over, we bade a tearful farewell to each other, Flip turned suddenly into a friend, and Nigel Kirkpatrick, Ned Northcote, Frankie Wright, promised to exchange letters with me from Marlborough, Repton, and Radley. But it was three years before I wrote another letter.

20 *Dark Ages*

If we had written, all our letters would have told the same story. The lively aristocrats of the cubicles and the sixth-form room were reduced to serfdom, cultivated Greeks pitched into the Carthaginian slave market. We began to adapt ourselves to our new indignity; C. V. Connolly, Esq., K.S., New Buildings, Eton College, Windsor.

The seventy Eton scholars lived together in a house, part Victorian, part medieval, where they were governed by the Master in College who had under him the Captain of the School and nine other members of Sixth Form, who wore stick-up collars, could cane, and have fags. All boys were divided into elections according to the year in which they won their scholarship; the elections moved slowly up the school *en bloc* and each represented a generation.

Below the top twenty came another thirty boys or so who formed the bulk of college and then the bottom twenty about fifteen of whom were doing their compulsory year of fagging, and who, while all the others had rooms, lived in wooden cubicles in Chamber.

The whole school, ruled in theory by Sixth Form and the Captain of the School, was governed by Pop or the Eton Society, an oligarchy of two dozen boys who, except for two or three *ex officio* members, were self-elected and could wear coloured waistcoats, stick-up collars, etc., and cane boys from any house. The masters could not cane. They punished by lines, detentions, and 'tickets' or chits of misbehaviour which had to be carried to the housemaster for signature. Serious offences or too many tickets meant being complained of to the head-master and might end in a birching.

This system makes Eton the most democratic of schools, for it is a school where all the prefects except the Sixth Form (who are only powerful in College) are self-elected. The boys get the government they deserve.

In practice Eton was not a democracy for the system was feudal. The masters represented the church, with the headmaster as Pope; the boys, with their hierarchy of colours and distinctions, were the rest of the population, while the prefects and athletes, the captains of houses and the members of 'Pop' were the feudal overlords who punished offences at the request of the 'church' and in return were tacitly allowed to break the same rules themselves. Thus a boy had two loyalties, to his tutor and to his fagmaster or feudal overlord. Sometimes the 'church' could protect a young clerk, making the lot of a serious little boy more bear-able, in other houses the housemaster was powerless, the 'church' weak and unable to control the feudal barons. At other times there were strug-gles between master and boy which ended in Canossa.

On the whole the feudal system worked well. The boys elected to Pop, those who combined goodness at games with elegance, vitality, and a certain mental alertness, were urbane and tolerant; it was among the house-barons that bullies and stupid types were to be found.

A fag in Chamber I was in the lowest ranks of serfdom. Though fagmasters were usually chivalrous to their own slaves, mine was not, nor had we privacy, for our spare time was at the mercy of our rulers, who could send us far into Windsor to buy them food and beat us if we made a mistake over it. I had not often been beaten at St Wulfric's, at Eton it became a hideous experience, for even the little boy who was

'Captain of Chamber' could beat us, not with a cane but with a piece of rubber tubing. There was a 'Chamber Pop' who also could beat one in a body for a breach of privilege.

I felt quite lost and friendless in this world and sought out Meynell, the boy selected by Sambo to keep an eye on me. An eye was a euphemism for here was the familiar blend of character and prettiness, a tousled wire-terrier of a boy, tough, humorous, a natural leader and political commissar. We were all unhappy and had such a feeling of persecution that we bullied each other to forget it. I was sixty-ninth in college order and among the most bullied boys in my election where Meynell was ringleader. He invented tortures as a perpetual inquest to see if we had 'guts' and was much liked in the elections above him who considered him a 'good influence'.

Nobody would have believed that he could make me stand on a mantelpiece and dance while he brandished a red-hot poker between my feet and said: 'What is your name?' 'Connolly.' 'No – what is your real name? Go on. Say it.' 'Ugly.' 'All right, Ugly, you can come down.' He was aided by a few boys who hoped that their sycophancy would save their skins and by another bully called Highworth. Highworth was not a torturer like Meynell, but a conceited, rakish, conventional boy who could not bear anyone to be eccentric or untidy. He should never have been in College, he was a natural Oppidan.*

I spent much of my spare time in School Library, sheltering among the poets. I had discovered the Celtic Twilight and in proportion as I was unhappy, I took it out on the *Lake Isle of Innisfree*, the *Little Waves of Breffny*, *Glencullen* and other escapist poems, to which I added the *Golden Journey to Samarkand*. I tried to make friends with one other bullied boy but he reciprocated too violently, showed me his own poems, and sniffed at the back of his nose. Instead I fell for a boy called Wilfrid, the faun type over again with green eyes, nectarine colouring who was quick to divine in the little black-gowned, dirty

* Oppidans were the thousand other boys not in College who paid the full fees. Oppidans could be brilliant scholars but they could never experience the advantages and disadvantages of the intensive intellectual forcing-house which College was.

colleger a potential admirer, even as a beautiful orchid accepts the visits of some repulsive beetle. He was an Oppidan, good at games and older than me. It was only possible to see him leaving his classroom about once a week or sometimes coming out of Chapel or at Absence when the whole of our Feudal society assembled in School Yard. If he was with anyone important he would cut me; if not he would make a joke or two at my expense while I grinned like a waiter. My daydreams centred round him. I looked up his home address, found out about his family, and copied his initials on to bits of paper. It was something to be in love at last.

The beatings were torture. We were first conscious of impending doom at Prayers when the eyes of Sixth Form would linger pointedly at us. They had supper in a room of their own and a special fag, 'Senior', who was excused ordinary duties, like other police spies, was sent from there to fetch the 'wanted' man. From Upper Tea Room 'Senior' set out on his thrilling errand, past the boys chatting outside their rooms. 'Who's "wanted"?' 'Connolly.' 'What, again?' At last he reached the fags who were shivering with terror – for this was always an agonizing quarter of an hour for them – in their distant stalls in Chamber. Those who were sitting in their tin baths paused with the sponge in the air – they might have to get out again to dress. The talkers ceased their chorus simultaneously, like frogs, even the favoured who were being tickled in their stalls by the Master in College stopped giggling and fear swept over the wooden partitions. 'It's Connolly.' 'Connolly, you're "wanted".' 'Who by?' 'Wrangham.' 'That's all right. He won't beat me, only tick me off. He's my fagmaster.' 'He's going to beat someone. He's got the chair out.'

The chair was only put in the middle of the room when beatings were to take place and sometimes the fag was sent beforehand to get the canes with which he would himself be beaten.

The worst part was the suspense for we might make a mistake the day before and not be beaten for it till the following evening. Or we could get a day's grace by pleading a headache and getting 'early bed leave' or by going out to the shooting range, the musical society or to a mysterious evening service, held once a week to expedite the war which was much frequented by guilty consciences, called Intercession. The huge chapel was dark and deserted, the gas mantles plopped, the stained-glass windows glittered, the headmaster droned the prayers from the altar. I too was praying. 'Please God may Wrangham not "want" me, please please God may Wrangham not "want" me or may he forget about it by tomorrow, and I will clean my teeth. And make me see Wilfrid. Amen.'

Often mass executions took place; it was not uncommon for all the fags to be beaten at once. After a storm of accusation to which it was wiser not to reply since no one, once the chair was out, had been known to 'get off', the flogging began. We knelt on the chair bottoms outwards and gripped the bottom bar with our hands, stretching towards it over the back. Looking round under the chair we could see a monster rushing towards us with a cane in his hand, his face upside down and distorted – the frowning mask of the Captain of the School or the hideous little Wrangham. The pain was acute. When it was over some other member of Sixth Form would say 'Good night' – it was wiser to answer.

These memories are associated for me with the smell of Sixth Form supper and with the walk back through the spectators to the bed that pulled down from the wall, with the knowing inquiries of the vice-haunted virginal master in college, a Jesuit at these executions, and the darkness that prisoners long for.

The Captain of the School, Marjoribanks, who afterwards committed suicide, was a passionate beater like his bloody-minded successors, Wrangham and Cliffe. Meynell began to receive anonymous notes which made certain suggestions and showed 'character' by taking them straight to his fagmaster. The Captain of the School was told and the culprit was ordered to confess; nothing happened. Then another note arrived. The sender, clearly very high in the school, was never discovered, but in one satisfactory evening Marjoribanks had beaten all the lower half of college. Thirty-five of us suffered. Another time we were all flogged because a boy dropped a sponge out of a window which hit a master, or we would be beaten for 'generality' which meant no specific charge except that of being 'generally uppish'.

The result of these persecutions, combined with Chamber beating and bullyings, was to ruin my nerve. My work went off, and I received several 'tickets' which I had to present to my tutor, in itself a torture. To this day I cannot bear to be sent for or hear of anyone's wanting to see me about something without acute nervous dread.

My own election was broken under the strain of beatings at night and bullying by day; all we could hope for was to achieve peace with seniority and then become disciplinarians in our turn. But there was one ray of hope. The election now in power was a reactionary one which would be succeeded as it passed on by a gentler crowd, and our own senior election, the year above us, whom as yet we hardly knew, contained heroic fighters for liberty and justice. It bristled with Pyms and Hampdens and the feudal system was powerless there.

I had another stroke of luck. After a 'chamber pop beating' from Meynell and four other boys, he began a heart-to-heart – 'Ugly, why are you so filthy, what is the matter with you?' After the tears which followed I succeeded in making him laugh, and revealed my capacity as a wit. I was able to expand it and soon I could make not only Meynell laugh, but Highworth: they began to leave me alone, bullying me only when they could not find anyone else, but even then sparing me, if I seemed unsuspecting and confident and did not smell of fear. At last I made them laugh at the expense of their victims and my sarcasm became useful. One evening in my second term, after the Armistice had been signed, Meynell asked me to call him Godfrey. From then I was safe, my prayers at 'intercession' were answered. I had become a bully too.

Highworth's father and Meynell's and my own had all been professional soldiers who had employed the methods of the parade ground for the disciplining of their sons. We now became the rulers of Chamber, in which Godfrey Meynell was the Hitler, Highworth the Goering, and I the Goebbels, forming a Gestapo who bullied everyone we could and confiscated their private property.

After two terms of being bullied, I had, with occasional relapses, a year of bullying until, owing to some bad tactics, I let both Godfrey and Highworth combine against me. Yet we were fond of each other and our triumvirate was racked with jealousy. Highworth was a big neat handsome boy, good at games, a fast bowler, fond of girls and dirty stories. Godfrey was untidy, lazy, yet energetic, sentimental and self-reproachful, a puritan with a saving grace of humour, a border baron half-converted to Christianity whose turbulent life fitted exactly into the pattern of Eton feudalism for he was an example of character and prettiness in authority; his courage was tremendous, to play football under his captaincy, on a losing side, was a sensation. For an hour and a quarter he blamed, praised, and appealed to our feelings, leading rush after rush against boys bigger than himself, poaching any kicks he could get and limping off the field with his arm round my neck. 'My God, you went badly today, Nolly – haven't you any guts – to think we lost to those bastards by three to one' and tears of rage would roll down his cheeks. 'Next time we've got to win – we've got to – understand, Flinchface?'

His personality dominated us because it was the strongest and because it was the incarnation of schoolboyness; the five hundred years of Eton life had gone to make it, the Gothic windows, the huge open fireplace, the table in the middle of Chamber round which our life centred, had been brought into being for him. He was emotional and as Captain of Chamber would 'beat' me for untidiness, half miserable at having to flog his best friend, half pleased at fulfilling a Roman duty, only to suffer remorse at the condition of his own belongings. 'God knows what I'm to do – I can't let you beat *me* – I haven't the authority – if I ask you to hit me as hard as you can I might lose my temper and knock you down. We'll have to make Wayne and Buckley tidy our stalls for us in future.'

Godfrey's relaxation was reading Homer; he adored the Odyssey, for the Homeric world was one in which he was at home and the proverbs of 'the wily Odysseus', to the disgust of the able but Philistine Highworth, were never off his lips. 'Oh, babababarbaba babababarbaba,' he

42

would storm; 'for God's sake stop spouting Greek – I can't understand a fellow with guts like you Godfrey wanting to quote that filthy Greek all the time – and as for you, Cyril, you're worse – nine bloody bean-rows will I have there and a hive for the honey bloody bee – my God it makes me crap.'

Between two such personalities it seemed that I never would have a chance to develop, or find room to reach out to the sun, but I had two pieces of good fortune. Highworth, always sexually precocious, laid hands on a confirmation candidate in the confessional state and was sent away for two terms and Godfrey got pneumonia. He was in the sick-room for a month and while he was ill his trampled satellites plucked up their courage. I made friends with three of them and when he came back, we presented a united front against further bullying. Godfrey himself was deeply altered by his illness, his mischievous rest-lessness left him; being ill for so long and perhaps discovering how little he was missed and how well people got on without him, how transitory was power, had changed his character. For the rest of his time at Eton (he left early for Sandhurst), he was hardworking and modest. He never recovered his leadership but became liked by all those who once had gone in fear of him. The border baron, the prince of the dark ages, had undergone a change of heart, a genuine conversion.

Godfrey afterwards joined his father's regiment, went out to India, and had himself transferred to the Indian Army, for he disliked the social side of army life and wanted to be in closer contact with the men he loved. From there he went with his gurkhas to Waziristan, still reading Homer, and was killed in action on the frontier, winning a post-humous V.C.

> Liquenda tellus et domus et placens
> Uxor . . .

Encased in the shell secreted by my cowardice, I have thought about his death on that untenable hillside, outnumbered, putting heart into his troops by assuring them that help would reach them, though well aware that help could not, and dying covered with wounds after fighting all day.

Such an end seems remote from the literary life, yet it was the end of one my own age, with whom for four years I had been shaken about like stones in a tin. To a parent passing through College there must have seemed nothing to choose between Godfrey and myself, two small boys in Eton jackets cooking their fagmaster's sausages, both untidy, noisy, and mouse-coloured and yet in each a fate was at work; two characters, reacting differently to the same environment, were shaping their lives. The qualities I admire are intellectual honesty, generosity, courage, and beauty. Godfrey was grave. I was not.

Such was the reward of leadership, the destiny of character – not the position of business responsibility which St Wulfric's had promised us but a premature and lonely death with the barren glory of a military honour.

~

The boys in my election with whom I now made friends were Charles Milligan, Kit Minns, and Jackie O'Dwyer. Charles became of morbid interest through being caught smoking which made him seem romantic and subversive. He was the Extreme Blonde with delicate features and an air of neatness and languor. Minns, a peacable Oriental-looking boy, surprised the Gestapo by refusing to be bullied. He was quiet and good-natured but when threats or force were employed he would not move. The Gestapo were puzzled; we felt like hunters up against a new animal for Minns was invincible, not through his badgerlike strength, but because he knew he was right. For the first time we felt guilty, aware that our bullying proceeded from a sense of inferiority deepened per-haps by sexual ignorance, and confined ourselves henceforth to the official victims.

O'Dwyer was nearly always in tears but he was affectionate, witty, and genial and I secretly made friends with him. We arranged that if he publicly stood up to the Gestapo in my presence I would try to prevent him being punished. The moment came. Godfrey, as usual, was late in changing for afternoon school. 'My God, I've lost my braces.' He

looked round, then marched up. 'O'Dwyer, give me your braces.' 'No.'
'Take off your braces and give them me at once.' 'No.' This was
unheard of: Godfrey glowered at O'Dwyer, who stood rooted to the
spot with the tears streaming down his face. After a silence, Godfrey
turned away and claimed some braces elsewhere. Another serf was on
the road to emancipation. Not unnaturally our election had a bad name
though no one quite knew what was going on in it.

I was now fifteen, dirty, inky, miserable, untidy, a bad fag, a coward
at games, lazy at work, unpopular with my masters and superiors,
anxious to curry favour and yet to bully whom I dared. The rule of the
election system was that we spoke only to the boys of our own year; we
could be beaten for speaking first to a boy in an election above and were
expected to enforce the same discipline on those below. All our election
were most formal with the year that had arrived beneath us. I got a bad
report and was described as 'cynical and irreverent'; *'tu ne cede malis'*,
wrote Mr Stone, *'sed contra audentior ito'*.

My parents were upset, heads were put together, and the blame was
thrown on Orwell, who was supposed to be my 'bad influence' though
now I hardly ever saw him. We had been for walks on Sundays but we
belonged to two different civilizations. He was immersed in *The Way of
All Flesh* and the atheistic arguments of *Androcles and the Lion*, I in
the Celtic Twilight and Lady Gregory's resurrected Gaelic legends. His
election found us (Meynell excluded) brutish and savage. They were
anxious to talk to their junior election and subvert in that way the
reactionary 'election' system but they did not know how to begin for we
were hardly the material on which liberal opinions could be tested.

The moral leaders of my senior election, known as 'the caucus', were
Denis Dannreuther, Roger Mynors, Robert Longden, Gibson and
Cazalet. Orwell was rather extreme and aloof, and Farlow, the most
original and vigorous member, too rough and cynical for the lofty inner
ring of whiggery. These two precocious boys were bosom friends:
Farlow a boisterous sceptic who applied 'cui bono' – 'who benefits by
it' – as a criterion to the whole school system and Orwell perpetually sneering at 'They' – a Marxist-Shavian concept which included

Masters, Old Collegers, the Church, and Senior reactionaries. This did not prevent him knocking Highworth down once when he found him tormenting me. One day at the end of my sixth term I found myself 'staying out' in the sick-room with Roger Mynors. Day by long day we made friends, discovering in each other the inevitable passion for the Isle of Purbeck, for chalk streams and geography, and for the first time I underwent the civilizing influence of my senior election. They were a most remarkable set of boys, and included a batch of five scholar athletes, animated, unlike the rulers of college, by post-war opinions. They hated bullying, beating, fagging, the election system, militarism, and all infringements of liberty and they believed in the ultimate victory of human reason. They were polite to each other and formed an oasis of enlightenment, with one set of baby reactionaries underneath them and another, more dangerous, in the year above.

Mynors did not drop me when we came out of the sick-room and an epidemic of mumps thinned out my own election, enabling Charles Milligan, Jackie O'Dwyer, and myself to push forward together. Jackie was clever, lazy, good at games, and attractive. He represented a type which is found in every school, the affable genial kind of boy whose life is a succession of enthusiasms; for dab cricket, for learning all the peers by sight, the variations of the house colours, the results of the Harrow matches or the batting averages of the eleven. He was sunny and tolerant, suspected of 'not going hard' in the more painful sports and, like myself, greedy. We ate quantities of bananas and cream and all day played a game called 'passage fives' under a white fused light in the echoing mump-stricken corridor. Roger Mynors walked about with me and called me the 'little ray of sunshine'. The affectionate and civilized head boy of St Wulfric's tentatively reappeared and that Easter, after my fourth term, I wrote O'Dwyer a letter. The dark ages were over.

21 *Renaissance*

It was now the summer of 1920. I was no longer a fag and had a room of my own. Neither ruler nor serf, I now formed part of the central bourgeoisie of College. I first saw Nigel by the letter slab and from that moment I was as much changed as Godfrey by pneumonia. The 'pair system' reappeared in my life, the faun, the dream brother. That afternoon we played in a knock-up cricket match and each made twenty-five. Nigel had all the familiar features, dark hair, green eyes, yellow skin, and a classic head with the wistfulness of a minor angel in a Botticelli, but, being a colleger, he was not stupid like Wilfrid or Tony; in spite of the year and a half between our ages, companionship was possible.

To say I was in love again will vex the reader beyond endurance, but he must remember that being in love had a peculiar meaning for me. I had never even been kissed and love was an ideal based on the exhibitionism of the only child. It meant a desire to lay my personality at someone's feet as a puppy deposits a slobbery ball; it meant a non-stop daydream, a planning of surprises, an exchange of confidences, a giving of presents, an agony of expectation, a delirium of impatience, ending with the premonition of boredom more drastic than the loneliness which it set out to cure. I was now entering adolescence and for long was to suffer from that disfiguring ailment. My sense of values was to be affected, my emotions falsified, my mind put out of focus, my idea of reality imposed on reality and where they did not tally, reality would be cut to fit.

Nigel was in my sub-junior election. This meant that although I could be seen about with my junior election, I could not be seen alone with him. One way I could talk to him was by availing myself of co-ordinated visits to the shooting gallery, glimpses on the way to meals, leaving chapel, at absence or other ceremonies of the community. The other was to frequent my junior election and make use of the etiquette by which they were allowed to go about with him. This meant altering my ideas about the election system, in fact, ceasing to be a reactionary. The change in emotional life led, as is often the case, to a new political alignment.

I first made friends with the two civilized members of my junior election, Peter Loxley and Walter Le Strange, and through them was able to see something of Nigel and his red-haired friend Freddie Langham. At the same time, growing more liberal, I became more accept-able to the election above. Denis Dannreuther and Robert Longden took me up and afterwards King-Farlow and George Wansbrough. At the end of the term I sat next to Nigel at a house-match. (I could not give a picture of Eton if I did not emphasize how much time was devoted to planning meetings with people of another year or in another house; the intrigues were worthy of Versailles or Yildiz.) At the house-match I asked Nigel who he liked best in the school. Langham? 'Second best,' Loxley? 'Fourth best,' and so on. He also asked me. We realized that we had both omitted 'first best' and that the only people we had not mentioned had been each other. I experienced the thrill not untinged with apprehension by which the romantic recognizes recipro-cated love.

Then came Camp, where my parents, who lived near, gave dinner-parties for Godfrey and my new friends, Mynors, Runciman, Wans-brough, Longden, and Dadie Rylands. Our house was a refuge from Camp and, making up my little dinner-parties, I tasted the joys of being a political hostess and laid my plans for the future.

The Christmas term of 1920 I was launched. Looking back at my schooldays I am conscious of a rhythm about them, every year cul-minated in the summer term; it was the term when things happened, the climax of emotions, successes, and failures. I never felt well in the sum-mer term. The Thames Valley climate was lowering, I was enervated by the profusion of elms and buttercups and sheep-turds, the heat and the leisure. The summers at Eton were too pagan, one collapsed half-way through. Those hot afternoons punctuated by the 'toc toc' of bat hitting ball when I sat with a book in the shade of Poets' Walk, a green tunnel that has etiolated so many generations of poets, or wandered through the deserted college buildings, where the chalky sunbeam lay aslant the desk, were deleterious. Christmas terms meant consolidation and new beginnings; Easter was a season of promise; the games that I was good at were fives and squash; I liked the Easter terms best. Christmas was a primitive, Easter the quattrocento, and summer the decadence.

To this day I can tell whether a person is school-minded: whether they are cowardly, gregarious, sensitive to pupil-teacher relationships, warm, competitive and adolescent – or whether they are schoolproof. The art of getting on at school depends on a mixture of enthusiasm with moral cowardice and social sense. The enthusiasm is for personalities and gossip about them, for a schoolboy is a novelist too busy to write. Orwell, for example, with his 'non serviam', or Steven Runciman who divided the world into two groups, the stupid and the sillies, lack the ape-like virtues without which no one can enjoy a public school. I possessed them, and from now on was happy and successful. I joined the College Literary Society, for which we wrote poems and criticism.

Two of my new friends in super-senior election belonged, Dadie Rylands and Terence Beddard, whom I called, as one was so much more censorious than the other, the Old and the New Testament. Dadie was a charming, feline boy; he lent me modern poetry to read in the Chap Books which were then coming out. He liked Rupert Brooke and introduced me to the Georgians. My possession of these Chap Books awoke in Highworth envy tinged with incomprehension. 'My God, Cyril – if I'd known you were going to turn into a bloody aesthete and go bumsucking after people like Rylands! There's Godfrey turned pi as hell and all the rest of our election without any guts – and now you start letting your hair grow long and reading those bloody chapbooks. Rupert Brooke! Ow boo-hoo boo-hoo, stands the church clock at ten to bloody three and is there honey still for bloody tea!' After this I lost my temper and for the next year never spoke to him. Handsome and neat as ever, with several cricket colours and many Oppidan friends, he had hopes of getting into Pop, and yet was bewildered, isolated from the rest of us by his lack of adolescence.

One day I wrote a pines-and-heather poem myself for the Literary Society which was favourably criticized. The last couplet was:

> And, winging down the evening sky,
> The herons come to the heronry.

Dadie said that by accident I had written a couplet as good as anything in Rupert Brooke. Godfrey took me aside and said that he wished he could have written the poem, that it expressed everything he felt and that he did not know anyone else could feel. Even Terence Beddard, a dandy with a romantic side and a gift for satire, was impressed – but Highworth never saw it.

Terence and I did classics up to Mr Headlam in the same division, we satirized Georgian poetry and the literary society in our spare time and invented a Georgian poet called Percy Beauregard Biles. Terence was a Byronic character, the first one I had met; he was a Mercutio, a foppish, melancholy, and ironical dandy. I used to go along to talk in his room and we discovered a common interest in Nigel. By then I liked Freddie Langham almost as much; he was more engaging, intelligent, and whole-hearted than Nigel who could embarrass me by displaying a senti-mentality which I shared. He was also inclined to grow weepy, and religious. We sometimes walked across School Yard at night and lay on our backs looking up at the buttresses of the chapel for it was a dis-covery of mine that the height of the Gothic could be appreciated in that way.

'I suppose we are the only people in College,' said Nigel, 'who ever look at the stars. The others are all fools. We are the only two who are humble.'

By the next term Terence had left. He had had great influence on me, bringing out a side – Don Juan with a touch of Wilde – whose deve-lopment made my life more interesting but also more theatrical and egocentric. For years afterwards I wrote to him, about 'Le Rouge et Le Noir' as I called Freddie and Nigel. Nigel sulked that term and grew more religious than ever. My friends were Denis Dannreuther (the head of my senior election), Charles Milligan, and Freddie Langham; the

Dark Friend, the Extreme Blonde and the Redhead were rallying.

Denis was an exquisite classical scholar, one of those rare people who combine a brilliant and logical mind with genuine moral feeling and who become more than a careerist. We talked ethics and College politics, for the political situation was fascinating. There was party government in the struggle between pre-war and post-war – between right and left. The armistice and the end of the war had released a wave of scepticism and revolutionary feeling over Eton where a book like *Eminent Victorians* made a particular sensation. The Left Wing or Liberals, as we called ourselves, in opposition to the Reactionaries, had a clear view of the situation.

(1) The war and the corresponding increase of militarism had affected the freedom of Eton boys. Emergency measures had been enforced and not repealed, lights went out earlier, discipline was stricter and privileges had been given up in the crisis which had never been restored. The tightening up of discipline involved a cynical view of boy nature, which, especially in College, was to be deplored. Those responsible were the ushers, among whom were certain Vile Old Men who wished to wrest from the boys all liberty and independence and who were aided by our vacillating Master, a sex-obsessed prude who extorted information about boys' morals from hysterical confirmation candidates and practised other Jesuitical abuses. Behind him was that fine casuist the Headmaster and of course the Old Tugs – old collegers who belonged to the stoic pre-war generations, the pillars of the *ancien régime*.

(2) The corner-stone of this régime was the election system, which did not exist in the houses, was of quite recent origin, and harmful in that it created a false authority, separating people who ought to be mixing with each other, preventing a 'bad' election being improved by a 'good' one and creating a sense of guilt in those who had innocent relationships outside. The theory that the election system prevented bullying was untrue, since bullying, like immorality, was commonest among boys of the same age. The election system therefore must be abolished from the top, and boys be allowed to talk to whom they liked.

In this daylight the danger of immorality would be less than in the present atmosphere of privilege and intrigue.

(3) Corporal punishment was a relic of barbarism. It was as bad for those who administered as for those who received it. That torture also must be abolished from the top while mass floggings and generality beatings of the kind we had been subjected to were inexcusable.

(4) The fagging system must be modified. The summoning of boys from Chamber to distant parts of College, the last one to arrive being sent off to Windsor for a walnut cake, made too great inroads on their time and the knight-and-squire relationship between fagmaster and fag was sentimental.

(5) The privileges of College Pop or Debating Society were invidious. There was too much canvassing and blackballing, the elections made too many people unhappy.

(6) Games and colours were over-important. Their influence was exaggerated and must be fought. They should not be competitive or compulsory.

(7) The Corps was a joke; it had no business to be compulsory and any tendency to increase militarism among a war-weary generation must be exposed and ridiculed.

(8) Boys must be appealed to through reason. They must be given the benefit of the doubt; their fundamental goodness and good sense must be believed in, however contrary to appearances.

To this the reactionaries replied as they always have; that human nature could not be changed, give people an inch and they would take an ell, that 'one must draw the line somewhere', that if games and discipline were relaxed orgies would break out, that corporal punishment was the only check on self-satisfaction and answered a bully in his own coin, that boys were conservative and hated giving up any of their hard-won privileges, that life was a Vale of Tears in which liberalism did not work.

At that time College Pop, unlike School Pop, still had debates and some of my senior election had been elected members of it. There had been two classic debates, on the 'election system' and on corporal punishment, that had almost ended in blows. The liberals at the bottom, Denis, King-Farlow, Roger Mynors, Bobbie Longden, and Gibson had been supported by Miles Clausen and Christopher Hollis, the liberals at the top. The election in between that would shortly be coming into power was reactionary, except for Rylands and for one or two others who were non-political.

As the last liberals left the top of the school and my reactionary super-senior election came into office, the position of the liberals in senior election, and the few others, like myself, Charles Milligan, Le Strange, and Loxley grew unpleasant. Reprisals were due and our few protectors were leaving. Without Beddard and Rylands I had no friends among those coming into power and at the advanced age of seventeen I received a beating for 'uppishness'. Here are two letters of the time.

Easter, 1921

My Dear Terence,

Home and Morbid. Since I wrote I have become clean gone on Nigel again. It's really too awful. I told you his attitude this half has been sulky with flashes of niceness – well, Monday I lectured him about it, and got out from him – A, the fact that he despised me. B, that his ideal was to be completely indifferent – this he kept up continually till on Thursday afternoon I got him alone in Lower Tea Room and discovered that 'he was aiming at obtaining spiritual perfection, and that he regarded me as a distraction to be avoided, that I brought along other distractions (Loxley and Le Strange) and tried to talk about nothing with him and Langham.'

All of which is true. I spent the last three days trying not to show him (Freddie) that I liked N. more (which I did since last Monday). N. told me that he thought it impossible to like everyone and that he wanted to cut down his acquaintances to a small but select circle and he did not want me to be one but he was afraid my personality was too strong. Well, I then had him on toast. I said that he must have a pretty rotten sort of perfection if it had to be guarded from plausible antichrists like me (that is his unexpressed idea of me), that he treated me like a muck-heap in the corner of his room which he shunned instead of trying to clear up – that he was running away from temptation instead of fighting it, that he was completely selfish, and instead of trying to make others better was only trying to safeguard himself – as for his beastly set, he, I suppose, believed in the parable of the good Shepherd? Yes he did – Well, which did the shepherd admire most, the 99 good sheep or the wandering one? He had to admit he would admire the 99 more. But which did he like most and take most steps over? Moreover who did he suppose liked the shepherd best, the 99 good sheep or the wandering one?

He had to give in and admit he was quite wrong and unchristian . . . I showed him that, temporarily at any rate, I preferred him to Langham. This morning I found him in Lower Tea Room and said goodbye, he asked me to write to him and seemed to have forgiven me. Now I can think of no-one else. Do you know the Greek epigram 'delicate are the fosterlings of Tyre but Myiscus outshines them as the sun the stars'; it seems to me that suits him, there is a husky look about him which the name Myiscus brings out and his good looks are typical sun products, not rosy or effeminate.

Langham is now very nice and attractive but relegated to second place, and now I am not glad at getting home but sorry at not seeing N. I am altogether rather fed with last half – I talked exclusively to a set consisting of Dannreuther, Minns, Milligan, Eastwood, Langham and N., with no one else have I talked anything but trivialities. I got on badly with N. and quarrelled with Highworth. However I got my first 'stinker' [Distinction in Trials] the story of which I must tell you when I have more time. I never dreamt I could go clean gone on the *same* person. Wish me luck in my new venture. I hope I can get him gone on me again but I dread lest I should then cool myself. N. despises you I think even more than me. χαιρε.

Tuesday

My Dear Terry,

I wrote you two letters lately. Re N. I think it was being treated the right way set me gone on him again. What I like is a winning fight – well at first I got that, then nothing to fight for, then a losing one. Now I am straight again. It is not true to say the unattainable is the spice of life, it is attaining the unattainable. I never enjoy doing a thing until I have made sufficient difficulties – given that I am colossally conceited, I only realized it lately. Tuppa (Headlam) and Crace both saying I was v. able bucked me up enormously. I used to think I could never do more than obtain a superficial knowledge of a few things. Now I think there is *nothing* I cannot do, though very few things worth taking the trouble to (don't end sentences with prepositions).

You ask how life is? Chaos. I am in the state of mind of not being able to get at anything, the only thing that is true is that *(a) every*thing is true *(b)* everything is false.

Tuppa's formula of Some People . . . Others . . . seems to be the only generality worthy of acceptance. I am house-hunting for a way of life, it is fun in a way but the agents do not know what I want and the houses that sound most attractive are hideous to look at close, others are beyond my income.

I wrote to N. and sent him my photo, with a lot of explanation of my present state, which seems to worry him. I said I thought I lived for the best form of happiness: learning to appreciate the first rate and know the sham, learning to look for beauty in everything, sampling every outlook and every interest (bar stinks and maths), trying to stop people being lukewarm and liking the second rate, trying to make other people happy, but not doing so at the cost of my own happiness, or concealing it when I am being generous. Publishing all the good I do. I suppose I am too cautious to risk investing in treasure in heaven. Roughly these are my ideals. I said how much more I liked him than I used to, and that he must treat me as a nice dog, not worship or despise, but sympathize. I said I really had no aim in life (by the way I am trying to analyse after doing anything my motives for doing it and so deduce what my outlook is – unwilling to accept my own introspective failure). I think the fact that one does things and cannot analyse motives or reconcile them to averred principles goes a long way to proving fatalism. I love extremes, either I would be a Catholic fatalist, or an atheist. (I did not say that to N. at the time.) I began 'Dear Nigel' and signed by photo 'Cyril'. I got:

Dear Connolly, I feel very honoured that you (then in pencil) *consider me*

worthy of ink. You see I don't think you are. I did not ask for the picture,
but as you sent it there remains no other course for me than to say
'Thank you' (you notice the improvement in style on the last letter!).
By the way I wish you would leave paragraphs in your so-called letters.

I want you to understand that I consider your spiritual welfare a thing
that it is my duty to improve. I will allow that I have felt a certain
amount of pitying affection for you. I saw last half that you were a waste
paper basket for wrong ideas and that something ought to be done for
you. I should have tried to do this had I had a chance of seeing you alone
and discussing. But you, quite blindly and utterly incapable of putting
yourself in my position, always brought company with you and went into
Langham's room, where your frivolity, barely keeping within the bounds
of decency, was to me so utterly despicable and repulsive to my
principles, that I was bound to adopt the attitude which you called a
pose. If it hadn't been for Langham I might have quarrelled with you
quite nastily – but of course you are not appreciating anything I say.
Think of all the millions of times last half you came into MY stall
ALONE.

If you come next half alone I shall not generally consider you a
distraction, but you must be quite prepared to be sent away, and I want
you to understand you are not going to come before either my work or
my religion and I want you to realize that anything in the nature of
company or popularity is quite repugnant to me. Langham is quite nice
and sociable, but as yet I do not know much about him and am beginning
to wonder if there is much beneath the surface. Be it far from me to
worship you! You state that you have no aim in life as yet and are trying
to find one, well why not take the plain one with which you have been
fed from your youth up. (A. Because it is plain. B. Because I have been fed
with it from my youth up.) *I.E. The Christian One. You can form a pretty*
average good ideal from this I should have thought. Of course you must
know all about it and you can do this by systematic bible reading. Form
your principles on what you read, and do everything in principle. Imagine
your ideal, which after all is set down in the N.T. You need not call it
God, if you dislike the word, but think of it and act on it always.
If you like, take it as a matter of interest. Think how frightfully dull your

present aimless life is (is house-hunting dull?) *compared with what it might be. If you have an aim in everything you do you will find you have an extraordinary pleasure at every success achieved, renewed confidence, and firmer principles. For instance I can assure you I gain real genuine pleasure in turning you out of my stall when I want to talk to you, but have some work to do. In your condition you are perfectly lonely and, whenever you are in trouble you have nothing to fall back on, no one to help you, and you act on inspiration. When I am in trouble I always know what to do through my principles. I consult with God and so am acting definitely, and not in an aimless helpless way.*

Try this, will you? Call it imagination at first if you like, but if you are sincere you will soon be convinced that it is more than that.

You must see for yourself how thoroughly unsatisfactory your present state is.

Now I am sure you will laugh at me for all this.

N.

A wonderful letter for a boy of fifteen and I think he means it. I wonder why he is so deliberately rude and impersonal. I don't think his ideal is so very good, he says God is his principle while the Christian idea of God is Love. His is more Petrine than Joannine Christianity. I think unless I can make him take an interest in poetry, painting, etc. he will become an awful Puritan. If he cares only about religion he will become narrow-minded too. I know he does despise all popularity, but then he is good-looking enough to be able to. The only respectable Christianity is Broad Church or R.C., and here we have a modern P. father in embryo. Moreover he talks as if he will drop Freddy as soon as he is sure there is nothing in him, though Langham likes him best in the election. I want to make Langham interesting and wrote to him telling him to go to the National Gallery before he answered. He has not answered but I think he is too young to enjoy writing letters.

I am becoming quite a Socrates in the lower half of college. I do want people to like talking religion and morals, to read good books, like poetry and pictures, and think for themselves. N. merely retires further into his shell as when he wouldn't answer my questionnaire for my religion chart. You see I think my ideals are superior to his. Of course they are founded on the assumption that there is no conscious immortality, that happiness is the mean between good and evil (in their usual sense), that the greatest happiness is to be found in novelty. I think self-sacrifice is the greatest happiness when you are at an age to appreciate it, at present it must be ostentatious and announced to everyone. I think in Art it is at first necessary to accept the decision of others. I have to go before a picture and say 'this is a great picture, I must learn to like it', till, aided by my own good taste, I do like it. I think my ideals have deteriorated . I used to think Perfection the aim of life, now I think it is Perfection in Happiness. Adversity is like a purge, it is good for you at the time and you are the more able to enjoy life when you have done with it, and it gives me a chance to demonstrate my atheism. I think I must try and be a Stoic in adversity, and Epicurean in prosperity. Baudelaire says somewhere:

> From the crude ore of each minute
> Draw the pure gold that is in it.

Gangue is the word for 'ore'.

I would love to have tea with you at Rumpelmayer's when you come back on the 24th when I go to stay with Loxley in town. I am so hard up for a sufficiently debauched confidant that you must excuse these long rambling epistles. Biles has written a bawdy ballad in exile. It begins –

> O to be back at school again
> To gossip and laugh and swear –

I must go to bed now. A Riverderci.

PS.

> Is it so small a thing to have enjoyed the sun
> To have lived light in the spring
> To have loved, to have thought, to have done,
> To have advanced true friends, and beat down baffling foes?

That we must feign a bliss
Of doubtful future date
And in pursuit of this
Lose all our present state
And relegate to worlds yet distant our repose?

The summer of 1921 my life was once again changed by Nigel. At first we got on well. We agreed that I should introduce him to art while he would convert me to religion. But the relations between adolescents are variable, and Nigel, who had perhaps overreached himself with religion, cared that summer only for cricket, and despised all who were not cricketers. One day we quarrelled. I said our friendship must be All or Nothing; he said, 'Very well, I choose nothing', and I left his room. After a day I tried to make it up. 'Nothing' was not having the effect I hoped for. Nigel was brutal and called me a dirty scug (boy without a colour). I left him in a hysterical mood and went and broke a chair in Upper Tea Room. Then I rushed to Freddie and Denis for sympathy. I was fond of Nigel and fond of myself, and he had injured both these idols.

The rest of the half I kept on making overtures to him which he rudely ignored. Sometimes I was rude too and used to seek him out in order to cut him. He would make loud personal remarks and kick Walter Le Strange if he was walking with me for he had now got a cricket colour and made Oppidan friends. The effect of this quarrel on me was threefold. I was unhappy and for the first time in my life rebuffed; the guardian angel who looked after my relationships had forsaken me. My one ambition was to get over my feeling for Nigel and avenge myself by making him regret having quarrelled with me. I wanted to become the most useful and desirable person in his world, indispensable to his vulgar ambitions which I would help him to gratify as contemptuously as Lord Steyne assisted Becky Sharp to a new necklace. In my daydreams I acquired all the colours under the sun. I put him up for Pop.

The three results were that I became more social, that I worked harder, that I grew sceptical and pessimistic about the world. I was determined that Nigel must see me only with people he would himself like to know. I hugged closer to Denis and to King-Farlow, who was my fellow history specialist. He was robust, tough, cynical, good at games, energetic, and vulgar. We were both absorbed in Renaissance history and translated everything we learnt into our own lives; after reading Machiavelli I practised Machiavellianism, drawing up analyses of whom I should sit next, whom make friends with; of how to separate So-and-so, how to win over somebody else. Every man had a price. It was necessary to discover his ruling passion and play on it. The test of action was whether it led to one's own advantage, i.e. was justified by political necessity. One must learn to keep 'one's thoughts secret in an open face'.

Thus all college must be cultivated for I could never tell who might prove an asset in the humiliation of Nigel – that humiliation which was to consist in giving him the things he valued and which I despised and in being the only person who could give them him. He now went around with my enemy Highworth. They talked invariably of cricket and cast black looks in my direction so I made friends with Highworth again. Machiavelli would have approved. Highworth, outwardly successful, was still bewildered, and oppressed, I discovered, by the thought of the Vale or official leaving poem he would be expected to write at the end of the term and to which his attitude to poetry could scarcely contribute. I offered to compose it for him. I tried to make Nigel jealous by cultivating Freddie Langham whom I liked more and more; I could not make friends with cricketers as College did not possess any but I made up to our rowing men, two of whom were in the Eight. Farlow also had some rowing and football colours, and I felt less of a scug as I swaggered with him past Nigel's room.

It was the fashion to have photographs of our friends signed and installed on the mantelpiece. I had sent Nigel mine. He refused to give me his. I took one and he said that I had stolen it. I collected photos after that like an old hostess collecting celebrities. I cultivated anyone who was a rarity or who had not been taken, persuading them to get done for me and rushing off with the new scalp. Machiavelli functioned. I found I could charm people merely by asking them questions, and seeming interested in them, and at the end of the term I was elected to College Pop.

The election had been stormy and it was through my friendship with the rowing men that I got in for had I been put up by any of the liberals I would certainly have been blackballed. The political situation was now acute. Super-senior election were in power and beatings were frequent. To our indignation they beat Orwell for being late for prayers, then another member of senior election whom they considered uppish, finally, and on the most flimsy pretexts, Whittome and myself. Orwell and Whittome were boys of eighteen; they were just outside Sixth Form, and were beaten by boys of the same age in their own senior election, as if they were fags.

The feeling ran so high against the Captain of the School, the odious Cliffe, and the six other reactionaries in his election that they were cut to a man. Denis's speeches at College Pop debates were reinforced by the contempt of Mynors, the intransigence of Farlow, the indignation of Cazalet and Gibson. At the end of the term it was customary to pass votes of thanks on those who were leaving from College Pop, on the President, Treasurer and Secretary, the Keepers of College Wall and Field. For the first time in history these votes of thanks were black-balled. The genial ceremony collapsed; Cliffe the Captain of the School, Lea the Cadet officer of the Corps, Babington-Smith and the boys who beat Farlow and Orwell and Whittome on trumped-up charges for political reasons faced the unprecedented verdict. Name after name was read out, the vote of thanks proposed and seconded, the ballot box passed, the blackballs counted, and the transaction noted down in the annals. At Farlow's 'leaving tea' a day or two afterwards a lampoon of mine which drew attention to the idiosyncrasies of the seven black-balled reactionaries was sung with rapture. The Master in College protested against the breach of tradition, the Old Tugs got to hear of it, the Vile Old Men took it up, and there were whispers about Bolshevism which almost reached the newspapers.

Meanwhile I had succumbed to the disease of scepticism. My health was excellent but I could not get rid of ideas of mortality, futility, and death. What was the use of existence? Why did one do anything? All was vanity. Stupidity governed the world and human life was a blot on creation. I searched the classics for confirmation of my scepticism and found an overwhelming support. Job and Ecclesiastes and the author of the Wisdom of Solomon agreed with me; the Greek lyric poets and philosophers proclaimed it, Horace confirmed them as did Voltaire and Gibbon and Villon and Verlaine. I wrote a paper on Pessimism for the Essay Society. Only two kinds of thought existed, a pessimism which anticipated better things (Christianity) and my own – which did not. But if one believed this then one should kill oneself, which, of course, I was not prepared to do. Why not? Because of the consolations of friendship and learning, because suicide played into the hands of the Jealous God. One lived on to spite him.

For years I throve on this black doctrine for, although it originated with me owing to a rebuff from Nigel and a Thames Valley summer more virulent than usual, it happened that I had caught the fashionable malady of the period. Futility was the rage. With Farlow I concocted a play which was to expose history. We had been set a 'work of the imagination' to show to housemaster and history tutor, and we collaborated on a revue about the Renaissance, interspersed with songs and satirical sketches which showed knowledge and reading, vast cynicism and an unsuspected talent for horseplay. The Popes, the Emperors, the Medici, the Doges, the Kings of France and England, the Constable of Bourbon, Calvin, Luther, Zwingli and Savonarola, the King of Spain, the Borgias, Leonardo and Michelangelo were treated to the same knockabout. It was the first creation of my new-born scepticism and the most important. Nobody liked it but ourselves, least of all our tutors, who refused to sign it, Mr Gow making only the ambiguous comment 'perveni ad umbilicum' and I had instead to write a little purple essay 'On a Crucifixion attributed to Antonello da Messina'. But in the Specialists examination called the 'Grand July' I did well and came out eleventh in the whole school. My gloom was not proof against this, although my philosophy withstood it. What did it matter, eleventh or eleven hundredth? Was death deferred a day? Would anyone care in a hundred years? *Cui bono?* 'Can I forget

Myiscus, who is in all beautiful things?'

> Now years three and 'halves' ten
> Have hastened by and flown
> And soon there will be other men
> But I shall be forgotten then
> My very name unknown.
> And no more careless evening hours
> Of slippered armchair ease
> No glimpse of tea things in the towers,
> No cans, no steam, no shouts from showers,
> No shorts, nor muddied knees.

as I made Highworth protest, echoing Mimnermus, in his commissioned Vale. At Camp that year my depression was entire. Nigel was not there nor Freddie nor Denis; I was glad to be able to get away on a motor-bicycle and drink a glass of port with one of my rowing friends at Ludgershall. I could only bear to talk to Jackie O'Dwyer; like some mad monarch with his favourite; even Farlow, in whose tent I was, lost patience with me, for like many Etonians, although cynical, he detested inefficiency. Nothing was worth doing but it was not worth doing badly. We argued till he used to yell, 'Here, Private Connolly, you who appreciate the beauty of our English hedgerows, you who claim that pleasure and pain are the same thing, go and empty this bucket.' I kept a volume of Gibbon in my uniform and read it when I could. My other bible was La Rochefoucauld whom I remember reading when the victorious Eight came back drunk from Henley. I found his opinions most reasonable for I was one to whom the existence of good seemed already more mysterious than the problem of evil.

In an old French exercise book of mine during this summer Walter Le Strange, my Anglo-Irish aesthetic friend in junior election, was keeping a diary, a valuable contemporary document.

* The Stoa was the group of lookers-on at College cricket. They read and talked under the elms, which constituted 'taking exercise'. Pride is a boy called John Carter who leads his side out to field. I am Apollo, Man is the author, Tyrannus the Master in College, Satyr Clutton-Brock, Cato Farlow, Rome Gibson, and Cynicus Orwell.

9 June. In the afternoon repaired with Satyr and Apollo to the Stoa.*
Pride was leading forth his chorus of Athleticism's devotees. 'Ora pro
nobis,' he cried. 'No anglo-catholicism' thought Man. Satyr fed him
on strawberries while he read *Wuthering Heights*, and, that finished,
The Newcomers. Discussions on Socialism and Tyrannus followed.
Yesterday Man and Calm and Conservation and Calculus discussed
Slavery and Fagging. Both are utterly foul. Everybody here seems to
think

  (a) White men are better than others.
  (b) England is everything.
  (c) a 'gentleman' is *the* thing. Also all or mostly all worship
      Athleticism.

Cynicus and Man listened to a revue – 'The Renaissance' – by
Apollo and Cato. Apollo good, especially the lyrics, Cato inclined to
drag but his horseplay satire superb. The conversation in Hall turned
on the pecrage. How ignorant they all are, even Pride.

  11 June.

> Barnaby bright
> Barnaby bright
> The longest day
> And the shortest night.

A bright day indeed. The trees along the field and by Jordan
looked splendid from the Stoa where I lay throughout the afternoon,
near the Ball Alleys. Apollo was on my right. He too knows my loved
acacia and has apostrophized it, he says, in verse. I am glad I did not
try Shaw before. I am just in the state to understand him. Two years
ago the preface to Androcles would have shocked me and upset me.
A year ago I should have fallen too easy a prey to it. Today I rejoice.
Shaw wants just what I want. An equalizing philosophy of life –
politically and intellectually, morally and socially a panacea, in fact
an elixir. Stevenson's Velasquez is very interesting. I looked at the
Prado reproductions with Apollo again today. How *ravissant* is
Mercury and Argus. An English hamlet may be pretty, the country
here – take Chamber Field over-strewn with buttercups and clover, or
Fellows Eyot with its poplars – is beautiful. But O, for the Wicklow

hills. I never realized till now the true glory of the Sugar Loaf – of Gilt Spear's top, or of the heights between Glencullen and the Scalp.

Evening full of the linnet's wings.

Sunday. Tea with the Alabasters. Then talk turned on the *Beggar's Opera*, which I have not seen. Apollo – with whom I walked in the evening – talked of introspection and confidences. Is introspection a good thing? I think it is. Why, I wonder, does one always feel a superiority to others? Not always, but frequently at least. Apollo, I fear, does it too much. Yet I like him.

13 June. Apollo, Beatrice d'Este, Rome* and I argued most of the afternoon about religion. Very interesting. The result: 'Man must worship something by an inborn instinct.' Surely he can drive this instinct out of him. Later on Satyr, Beatrice d'Este, Scaife and I gossiped with Rome. The conversation turning on Pride, Scaife gave demonstrations of his foul ways and words, whereupon Tyrannus entered and in his hypocritical friendly way adjured Rome to cease. Rome with much coldness, though quite politely, dismissed him, and we continued our conversation. This evening, however, Greedy-for-Power [Lea] 'wanted' Rome and Scaife, accused the one of filthy talk and the other of encouraging it. Rome told the story of how it happened. He was dismissed. But – and I burn to think of it – Scaife was whipt – whipt like a mere slave – that is, an oppressed fag, or lower boy, by that unutterable brute, Greedy-for-Power, for a sin of which Rome had proved him guiltless. O may all tyranny perish. May everyone be free! Let not the wretched new boy be oppressed and mishandled just for the convenience of the idle Capitalists, that is to say, the self-made priests of Athleticism, of the Public School Spirit of Imperialism.

27 June. Peter (Loxley) came back tonight. Full of racing and tennis. I wish sometimes I could interest myself in such things. Of course not worship them. I have been reading the *Loom of Youth*.

* Beatrice d'Este = Raymond Coghlan.
  Rome = Gibson, who was a Catholic.
  Scaife = 'Cully' Cox.

It is all so true in its way. Everything seems melancholy. Is life worth living? Where can one get help? One cannot paint for ever, it only makes you into that aesthete, loose tie, velvet coat sort of thing. Poetry makes you excited, or else sadder. O to do something! But how can a Nobody do anything worth while? Help is from within. Perhaps if one saw everybody as good. It is so hard – but it is beautiful. Therefore it is meet and right to do. 'Les sanglots longs' – but they do it always. 'I will arise and go now, and go to Innisfree . . .' O if only I could quit this place, with its society, its 'gentlemen', its absurd church. Where is a true religion? O for peace. Even this journal is hypocritical.

2 July. There is only one God here. Athleticism and his law is 'Believe – or Be cast out.' Even now I hear the shouts and cheers, as of barbarism. Baths are banged. Boys shout. Such a display of rowdyism I have seldom heard. The Mob! The Howling of an Angry Mob. Awful. But a joyful mob is worse. The Eight have won the Ladies' Plate at Henley. Three of them are in College – 'jolly boating weather – we'll cheer for the best of schools'. It seems sad to think that a great crowd of boys – of cultured boys – should pour out their spirits thus. O Athleticism! Athleticism! The din is now outside my door. Horror! Horror! Baths are banged and banged – cheers – cheers. So help me!

The noise has been quelled. It is sad that N. [Nigel] should have been so completely corrupted by athleticism. We were quite friendly once. But now he is so devilish superior. And rude, too. What have I done? I despise Athleticism – but not Athletics, yet I have never said *he* should not worship it just because I am interested in the things that really matter. Need he be so really uncivil?

3 July. A boiling Sunday. The heat was most oppressive. I talked chiefly to Cyril, Peter and Farlow. These questions of fagging and of College Politics are very interesting. So is reading the Greek gospel. Belief seems to be based on such slender grounds. It is extraordinary how unchristian are the lives of all those boys who 'profess and call themselves Christians', Carter, Maud, N. But there is an awful danger for us too. One is so inclined to become a Pharisee – an utter prig. The milder forms of this athleticism are not harmful for the young.

They do no lasting good. But they tend to present happiness. But everyone seems to imagine that athletics means success. Get a cricket colour and you are made for life. Half a dozen people come up to you. 'I say, isn't it good for College having two Sixpennies.' What could be more ridiculous? No one seems to take any interest in the fact that College has bought a Dürer, or that the Hervey English Verse Prize was won by a Colleger in C.

Carter's ignorance showed itself again yesterday. 'Why Lord John Russell and not Lord Russell?' he asked. But I mustn't be a snob. The Hermit [Martineau] – it appears from a conversation of this evening – is an ultra-reactionary. He disapproves of boys in B playing ping-pong in Sixth Form Passage.

Last Sunday Farlow gave a tea-party in Lower Tea Room, after which the party sang songs, including a topical one by Cyril. All very pleasant, but Carter made himself somewhat objectionable to his host. On the Friday evening there had been the usual College Pop election. Cyril got in. Peter was put up three times and blackballed, I ditto twice, Carter was put up and got seven (five excludes). All this gave us much subject for conceited conversation. Peter seemed rather sad not to have got in. I was also sorry for myself. Our conceit grew vehemently. On Monday, to the general consternation of many, Carter was awarded his College Cricket. This means he will be second keeper next summer, and so in a position to make even more of himself than at present.

~

That summer I went abroad for the first time. My father took me to Paris and the Belgian coast. We stayed off the Rue de Rivoli and ate in restaurants with purple menus, screened from the pavement by tubs of sooty privet. I did not care for Paris, I was frightened there, it was too hot and I thought people's feet smelt, I liked only the Louvre where I felt at home, Notre Dame, and Versailles which, as I wrote at the time, 'suited my mood'. 'French revues are funnier than English,' I wrote to

O'Dwyer, 'but after eight o'clock this town is as full of whores as camp was of wasps' – then I reverted to the interminable College politics. Carter, Nigel's great friend, in my junior election disliked me and my two cronies there, Loxley and Le Strange. There was a chance of him getting into College Pop. It was against my principles to blackball anyone yet somehow five people had to be found who would; Cazalet and Farlow, alas, had left – 'You have to remember, my boy,' I enjoined O'Dwyer, 'that nowadays you are Cazalet, and I am Farlow'.

One event in Paris upset me. On a sultry evening as I was walking back to my hotel after dinner, I was accosted outside the Café de la Paix by a pimp with a straw hat and an umbrella. He offered to take me to a music-hall. I was too nervous to refuse and he then informed me it would be 'rather a rough kind of place, you understand'. I was now too frightened and excited to turn back and he took me to a brothel in the Rue Colbert. I was overcome with guilt and apprehension as I sat with the pimp in the little gilded *salon* while he spoke to the Madame. The mechanical piano played, at last the girls filed in and I was asked to choose two of them. Voiceless I pointed with a trembling finger. They stayed behind and a bottle of champagne appeared. We all had a glass and then another bottle. Drink made no impression, I was paralysed with fear, partly of being hit on the head and waking up in Buenos Aires, partly of saying the wrong thing. Then it was suggested that I should go upstairs with the two ladies. It was then a new panic arose. How much was all this? In a shrunken voice I asked for the bill. '*Quoi. Déjà?*' '*Oui, oui, oui. Toute suite.*' I explained to Madame that I did not know if I would have enough money to pay. She was astounded. 'But I thought Monsieur was a gentleman! When the bill arrived it was for almost ten pounds, mostly for champagne and with a bonus of course for the pimp. I explained that I could not pay at once, that the ladies must leave immediately, that I would give her all the money I had (about four pounds), and find the rest within the week. I gave her my card, on which I had written the address of my hotel. My father was waiting up for me and I told him I had lost my way.

The rest of my time in Paris was spent in anguish. At any moment I expected to see Madame and the pimp arrive to ask for me. Meals in the hotel were a torture which I could not bear for I would be sure to see the pimp with his umbrella or Madame with my visiting card directed to our table by the concierge. No time of day was safe. I wrote to my grandmother who, I knew, was giving me five pounds for my birthday and asked her to send it to Paris in advance as the shops were better there than they would be in Belgium and I wanted to buy some presents for my friends. It seemed as if her letter would never arrive; my worst moment was in the Musée de Cluny, beside the iron crown of Receswinth. I went out and sat in a cold sweat on a bench in the garden.

Next day the money arrived and I rushed round to the brothel. It was eleven o'clock in the morning; no one remembered me, another Madame was on duty and listened in bewilderment while I explained, stuffing money into her hand, and wondering if it would seem impertinent to ask for my card back. At last I was safe. I bought Charles Milligan, Denis, and Freddie a few cheap presents and shortly afterwards attained my eighteenth birthday, still without having kissed anyone. The Belgian coast was a relief after this nightmare, and Bruges, with its brackish canals and Flemish primitives, like Versailles, 'suited my mood', for I would try no more conclusions with the Present.

Boys do not grow up gradually. They move forward in spurts like the hands of clocks in railway stations. Most of those in College advanced in this wise though in many the sap of youth ran down after their efforts. In my own case the autumn of 1921 and spring of 1922 were a high renaissance. They were not the happiest days of my life but I was as happy then as I was able to be.

I started the new term as 'a bit of a chap'. I was in a 'mess', that is to say I took tea in Charles Milligan's room with him and Minns and a fag to look after us, instead of having it in Tea Room. This was an advance in civilization as one had privacy and could have masters to tea and get on better terms with them. I was also in College Pop and got my 'shorts' for football, whereupon Nigel spoke to me again. We were delighted to be friends, my scepticism was now permanent but I had accepted the vanity of life and the worthlessness of human nature so fundamentally that I no longer felt bitter or with a grievance against society. 'Our mess has china tea – down by the streamside' I used to sing, and we gave exclusive tea-parties. Denis was in Sixth Form. All the election above him had now left except the youngest member, who was Captain of the School, a clerical reactionary held in check by Denis, Mynors, Gibson and Longden.

22 The Background of the Lilies

So far it would appear that work played a small part in our lives; this was not so, however; for the first two years most boys did not enjoy their work and found it a tedious drudgery. It was not smart at Eton to work; to be a 'sap' was a disgrace and to compete for prizes eccentric. Everybody used cribs though the punishments for being caught were severe. For boys at Eton wanted one thing, popularity, and the flaw in the Eton education was that work was unpopular. Indeed for twenty years I was never to grasp that the love and friendship which I sought were in this world the rewards not of seeking them but of hard work and success.

It is hard to see how such conditions arise. They are prevalent in most schools although boys are more bored and more unhappy than ever when they do not work. Even in College, among the seventy scholars, 'sapping' was discredited and we were infected by the fashion from without, behind which lay the English distrust of the intellect and prejudice in favour of the amateur. A child in Ireland, a boy at St Wulfric's, a scholar at Eton, I had learnt the same lesson. To be 'high-brow' was to be different, to be set apart and so excluded from the ruling class of which one was either a potential enemy or a potential servant. Intelligence was a deformity which must be concealed; a public school taught one to conceal it as a good tailor hides a paunch or a hump. As opposed to ability, it was a handicap in life.

At Eton this was emphasized by the stigma attaching to Collegers which although an economic prejudice found expression as an anti-intellectual one and of which a ridiculous aspect was the contempt in which boys held masters, a relic of the eighteenth century when boys brought their own tutors to Eton and treated them, as the term 'usher' still indicated, little better than their servants. In this direction the feeling was strong; masters who were old Etonians, who were rich like John Christie or well-born like Georgie Lyttelton, escaped but in general the boys assumed that most of the staff had never held a gun or worn a tailcoat, that they were racked by snobbery, by the desire to be asked to stay with important parents or to be condescended to by popular boys. An Eton division consisted of thirty boys, five of whom wished to learn something, ten of whom wished to do what everybody else wanted, and fifteen of whom spent their time searching for the usher's weak points and exploiting them with the patience of prisoners of war tunnelling out of a camp. What Proust called the '*lâcheté des gens du monde*' was never so apparent as at Eton, where the life of a teacher like Aldous Huxley was made intolerable because of his defective sight.

The teachers in the middle parts of the school devoted themselves to cramming and keeping order; inspired teaching, owing to the intransigence of the boys, could appear only at the top, where there were five real teachers: the Headmaster, Mr C. M. Wells, Mr G. W. Headlam, Mr G. H. K. Marten, and Mr Hugh Macnaghten. They are worth considering.

At Eton, as at other schools, there existed the ordinary education for the average boy but there grew up as well an inner culture, the eleusinian mysteries of learning, to which favoured boys were admitted and which was maintained by teachers such as these and by a few important outside figures, the Provost, Mr Luxmoore, Mr Broadbent; the pure eighteenth-century Etonian tradition of classical humanism, which could be learnt nowhere else. Most of the boys went through the school without knowing of its existence, without having heard of esoteric figures like William Johnson Cory or Mrs Warre-Cornish, Howard Sturgis or Austen Leigh, but by 1921 (the year for me when 'modern history' begins) I was being initiated; I would dine with the Provost and the

Headmaster, or Mr Headlam and Mr Marten would come to tea.

The first of the big five a Colleger came up to, when about sixteen, was Hugh Macnaghten. Although a fine teacher, his learning possessed the faults or rather the literary vices of his time. He was an ogre for the purple patch, the jewel five words long, the allusion, the quotation, the moment of ecstasy. In fact he was embedded in the Milton-Keats-Tennysonian culture, that profuse and blooming romanticism of the 'bowery loneliness',

> The brooks of Eden mazily murmuring
> And gloom profuse and cedar arches

which had dominated English literature until the death of Flecker and Rupert Brooke.

The Eton variety was diluted with Pre-Raphaelitism. Watts's *Sir Galahad* hung in College Chapel, Burne-Jones and William Morris had been Eton figures, and Mr Luxmoore painted fastidious water colours of his riverside garden in which the fair Rosamund would not have disdained to take her medicine. He was a disciple of Ruskin, the forgotten man of the nineteenth century.

Another field for the Pre-Raphaelite influence was in translating. Homer and Virgin were the pillars of an Eton education; it would be hard to derive more pleasure then or now than we obtained from reading them. But we read them with the help of two official cribs, Butcher and Lang for Homer, Mackail for Virgil. Lang believed that Homer must be translated into the nearest English equivalent which was an Anglo-Saxon prose reminiscent of the Sagas. He tried to manage on a Bronze-Age vocabulary, and the Mediterranean clarity of the *Odyssey* was blurred by a Wardour Street Nordic fog. Homer, in short, was slightly Wagnerized. Mackail, who had married Burne-Jones's daughter, gave to his Virgil an eightyish air, the *lacrimae rerum* spilled over and his Christian attitude to paganism, that it was consciously pathetic and incomplete, like an animal that wishes it could talk, infected everything which he translated with a morbid distress. Dido became a bull-throated *Mater Dolorosa* by Rossetti. His translations from the *Greek Anthology*, one of the sacred books of the inner culture, the very soil of the Eton lilies, were even more deleterious. They exhaled pessimism and despair, and overripe perfection in which it was always the late afternoon or the last stormy sunset of the ancient world, in which the authentic gloom of Palladus was outdone by that attributed to Simonides, Callimachus, or Plato. Meleager was the typical Pre-Raphaelite lover.

To put it another way, a sensitive Etonian, with a knowledge of Homer and Virgil through these translations and a good ear, would be unable to detect in poems like *Tithonus, Ulysses*, or the *Lotus Eaters* any note foreign to the work of Homer and Virgil. If he had been told that 'a spirit haunts the year's last hours' was a word for word translation of Virgil, he would have accepted the fact. The two classics had been 'romanticized' for him, impregnated with the cult of strangeness, of the particular rather than the general and of the conception of beauty characteristic of the Aesthetic Movement as something akin to disease and evil.

Macnaghten accentuated this. He told us that the most beautiful word in the English language was 'little', he liquidated his 'r's' in reciting and intoned poetry in a special way . . .

> and hear the bweeze
> Sobbing in ver little twees.

Jolly good! he would exclaim, and to hear him chant 'Ah, poor Faun – ah, poor Faun' was a study in pity which made his severe and even harsh discipline appear the more surprising.

The other subject of this inner cult was Plato. His humour and sophistry were the delight of those who expounded them to the bewilderment of those who listened. His theory of ideas and essences, his conception of body and spirit, the romantic dualism on which he insisted formed the ruling philosophy. Platonism was everywhere, popping up in sermons and Sunday questions, in allusions to Neoplatonism, in essays by Dean Inge, at the headmaster's dinner-parties or in my tutor's pupil-room. Socrates roamed through the classes like a Government inspector and even Virgil and Tennyson withdrew before him. But it will be remembered that Plato himself, in the Republic, turned against the poets and advocated censorship and discipline. This contradiction extended through our school-life and emerged in its attitude to sex.

For there was no doubt that homosexuality formed an ingredient in this ancient wisdom. It was the forbidden tree round which our little Eden dizzily revolved. In a teaching conscious and somewhat decad-ently conscious of visual beauty, its presence in the classics was taken for granted; it was implicit in Plato's humour and aesthetic. Yet Eton, like all public schools, had no solution for sex. If boys had such intercourse between the ages of fourteen and eighteen, no matter with whom or with what, they had better go. The School could do nothing for them. 'Created sick, commanded to be sound', the majority floundered through on surreptitious experiments and dirty jokes but there were always a number who, going further, were found out and expelled.

The extent to which sex-life is necessary and should be permitted to growing boys remains uncertain. The Eton attitude was in line with that of other authorities and with the wishes of most parents, for the dilemma is inherent in all education, lurking in the playing-fields and vinegar-scented cloisters of our seats of learning as, in the preaching of the careful Pater, beckon the practices of Wilde.

The result was that boys learnt to walk a tightrope; the sentimental friendship was permitted in some houses and forbidden in others, allowed to some boys and denied to their fellows or permitted and then suppressed according to the changing views and vigilance of the housemaster. No one could be sure on what ground they trod. There was Macnaghten who, spartan in body as he was soft in mind, would give an annual and long-anticipated lecture attacking those friendships at a point in Plato's *Euthyphro*; at the same time we were made to put into Latin verses a sentimental poem addressed by Dolben to the then Captain of the Eleven. One thing was certain; the potentially homo-sexual boy was the one who benefited, whose love of beauty was stimulated, whose appreciation was widened, and whose critical powers

were developed; the normal boy, free from adolescent fevers, missed
both the perils and the prizes; he was apt to find himself left out. There
is much celibacy in public schools and, where many housemasters are
not married, it is possible to say that their teaching will encourage
continence officially and homosexuality by implication, sending up to
the universities, from whence they will immediately rebound as masters,
that repressed and familiar type, the English male virgin.

Another effect of Macnaghten's teaching was to associate English
literature with Latin verses. We came to think of poetry in terms of tags
and useful epithets, and to consider the best poetry as being in the form
of the sonnet or sixteen-line lyric. Macnaghten would not treat Latin
verses as a crossword puzzle; he insisted that we put feeling into them,
that we exercised our dreams of literary composition through the
medium of another language. In his taste he was a true escapist; everything he admired reeked of the death-wish, port after stormy seas, holy
quiet and romantic fatigue. No one who did his verses well could write
poetry afterwards. There would be one slim Eton-blue volume with a
few translations, a *Vale*, and a couple of epigrams, then silence. For the
culture of the lilies, rooted in the past, divorced from reality, and
dependent on a dead foreign tongue, was by nature sterile.

It may be wondered why I call Macnaghten a good teacher. The
reason is that although he concentrated on moments of beauty, he did
not neglect the encircling drudgery, and because, although his taste was
uncertain, he would permit no blasphemy. To laugh at anything he
thought good meant punishment. He chastened the hooligans (even
Highworth could but mumble) and he insisted on the modesty, the
abnegation without which great art cannot be appreciated. 'Up' to him
boys for the first time had the experience of literature and every now
and then, in the dusty classroom, grew aware of the presence of a god.

Wells taught the classical specialists; he was a fine cricketer and a
judge of claret, a man of taste with a humour of understatement in the
Cambridge style. The Headmaster was theatrical, he liked knotty points
and great issues, puns and dramatic gestures. He was a worldly teacher,
a Ciceronian, an All Souls Fellow and we felt we were learning Divinity

from a Prince of the Church. He was fond of paradoxes and we learnt to turn out a bright essay on such a subject as 'Nothing succeeds like failure' or 'Nothing fails like success'. The exaggeration of his teaching was repugnant to the classical specialists and such was the moral weight of William Egerton, Denis, or Roger Mynors, that he became a naughty boy 'showing off' in their presence although his entry into any other class-room would petrify us with fear.

His was the cult of that light verse which had always been the official poetry for despite Gray, Shelley, Swinburne, and Bridges, the kind of poetry which Eton took to its heart was either the sentimental lyric, the translation (of which Cory's *Heraclitus* is the example) or the facetious. Praed, Clough, Calverley, W. S. Gilbert, and the sacred J. K. Stephen were the official bards and if the Headmaster had had to include a living writer he would have added Father Ronald Knox.

Thus, although the *Eton College Chronicle* made an appeal to premature essayists and the fourth leader of *The Times* was within the grasp of its editors, critical or creative writing there was none. Humorous 'Ephemerals' had a sale; but in spite of tradition, and the encouragement given to them, the Arts at Eton were under a blight. Figures of the post-war world such as Aldous Huxley and Maynard Keynes had been in College, but we would never have known it. They were not recognized, they did not wear like Maurice Baring, Arthur Benson, Percy Lubbock, or J. K. Stephen, a halo in the pale-blue canon.

Into this world the history teachers introduced a note of realism. Marten was a model of clarity and enthusiasm; he was the sanest of schoolmasters but for that reason had less influence on us than a teacher like Headlam who did not aspire to be impartial.

If the Headmaster epitomized All Souls, Headlam was typical of Balliol, but it was not Balliol that made him impressive, so much as the fact that in his class-room there was at last evidence of a Pre-Ruskinian culture, of the eighteenth century. His favourite writer was Horace, the book he gave to us on leaving was *Boswell's Life of Johnson*. To us he was an enigmatic figure, he seemed to go some of the way towards futility and yet while our conclusions from the axiom All is Vanity were 'nothing is worth while, except art', 'except friendship', 'except pleasure', or 'except wisdom', his seemed to be 'except success – except doing a job efficiently'. He appeared cynical but that may have been only because he was un-Tennysonian. Although irritable in the early morning he was more tolerant than other masters; his tolerance at times seemed apathy, a product of disillusion, yet he hated idleness, dishonesty, and that frivolous complacency to which growing boys are addicted. He brought common sense and reasonable worldly values into his relations with boys with the result that his house was the best at Eton and, as he surveyed the row of Pops in it with affected vagueness, he must have enjoyed the bewilderment of other housemasters.

All the history specialists imitated him, his affectations of saying 'Erse' instead of 'Yes' and 'Toosda' for Tuesday, his apparent lack of interest in games and exercise (although he was a good fives player and his house held the football cup), his attitude of *nil admirari*. He was a Tory in politics, where again he seemed to stand for tolerance, efficiency, and a hatred of fuss. 'You must learn that there is no justice in this world,' he was fond of saying, perhaps setting the wrong boy a punishment to illustrate it and 'You must always remember that nobody is indispensable,' was another of his maxims.

Was he a Balliol careerist, with the affectation of laziness and indifference that was considered the Balliol manner and by which we were taken in, or a split man in whom an efficient and ambitious self was being watched by a cynical spectator? Or was he an evocation of the eighteenth-century Tory or of ancient Rome? In appearance he was dark, handsome and rather fat, not unlike the Roman poet whom he interpreted; his expression was blasé and judicial, his voice and smile were charming, his eyes, sombre in repose, when angry, kindled into fire.

All masters lost their tempers; there were some whose rages were comic spectacles, others who became maniacs, fascinating to watch but dangerous if one got in the way; with the Headmaster or Macnaghten there was a sensation of panic owing to the severity of the penalties which they could enforce, but with Marten and Headlam alone did one get a feeling of shame; they were teachers whose rebukes of one boy enlisted against him the sympathy of the class, and 'To do poorly' up to Headlam, or be 'tiresome' with Marten, was distressing for at last we were attaining a level where it was not impermissible to work.

In the aestheticism which was gathering round me, part backwash of the nineties, part consequence of my Celtic romanticism being worked upon by the Pre-Raphaelite background of the Eton lilies, Headlam's sober intellectual energy, his Roman values, offered a gleam of mental health. But, to an aesthete, what appealed in Headlam was his irony, his way of making a reference to authority sound ridiculous (due, one suspected, to an antipathy to the Headmaster which was pronounced among the senior old Etonian housemasters) and to his fondness for what he called gestures – 'That would be a good gesture – the Massacre of St Bartholomew was a bad gesture.' The good gesture, the noisy piece of self-sacrifice, was one of the few lines of conduct sanctioned by my futilitarianism. It must be like Sidney Carton's, magnanimous, public, and useless.

By the time I had left Eton I knew by heart something of the literature of five civilizations. It was a lopsided knowledge since we were not taught literature and since the only literature which appealed to me was pessimistic but it is worth analysing, since, although many of the books had been read for hundreds of years and others seemed my own discoveries, taken together, they give a picture of fashionable reading-matter just after the last war.

I was fond of the Old Testament, disliked the New. My favourite books were Ecclesiastes and the Wisdom of Solomon in which I recognized the melancholy and tired distinction of an old race, the mysterious Ezekiel and that earthy mystic, the first Isaiah. Job was too much thrust upon me and the Lamentations of Jeremiah I found in faulty taste. All these I read with more pleasure in the sonorous Latin of the Vulgate. They were among the books I lived in through the winter evenings.

In Greek literature I had read the *Odyssey* with passion, but not the *Iliad*, I admired Aeschylus, particularly the *Agamemnon*, and Sophocles, particularly *Oedipus Rex*; Euripides and Aristophanes I disliked, and Plato, except his epigrams and the *Symposium*. I enjoyed the lyric poets, Saphho and Archilochus, and adored the Mackail selection of the *Greek Anthology*, Theognis, Plato, Callimachus, Palladas, and Meleager; I knew all the sceptical epigrams by heart and most of those about love and death and 'the fate of youth and beauty'. In all my books I had written after my name 'τίς τίνι ταῦτα λέγέις' (Who are you that say this, and to whom?). Mackail's *Anthology* (in the one-volume edition with the long preface) might have been described as the Sceptic's Bible. I was also fond of the bloomy Theocritus and the *Lament for Bion*.

In Latin literature I read Horace and Virgil but did not enjoy them till later for Horace, except by Headlam, was not inspiringly taught and Virgil associated with too many punishments and in his moments of beauty with Macnaghten's vatic trances. Although I had learnt Latin all my life I still could not appreciate it without a crib and it was the arrival at the end of my time of the Loeb translations, sanctioned by the authorities, that put its deeper enjoyment within my grasp. Virgil and Horace, without them, had been too difficult, too tearstained. Horace besides was more connected with character than with prettiness. We were slow to appreciate him as a verbal artist.

> Fortes creantur fortibus et bonis
> Est in juvencis, est equis patrum
> Virtus

'Brave men are bred from the good and brave, there is in cattle, there is in horses,' Headlam would rasp, 'the virtue of their sires,' and the history specialists, conscious that though not poets, they were the stuff about which poetry was written, seemed to preen themselves for a moment in the afternoon drowse.

My favourite was Catullus, whose poetry 'suited my mood', and therefore the mood of the age. It was cynical, romantic, passionate and bawdy and I could substitute my own name for his. '*Otium, Cyrille, tibi molestum est*', '*Sed tu, Cyrille, destinatus obdura*'. I liked the world of Suetonius and Tacitus but the Latin prose-writer for me was Petronius

Arbiter. I had four editions of the *Satyricon*. The best I had bound in black crushed levant and kept on my pew in chapel where it looked like some solemn book of devotion and was never disturbed. To sit reading it during the sermon, looking reverently towards the headmaster scintillating from the pulpit and then returning to the racy Latin, 'the smoke and wealth and noise of Rome' was 'rather a gesture'.

I also liked Martial, crisp and Iberian but resented the sanctimonious Juvenal, I was excited by the *Pervigilium*, I struggled through the convolutions of Apuleius and admired the pagan chapters of the *Confessions* of Saint Augustine.

In French I cultivated the Troubadours but was disappointed, as I was by those four old bores, Montaigne, Rabelais, Boccaccio, and Burton. The deceptively simple verses of Villon I loved, with the Poussin landscapes of Chénier and the garden sadness of Ronsard and Du Bellay. Then came a few lines of Racine, all *Candide* and *Manon Lescaut*, and an unrepresentative selection of Flaubert, Gautier, Hugo, and Baudelaire, no Rimbaud but a close study of Verlaine, Heredia, and Mallarmé.

I was fortunate to read French with Mr de Satgé; he loved beauty and, while working with him, I apprehended that remoteness of great poetry from life which is inherent in the exaction of the form and creates literature, '*la treille où le pampre à la rose s'allie.*'

In English I began with Spenser sleeping in his coils, I knew little Shakespeare but I worshipped Hamlet, who seemed the Prince of Scepticism and Gestures ('How now, a rat in the arras!'), and of course Marlowe. Shakespeare's sonnets I absorbed. They formed, with Omar Khayyám and the *Shropshire Lad*, limited editions, called 'the Medici Books', which, unhealthy though they were in bulk, one could yet obtain as prizes. Webster was my favourite Elizabethan, then came Donne and after him Marvell, Herrick, and Sir Thomas Browne. Milton was the poet in whom my appreciation culminated. Then a gap until Blake, the *Marriage of Heaven and Hell*, and, still later, Tennyson and Matthew Arnold. I knew nothing of Pope, Dryden, and Crabbe, and I had a prejudice against the romantics; Keats turned my stomach,

Shelley was ethereal, Byron vulgar, and Wordsworth prosy. What I required from an author was the authentic romantic thrill and the prestige of obscurity. After Tennyson was Housman, who came down to lecture to us on Erasmus Darwin and then Bridges, Yeats, Brooke, de la Mare, Flecker, Masefield, *The Spirit of Man*, and a repository of Georgian cliché called *Poems of To-day*.

In prose, after Sir Thomas Browne, came Boswell, Gibbon, and Sterne, then Pater (so clear in his thought, so evasive in his conclusions), in whose Sebastian van Storck, with his refusal 'to be or do any limited thing', we recognized a fellow sufferer. Lastly the usual modern mixture – Samuel Butler, Shaw, Compton Mackenzie, James Stephens, Belloc, Buchan, Conrad, Lytton Strachey, and Aldous Huxley. Orwell lent me *The Picture of Dorian Gray*. But I could not swallow it. It was not necessary.

I was as fond of painting as of poetry and haunted the National Gallery. My taste was conservative. I knew of no French painter except Corot and it was typical of the civilization of the lilies, the limitations of good taste, that I had such knowledge of the masterpieces of the past yet remained timidly at sea among the creations of the present.

23 *Glittering Prizes*

The result of scepticism, of escaping from the world via the pursuit of knowledge, was that I unexpectedly won the Rosebery History Prize. The gain was about twenty pounds' worth of books, but those available, with their horrible bindings, so shocked me that I obtained special permission to get Medici prints. The Man with the Glove, Beatrice d'Este, and The Duke of Cleves now looked down on my bureau. After an intrigue with Denis I was given my 'liberties', the privileges of not wearing a hat, of fagging boys, of having supper by themselves, accorded to the next six in college, after Sixth Form. When a boy not in Division One (Sixth Form and Liberty) won the Newcastle, a classical prize, he was co-opted into it; in getting the same reward for the

Rosebery I had advanced the prestige of the History Specialists, a prestige which was rising at the expense of classics, languages, and science. History was easier and more interesting, it was the fashion. Most of the important boys were history specialists, and Mr Headlam's division had ended by becoming a field of the cloth of gold for the feudal chieftains. Of the eleven hundred boys about twenty-five were in Pop and eight of these were 'up' to him. After I got the Rosebery they began to notice me.

In every division there is room for one boy to reconcile popularity with hard work. He is the brilliant idler, a by-product of dandyism. 'Petronius deserves a word in retrospect. He was a man who passed his days in sleep, his nights in the ordinary duties and recreations of life: others had achieved greatness by the sweat of their brows – Petronius idled into fame.' This archetype of scepticism came to my aid; by imitating his example and doing my work illicitly at night by candle my days were left free for social intercourse. I had an excellent memory. I could learn by heart easily, gut a book in an hour and a half of arguments, allusions, and quotations, like a Danube fisherman removing caviare from the smoking sturgeon, and remember them for just long enough to get down in an examination paper. I was the perfect examinee. The Oppidans began to take me up. I answered difficult questions and discovered smutty passages for them and if I was caught reading a book in class, it would be something as spectacular as the *Epistolae Obscurorum Virorum*. Once a week we had to recite a few lines of poetry that we learnt by heart; most boys depended on poems they had learnt before.

> Thereisswee musichere thasofterfalls
> Thanpetalsof blowroseson the grass . . .
> On the grass

At the end I would stroll up with modest confusion and recite a long Greek chorus chosen for its pessimism, for not to be born was best of all.

My strong point was still being funny. I was working hard enough to

be permitted some licence, and I could make jokes about our subject –
for the history we studied was the history of personalities – in which
even Oppidans could join. I was at my best when being taken up,
grateful but not servile, sunny but not familiar and with the schoolboy's
knack of living in the moment. I had the advantage of beginning at the
top, the only Oppidans I knew were already in Pop, I had no inferiors
with whom I had been associated, no ladders to kick down. Antony
Knebworth was the first to make friends with me. He had won the other
Rosebery prize and was a Byronic figure of overpowering vitality who
with his crony, Nico Davies, seemed to make more noise than a whole
division. He and Nico were the most successful types of normal schoolboy; they were in all the elevens, ran their houses, were able and rather
lazy at their work, conventional, intolerant, and sentimental; they were
easily moved to laughter, rage, or tears, strict enforcers of privilege and
always appealed to by the headmaster when there was a question of Pop
'using its influence'.

A less schoolminded couple were Teddy Jessel and Edward Woodall;
they were dandies in the pure sense, with a sober worldly gravity. Jessel
had a touch of the 'Arbiter' himself, he was critical of errors of taste,
especially on the part of masters whom he treated, with two exceptions,
as a set of lower-middle-class lunatics. He disliked Collegers, finding
them dowdy and 'pi', and he was fond of remarking how swiftly their
cleverness evaporated. 'A brilliant scholar, won the Newcastle three
times running,' he would exclaim, imitating a master's complacent tones,
'and now he has passed second into the Office of Works.' With me,
however, he was more tolerant, Horace Walpole to Gray, Townley to
Pontifex. The other important Pop was Alec Dunglass, who was
President and also Keeper of the Field and Captain of the Eleven. He was
a votary of the esoteric Eton religion, the kind of graceful, tolerant,
sleepy boy who is showered with favours and crowned with all the
laurels, who is liked by the masters and admired by the boys without any
apparent exertion on his part, without experiencing the ill-effects of
success himself or arousing the pangs of envy in others. In the eighteenth
century he would have become Prime Minister before he was thirty; as it

was he appeared honourably ineligible for the struggle of life.

Relations with Oppidans were more superficial than with Collegers. They were easy-going extroverts lacking in super-ego who regarded friendship as a question of equality and shared interests; only Collegers treated it as a philosophy, an end in itself. Meeting Oppidans was like going to smart luncheons where people seem more intimate than they are; returning to College was going on from lunch to spend all the afternoon with a bourgeois intellectual friend of long standing. Friendship, among Oppidans, was a luxury – a touch of failure, inequality, absence and it perished. In College it was a necessity of our strange monastic society, a religion invented by sensitive boys under hard conditions and which existed to combat them.

The term which was my happiest now drew to an end. College politics were absorbing and occupied our anxious elders outside to the extent that we christened these busybodies 'The College Investigation Society' and wrote bawdy songs about them. Le Strange summed up the feeling of the minority:

> 20 Nov. There are two great troubles: political and religious. What is one to believe? The religious services here are just awful. Singing absurd meaningless hymns among ugly windows and pictures, with hopeless tunes, and then the intoned droned prayers – all meaningless.
>
> If there is a God he can't be like the Yahweh of the Old Testament. Yet was Christ God? I think not. If there is no God – only a fiction of man's brain, what are we to do with life? Is there another life? Will it be a punishment or reward for this life? No! Then must we be good? Why not rest – peace is what I need. To get away from all the noise and squalor of the world out on to the hills – if there is any god it is Pan – but we cannot worship him except by letting ourselves be absorbed. He is deaf to prayers. He goes on his way regardless. There cannot be a benevolent God. It is impossible in all this squalor. Should one try to improve the squalor? Dorian Gray is an extremely interesting book but of course Lord Henry Wotton must be wrong. I have also just read *Potterism*. It is dreadful the morbid state into which people get whatever they do. Either they become jingoists like Kipling or else they

think of a vanished golden age – like those patriot poets in Ireland.

All the questions of freedom – ethnologically, and of Disarmament are so interesting, but the world is so parochial that one can never think of them.

All my time is taken up with talking of: Athleticism, College Pop, and Fagging. They all run into one another.

Peter and I were both elected to Coll. Pop at the beginning of this half, after being blackballed last summer. So was R. Cyril got in last half. We all arranged to keep Carter out. He was so awful, sarcastic, reactionary, etc. After all, he had his College Cricket, that was sufficient. Now he had got his Wall too. Poor R. has been turned out of that, he is a barbarian and to be foiled of his barbar triumphs must be hard. Everything here is done on an athletic standard. I am still in Lower College with those small boys, good enough in themselves – But O! the ignominy of it. Thank God Peter is also in L.C. O Peter is splendid! unselfish, generous. It must be wretched for him too. But I can't make myself think of that.

I want to reform College when my time comes – to make the fagging better if I can't abolish it, and corporal punishment too. Why should this heaven be made a hell just for the sake of old traditions and to make the British public school type? Ought I to keep Carter out? He has been good to me – but his influence is bad in College. He stands for Athleticism and Good Form and all the rubbish joined with that. And still at the back of all these questions of reform and improvement and an intellectual rather than an athletic standard and so on, is the moral question.

Is anything worth while?

Should one live for the greatest happiness of the greatest number, avoiding all classes and creeds – or live so as to get the greatest peace for oneself? The second is so easy, and yet conscience goes against it. What is conscience? Is it only some hereditary tradition to be spurned with patriotism, etc.? The English Gentleman. What an opprobrium that is. O pray, if you have a God, for peace of mind. If we live for others we spoil ourselves. If we live for ourselves we harm others. The only course is to give oneself up to art or literature or such. But then that doesn't pay, and I suppose – *Il faut vivre.*

We shared Walter's contempt for the politics of the outside world; politicians were monsters of inefficiency and self-interest, we underwent the general post-war disillusion and would have been surprised and humiliated to be told that through the medium of college politics we had ourselves become politically-minded. I was fond of quoting Halifax: 'The Government of the world is a very great thing, but it is a very coarse thing compared with the fineness of speculative knowledge.'

My mother took me to Switzerland for the Christmas holidays of 1921. We spent them at Mürren. I was mad about skiing, the hotel was full of pretty girls. I skied, made friends, and fell in love but still managed to work for some part of the day. I had often met girls in the holidays but when I was back at Eton they had failed to retain a hold on my imagination; if I had asked them to come down to see me I would then find excuses to put them off. Their reign would come later. Staying in the same hotel, however, was Antony Knebworth and we saw something of each other. For the first time I was aware of that layer of blubber which encases an English peer, the sediment of permanent adulation. Antony was high-spirited and even when he rearranged all the shoes outside the hotel's two hundred bedrooms he could do no wrong. The meeting had consequences for me. The alpine heights, unfriendly, like too healthy climates, to all forms of art, were also unpropitious to philosophic doubt. My scepticism retreated; the shutter between myself and the rest of the world was raised and, under Antony's protection, I enjoyed a social success.

It was now decided I must try for a history scholarship; at first Cambridge was indicated. Most Collegers went on to King's, where there were safe scholarships for them and a reprieve for several more years from expulsion from the womb; Farlow was there and Rylands, Walter Le Strange was going on and eventually Nigel and Freddie. Some of us had been to Cambridge the term before to see the production of the *Oresteia*, and we had found it exhilarating and cosy, for, subject to a little permutation, the sentimental friendships from College continued unabated with undergraduates from other schools forming an audience, who, at a pinch, could contribute new blood to the cast.

On the other hand, Headlam advised Oxford, of which we had caught a glimpse marching down the High on a wintry field-day, while the old Etonians waved to us from their college porches. Denis and Roger Mynors and Bobbie Longden were all going up for scholarships there and besides Oxford was 'better for history'. In the end out of admiration for Headlam I chose to try for Balliol and as a gesture because it was the more difficult. For the same reason I concentrated on medieval history; we were taught European history from the Renaissance and 'medieval' history meant teaching myself, another 'gesture', which also provided the escape that I wanted my work to be. In history I was on the side of the underdog; I liked the past, the personal element, the Ages of Faith, the policies with no future. Most stimulating were the Dark Ages, there was 'no damned merit' about them, they were obscure, their futility a standing criticism of humanity. I admired the Childerics and Chilperics of the Merovingian dynasty, the chronicles of Liutprand, the crimes of Brunnhild and Fredegonde.

Each night, by my outlawed candle, I read all Gibbon, all Milman's *History of Latin Christianity*, I specialized in the heresies of anarchists and Albigensians but I was interested in them all, in the Manichaeans, in the heresies of Abelard, of my hero Frederic Stupormundi, the Flagellants and in my favourite Neminians who believed in a religion of 'No Man' because 'No Man living hath seen God', and 'To No Man is it given to escape Death'.

Reading late by candle was bad for the nerves for it had to be hidden in one's bed or a chink of light might be seen under the door and, like many lazy people, once I started working I could not stop; perhaps that is why we avoid it.

The result of cramming was that a noise of any kind sent me into a temper and that ordinary schoolboy chatter drove me mad. I could speak only to Denis, Charles Milligan, and Jackie O'Dwyer; in other company I would glower and pull out a book. With the Oppidans, how-ever, my ill humour vanished, I became engaging and witty.

I now admitted to myself my ambition to get into Pop and planned my campaign. My handicap was that I had no athletic distinctions, nor was I in Sixth Form from which a certain number of Pops invariably had to be chosen. My only hope was to be elected as wit. Although it was but a small section of Pop who thought me funny, they were influential. My tactics were to seem as important as I could in College, so that my Oppidan friends would not feel that I was too powerless in my own field to deserve recognition abroad. There were two Pops already in College, the lion-hearted Gibson, a fellow history specialist, and Robert Longden, one of those angel-faced Athenians whom the school delighted to honour. I was very fond of both of them and had known them for a long time. I would walk away with Gibson, arm-in-arm, from divisions and seeing me with the only two 'possible' people in College, the Oppidans felt they were safe in going about with me by themselves. I mention this technique in case others who wish to be elected to things may find it helpful. It was not very difficult for if the Oppidans observed me with the right Collegers, the latter also saw me with the right Oppidans and both felt pleased with their discrimination.

Deeper than this lay my friendship with Teddy Jessel which arose out of a certain boredom he felt at Eton through not being adolescent. I amused him because he stimulated me.

If I should get into Pop I told my conscience, my morbid spiritual director, I would make amends, for I should be free to talk to whom I liked, and then no one could stop me. There could be no further social ambition. Meanwhile I watched my step.

The scholarship examinations drew near. With Denis, Robert Longden and Roger Mynors I stayed in Balliol and did two papers a day, of which the most important was the English Essay. The subject was *Compromise* which was a favourite of mine for I had already written one essay on it and had quotations ready by which I could prove that compromises were failures and that, even if they were successes, it was one's duty to remain uncompromising. The Ages of Faith came to life under my pen. But as Denis and I walked about the Quad or lunched with the Balliol contingent of Old Collegers, as we inspected the dingy rooms with no pictures and few books whose furniture was a dark green tablecloth burnt by cigarette ends, a blokey armchair and a small cold bedroom looking out on a Neo-Gothic quad, a doubt assailed us. Here we were, urbanely pouring out the content of our well-stocked minds for six hours every day. *And for what?*

The sheets had not been aired in my bedroom. I got rheumatism in my shoulder and could hardly hold a pen during the later papers. The dons impressed me but the undergraduates I encountered made me long to return to my suspended boyhood, to Charles and Jackie and Nigel and Freddie, my books and Medici prints, the view from my window of wine-dark brick and the chestnut tree in Weston's Yard.

> College spirit [I noted down] is antagonistic to Balliol spirit in its suppression of the political, lack of emphasis on conversation, hatred of 'giants at play' and in its attention to reading and the reading of dead rather than living authors. It appears more akin to Cambridge, but with less emphasis on the bawdy Elizabethans.

We were all four school-sick (Oxford reminded me of Wellington) and radiant when the train brought us back down the Thames valley. The term ended in athletics. I went in for school fives with Longden and then the scholarship results came out. Denis and Roger had got classical scholarships at Balliol, Robert at Trinity, and I had won the Brackenbury History Scholarship. There was excitement, the history specialists cheered, and a whole holiday was given. Then came the last Sunday of term and the morning of the Pop election. I sat in my room with Charles. We had planned to go abroad together for Easter, our parents had given permission and in a few days we would realize our dream of a visit to Provence. I longed to see Avignon, the scandalous history of whose popes was as clear to me as the lines on my hand, for although I had now been abroad twice, to Paris and to Switzerland, I had never travelled alone before.

We knew that Gibson and Longden planned to put me up for Pop. The suspense grew heavy, our voices languished. Pop elections took hours, for the same boy would be put up and blackballed seven or eight times, a caucus of voters keeping out everybody till their favourite got in. Only the necessity of lunch ended these ordeals. Suddenly there was a noise of footsteps thudding up the wooden staircase of the tower. The door burst open and about twenty Pops, many of whom had never spoken to me before, with bright coloured waistcoats, rolled umbrellas, buttonholes, braid, and 'spongebag' trousers, came reeling in, like the college of cardinals arriving to congratulate some pious old freak whom fate had elevated to the throne of St Peter. They made a great noise, shouting and slapping me on the back in the elation of their gesture and Charles drifted away. I had got in on the first round, being put up by Knebworth, but after they had left only the faint smell of Balkan Sobranie and Honey and Flowers mixture remained to prove it was not a dream.

At that time Pop were the rulers of Eton, fawned on by masters and the helpless Sixth Form. Such was their prestige that some boys who failed to get in never recovered; one was rumoured to have procured his sister for the influential members. Besides privilege – for they could beat anyone, fag any lower boy, walk arm-in-arm, wear pretty clothes, sit in their own club and get away with minor breaches of discipline – they also possessed executive power which their members tasted often for the only time in their lives. To elect a boy without a colour, a Colleger too, was a departure for them; it made them feel that they appreciated intellectual worth and could not be accused of athleticism; they felt like the Viceroy after entertaining Gandhi. The rest of the school could not understand that a boy could be elected because he was amusing; if I got in without a colour it must be because I was a 'bitch'; yet by Eton standards I was too unattractive to be a 'bitch' – unless my very ugliness provided, for the jaded appetites of the Eton Society, the final attraction!

When I went to chapel I was conscious of eyes being upon me; some were masters, cold and censorious; they believed the worst; others were friendly and admiring. Those of the older boys were incredulous but the young ones stared hardest for they could be beaten for not knowing all the Pops by sight and mine was a mug they must learn by heart. Everybody congratulated me. The only person not to was Denis. He himself had been co-opted in as future Captain of the School and he could not believe that my election to such an anti-intellectual and reactionary body could give me pleasure. I thought that it was because he was envious, since he had been elected *ex officio*. My intravenous injection of success had begun to take.

Before we went abroad I visited St Wulfric's. I was now Old Wulfrician No. 1 whose triumphs were chronicled in the school magazine but although Flip and Sambo were charming, I was uneasy as I surveyed the eighty little boys in their green jerseys and corduroy knickers. I taught the Sixth Form, I wandered round classrooms and playing fields, the drill ground, the gooseberry bushes, the chapel. It seemed inconceivable that I could have felt so deeply, that I could have been a boy there myself, that Tony Watson had existed or the Manx Shearwater. Flip was confidential; I saw her angry with one or two boys, then when they had gone, she would laugh about them, and say what a lot of nonsense one had to tell them at that age, how difficult it was to keep them in order. Had I dreamt then about my favour-charts? Had I imagined it all, like a savage who believes that a tree or an old bone is ill-disposed to him? I could not be sure for it was clear that these monsters whom I had feared when I was ten had become delightful and reasonable people now I was eighteen – or would my 'favour' change and Flip be revealed again as Avenging Juno? I was bewildered.

All the boys seemed happy; there were several peers and a Siamese prince; once more the School had won the shooting trophy and the Harrow History Prize. It was a mystery. I felt like the English lady at the Paris exhibition whose mother was taken ill in her hotel and who came back with a doctor to find her name absent from the register, the rooms re-let, re-papered, refurnished and the hotel staff adamant that mother and daughter had never been seen. I wired to Charles to fetch me a day early and we crossed to Dieppe. Sambo's farewell was vivid. 'Don't forget, Tim. A Balliol scholar has the ball at his feet.' Already I felt embarrassed to know what to do with it.

~

We stayed our first night near the Gare St Lazare and visited the Folies Bergères. In the interval we roamed about the Promenoir and sat down at a table with two thin dark prostitutes. It was a great moment and seemed to wipe out my humiliation of the year before. We gave them drinks and were extremely polite, in the *Sinister Street* manner, for who knew, they might have as many different editions of Petronius as I? We wore blue suits, camel's hair waistcoats, and dark blue overcoats with a waist at the back; we smoked cigars and drawled a little, for I was in Pop, and Charles, in Sixth Form, was blonder and neater and vaguer than ever. He might have entertained prostitutes at the Folies Bergères all his life.

Suddenly Egerton and Rylands came up. We were uneasy and left our guests, for 'Pussy' Egerton, now a scholar of Trinity, had been the Captain of the School and in the Eleven; he was 'the hell of a chap' and the Colleger who had best fitted into the background of the lilies, correcting the headmaster, sleeping through difficult construes, to wake up and suggest an emendation with that boom of laziness which was a trait in the 'To him that hath shall be given' Eton type. Rylands, his great friend, was more exaggerated, more literary. He was going to be the Duchess in the *Duchess of Malfi* next year, he told us, and he talked of 'Lytton' and 'A.C.B.'

Afterwards we went back to the hotel and lay awake in the dark. My face itched, and I could feel lumps under my fingers. I scratched, and heard a noise in the silence. Charles was scratching too.

'Charles.'

'Yes.'

'Are you awake?'

'Yes.'

'So am I.'

'Charles.'

'Yes.'

'Do you know how one catches it?'

'Yes. I think so. From shaking hands – or touching them or drinking out of the same glass.'

'My God – it's come out on my face already.'

'And mine.'

'I shook hands with mine.'

'Mine wore gloves – I felt fairly safe.'

'But don't you think she wore them because she *had it there*?'

'Christ! How awful – and my face itches too.'

'Have you got anything we can put on?'

'Only some Icilma.'

'It's better than nothing – in the morning we can go to a doctor.'

'Or should we go now?'

We put on the light and looked at each other. Charles sat up in his white Egyptian cotton pyjamas. They were mosquito bites. We joked about them with nervous vigour, and caught the morning train to Avignon.

There is the first time we go abroad and there is the first time we set eyes on Provence. For me they almost coincided and it would be hard to express what I felt that evening, in the garden above the Papal Palace. The frogs croaked, the silver Rhône flowed underneath, the Mediterranean spring was advancing. I have been back so many times, as a spring ritual, to that palace, to Hiely's restaurant with its plate-glass windows, to the Greek Theatre at Arles, the hills of Les Baux, the ruins of St Rémy, to the Rhône with its eddies and islands and the cypress hedges where the cicadas charge the batteries of summer that I can no longer remember what they looked like for the first time. I know only that they are sacred places, that the country between the Mont Ventoux and the Canigou, from Avignon and Vaucluse to Figueras and Puigcerdá, is the expression of the complete south, the cradle of my civilization.

We hired bicycles at Villeneuve-lès-Avignon and visited Nîmes and Tarascon and Beaucaire. Then we had to make a decision. Should we go on to the Riviera or down the east coast of France towards Spain? Charles inclined to casinos but we chose Spain because it was cheaper and spent the next night at Narbonne. The town was gloomy, the mistral blew, Charles broke the chandelier in our room and tried to hide

the pieces. At the last moment they were found and a large item added
to the bill. The mistral made travelling impossible. We sat in the train
going past platforms where the acacias and cypresses were plastered
back by the wind and where even the names of the stations seemed
fretted by the mistral; Agde, Leucate, Fitou, Palau del Vidre. The
lagoons fascinated us, for it was the country of *Mariana in the South*.
The strip of sand, the reeds, the sea lavender, the wind and sun brought
back South Africa; there was the Mediterranean, a dark streak beyond
the lagoons like the edge of a pineta and close at hand the stakes in the
water, the white beds of flaking salt, the barren rocks of the Corbières.
We reached the red soil of Rousillon, the fortress of Salses, the cathedral
of Elne where a Byzantine empress lay buried, Collioure with its phallic
church tower, dingy Port-Vendres, Banyuls and after many tunnels the
frontier at Cerbère. We could go no farther without a visa.

Next morning we scrambled up to the top of the hill from the beach,
blown flat against the ground by the mistral but able to feel we had
looked into Spain. Below us was an identical stony hillside dotted with
asphodel, Port Bou with its cove, Cullera and Llansa, the mountain
peninsula that runs out to Cadaqués and the plain of the Ampurdan.
For one moment we surveyed it, then we were blown off our feet.
Unable to stay on in Cerbère, we retreated, still battered by the mistral,
from the station with its queues of Catalans, in berets and rope-soled
shoes, their rugs slung over their shoulders, to the palms and cafés of
Perpignan. I was getting school-sick for Eton.

> *Où sont les gracieux galants*
> Whom I saw last month ago?
> And here at Perpignan I want
> To see them all again, although
> 'Twas not with such an easy flow
> Of mutual intercourse enjoyed . . .
> In fact I often was, I know,
> By ἔρις not ἐρῶς destroyed.
> And how does my dear Denis fare

Called 'proud' by Dadie, whom we met
The prey of Folies Bergères
And wooed by many an Amoret
Who said '*Dormirez-vous*, you pet'
But Egerton, with *visage noir*
Repulsed the sirenaic set
Who circle in the Promenoir.

Our journeys back were unpleasant. We both ran out of money and because of our tickets had to return by different ways. I travelled by Toulouse, carried my suitcase across Paris, got to London in the evening and rather than confess that I was penniless, spent my last five shillings on dining alone in Soho and then retired for the night to St Martin's-in-the-Fields. It was cold and uncomfortable; the people coughing all round me and wrapping themselves up in newspapers kept me awake. The next morning I met Charles at Victoria. He was coming back by Avignon but had overslept and gone on to Marseille where they had tried to make him pay the difference. He had only a bag of dates on which he had been living and we took them to the Park and finished them before going round to his home in Upper Brook Street.

24 *Vale*

When we went back to Eton the news of our travels had preceded us. We were sent for by the Headmaster and rebuked for having visited the Folies Bergères which was not the sort of place where Etonians go. Charles's visit in his sleep to Marseille was misconstrued by his tutor who asked him if he was aware that it was a centre of the white slave trade? I had been staying on my way back with my aunt and her butler had packed the magazines which were by my bed, including a copy of *La Vie Parisienne*. My tutor was horrified; it was bad enough to glance at such drawings he explained, what made it worse was that they were so 'diabolically clever'. He also took away *Tristram Shandy* and an uncut Rabelais.

Denis, Robert Longden, and Roger Mynors now formed the principal mess. Charles and I now messed alone; Denis was Captain of the School but for the first month of my last term I lived among Oppidans. 'Since God has given us the Popacy let us enjoy it,' was my motto after Leo the Tenth's. I was ashamed to hire classical records now from the music shop and on summer mornings I would go down there with Edward Woodall, Robin Gurdon, and Teddy Jessel to play 'Say it with Music' while the fox-trot floated away on the sunlight and we commented on the looks of the passers-by.

It was a custom to walk up to a hotel in Windsor and sit in the garden, drinking and smoking. These were serious offences but the Pops took them for granted and never went about without a full cigarette case. At lunch they sat beside their housemasters, breathing port and tobacco over them and making patronizing conversation. I soon discovered that my notion of being careful whom I went about with till I was in Pop and then making friends with whom I liked was quite impracticable. The Pops like all tyrants clung together as afraid of what the school thought of them as the rest were of the Pops; those who had nothing in common and disliked each other hurried when they met to link arms against an invisible danger.

Thus only boys in Pop were allowed to walk arm-in-arm. When I was not in Pop but was walking with Teddy Jessel or Robert Longden I would await the gesture, the arm first raised and then shot forward to bring the sleeve and cuff down within grip of the fingers and then the whole arm inserted, like a bishop laying on hands, with a sacred stealing motion through my own. It was a solemn moment when this public favour was conferred but when I was in Pop and enjoyed the same privilege I found that my arm seemed unwilling to experiment, and felt at ease only when another braided Pop sleeve reposed in mine.

Soon everybody in College began to seem insipid and dowdy for I saw them through Oppidan eyes and only the fastidious Charles and the genial Jackie were proof against the insolent fashionable stare. 'How petty everything is,' wrote Walter Le Strange. 'Even people one would never suspect of it seem afraid of Cyril, speaking of him only in hushed whispers.'

Some of the Pops had been worried about my not having a colour and the Captain of the Boats was persuaded to give me a rowing one; like an oligarchy the Eton Society went in terror of letting itself down. For a month I was a model member of that corrupt and glittering eighteenth-century clique and I forgot for the first time in my life that I was a 'highbrow', and that highbrows are cut off from the world.

During this month I managed to emancipate myself from the Irish bogey through the Anglo-Irish boys at school who were cousins of mine and whom I met at my aunt's. Being in Pop was a distinction even the Anglo-Irish had to recognize and one day I realized that I was the most important boy there, that they wanted to know me not I them, that I need not rack my brains to think of something to say about horses, it was for them to try to talk about the all-Colleger performance of *She Stoops to Conquer* in which I was playing an exhibitionist role.* A voice told me that Clontarf, rebuilt with livid stained glass in the Isle of Wight Gothic of the sixties round an old ivied tower, was an ugly and unimportant house in a Dublin suburb, that History, after taking one look at the Vernons, had moved across the Channel and that whoever might now receive her favours, it would not be the lately landed Anglo-Irish Gentry.

Alas, in my excursion into the ruling class I had reckoned without an old enemy – the Thames Valley summer. Buttercups, lilac, elms, and steamy evenings had returned and were preparing their annual coup. They used a roundabout method.

It was the privilege of College Pop not to have to stamp their own letters. One member offered to 'keep the stamps' and to him a fag would bring the letters from the letter-box, stamp them there and enter

---

* *Mrs Hardcastle*. The signatures on my programme at this extreme moment of dandyism are revealing. Dunglass, Knebworth, Teddy Jessel, Robin Gurdon, Maurice Bridgman, Edward Woodall, Greville Worthington, Guy Wainwright – all history specialist members of Pop, Brian Howard (aesthete), Bernard Brassey (toast of the day), and three fags, Alsop, Coleridge and Ford to represent College with Nigel and his friend O'Connor. Five of these and three members of the cast would meet violent deaths before they were forty. *Quelle époque!*

the amounts due in a book. When stamps ran out, the stamp-keeper would go round and ask people for what they owed him. At that time I kept the stamps for College Pop but I spurned the dunning of people for money and announced that I would pay for the stamps myself. One or two conscientious boys gave something, the rest accepted this typical 'gesture' as a mixture of idealism, laziness, and the desire to show off. '*Qui veut faire l'ange fait la bête!*' I soon ran out of stamps and having some letters brought to me to post, I remembered that any placed in the letter-box in the rooms of the Eton Society were franked in the same way. I sent the fag down with them. That afternoon, when the letters were collected, somebody in Pop chanced to go through them, and noticed that several were to the parents of Collegers. The old hostility broke out. 'Why the hell should those bloody bastards in College post their letters here – why should we stamp letters addressed to all the bloody villas in Tooting, etc., etc.'

The Pops assumed that they had been posted by Denis, whom they disliked, to oblige his friends and made remarks about him. I heard of the proceedings but at some time in the St Wulfric's or Dark Ages period my nerve had gone. I felt the old panic about 'owning up', 'going straight', 'generality', and 'being wanted' – I could not explain, only wait for it to blow over. Eventually – by elimination – they discovered who it was. Nico Davies and Knebworth rebuked me in a friendly way. I tried to apologize but was seized with a hopeless feeling of guilt. How could I explain? I had betrayed Pop; I had let down the friends who had made the experiment of electing me.

From that moment my vitality failed as I had seen it fail in others, I felt uneasy whenever I was with Pops, and could no longer face the rakes in the Hotel Garden. I made the mistake, common in youth, of not understanding that people who like one for oneself will overlook occasional lapses. I felt that the Members of the Eton Society liked me only in so far as I conformed while someone more mature would have known that the affair was trivial and that they liked me because they knew I could never conform. Driven underground for a year by success, my persecution mania had found an outlet.

In College my self-confidence still held out but even as I had fallen victim to scepticism a summer before, so now I succumbed to aestheticism. It was in the air; the season, the lime-flowered summer evenings undermined me and I fell. I wore, instead of a blazer, with my grey flannel trousers, a black dinner-jacket, and a panama hat. The fashion was not followed. I read *Marius the Epicurean* and *À Rebours* which sent me on to silver Latin and '*faisandé*' prose. I studied the philosophy of Aristippus of Cyrene and smouldered with the 'hard gem-like flame'. I believed in living for 'golden moments', in 'anything for a sensation' and read Baudelaire, Verlaine, Hérédia, Moréas, and Mallarmé at French Extra Studies with de Satgé, from whom I borrowed *Limbo* and *Crome Yellow* which I got into trouble for reading.

I went to the rose-show at Windsor and had an intense experience looking at the whitest of white roses; after that I always had some Frau Karl Druschki's in my room. Rancid with boredom, I burnt melancholy texts around the wall with a poker. 'Let us crown ourselves with roses before they be whithered' (*Coronemus nos rosis antequam marcescant*) from the *Wisdom of Solomon*, '*Finis venit, venit finis, evigilavit adversum te et ecce venit*' from Ezekiel, and from Mallarmé '*La chair est triste, hélas, et j'ai lu tous les livres*'.

I now admired the twelve Caesars with their enigmatic deathbed sayings charged with power and satiety and the last king of France – '*mettens-nous à la fenêtre et ennuyons-nous,*' exclaimed Louis XIII. '*Nous ne sommes pas heureux à notre âge*' added Louis XIV. Louis XV left no wisdom, but I learnt that on receiving the news of each defeat in the Seven Years War '*Il ouvre ses grands yeux tristes, et tout est dit.*'

A favourite and succulent character was Audubon, in Lowes Dickinson's *Modern Symposium*.

> And just there is the final demonstration of the malignity of the scheme of things. Time itself works against us. The moments that are evil it eternalizes; the moments that might be good it hurries to annihilation. All that is most precious is most precarious. Vainly do we

cry to the moment, '*Verweile doch, du bist so schön!*' Only the heavy hours are heavy-footed. The winged Psyche, even at the moment of birth, is sick with the pangs of dissolution.

Walter Le Strange corroborated.

25 June. Seven months since I have seen you, sweet book! Cyril has had you – thank God they were no profane hands that touched you, or unholy eyes that read my heart. When I last confided to you I had sunk to depths of aesthetic affectation deeper than I realized at the time. Now I am (I flatter myself) more level-headed. Cyril has once more consented to *know* me, after some months of estrangement. His conversation is as butter and honey after bread and dripping. Unfortunately, instead of what was, for me at least, friendship, there is now worship. For then we were outwardly (I flatter myself again) equal, now I am (to the world, not mentally, I hope) unchanged, while he has Success. Niké disdains me. I let Cyril influence me more than I mean to. I know all influence (especially an enervating one like his) is bad. But Cyril is so pleasant I cannot resist him even if I wished to try. (O Hypocrite that I am, this is written for his eyes.)

12 July. Life should be lived, wildly and feverishly within, outwardly with absolute calm and composure. Nor ought one's true opinions to be given to anyone. Everything should bow to expediency and efficiency. How weak I am! In the evening I make huge resolves, in the morning I remember them and disregard them.

15 July. Since last I wrote the whole world seems to have been spread before me. I have seen incense burnt on the altar of Dionysus and heard the Antigone acted in the original tongue of Sophocles. I have dined with the Headmaster and talked of Italian Art. Cyril has shown me the most beautiful flowers in the world. I have knelt on the floor looking at a medieval map beside a Prince Palatine. I have had my 18th birthday. I have four ambitions of which only the third is likely to come true.

(1) To get a scholarship at King's in December.

(2) To get my College Wall.

(3) To see Florence and Venice.

(4) To be in Pop next summer half.

To myself I appear a Messiah.

To my friends an ineffectual angel with a touch of the idiot.

To my enemies a negligible knave.

Coronemus nos rosis antequam marcescant. But I only do it because it is the thing to do.

Vain attempts to attract Maud.

The Beggar's Opera and *Dear Brutus* both tend to show 'the utter futility of doing anything under any circumstances'.

Le Strange at least kept his diary but all my own attempts to write were doomed to failure. I didn't see how one could write well in English, and my Greek and Latin were still not good enough. I took to writing jingles in which a Greek verse was brought in to rhyme with the English; it was not till a year or two later that I was able to discard English and express myself in Greek epigrams for to compose in a dead language was the creative activity toward which my education was inexorably tending. Meanwhile there was French.

> Roses blanches
> Qui se penchent
> En songes
> Elles m'ont chanté
> Des enchantés
> Mensonges.
>
> Que la vie est brève
> Rêve d'un rêve, etc. etc.

This was the summer's only inspiration.

Meanwhile a strange pink album had appeared called the *Eton Candle*. It contained poems and some precious stories, contributions from Max Beerbohm and those suspect old Etonians, Aldous Huxley, Osbert and Sacheverell Sitwell. One day Teddy Jessel introduced me to the editor, a boy in his house with a distinguished impertinent face, a sensual mouth and dark eyes with long lashes. He wrote to ask me to tea. I accepted, on Pop writing paper, and went round one summer afternoon to find *foie gras* sandwiches, strawberries and cream, and my postcard of acceptance prominently displayed on the mantelpiece. Seeing it up there for the world to know that Brian Howard had had a Pop to tea with him, I was miserable. I felt that once again I had let the Eton Society down. It was natural for Teddy Jessel to know Brian who was in the same house. The question was, *Who else did?* I swallowed down my tea like a lady who is offered a swig by a madman in a railway tunnel and bolted.

Afterwards when I saw Brian alone I would talk to him; when I was with other Pops I avoided him, as in the Dark Ages Wilfred had avoided me. I need not have worried for he soon became the most fashionable boy in the school but, as it was, though I grew to know him better, his politeness overwhelmed me. He belonged to a set of boys who were literary and artistic but too lazy to gargle quotations and become inoculated with the virus of good taste latent in Eton teaching and too disorderly and bad at games to be overburdened with responsibility and who in fact gained most from Eton because of the little they gave. There was Harold Acton, a prince of courtesy, his brother William, Robert Byron who was aggressive, and played jokes on the Corps, the two Messels, Antony Powell, the author of *Afternoon Men* and Henry Green who has since described them in his novel, *Blindness*. They were the most vigorous group at Eton for they lived within their strength, yet my moral cowardice and academic outlook debarred me from making friends with them.

College politics were now less exciting, for we were not in opposition but in office. Denis was Captain of the School; beatings stopped, fagging was light, the election system languished. College Pop had now extended the privilege of using its library to the Upper Half of College, and so to belong no longer brought that increase of privacy which, at Eton, formed the substance of promotion. Being in Liberty and in Pop but not in Sixth Form, I was in an irresponsible position, a school but not a house prefect. I looked on myself as a kind of Charles James Fox or Wilkes, a Whig to the left of the Whig position although I was more of an anarchist than a Liberal for I disbelieved in power and authority and thought them evil and believed that the natural goodness of human reason must triumph without them.

The deadly sin, since I was in Pop, was 'Worldliness' and I preached against it whenever I could. As with many anarchists, there was some vanity in my make-up. I did not want to cooperate or be cooperated with and began to take umbrage with Denis, Roger, Robert Longden, the Periclean Caucus who governed College.

Thus after the reform of College Pop into a debating society, I resigned as a protest against compulsory debates although the motion, 'that death was preferable to life', was one very dear to me. A blasé *grand seigneur*, I called everybody in College by their Christian name and at Liberty Supper I would hold 'wantings', which were parodies of the dread affairs of my youth, and on occasion a mock beating in which the victims kept their gowns on, and the canes, carefully notched beforehand, broke in half at the first stroke. It was a silly way to behave as rumours spread which made more difficult the genuine reforms of the Caucus. Anybody could play about with discipline in that way since however much one might rag 'wantings' and fagging, there was no question of boys not turning up for the wanting or not running to be fagged.

I made friends with many of the fags; in my jaundiced state I enjoyed their simplicity and vitality, besides, I wanted them to be happier than I had been myself. I was sometimes suspected of other motives by my ambivalent housemaster which made me scornful and defiant. He had complained once of my 'infernal pride' and I at last lived up to it. I hated history by now; it stank of success, and I buried myself in the classics. I was bored and unhappy but there was no equal in whom I could confide. I was afraid Denis would fail to understand, the virtuous Caucus might lecture me, my housemaster was antipathetic, Headlam could have helped me but I was too frightened of him. He had pointed out to me the seats which the Sitwells had occupied in his class-room but on the other hand he had condemned as morbid 'Ere blowsy tediousness of summer days', the last line of a sonnet I wrote.

Urquhart came down from Balliol and had tea with me; he seemed with his easy-going good-mannered confidence and aroma of the days of Greville and Palmerston to promise release into an adult world of intellectual excitement and sensible activity – but after he had gone the white roses, the green bananas, the clove carnation soap and the dismal mottoes resumed their power, and I even engaged a fag to sing Gregorian chants outside my room, like Saul with David.

I was eighteen and a half; I had never had sexual intercourse, I had never masturbated. 'Lilies that fester smell far worse than weeds,' perhaps even St Wulfric's, even the Eton authorities had not required a chastity so strict.

The end of term arrived. There was still Camp, which was one long operatic farewell for me but parting was imminent. I had a spectacular leaving tea, to which my friends were invited in platonic couples and where I played the *Après-midi d'un faune* on my gramophone.

> Cyril's leaving tea. A beautiful evening, tea and fair faces and good music [wrote Le Strange]. Then Liberty Supper, the last alas! How banal Liberty suppers will seem next half – *Cyril est épatant, mais comme toujours à la grande manière.* N. got his 22 today. He has gone completely off, as has Maud who used to be so very nice.

There was the last chapel where for the last time I refused to bow my head in the creed and read Petronius through the leaving hymn, walking afterwards under the limes with Teddy Jessel. The cant of leaving infuriated him, the sentimental farewells, the warnings against the prostitutes of Jermyn Street, and hypocritical anxiety of the stupider Pops worrying about their successors. The gruelling election had lasted all that morning, with partisans of one boy putting in two or three blackballs each against nominees of others until one understood why the College of Cardinals, on such occasions, was locked in and given no food. My principles still kept me from blackballing anyone but I enjoyed the excitement. Charles my old friend and mess-mate was elected, and the second time round I put up Nigel to realize my insolent daydream of the year before.

In spite of the reconciliation our friendship was in abeyance; it would seem that in the quarrel I had expended all the emotion I was capable of feeling. I remembered how at one time noticing the shape of his ear in chapel had moved me and now he was only a bouncing fellow who had just missed the Eleven. He was not elected till a year later but his gratitude put me to shame.

In *College Annals* Denis wrote the account of his stewardship.

> The past year has been conspicuous more for an alteration in the general tone of College than for any remarkable achievements. It has always been the hope of my own Election to destroy the inter-election enmity, as it existed a few years ago, to abolish the scandals of College Pop, to reduce the number of beatings to a minimum, and generally to substitute a more harmonious system of government for the old methods of repressions and spite.
>
> The actual changes that have occurred may be summed up thus:- When I was a fag it was considered a poor night for the 'senior' if no one was beaten, and 'wantings' occurred every night, whereas this last half it does not happen to have been necessary to use corporal punishment at all, scarcely a dozen to twenty 'wantings' the whole half. As regards College Pop, instead of being a miniature Eton society with exclusive right to Reading Room, it has been reformed with the intention of making it a debating society proper, and I have hope that the new rules will not allow it again to degenerate into a selfish body of College 'chaps', like School Pop . . . It is early yet to judge of the success of these experiments, and the universal prediction of the 'old men' *may* be verified, but I can at least honestly record that College has been in every way *happier* this year than at any time in the last six years.

The verdict of subsequent Captains of the School on our shortlived and unpopular experiment in happiness can be found in Mr Eric Parker's *College at Eton* (Macmillan, 1933). *College Annals* also included a short autobiography of every colleger, usually a list of his athletic distinctions, but, under our decadent administration, more general in tone. Thus Farlow added his slogan, '*cui bono*' to his list of triumphs, Charles included his gesture in resigning from the Corps and

Le Strange ended up 'other minor scholastic achievements there were too, which it would be tedious to enumerate'. I added a list of favourite authors, favourite flower, rose (white), and my new motto, 'I hate everything public' (σικάινω πάνια τὰ δημόσια), concluding: 'A sentimental cynic, superstitious atheist, and Brackenbury Scholar of Balliol College Oxford'.

Although I affected not to care I dreaded leaving; one part of me was bored and looked forward to moving on, the other clung to the past. Once more I had built up a private civilization of reason and love at a temperature warmer than the world outside; once again it had to be shattered. 'We whose generations are ordained in this setting part of time are providentially taken off from such imaginations' – but I could not repress a dread of the future, of the uglification of life, of Oxford bedrooms and dour undergraduates. Eton is one of the few schools where the standard of comfort is almost in advance of the universities and unlike most boys, Denis and Robert and I were not looking forward to more liberty than we enjoyed already, to more interesting friendships, or to a room of our own for the first time. Also we were attached to the past and used to a world of boys, boys with a certain grace who like the portraits in the Provost's Lodge wore their eighteenth-century clothes with elegance. The world of matey young men with their pipes and grey bags, the blokeries to which we had been allotted, filled us with despair; we mourned with apprehension, 'Not the dead but the ἥβας ἄνδος απολλῦμενον – the flower of youth perishing.'

I was now entering the third hot room of English education; from St Wulfric's I had got a scholarship to Eton, from Eton to Balliol and from thence there would, I supposed, be other scholarships awaiting me; I could not imagine a moment when I should not be receiving marks for something, when 'poor' or 'very fair' or 'Beta plus' was not being scrawled across my conduct-sheet by the Great Examiner. And yet already I was a defeatist, I remembered Teddy Jessel saying to me by the fives courts, in my hour of triumph: 'Well, you've got a Balliol scholarship and you've got into Pop – you know I shouldn't be at all surprised if you never did anything else the rest of your life. After all, what happens to old tugs? If they're clever they become dons or civil servants, if not they come back here as ushers; when they're about forty they go to bed with someone, if it's a boy they get sacked, if it's a woman they marry them. The pi ones go into the church and may become bishops. There goes Connolly, K.S., a brilliant fellow, an alpha mind, he got the Rosebery and the Brackenbury, and all the other berries, and passed top into the Office of Rears!'

There was much truth in this, in fact were I to deduce any system from my feelings on leaving Eton, it might be called *The Theory of Permanent Adolescence*. It is the theory that the experiences undergone by boys at the great public schools, their glories and disappointments, are so intense as to dominate their lives and to arrest their development. From these it results that the greater part of the ruling class remains adolescent, school-minded, self-conscious, cowardly, sentimental, and in the last analysis homosexual. Early laurels weigh like lead and of many of the boys whom I knew at Eton, I can say that their lives are over. Those who knew them then knew them at their best and fullest; now, in their early thirties, they are haunted ruins. When we meet we look at each other, there is a pause of recognition, which gives way to a moment of guilt and fear. 'I won't tell on you', our eyes say, 'if you won't tell on me' – and when we do speak, it is to discover peculiar evidence of this obsession. For a nightmare I have often had has been that of finding myself back; I am still a boy at Eton, still in Pop, still in my old room in Sixth Form Passage but nobody remembers me, nobody tells me where to go. I am worse than a newboy, I am a new oldboy, I go into Hall and search for a place to eat, I wander in schoolrooms trying to find a class where I am expected. When I first used to have this dream I had only just left Eton, I knew most of the boys and the masters and the nightmare then took the form of everyone, after my place had been filled, my gap closed over, having to pretend they were glad I had come back. As time went on nobody remembered me and the dream ended with my ignominious ejection. I have found other old Etonians who have had the same experience; some dream they are back in their old rooms while their wives and children hang about outside to disgrace them.

Once again romanticism with its deathwish is to blame, for it lays an emphasis on childhood, on a fall from grace which is not compensated for by any doctrine of future redemption; we enter the world, trailing clouds of glory, childhood and boyhood follow and we are damned. Certainly growing up seems a hurdle which most of us are able to take and the lot of the artist is unpleasant in England because he is one of the few who, bending but not breaking, is able to throw off these early experiences, for maturity is the quality that the English dislike most and the fault of artists is that, like certain foreigners, they are mature.* For my own part I was long dominated by impressions of school. The plopping of gas mantles in the class-rooms, the refrain of psalm tunes, the smell of plaster on the stairs, the walk through the fields to the bathing places or to chapel across the cobbles of School Yard, evoked a vanished Eden of grace and security; the intimate noises of College, the striking of the clock at night from Agar's Plough, the showers running after games of football, the housemaster's squeak, the rattle of tea-things, the poking of fires as I sat talking with Denis or Charles or Freddie on some evening when everybody else was away at a lecture, were recollected with anguish and College, after I left, seemed to me like one of those humming fortified paradises in an Italian primitive outside which the angry Master in College stood with his flaming sword.

> Procul abest Fridericus, Fridericus capite rubro
> Procul abest Nigel, qui solebat mecum ire
> Procul absunt pueri qui clamant in cubiculis eorum
> Qui sedent super focos pulchri sine arte
> Pulchri sunt sed nesciunt, nec decoris eorum habent scientiam –
> O Roma, urbs beata, lumen ultra mare.

Since I was unable to write in any living language when I left Eton I was already on the way to becoming a critic. My ambition was to be a

---

* Even the Jews in England are boyish, like Disraeli, and not the able creators of adult philosophies like Marx or Freud.

poet but I could not succeed when poetry was immersed in the Georgian or Neo-Tennysonian tradition. I could but have imitated Housman, Flecker, Brooke, de la Mare, or Ralph Hodgson. By the time Eliot and Valéry came to save my generation from the romantic dragon it had already devoured me. I was however well grounded enough to become a critic and drifted into it through unemployability.

In other respects I had been more deeply scarred. The true religion I had learnt at Eton and St Wulfric's had not been Christianity nor even Imperialism but the primitive gospel of the Jealous God, of φθονερόν – a gospel which emerged as much from the Old Testament as from Greek tragedy and was confirmed by experience. Human beings, it taught, are perpetually getting above themselves and presuming to rise superior to the limitations of their nature; when they reach this state of insolence or ὕβρις, they are visited with some catastrophe, the destruction of Sodom or the Sicilian expedition, the fate of Œdipus or Agamemnon, the Fall of Troy or the Tower of Babel. The happiness, to which we aspire, is not well thought of and is visited with retribution; though some accounts are allowed to run on longer than others, everything in life has to be paid for.

Even when we say 'I am happy' we mean 'I was' for the moment is past, besides, when we are enjoying ourselves most, when we feel secure of our strength and beloved by our friends, we are intolerable and our punishment – beating for generality, a yellow ticket, a blackball, or a summons from the Headmaster – is in preparation. All we can do is to walk delicately, to live modestly and obscurely like the Greek chorus and to pay a careful attention to omens – counting our paces, observing all conventions, taking quotations at random from Homer or the Bible, and acting on them while doing our best to 'keep in favour' – for misfortunes never come alone.

Consider Jackie; playing fives with me one afternoon he said 'Damn and blast' when he missed a ball. The Headmaster, who was passing, heard him and told Sixth Form. That night he was beaten. In the excitement of the game he had forgotten to prepare his construe. Others had prepared theirs but after the silence before boys are put on to construe, when all diversions have been tried in vain, it was he who was called upon. He was ploughed and given a 'ticket' 'Failed in Construe' to get signed by his tutor. He had not the courage to show it him, forged his tutor's initials on the bottom and handed it back. By chance the two masters met, the ticket was mentioned and the fraud discovered. Within three days of the game of fives the Praepostor came with the terrible summons. 'Is O'Dwyer K.S. in this division? He is to go to the Headmaster at a quarter to twelve.' The wide doors are open which means a birching will take place. The block is put out. Two boys in Sixth Form are there to see the Headmaster does not raise his arm above the shoulder, and an old College servant to lower his trousers and hold him down. 'Call no man happy till he's dead. Next time it may be me.'

Morally I was not in advance of this abject religion; I rejected Christian ethics yet was not enough of a stoic to adopt pagan standards in their place. I was a *vierge folle* full of neurotic pride and this gave to my thinking a morbid tinge.

Politically I was a liberal individualist with a passion for freedom and justice and a hatred of power and authority but I disliked politics and wished for nothing better than to talk to my friends, travel abroad, look at Old Masters and Romanesque cathedrals, read old books and devote myself to lost causes and controversies of the past.

The cause of the unhappiness I had come across I put down as Competition. It was Competition that turned friends into enemies, that exhausted the scholars in heart-breaking sprints and rendered the athletes disappointed and bitter. 'Never compete' was my new commandment, never again to go in for things, to be put up and black-balled, to score off anyone; only in that way could the sin of Worldliness be combated, the Splendid Failure be prepared which was the ultimate 'gesture'. Otherwise when free from guilt and fear I was gay, with evening high spirits hardly distinguishable from intoxication and which rose and rose until the shutter fell, a glass which cut me off from loving friends and imagined enemies and behind which I prepared for that interview with the moment, that sacred breathless confrontation from which so little always results, and so much is vainly expected. I was also an affected lover of sensations which I often faked, a satirist in self-defence, a sceptical believer in the Heraclitan flux, an introspective romantic-sensitive, conceited, affectionate, gregarious and, at the time of leaving Eton, the outstanding moral coward of my generation.

Sometimes I imagine Eton replying to these criticisms, the voice of 'Henry's holy shade' answering me with the serenity of a dowager.

'Yes. Very interesting. It was one of my masters, I think, who said, "Connolly has a vulgar streak" – but we won't discuss that. As I understand, you blame us because our teaching encouraged aestheticism and the vices that are found with it and then punished them when they occurred. Has it ever occurred to you to blame yourself? You say winning a scholarship and getting into Pop turned your head, and set you back ten years. Well, I'm sorry for you. Other boys achieved this and more and were not harmed by it. Look at Robert Longden. The same age as you are and Headmaster of Wellington and Lord Dufferin, almost in the Cabinet. You complain that my teaching is cynical and concentrates on success. Don't forget what Jowett said, "There are few ways in which a young man can be more harmlessly employed than in making money." Not that I altogether approve of Pop myself, but since your time its morals have improved and its powers been restricted. The state of College has improved too; that Bolshy epoch, when some of the post-war unrest reached our little backwater, is a thing of the past.

'I think if you had been less vain, less full of the wrong sort of pride and with a little more stuffing, you would not have been attracted to the "primrose path". You would not have let a little success get the better of you. Don't forget we put you in a strong position. The great world is not unlike the Eton Society. Their values are the same. You could have made lasting friendships with people who will govern the country – not flashy people but those from whose lodges, in a Scotch deer-forest, great decisions are taken. You Bolshies keep on thinking the things we stand for – cricket, shooting, Ascot, Lords, the Guards, the House of Commons, and the Empire – are dead. But you all want to put your sons down for Eton. It's twenty years now since you came here. Even then people talked about this world being dead but what is more alive today? your Bolshevism or the English governing class, the Tory Party?

'But let's leave Pop, let's suppose it is no good in after life to a boy – excuse me – with your income. There was always a Balliol scholarship. Why didn't you follow that up? I see you show a tendency to sneer at the government offices and the diplomatic service. And yet they rule the country more than ever. If "Pop" leads to the Cabinet, "College" leads to the Permanent Under Secretaryships, the plums of the administration. It was the old Colleger type, prelate, judge, or civil servant who turned out the late king (not an old Etonian) with such absence of friction. They decide who's to be given a visa or permitted to land; they open the mail and tap the telephones. I shouldn't sneer at them. You imply our education is of no use to you in after life. But no education is. We are not an employment agency; all we can do is to give you a grounding in the art of mixing with your fellow men, to tell you what to expect from life and give you an outward manner and inward poise, an old prescription from the eighteenth century which we call a classical education, an education which confers the infrequent virtues of good sense and good taste and the benefit of dual nationality, English and Mediterranean, and which, taking into account the difficulties of modern life, we find the philosophy best able to overcome them.

'You complain that Ruskin's cult of beauty and Tennyson's imagery of water and summer still predominate; but we can't help our buildings being beautiful or our elms stately. If you think boys are happier for a retarded development in unfriendly surroundings, you should have gone to Wellington. You say we are sterile and encourage composition only in dead languages. Shelley and Swinburne and Dr Bridges wouldn't agree with you. And what matter, if the spirit is alive. Take this:

> Quam breve tempus abit quod amando degitur! Instar*
> Momenti fugiens vix superat.

* Que l'heure est donc brève
Qu'on passe en aimant
C'est moins qu'un moment
Un peu plus qu'un rêve
Le temps nous enlève
Notre enchantement.   Anon.

Exquisite! It is by Mr Broadbent. Something you were too bathed in your masochist Celtic twilight to appreciate. You were never a very good classical scholar. Too lazy. You would not grasp that, as one of my masters writes, "No education is worth having that does not teach the lesson of concentration on a task, however unattractive. These lessons if not learnt early, will be learnt, if at all, with pain and grief in later life." Now I expect you have found that out, as you will one day find out about character, too.

'About the civilization of the lilies, Percy Lubbock and Santayana say very different things from you. However, we bear no ill-will. We shall be here when you have gone. Come down and see us some time. I admit we have been disappointed in you. We hoped that you would conquer your faults but we can't all be Pitt or J. K. Stephen and, in spite of what you say, we have since turned out a writer who has been able to reconcile being a "live wire" with loyalty to the school tradition, even on the Amazon.'

~

I have concluded at this point, for it marks the end of my unconscious absorption of ideas, besides there was now nothing new which could happen to me. Although to the world I appeared a young man going up to Oxford 'with the ball at his feet', I was, in fact, as promising as the Emperor Tiberius retiring to Capri. I knew all about power and popularity, success and failure, beauty and time, I was familiar with the sadness of the lover and the bleak ultimatums of the beloved. I had formed my ideas and made my friends and it was to be years before I could change them. I lived entirely in the past, exhausted by the emotions of adolescence, of understanding, loving and learning. Denis's fearless intellectual justice, Robert's seventeenth-century face, mysterious in its conventionality, the scorn of Nigel, the gaiety of Freddie, the languor of Charles, were permanent symbols which would confront me fortunately for many years afterwards, unlike the old redbrick box and elmy landscape which contained them. I was to continue on my useless assignment, falling in love, going to Spain and being promising indefinitely.

Somewhere in the facts I have recorded lurk the causes of that sloth by which I have been disabled, somewhere lies the sin whose guilt is at my door, increasing by compound interest faster than promise (for promise is guilt – promise is the capacity for letting people down); and through them run those romantic ideas and fallacies, those errors of judgement against which the validity of my criticism must be measured.

For the critic's role was implicit in this Georgian boyhood.

> Beneath the hot incurious sun
> Past stronger beats and fairer,
> He picks his way, a living gun
> With gun and lens and bible
> A militant enquirer;
> The friend, the rash, the enemy,
> The essayist, the able,
> Able at times to cry.

It is too early to tell if he has been misled by the instinct for survival. It may be that, having laid the ghost of his past, he will be able to declare himself and come out in the open – or it may be that, having discarded the alibi of promise, it will only be to end up in the trenches or the concentration camp.

> Determined on time's honest shield
> The lamb must face the Tigress,

and the Tigress may win for in spite of the slow conversion of progressive ideas into the fact of history, the Dark Ages have a way of coming back. Civilization – the world of affection and reason and freedom and justice – is a luxury which must be fought for, as dangerous to possess as an oil-field or an unlucky diamond.

Or so now I think; whom ill-famed Coventry bore, a mother of bicycles, whom England enlightened and Ireland deluded, round-faced, irritable, sun-loving, a man as old as his Redeemer, meditating at this time of year when wars break out, when Europe trembles and dictators thunder, inglorious under the plane.

July 1937 – *Aug.* 1938
 'Post fanum putre Vacunae.'

A London Diary
(1937)

There is no precedent for a diarist setting forth his qualifications. It is expected of him that he should be alert, full of curiosity, active, topical, and well-informed. I am none of these, being by nature incurious and slothful, with a tendency to hibernate in winter, not to get up till it is dark, leading in fact an obsessional life rather than an extrovert one, for I am a person whom certain ideas haunt for long periods, who reads and re-reads a certain book and then carries it about with him like an iodine bag. For the rest I am Anglo-Irish by extraction, continental in habits, thirty-three last September, and bear on my shoulders the round pyknic head of the manic-depressive without, as yet, giving way to the sterner symptoms. I suppose I belong to one of the most non-political generations the world has ever seen, for my adolescence, like that of most of my friends, was passed in the backwash of the war, in those years between the armistice and the slump when the whole intelligentsia seemed to be trying to forget that politics and militarism had ever existed, and when it was the ambition of everybody I knew to recreate the liberal atmosphere and the artistic intensity which had gone before. The Oxford I knew was that of Oscar Wilde, divided into camps of philistine and aesthete; politics consisted of an occasional walking tour in Albania; poetry was a sandcastle of Flecker and Housman being rapidly washed away by the rising tide of Yeats and Eliot, prose was written by Proust, Valéry, Firbank, Huxley and Norman Douglas; the painter we admired most was Poussin. The dominating note was a certain neo-classicism which did not extend to our conduct, which was dubious and extravagant, any lapses being justified by the magic phrase 'well anyhow I/he (but never she) have/has preserved my/his *intellectual integrity.*' We would no sooner have attended a political meeting than we would have gone to church and we were greatly impressed, in a ninetyish way, by money and titles and the necessity of coming into closer contact with them. This characteristic symptom of aesthetic materialism was perhaps a reaction from the privations of our wartime childhoods, for it must have been one of the few moments in history when a bottle of champagne or a good suit had an almost mystical quality, representing a return to a subtler and securer world with a more gracious sense of values. Such action as was necessary in the life of reading, mutual criticism, aesthetic satisfactions, and personal relationships for which we felt ordained was provided by foreign travel. In our favour it must be said that we had all been whirled about in the most stupendous hurricane of mass suggestion and mass bullying that has ever blown through history, and that the natural reaction of the proud and the intelligent was to hold themselves as aloof as possible from all popular movements in the future; to be a spectator was our form of protest after seeing what a mess the actors had made, for it did not seem possible, so used were we to the idea of a military autocracy, that we would ever be in a position to improve things ourselves. We spoke with admiration of the Manchus and the Cinghalese or the characters in Proust and Joyce who carried on a passive resistance to their vulgar overlords with the weapons: scholarship, taste, intimacy, wit, which a superior civilisation had put at their disposal.

≈

What has happened to that generation now? Some only needed the warning of the general strike to teach them how closely their isolation depended on economic security, others were finally converted to that point of view by the slump. The most realistic, such as Mr Evelyn Waugh and Mr Kenneth Clark, were the first to grasp how entirely the kind of life they liked depended on close co-operation with the governing classes. The rest of us wavered on. I have been especially interested in the fate of these waverers and have been trying to analyse in the last few days exactly what has sent into politics, and especially into left-wing politics, almost all my contemporaries who have not taken shelter in the civil service or the Catholic Church. To begin with, they have become politically minded entirely, I think, through foreign affairs, due to the essential difficulty of making contact with the English political classes which is experienced by people who were surfeited with English propaganda during the war. The first wave to go over were the Germanophiles; people who were happy in the socialist Germany of Stresemann and the Vienna of Freud; for them Hitler and Dollfuss were the turning point. Abyssinia was the limit for a far greater number – no spectator of that setpiece of injustice was able to remain neutral. For the few remaining ivory tower-holders there has been Spain. Of course, there have been other causes for the swing. For many it has been a question of expediency – there are many young people who realise that the Right will never reward or appreciate their talents, and many more who feel that their only chance of saving their skins is to obtain some kind of recognition for their views. They are the passengers who pull the communication cord, who try to grab the reins from the drunken driver. There are others for whom the consciousness of social injustice is a slowly working poison, those whom the pea is always prodding through the mattress till they can only see the magnificence of our rulers in terms of the indigence that it disguises.

～

And then again there is the typically English band of psychological revolutionaries, people who adopt left-wing political formulas because they hate their fathers or were unhappy at their public schools or insulted at the Customs or lectured about sex. And the even more typically English band, and much larger, of aesthetic revolutionaries; people who hate England for romantic reasons, and consequently the class which rules it, which makes the Gold Flake and the Player's, the radio programmes and the Austin Sevens, the beauty spots, the residential district, the camps and the cinemas, who select test-teams and preside at Ascot; as if by removing them it would be possible to remove the whole cabbage-like deposit of complacency and stupidity from the English race or the unrest from the hearts of those who dislike it. Only by a radical change in the English climate could these revolutionaries, the Jerusalem-builders, attain their object. But always one comes back to those two vast massacres of the innocents, Spain and Abyssinia. The Abyssinians slaughtered in their ignorance, like fur-bearing animals; the Spanish republicans cut down at the moment when a better life, when justice, freedom, and education seemed at last obtainable by them.

The Art of Travel
(1931)

Travel is a neglected art. For we cannot dissociate the idea of travelling from the conception of the tourist, the man who goes to see something, who acquires merit by visiting the leaning Tower. The traveller's interest is subjective, the tourist's is objective – he carries on the pilgrim tradition, the tradition that one is a better man, or rather that one is excused so many unpleasant duties by visiting the modern holy places. The French, with their cursus honorum, and the Americans, who made the voyage to Europe a class distinction, are the worst offenders. For the Frenchman there is 'le voyage à l'Acropole,' at present under a cloud, and then, in ascending precedence, Morocco, Syria, Chicago, Lake Chad, Udaipur, Cambodia and the Taumotu Archipelago, the last probably carrying with it unheard of exemptions. With us, however, the voyage à la mode is not yet compulsory. True, at one time the most sedentary taste-mongers of the metropolis could all be found on the road to Isfahan, but now they are back in their museums, and travelling, in fact, is rather out of style. So much has been written about this – the snobbish, cultural, spurious element in travel, that despite the economic interest of the subject at present we must abandon it altogether to get back to the real nature of the art.

Travel, in fact, is not a hobby, but a drug. Both stimulant and opiate, it is the noblest form of self-expression that yet diminishes the self. Here is the mystery, the magic power of the art, for by virtue of his anonymity the traveller is able both to find and to forget himself on his way. He arrives at a place where no one knows who he is, and where he is consequently anything that he chooses to be. Self-assertion, self-negation, self-deception are the properties of the traveller, and he is able to realise simultaneously his two most innocent dreams, the illusion of action, the illusion of flight. For the voyage gives to sedentary and thoughtful people everything which they envy in the heroic careers. Decisions have constantly to be made, plans to be constructed; while if one travels with friends, there is a mob that has to be persuaded, and very often a mutiny that has to be put down. There are, besides, a constant procession of strangers who must be cajoled, threatened, bargained with, or bluffed, and with many of whom personal relations are reduced to a contest of wills – that unpunished duel. But most of all it is in the journeying, in the motion itself, that the illusions are blended, that the feeling of doing something, of belonging to the world of action, is united with the deeper and more dignified conception of flight.

The idea of the fugitive, of Cain the first wanderer, is closer to the real nature of travel than that of the adventurer and explorer. The healthy instinct of the child is to return to the womb. This longing for escape and obscurity persists in romantic and religious forms ('there is in God, men say, a deep and dazzling darkness') and becomes that love of death which is supposed to balance with our love of life. They have frequently been analysed, those utopias that homesick man invents for himself in an unfriendly world, but what has not been stated is that travel also has a Freudian basis, 'Partir, c'est toujours mourir un peu,' and that is why we like it. The voyage is a gesture of escape.

For this reason romantics travel, or if you prefer, habitual travellers are romantic – because the romantic, as the name implies, is engaged on flying from unpleasant facts, and, as with age, he is disillusioned with the ideals that he substitutes, so he comes to idealise that which alone was not disappointing, the machinery of flight. Alps, grottoes, waterfalls, I imagine, play a minor part – for those who are not flying from an environment are flying from themselves, or, worst of all, from their lack of self. And here we are back at the mystic quality, the flight from the ego and into the ego, the therapeutal nature of the art.

The modern romantic has a hard struggle to keep in love with himself. Behaviourism and other scientific doctrines, the machine age, corpulence, the office and the altar, all the evidences of materialism weaken his allegiance. Inevitably he falls out of love with his hero, and when he does, for the Cyprian is implacable, all his friends are quick to do so too. It is then that the voyage, that unfailing aphrodisiac, will set him on his feet.

For the traveller's world is egocentric; anthropomorphic: the sun rises and sets for him, and for his guidance signs and wonders are mysteriously at hand. In Marseilles, perhaps, he finds himself in the Rue du Jeune Anarcharsis, and this memento of the first royal traveller, the founder of the classical voyage, seems to confer a divine approval on his mission – and by acquiring the sense of mission, of being a projectile, a parabola whose transit in red ink over the black lines on a graph paper is the traveller's own cometary progress through the lives he intersects, the romantic may regain a sense of importance and yet be rid of that burden of free-will, that horrible choice in his movements which reduces many a hardened wayfarer to miserable inanition. Like Childe Roland, one should be a personage, hurrying to keep a predestined appointment. Dante presents a perfect example of this feeling.

> Lo giorno se n'andava, e l'aer bruno
> toglieva li animai, che sono in terra,
> de la fatiche loro; ed io sol uno
> m'apparecchiava a sostener la guerra . . .

Here is the illusion of action, everybody stops work, but I go on – with the 'guerra del camino' – the mimic warfare of travelling which turns the clerkly author into a conquering hero. And the magnificent self-motive! That 'io sol uno' – the appalling and superior loneliness of the romantic traveller in which, with twilight, his ego burgeons like a tropical flower, his personality spreads itself like a great bat!

Yet cures like this are rare. At first the voyage strips the traveller of the importance he enjoyed in his home, the sense of being appreciated and cared for, of every false accretion and artificial inflation of his personality, which must be reduced to its lowest terms before it is allowed to develop again. For the first time for years he is alone with himself and very soon he wonders what they have in common. Often, too, he may return cured only to have his self-interest, his Narcissus pool once more fatally disturbed. Another trip must follow and soon he is a hopeless case, a voyageur traqué, a travel addict.

No place can sustain the emotion of going to it. Arrival is an anti-climax. The Garden of Eden was floated down the Euphrates by the Flood, and became a barren island 'to teach thee,' as Milton explains, 'that God attributes to place no sanctitie, save what is thither brought by men.' Sightseeing is destroying travel, obscuring the pleasures of movement with restrictions – 'You must see this – you don't mean to say you missed that' – a host of irrelevant ordonnances have made hideous a once untainted art. It is now unseemly to boast of spending thirty nights in as many different beds, of waking up each morning in bewilderment. A premium has been put on curiosity instead of that talented incuriosity which is so much more discriminating. I was once told by a sightseer of the old school that I had 'damned myself' by not admiring the Fra Angelico in the Prado, the last place where one would wish to see it. Everywhere the traveller has let his art be ruined by the culture snob – 'How curious – how too amazing.' Tinted spectacles. Blink, blink. 'Where's the guide-book.' Flip, flip. 'I wonder if so-and-so came across this,' and, primed with reliquaries, the scrannel, death-dealing arbiter emerges into the sunlight from the church door. 'Extraordo! Extraorda . . .!' he hoots intelligently, and at the familiar, enlightened bray, the cabbies, touts and postcard sellers hurry round him. In contrast, I once heard an American say, 'Of course, I remember Oxford; wasn't that the place with the garden?' and the phrase conjured up a mediaeval map, a kind of crazy quilt of England which only a natural traveller, not a culture pilgrim, can devise.

I should like to restore mobility to the place it deserves, to produce a book of photographs with the slenderest commentary, a book called 'The Anonymous Voyage' that would exhibit the bones of travel, the simplest component elements, the boat, the train, the ferry, the street, the hotel. There would be the quality of different countries; the incidents of movement; leaving at dawn, lunching on the train, arriving in the evening, walking round the town and dining by daylight; drinking alone.

There is the hotel restaurant half-empty, the flat wan voices of American women – those school teachers who have a free year in every seven, and are found all over Europe wondering – wondering whether there is any way they can get their shoes shined, their mail forwarded, their baggage checked and sent on. The British couple enter in evening dress. He bows and props his paper up. At the long table with thirty places, the voyagers of commerce eat and wipe their mouths. The traveller finishes his bottle with the wire round it, takes a dried fig from the wicker basket, and rises pink in the face, and warm with appreciation for his absent friends. The waiters bow him out. The English stare. The manager's daughters giggle in the bureau. The last month's engineering papers are laid out in the reading-room. It is dark. It is getting late. It is time for bed. He is in Spain.

Spain of all countries best enforces on the traveller that strict regime of boredom, loneliness, and apathy which is part of his cure. As the religious retire to meditate on religion, so the traveller travels to undergo a purification, an ordeal by ennui, to study the problem of leisure, that awful interval between a meal and a meal. In Spain everything contributes to throw him on his own resources, and what unpleasant ground they are on which to fall! The long morning, the late heavy lunch, the anger-making wine, the coffee taken among the huge sample-laden trunks of the viajantes, all lead up to the siesta in a country where it is impossible to find anything to read. Lying flushed on the iron bed, the traveller recalls his grievances – social snubs, sexual rebuffs, intellectual humiliations, his memory trails back among them as the shadow trails across the wall. At five o'clock he goes out. The penance is over. In four hours he may dine!

So far I have supposed the voyager to be alone – but I will close with a few practical remarks – for one cannot be too prosaic in writing about travel now. The subject has been ruined by the box-office images, the smarm, the clever sentimentality of authorities like Morand, Maurois, Giraudoux and Valéry Larbaud, and to restore the art to dignity only a careful banality may be allowed.

There are two disadvantages to travelling alone. One misses one's friends too much, writes and waits for too many letters, and is not spiritually alone at all. It is better to travel with a companion than to voyage under another's shadow, and this removes the other disadvantage – the way small material obstacles; rudeness, bugs, and nights in the train, become so overwhelming that the vitality of the solitary traveller ebbs completely away. The first time I went to Spain I spent the whole of Easter in bed, broken by the unfamiliar life. For in any crisis of that kind, one's character, compact, like one's conscience, of the opinions of others, is always the first thing to go. The cure, incidentally, is to wait for impulse, the genius of the traveller, to return, and on its rising tide to be floated gently off the mud.

The best compromise is to travel with a party and feel alone among them, 'ainsi nous errions,' wrote Rimbaud, 'moi pressé de trouver le lieu et la formule!' Verlaine, you notice, is allowed to join in the wandering, but to the other alone is given the mission, the purpose, the 'object of the voyage' that forms so often require us to fill in.

Travelling with another person also diminishes misfortunes and reduces the embarrassments of night-life – a thing which most sightseers ignore. Yet in many countries night-life provides us with authentic colour and shows the peasant populations most at their ease. One may see local dances genuinely performed and a place like the Ba-Ta-Clan in Valencia is of a creole beauty. The aesthetic of night-life is, besides, through Baudelaire, Nerval, Beerbohm and Sickert an intellectual heritage of our generation, yet the majority do not enjoy it and consider abandoned to vices anybody who does. One can't enjoy travel without a vulgar streak, and hence a contemporary Ulysses has often to combat the inbred good taste of the cultured sightseer.

Another charm of travelling too is that you literally lead a double life. Besides the life of moving from place to place, with their conflicting impressions, there is an inner life of discussions and reminiscence which bears no relation to the other, and yet merges with it in a fugue or harmony which the solitary traveller can only faintly obtain by blending a certain landscape with the book he reads there. When more than two people travel together, this inner personal life becomes too rich for the outer environment; the jokes and allusions that arise generate a clique self-confidence that causes every example of beauty or forbidding strangeness, to dwindle and lose colour. Fear is a valuable ingredient in the sum of golden moments enjoyed, so the serious traveller must remain a child who is afraid of the dark – with companions he becomes too insensitive. A pleasure of the accompanied tour is the competition to which it gives rise. This, when openly admitted, quickens the observation beyond anything, for a voyage is a series of reminiscences bottled and laid down for the future, and by that time the bitterness will have evaporated from them.

An unrecorded danger on the way are the currents which set from small towns to the capital, from a country towards the one more distant. These are always sucking the impulsive traveller in, and he cannot be too careful in planning a tour, to choose a terminus that is also a geographic one. For this reason the beginner should visit Belgium, Brittany or the Château country first, for he will never see them otherwise.

It remains to say something about expense. The old derive a sadistic pleasure from advocating discomfort, but actually the sensation of being in a sleeper on the North Express is richer than that of travelling third on a nameless one. The imagination subsists on either, but in summer especially, the more luxuriously one travels the less one gets tired, and the farther one consequently is able to go.

Above all, one avoids meeting the inhabitants of the country, and of a whole fresh chunk of human ugliness and stupidity one is kept in ignorance. The great thing is to think about money constantly, for more than anything else the budget and the continental Bradshaw are the travellers' weapons against Time – Time that raises up a Hydra head to be killed every afternoon and morning. When not on the move the traveller should be either planning how to make two trains fit or both ends meet, calculating afresh his resources to the foreseen, though inevitable conclusion – and for many the voyage seems insipid till they have spent all their money. 'Je suis Arnaut qui plor e vau cantan,' and the masterpieces of contrast so dear to the expert traveller are not achieved till he has, penniless, to find his way home again.

For others it is the preparation for the voyage that is the most intense part of all. This can be artificially stimulated by books and time-tables, or the idea of a certain region may appear in the mind to suit a certain mood, and once there, be allowed to gather and fester like a boil, till only instant departure to the place in question can lance it. At present I would recommend people to go to Spain, while the exchange is low, and before the last peasants have been metamorphosed into citizens – let them visit places like Calpe, Orihuela, Mojácar and Almuñecar, before they are spoiled. Or if they like social crises, let them omit Spain and examine Vence. Vence, where two of the three English tea-rooms have been invaded by modern art, where the hard-boiled British colony of the hill-town has started a debating society, where English painters from Saint Paul, American rivals from the plain below, are fouling a last eyrie of Victorian civilisation, and where – from what, alas, unghostly paintings! – the ghost of Lawrence looks out on the puzzled invalids, the distinguished retirees.

But wherever people go, let them recapture the pleasures of motion: pleasures that will continue when towns and landscapes have become entirely standardised and interchangeable, and the objectives of the tourist long blotted out – the joys of buffeting along the carriages to the wagon restaurant, of rinsing grapes in 'eau potable' at the junctions, of standing in the corridor between Rome and Naples, or Vienna and Budapest. And there I may meet you, reader, for as long as I remain an artist, and an artist remains a member of the leisured classes who cannot pay for his leisure, I will be found economising through this long summer, on a train.

The Ant-Lion
(1939)

The Maures are my favourite mountains, a range of old rounded mammalian granite which rise three thousand feet above the coast of Provence. In summer they are covered by dark forests of cork and pine, with paler interludes on the northern slopes of bright splay-trunked chestnut, and an undergrowth of arbutus and bracken. There is always water in the Maures, and the mountains are green throughout the summer, never baked like the limestone, or like the Southern Alps a slagheap of gritty oyster-shell. They swim in a golden light in which the radiant ebony green of their vegetation stands out against the sky, a region hardly inhabited, yet friendly as those dazzling landscapes of Claude and Poussin, in which shepherds and sailors from antique ships meander under incongruous elms. Harmonies of light and colour, drip of water over fern; they inculcate in those who stay long in the Midi, and whose brains are addled by iodine, a habit of moralizing, a brooding about causes. What makes men divide up into nations and go to war? Why do they live in cities? And what is the true relationship between Nature and Man?

The beaches of the Maures are of white sand, wide, with a ribbon of umbrella-pines, below which juicy mesembrianthemum and dry flowers of the sand stretch to within a yard of the sea. Lying there amid the pacific blues and greens one shuts the eyes and opens them on the white surface: the vague blurred philosophizing continues. Animism, pantheism, images of the earth soaring through space with the swerve of a ping-pong ball circulate in the head; the woolly brain meddles with ethics. No more power, no aggression, no intolerance. All must be free. Then whizz! A disturbance. Under the eye the soil is pitted into a conical depression, about the size of a candle extinguisher, down whose walls the sand trickles gently, moved by a suspicion of wind. Whizz, and a clot is hurled to the top again, the bottom of the funnel cleared, in disobedience to the natural law! As the funnel silts up it is cleared by another whirr, and there appears, at the nadir of the cone, a brown pair of curved earwig horns, antlers of a giant earwig that churn the sand upwards like a steam shovel.

Now an ant is traversing the dangerous *arête*. He sidles, slithers, and goes fumbling down the Wall of Death to the waiting chopper. Snap! He struggles up, mounting the steep banking grain by grain as it shelves beneath him, till a new eruption is engineered by his waiting enemy. Sand belches out, the avalanche engulfs him, the horny sickles contract and disappear with their beady victim under the whiteness. Mystery, frustration, tragedy, death are then at large in this peaceful wilderness! Can the aggressive instinct be analysed out of those clippers? Or its lethal headpiece be removed by a more equitable distribution of raw materials? The funnels, I observe, are all round me. The sand is pockmarked with these geometrical death-traps, engineering triumphs of insect art. And this horsefly might be used for an experiment. I shove it downwards. The Claws seize on a wing, and the struggle is on. The fight proceeds like an atrocity of chemical warfare. The great fly threshes the soil with its wings, it buzzes and drones while the sand heaves round its propellers and the facets of its giant projectors glitter with light. But the clippers do not relax, and disappear tugging the fly beneath the surface. The threshing continues, a faint buzzing comes from the invisible horsefly, and its undercarriage appears, with legs waving. Will it take off? The wings of the insect bomber pound the air, the fly starts forward and upwards, and hauls after it – O fiend, embodiment of evil! A creature whose clippers are joined to a muscle-bound thorax and a vile yellow armour-plated body, squat and powerful, with a beetle set of legs to manoeuvre this engine of destruction. The Tank with a Mind now scuttles backwards in reverse, the stern, then the legs disappear, then the jaws which drag its prey. Legs beat the ground. A fainter wheeze and whirr, no hope now, the last wing-tip vanished, the air colder, the pines greener, the cone empty except for the trickle, the sifting and silting down the funnel of the grains of pearl-coloured sand.

Nature arranged this; bestowed on the Ant-Lion its dredging skill and its cannon-ball service. How can it tell, buried except for the striking choppers, that the pebble which rolls down has to be volleyed out of the death-trap, while the approaching ant must be collected by gentle eruptions, dismayed by a perpetual sandy shower? And, answer as usual, we do not know.

Yet the relationship between the Ant-Lion and the curving beaches of Pampelone suggests a parallel. This time at Albi. Here Art and Nature have formed one of the most harmonious scenes in Europe. The fortress cathedral, the Bishop's Palace with its hanging gardens, and the old bridge, all of ancient brick, blend into the tawny landscape through which the emancipated Tarn flows from its gorges to the Garonne. Here again one wanders through this dream of the Middle Ages, by precincts of the rosy cathedral where the pious buzz like cockchafers, to be brought up by a notice on the portcullis of the Bishop's Palace. 'Musée Toulouse-Lautrec.' Tucked in the conventional Gothic of the fortress is a suite of long rooms in which the mother of the artist, using all her feudal powers, forced the municipal authorities to hang the pictures of her son. Less fortunate than those of Aix, who refused Cézanne's request to leave his pictures to the city, the fathers were intimidated by the Countess into placing them in this most sacred corner, lighted and hung in salons whose decoration has concealed all traces of the unsightly past.

The concierge turns proudly to the Early Work – pastoral scenes and sentimental evocations of Millet – these he likes best; they are what the Count was doing before he left his home and was corrupted by the Capital. Then come the drawings, in which emerges the fine savage line of the mature artist, that bold, but not (as in some of the paintings) vulgar stroke, which hits off the brutality of his subjects, or the beauty of those young girls doomed to such an inevitable end. In the large room beyond are the paintings, a morgue of End of Century vice, a succession of canvases in which there is hardly daylight, and where the only creature who lives by day is the wizened little Irish jockey. The world of the hunchback Count is nocturnal, gas-lit, racy, depraved and vicious; the shocked Albigeois who pass through the gallery are riveted by the extraordinary picture of the laundress who checks over with the *sous-maîtresse* the linen from her Maison. As one goes from picture to picture the atmosphere intensifies, Valentin le Désossé and La Goulue become familiars, and the lovely girls blur into the dark of the Moulin Rouge, where one distinguishes a favourite figure, the long, sad, nocturnal, utterly empty but doggedly boring face of 'L'Anglais,' – some English habitué to whom constant all-night attendance has given the polish of a sentry at his post.

At the end of the gallery is a door before which the concierge smiles mysteriously, as if to prepare us for the Pompeian revelations. He opens it, and we emerge on a small terrace. The sun is shining, the sky is blue, the Tarn ripples underneath. Beyond the ancient brick of the bishop's citadel and the arches of the bridge stretches the landscape of the Albigeois – foothills of green corn, delicately crowned by pink hill villages, which merge into the brown of the distant Cevennes under the pale penetrating light of the near-south, the transitional-Mediterranean. A lovely and healthy prospect, in which fields and cities of men blend everywhere into the earth and the sunshine. One takes a deep breath, when obstinately, from behind the closed door, one feels a suction; attraction fights repulsion as in the cold wavering opposition between the like poles of a magnet. Deep in his lair the Ant-Lion is at work; the hunchback Count recalls us; the world of poverty, greed, bad air, consumption, and of those who never go to bed awaits, but there awaits also an artist's integration of it, a world in which all trace of sentiment or decadence is excluded by the realism of the painter, and the vitality of his line. In the sunlight on the terrace we are given the choice between the world of Nature and the world of Art. Nature seems to win, but at the moment of victory there is something lacking, and it is that lack which only the unnatural world inside can supply – progress, for example, for the view from the Palace has not altered, except slightly to deteriorate, for several hundred years. The enjoyment of it requires no more perception than had Erasmus, while the art of Lautrec is modern, and can be appreciated only by those who combine a certain kind of aristocratic satisfaction at human beings acting in character, and in gross character, with the love of fine drawing and colour.

Not that Lautrec was a great artist; he is to Degas what Maupassant is to Flaubert, one who extended the noble conception of realism by which a great master accepts the world as it is for the sake of its dynamism, and for the passive, extraordinarily responsive quality of that world to the artist who has learnt how to impose his will on it. The world of Lautrec is artificial because it excludes goodness and beauty as carefully as it excludes the sun. But it is an arranged world, a world of melancholy and ignorance (figures melancholy because ignorant, patient in the treadmill of pleasure), and so the artist drags us in from the terrace because force and intelligence dominate that arrangement. And once back, we are back in his dream, in a hunchback's dream of the world; the sunlight seems tawdry, the red brick vulgar, the palace ornate; the crowd who stand in their tall hats gaping at the blossoming Can-Can dancers are in the only place worth being.

Now I understand the Ant-Lion. It is in Nature and with a natural right to its existence. There is no conflict between them; it is an advanced gadget in the scheme which includes the peaceful hills and the beach with its reedy pools of brackish water. Nor is there any opposition between Lautrec and the landscape of Albi. Albi was the oyster, and the contents of the museum are the Pearl. The irritant? The action of a physical deformity on an aristocratic, artistic but unoriginal mind which was happiest in the company of its inferiors, and which liked to be surrounded by the opposite sex in places where the deformity could be concealed by potency, or by the distribution of money. The result, a highly specialized painter, one of Nature's very latest experiments. And yet even that peaceful landscape was the home in the Middle Ages of a subversive doctrine, the Albigensian heresy; a primitive anarchism which taught that men were equal and free, which disbelieved in violence and believed in a chosen priesthood, in the Cathari who attained purity by abstinence, while they encouraged the Count's royal ancestors to come through excess and indulgence to heavenly wisdom. It was they who believed that the human race should cease to procreate, and so solve the problem of evil, who were massacred at Muret and Lavaur, and whom Simon de Montfort slaughtered with the remark, 'The Lord will know his own.' And the Heretics were right. Had a revolt against procreation spread outwards from Albi the world would have become an empty place, nor would such obstinate human beings who survived have been driven to kill each other for living-room, victims, for all we may know, of some deeper instinct of self-destruction which bids them make way for a new experiment, the civilization of the termite or the rat.

Much has happened since the summer. To-day the Maures are out of bounds, the Museum closed, and many generalizations based on incorrect assessment of the facts fallen to pieces, but (since the operations of the Ant-Lion have now been extended) it seems worth while to recall that the statements on the life of pleasure which Lautrec took from his witness at the Tabarin and the Moulin de la Galette, and which he so vigorously recorded on canvas, are still available to the traveller of the future, and assert their truth.

December 1939

The Unquiet Grave
(1944/5)

A Word Cycle by Palinurus

Introduction

It is nearly ten years since *The Unquiet Grave* was begun, long enough for a book to cease to be contemporary and to start settling down to a position in time. With this new and revised edition, an opportunity is presented to show how and why it came to be written and to take on its present form. This may answer some of the criticisms to which Palinurus has not had a chance to reply; such as that *The Unquiet Grave* is merely an anthology, a collection of extracts chosen with 'outremer' snobbery and masquerading as a book or that, if book it be, then it is both morbid and depressing.

The Unquiet Grave is inevitably a war-book. Although the author tried to extricate himself from the war and to escape from his time and place into the bright empyrean of European thought, he could not long remain above the clouds. He was an editor living in Bedford Square who kept a journal in three little note-books provided by his wise printer between the autumn of 1942 and the autumn of 1943. As a man, he was suffering from a private grief – a separation for which he felt to blame; as an editor, he was struggling against propaganda (the genial guidance of thought by the state which undermines the love of truth and beauty); as a Londoner, he was affected by the dirt and weariness, the gradual draining away under war conditions of light and colour from the former capital of the world; and, lastly, as a European, he was acutely aware of being cut off from France. And so in keeping a journal for what a Russian peasant would have called his 'back thoughts', he was determined to quote as many passages as he could from the French to show the affinity between their thought and ours, and to prove how near and necessary to us were the minds and culture of those across the channel who then seemed quite cut off from us, perhaps for ever. To evoke a French beach at that time was to be reminded that beaches did not exist for mines and pill-boxes and barbed wire but for us to bathe from and that, one day, we would enjoy them again.

We must understand the author's obsession with pleasure at a time when nearly all pleasures were forbidden. Besides his love of France, Palinurus also wished to proclaim his faith in the unity and continuity of Western culture in its moment of crisis. He chose his quotations to illustrate how we have gone on thinking the same things since the days of the ancient Greeks, how the present can always be illuminated by the past. He looked for sanctions rather than originality.

Meanwhile the three note-books filled up, while the personal sorrow came to a head and disappeared into a long false lull, like an illness. Working on the manuscript for another year, Palinurus began to see that there was a pattern to be brought out; in the diaries an art-form slumbered – an initiation, a descent into hell, a purification and cure. The various themes could be given symphonic structure and be made to lead into and suggest each other until every paragraph became fitted into an inevitable position in the pilot's periplus (or intellectual voyage) from which it could not be moved. Stained by the juice of time, the second autumn was not quite like the first; the returns of grief or pleasure or religion acquired a richer orchestration, the writing had developed the writer. There was so much to cut or to improve; the exploration of the Palinurus myth (which is mentioned incidentally in the first article the author published) led on to others, until one seemed always to be pursuing some new clue. It seemed also the moment to collate once and for all the findings of depth-psychology with subjective feelings even if a loss to literature were the result. Finally the whole book had to be re-set. *The Unquiet Grave* by now consisted of thirty long galley-proofs scissored into little pieces like a string of clown's black sausages, covered with insertions and deletions and spread out on the floor to be arranged and rearranged into a mosaic. The coils of print seemed to move with a life of their own. With incomparable devotion, Lys Lubbock and Sonia Brownell, the two secretaries at *Horizon*, had typed the whole manuscript out twice and at last it was published from here in December 1944 with four collotype plates in a limited edition of a thousand. Lys and Sonia sold copies over the counter, the demand grew and the expenses of the two printings were recovered. The identity of the author-publisher was never regarded as a top secret. By publishing the book without his name, however, more reality was given to the Palinurus myth and the anonymity acted as a coat of varnish to protect what might otherwise seem too personal a confession.

The plot of the book is contained in the title. *The Unquiet Grave* first suggests the tomb of Palinurus, pilot of Aeneas; it is the cenotaph from which he haunts us. 'The ghost of Palinurus must be appeased'. He is the core of melancholy and guilt that works destruction on us from within. But the title is also that of an old border ballad in which a lover haunts the grave of his mistress and troubles her sleep.

> The wind doth blow tonight, my love,
> And a few small drops of rain,
> I never had but one true love,
> In cold grave she was lain.

He remains by her grave for a year and a day (the period of the diary) until she dismisses him,

> The stalk is withered dry, my love,
> So will our hearts decay,
> So make yourself content, my love,
> Till God calls you away.

In the first part, 'Ecce Gubernator' ('Behold the pilot'), we are presented with a self-portrait of Palinurus, with his views on literature, love and religion, his bitter doubting attitude. Something is badly wrong; he has lost touch with his sub-conscious self, the well is obstructed; he is reminded of a gull fouled with oil. The presiding genius of this section is Pascal whose terrible sayings penetrate the mask and cause Palinurus to reveal himself and so allude for the first time to his private sorrow, 'Revisit pale Chelsea's nook-shotten Cythera'. Cythera was the Island of love; Shakespeare's word 'nook-shotten' can mean full of indentations, the 'shelfy coast' of the title-page or else full of nooks and alcoves. There follows the first allusion to Paris, 'lost love, lost youth, lost Paris; remorse and folly. Aïe!' Pascal and Leopardi dominate because when they died they were the same age as Palinurus (thirty-nine). Will he survive them? After considering opium as a remedy the pilot continues his downward rush towards the notion of suicide with which the section ends. 'Te Palinure petens' ('looking for you, Palinurus') begins with the worst period of the nightmare journey. The names of four friends who took their own lives are evoked, one, who shoots herself at this very moment, was the companion of the 'dark face' from the Île-Saint-Louis, most sacred of the holy places. Palinurus is soon driven to admit that all his trouble comes from Paris, and he mentions the Rue Delambre, the Quai D'Anjou (on the Island) and the Rue de Vaugirard as connected with his deepest feelings. Two new Genii preside over this section, Sainte-Beuve and Chamfort, who bring respectively philosophic resignation and cynical courage to dispel the pessimism of Pascal and Leopardi or the suicidal raving of Nerval. On page 86 comes the first ray of hope. 'Streets of Paris, pray for me; beaches in the sun, pray for me; ghosts of the Lemurs, intercede for me; plane-tree and laurel-rose, shade me; summer rain on quais of Toulon, wash me away.' In the last section this prayer is literally answered. The title 'La clé des chants' ('the key to the songs') also suggests Grandville's 'la clé deschamps'. The nature-cure. The ferrets and lemurs who represent the strength and beauty of the healthy libido as well as the innocent paradise, the happy pagan honeymoon of the doomed relationship make their appearance in a kind of litany. Here the presiding genius is Flaubert who enriches the sensibility and stoical courage which he shares with the others, with the joy of creation.

Baudelaire, one-time dweller in the Île-Saint-Louis, also haunts this section and their common friend Sainte-Beuve makes a farewell appearance.

The last movement opens with a series of alternating passages on the theme 'Streets of Paris', recalled by autumn mist in London, and 'Beaches in the sun' suggested by the late summer radiance. Mediterranean harbour scenes are followed by Atlantic sea-scapes, with allusions to Baudelaire at Honfleur, Proust at Houlgate and Flaubert at Trouville, where he met his 'fantôme' and dark inspirer, Madame Schlesinger. About the fortieth birthday of Palinurus the catharsis occurs; he re-lives the early stages of his love-affair: the walk to the apartment on the Île-Saint-Louis, the Paris of the expatriates, and the year in the South of France, the villa Les Lauriers Roses. Describing this Paradise Lost brings Eden up from the dark world of the subconscious where it has been festering into the daylight of art. The ghosts are laid and the avenging 'Lemures' become the affectionate lemurs, until the book closes with a long and reasoned apology for the pursuit of happiness, an affirmation of the values of humanism. Placated and placating, the soul of Palinurus drifts away; his body is washed up on a favourite shore. The epilogue, a pastiche of psychoanalytical jargon and Jungian exegesis, relieves the tension while closely examining the background of the myth.

As a signal of distress from one human being to another *The Unquiet Grave* went unanswered, but the suffering was alleviated. As a demonstration of the power of words, however, of the obsessional impetus in an aesthetic form to fulfil its destiny, the work was an object-lesson. All grief, once made known to the mind, can be cured by the mind, the manuscript proclaimed; the human brain, once it is fully functioning, as in the making of a poem, is outside time and place and immune from sorrow. 'La pensée console de tout.' If *The Unquiet Grave*, therefore, should leave an impression of being morbid and gloomy then its intention has not been fulfilled.

CYRIL CONNOLLY
London
December 1950

'Palinurus, a skilful pilot of the ship of Æneas, fell into the sea in his sleep, was three days exposed to the tempests and waves of the sea and at last came safe to the seashore near Velia, where the cruel inhabitants of the place murdered him to obtain his clothes; his body was left unburied on the seashore.'

LEMPRIÈRE

'Mox vero Lucanis pestilentia laborantibus respondit oraculum, Manes Palinuri esse placandos: ob quam rem non longe a Velia et lucum et cenotaphium ei dederunt.'*

SERVIUS, Commentary on the Æneid, Bk. vi l 378

'A shelfy Coast,
Long infamous for Ships, and Sailors lost;
And white with Bones':

Dryden's Virgil

---

*Soon the Oracle gave this answer to the Lucanians, who were suffering from an epidemic: The shade of Palinurus must be appeased! Whereupon they dedicated to him not far from Velia, a Cenotaph and a Sacred Grove.

The Unquiet Grave

Part One: Ecce Gubernator

The more books we read, the sooner we perceive that the true function of a writer is to produce a masterpiece and that no other task is of any consequence. Obvious though this should be, how few writers will admit it, or having made the admission, will be prepared to lay aside the piece of iridescent mediocrity on which they have embarked! Writers always hope that their next book is going to be their best, for they will not acknowledge that it is their present way of life which prevents them from ever creating anything different or better.

All excursions into journalism, broadcasting, propaganda and writing for the films, however grandiose, are doomed to disappointment. To put of our best into these forms is another folly, since thereby we condemn good ideas as well as bad to oblivion. It is in the nature of such work not to last, so it should never be undertaken. Writers engrossed in any literary activity which is not their attempt at a masterpiece are their own dupes and, unless these self-flatterers are content to write off such activities as their contribution to the war effort, they might as well be peeling potatoes.

'Les plus forts y ont péri. L'art est un luxe; il veut des mains blanches et calmes. On fait d'abord une petite concession, puis deux, puis vingt. On s'illusionne sur sa moralité pendant longtemps. Puis on s'en fout complètement et puis on devient imbécile.' – FLAUBERT.

Poets arguing about modern poetry: jackals snarling over a dried-up well.

How many books did Renoir write on how to paint?

To fashion a masterpiece, to weave a suit that will last some hundred years, it is necessary to feel, to think, and to write. These three activities must be co-ordinated. 'Bien écrire c'est à la fois bien sentir, bien penser et bien dire.' – BUFFON.

We cannot think if we have no time to read, or feel if we are emotionally exhausted, or out of cheap materials create what will last. We cannot co-ordinate what is not there.

What are masterpieces? Let us name a few. The *Odes* and *Epistles* of Horace, the *Eclogues* and *Georgics* of Virgil, the *Testament* of Villon, the Essays of Montaigne, the Fables of La Fontaine, the Maxims of La Rochefoucauld and La Bruyère, the *Fleurs du Mal* and Intimate Journals of Baudelaire, the Poems of Pope and Leopardi, the *Illuminations* of Rimbaud, and Byron's *Don Juan*.

Such a catalogue reveals its author. What is common in thought to these twelve writers? Love of live and nature; lack of belief in the idea of progress; interest in, mingled with contempt for humanity. All are what Palinurus has been called by his critics: 'Earthbound'! Yet they are more adult and less romantic than he. These masterpieces then (mostly high peaks of the secondary range), reflect either what he would like to be, or a self to which he is afraid of confessing. He would like to have written *Les Fleurs du Mal* or the *Saison en Enfer* without being Rimbaud or Baudelaire, that is, without their mental suffering and without being diseased and poor.

In feeling, these masterpieces contain the maximum of emotion compatible with a classical sense of form.

Observe how they are written; many are short and compressed, fruits of reflective and contemplative natures, prose or poetry of great formal beauty and economy of phrase. There are no novels, plays or bio-graphies included in the list, and the poetry is of the kind which speculates about life. They have been chosen by one who most values the art which is distilled and crystallized out of a lucid, curious and passionate imagination. All these writers enjoy something in common, 'jusqu'au sombre plaisir d'un coeur mélancolique': a sense of perfection and a faith in human dignity, combined with a tragic apprehending of the human situation, and its nearness to the Abyss.

We can deduce then that the compiler of this list should set himself to write after these models. Even though none of the conditions for producing a masterpiece be present, he can at least attempt to work at the same level of intention as the Sacred Twelve. Spiritualize the Earth-bound, Palinurus, and don't aim too high!

What follow are the doubts and reflections of a year, a word-cycle in three or four rhythms: art, love, nature and religion; an experiment in self-dismantling, a search for the obstruction which is blocking the flow from the well, and whereby the name of Palinurus is becoming an archetype of frustration.

As we grow older we discover that what at the time seemed to us the absorbing interests and preoccupations which we had taken up and thrown over, were in reality appetites or passions that had swept over us and passed on, until at last we come to see that our life has no more continuity than a pool in the rocks which the tide fills with foam and flotsam and then empties. Nothing remains in the end but the sediment which this flux deposits; ambergris valuable only to those who know how to use it.

'Dry again?' said the Crab to the Rock-Pool. 'So would you be,' replied the Rock-Pool, 'if you had to satisfy, twice a day, the insatiable sea.'

As we grow older, in fact, we discover that the lives of most human beings are worthless except in so far as they contribute to the enrichment and emancipation of the spirit. However attractive in our youth animal graces may be, if in our maturity they have not led us to emend one character in the corrupt text of existence, then our time has been

wasted. No one over thirty-five is worth meeting who has not something to teach us – something more than we could learn by ourselves,
from a book.

LOVE AND ANXIETY

A lover's warning:
'The sixth age is ascribed to Jupiter, in which we begin to take account
of our time, to judge of ourselves, and grow to the perfection of our
understanding; the last and seventh age to Saturn, wherein our days are
sad and overcast and in which we find by dear and lamentable
experience, and by the loss which can never be repaired, that of all our
vain passions and affections past, the sorrow only abideth.'
– SIR WALTER RALEIGH.

There is no pain in life equal to that which two lovers can inflict on one
another. This should be made clear to all who contemplate such unions.
The avoidance of this pain is the beginning of wisdom, for it is strong
enough to contaminate the whole of our lives; and since it can be
avoided by obeying certain rules approximate to those of Christian
marriage, they provide, even to the unbeliever, its *de facto* justification.
It is when we begin to hurt those whom we love that the guilt with
which we are born becomes intolerable, and since all those whom we
love intensely and continuously grow part of us, and since we hate
ourselves in them, so we torture ourselves and them together.

The object of Loving is to end Love. We achieve this through a series of
unhappy love affairs or, without a death-rattle, through one that is
happy.

A mutually fulfilled sexual union between two people is the rarest
sensation which life can provide. But it is not quite real. It stops when
the telephone rings. Such a passion can be kept at its early strength only
by adding to it either more and more unhappiness (jealousy, separation,

doubt, renunciation), or more and more artificiality (drink, technique, stage-illusions). Whoever has missed this has never lived, who lives for it alone is but partly alive.

We pay for vice by the knowledge that we are wicked; we pay for pleasure when we find out too late that we are nothing; its accounts are kept in small change, but the total is as large.

'Pleasure seizes the whole man who addicts himself to it, and will not give him leisure for any good office in life which contradicts the gaiety of the present hour. You may indeed observe in people of pleasure a certain complacency and absence of all severity, which the habit of a loose and unconcerned life gives them; but tell the man of pleasure your secret wants, cares, or sorrows, and you will find that he has given up the delicacy of his passions to the craving of his appetites.' – STEELE.

Beneath the mask of selfish tranquillity nothing exists except bitterness and boredom. I am one of those whom suffering has made empty and frivolous: each night in my dreams I pull the scab off a wound; each day, vacuous and habit-ridden, I let it re-form.

When I contemplate the accumulation of guilt and remorse which, like a garbage can, I carry through life, and which is fed not only by the lightest actions but by the most harmless pleasures, I feel Man to be of all living things the most biologically incompetent and ill-organized. Why has he acquired a seventy-years' life-span only to poison it incurably by the mere being of himself? Why has he thrown Conscience, like a dead rat, to putrefy in the well?

It is no answer to say that we are meant to rid ourselves of the self: religions like Christianity and Buddhism are desperate stratagems of failure, the failure of men to be men. They may be operative as escapes from the problem, as flights from guilt, but they cannot turn out to be the revelation of our destiny. What should we think of dogs' monasteries, hermit cats, vegetarian tigers? Of birds who tore off their wings, or bulls weeping with remorse? It is surely in our nature as human beings to realize ourselves, yet there remains this deadly flaw by which we feel most guilty when we are most confidently human, and are most to be pitied when most successful. Is this because Christianity is right? Or is it an ingrained effect of propaganda for the under-dog? When did the ego begin to stink? Those of us who were brought up as Christians and who have lost our faith have retained the Christian sense of sin without the saving belief in redemption. This poisons our thought and so paralyses us in action.

Communism is the new religion which denies original sin, yet seldom do we meet a Communist who as a man seems either complete or happy. And yet Original Sin, what rubbish! The Expulsion from Eden is an act of vindictive womanish spite; the Fall of Man, as the Bible recounts it, is in reality the Fall of God.

When I consider what I believe, which I can do only by proceeding from what I do not believe, I seem in a minority of one – and yet I know that there are thousands like me: Liberals without a belief in progress, Democrats who despise their fellow-men, Pagans who still live by Christian morals, Intellectuals who cannot find the intellect sufficient – unsatisfied Materialists, we are as common as clay.

But there can be no going back to Christianity, nor can I inhabit an edifice of truth which seems built upon a base of falsehood. The contradictions will out; hence the terrible record of the Church, which 'brings not peace, but a sword' – its persecutions, its cupidity, its hypocrisy, its reaction. These are inherent in its nature as a jealous, worldly, and dogmatic body; and because of them the Church, whenever strong enough to do so, has always belied its spiritual claims.

How privileged are Mahommedans! Small wonder there are more of them than of any other religion, and that they are still making converts; for their creed is extroverted – the more fanatical they become, the faster they relieve themselves by killing other people. They observe a dignified ritual, a congenial marriage code, and appear to be without the sense of guilt.

In my religion all believers would stop work at sundown and have a drink together 'pour chasser la honte du jour'. This would be taken in remembrance of the first sunset when man must have thought the oncoming night would prove eternal, and in honour of the gift of wine to Noah as relief from the abysmal boredom of the brave new world after the flood. Hence the institution of my 'Sundowner' with which all believers, whether acquainted or not, would render holy that moment of nostalgia and evening apprehension. In my religion there would be no exclusive doctrine; all would be love, poetry and doubt. Life would be sacred, because it is all we have, and death, our common denominator, the fountain of consideration. The Cycle of the Seasons would be rhythmically celebrated together with the Seven Ages of Man, his Kinship with all living things, his glorious Reason, and his sacred Instinctual Drives.

Ah, see how on lonely airfields and hill petrol-stations the images of Freud and Frazer are wreathed in flowers! From Wabash to Humber the girls are launching their fast-perishing gardens of Adonis far out on to the stream; with sacred rumbas and boogie-woogies the Id is being honoured in all the Hangars, the Priestess intones long passages of the liturgy to which it is most partial; boastful genealogies and anecdotes of the Pornocrats, voodoo incantations, oceans of gibberish from Maldoror and Finnegans Wake! In a rapture of kisses the river-gods return, then Pan and Priapus in their red bowler-hats give way to Human Reason, Human Reason to Divine Love, 'Caelestis Venus', and Divine Love to the gyrations of the Planets through the bright selfless wastes of the Aether.

'The ideal, cheerful, sensuous, pagan life is not sick or sorry. No; yet its natural end is the sort of life which Pompeii and Herculaneum bring so vividly before us – a life which by no means in itself suggests the thought

of horror and misery, which even, in many ways, gratifies the senses and the understanding; but by the very intensity and unremittingness of its appeal to the senses and the understanding, by its stimulating a single side of us too absolutely, ends by fatiguing and revolting us; ends by leaving us with a sense of confinement, of oppression – with a desire for an utter change, for clouds, storms, effusion and relief.'
– MATTHEW ARNOLD

This one-sided argument is often used against Paganism. It is false to assume that Pompeii and Herculaneum disclose what is finest in paganism, any more than Blackpool and Juan-les-Pins represent what is best in Christianity. A life based on reason will always require to be balanced by an occasional bout of violent and irrational emotion, for the instinctual drives must be satisfied. In the past this satisfaction was provided by the mystery religions, somewhat grossly by the cults of the Great Mother, more spiritually by the Eleusinian and Orphic mysteries. Where Apollo reigns, Dionysus will follow.

Ancestor, my old incarnation, O *Palinurus Vulgaris*, the Venetian red crawfish, langouste, or rock-lobster, whether feeding on the spumy Mauretanian Banks, or undulating – southward to Tenerife, northward to Sicily – in the systole and diastole of the wave: free me from guilt and fear, free me from guilt and fear, dapple-plated scavenger of the resounding sea!

My previous incarnations: a melon, a lobster, a lemur, a bottle of wine, Aristippus.

Periods when I lived: the Augustan age in Rome, then in Paris and London from 1660 to 1740, and lastly from 1770 to 1850.

My friends in the first period were Horace, Tibullus, Petronius and Virgil; in the second: Rochester, Congreve, La Fontaine, La Bruyère, La Rochefoucauld, Saint Evremond, Dryden, Halifax, Pope, Swift, Racine, Hume, Voltaire; whilst in the last period I knew Walpole and Gibbon;

Byron, Fox, Beckford, and Stendhal, Tennyson, Baudelaire, Nerval and Flaubert. – Afternoons at Holland House, dinners chez Magny.

Certain fruits of the earth awaken in me feelings which lie deeper than appetite. When I contemplate the musky golden orb of the sugar-melon or the green and brown seaweed markings of the tiger cantaloupe, the scales of the pine-apple or the texture of figs and nectarines, the disposition of oranges and lemons on the tree or the feign-death coils of the old vine-serpent, I feel a deep kinship with them, and also with the ripe sugar-cane, the banana in flower, and certain trees – especially the stone- or umbrella-pine, the sun-loving Norfolk Island pine, the leaning bamboo, the rough carob, the rusty cork-oak and the plane. For the hundredth time I note with wonder how the leaves and sprays of the plane-tree fall in the pattern of the hanging vine! 'Evincet ulmos platanus coelebs.' The bachelor plane shall drive out the elms. . . .

My desire is for wisdom, not for the exercise of the will. 'The will is the strong blind man who carries on his shoulders the lame man who can see.' – SCHOPENHAUER.

For me success in life means survival. I believe that a ripe old age is nature's reward to those who have grasped her secret. I do not wish to die young or mad. The true pattern of existence can best be studied in a long life like Goethe's – a life of reason interrupted at intervals by emotional outbursts, displacements, passions, follies. In youth the life of reason is not in itself sufficient; afterwards the life of emotion, except for short periods, becomes unbearable.

Yet, sometimes at night I get a feeling of claustrophobia; of being smothered by my own personality, of choking through being in the world. During these moments the universe seems a prison wherein I lie fettered by the chains of my senses and blinded through being myself.

It is like being pinned underneath the hull of a capsized boat, yet being afraid to dive deeper and get clear. In those moments it seems that there must be a way out, and that through sloughing off the personality alone can it be taken.

We love only once, for once only are we perfectly equipped for loving: we may appear to ourselves to be as much in love at other times – so does a day in early September, though it is six hours shorter, seem as hot as one in June. And on how that first true love-affair shapes itself depends the pattern of our lives.

Two fears alternate in marriage, the one of loneliness and the other of bondage. The dread of loneliness is greater than the fear of bondage, so we get married. For one person who fears being so tied there are three who dread being set free. Yet the love of liberty is a noble passion and one to which most married people secretly aspire – in moments when they are not neurotically dependent – but by then it is too late; the ox does not become a bull, nor the hen a falcon.

The fear of loneliness can be overcome, for it springs from weakness; human beings are intended to be free, and to be free is to be lonely, but the fear of bondage is the apprehension of a real danger, and so I find it all the more pathetic that it should be young men who dread loneliness and get married, and beautiful girls who worry most about becoming old maids.

First love is the one love worth having, yet the best marriage is often a second marriage, for we should marry only when the desire for freedom has spent itself; not till then does a man know whether he is of the kind who can settle down. The most tragic breakings-up are of those couples who have married young and who have enjoyed seven years of happiness, after which the banked fires of passion and independence explode – and without knowing why, for they still love each other, they set about accomplishing their common destruction.

When a love-affair is broken off, the heaviest blow is to the vanity of the one who is left. It is therefore reasonable to assume that, when a love-affair is beginning, the greatest source of satisfaction is also to the

vanity. The first signs of a mutual attraction will induce even the incon-
solable to live in the present.

Cracking tawny nuts, looking out at the tawny planes with their
dappled festoons of yellow and green, reading the Tao Tê Ching by a
log fire: such is the wisdom of October: autumn bliss; the equinoctial
study of religions.

Jesus was a petulant man: his malediction on the barren fig tree was
sheer spite, his attitude towards the Pharisees was one of paranoiac
wrath. He speaks of them as Hitler of the men who made the League of
Nations. Those parables which all end 'There shall be wailing and
gnashing of teeth' – what a tone for a Redeemer! I find such incidents
as the violence used on the man without a wedding garment or the
praise of usury in the parable of the talents to be understandable only
as outbursts of arrogance and bad temper. Though an inspired genius
as a mystic and an ethical reformer, Jesus is also completely a Jew; he
does not wish to break away from the Jewish framework of the Old
Testament, the Law and the Prophets, but mainly to enrich their ethical
content; consequently he imitates the intolerance of the Pharisees whom
he condemns ('O ye generation of vipers') and maintains the avenging
rôle of God the Father, which he claims to have superseded.

Impression of Jesus Christ after re-reading the Gospels: He *thought* he
was the son of God, he warmly disliked his parents, was a prig, a high-
spirited and serious young man (where was he, what was he doing,
between the ages of twelve and twenty-nine?). He felt a neurotic hatred
for the Pharisees, the family, his hometown and adultery, and he may
have been illegitimate (Ben Pandere)*; he had a macabre sense of

* The Jewish tradition was that he was the son of a Roman Centurion, Pantheras, the
Panther. Hence his aloofness to his 'father' and 'brethren', his ambivalent attitude to his
mother and to adultery. (His definition of adultery is very sharp, and he sets 'Thou shalt not
commit adultery' as the only commandment beside 'Thou shalt love thy neighbour as
thyself'. The question about the woman taken in adultery may have been put to him as a
trap by those who believed this story.) I have heard a friend say that the German scholar
Von Domaszewski claimed to have found on our Roman Wall the gravestone of Pantheras,

humour; was overwhelmingly grateful to anyone who believed in him ('Thou art Peter'), and extremely close to his elder cousin John, but though he moulded himself on him, was less ascetic. He was fond of wine and very partial to grapes and figs. More civilized than his cousin, he was yet deeply affected by his end, which warned him of what must happen to himself if he persisted. The death of John and the revelation of his own Messiahship at Caesarea Philippi completely changed him: impatient, ironical and short-tempered, he was a true faith-healer, sublimely inspired by his belief in himself and as tragically betrayed by it. I don't believe in his divinity, yet it is impossible not to believe in his greatness, his majesty, his fatalistic intuition and in that mixture of practical wisdom with sublime vision which alone can save our world. His faith carried him through to the end, then wavered. Was there a secret understanding with John the Baptist? John the Baptist, I feel, holds many clues. About the miracles I suspend judgement. Jesus Christ seems different from any other man because he was so certain that he was. But how different is he from Buddha, Joan of Arc, St Francis, the Nijinsky of the diaries and others who also thought themselves set apart and sent from God.

Buddha on the other hand is too oriental. His courage in living to a great age, among ageing disciples, confers a pedagogic monotony on his teaching. Besides, we can never absorb all the names associated with him; they are ill-accommodated to the Western ear. Only the Chinese wisdom has a natural affinity for the West, the Chinese are always practical. And Tao – a religion without words, without a saviour, without a doctrine, without a God or a future life, whose truth is in a hoof-mark filled with water – what more can one ask?*

---

which showed that his legion had been in Judaea about 4 B.C. The Christians maintained that 'Pantherou', son of the Panther, was a corruption of 'Parthenou', of the Virgin. There is a strange poem by Hardy on this theme.

* Taoism is a Monist reconciliation of the human being to the inhuman, inactive harmony of the universe. In return for this adaptation the Taoist resolves his conflict, and gains a sensation of power and tranquillity which he is loth to disturb. His quietism is akin to that of Zeno, Epicurus, Molinos and St John of the Cross, but is dangerously exposed to the corruption of *laisser-aller*.

'Repose, tranquillity, stillness, inaction – these were the levels of the universe, the ultimate perfection of Tao.' – CHUANG TZU.

Forty – sombre anniversary to the hedonist – in seekers after truth like Buddha, Mahomet, Mencius, St Ignatius, the turning-point of their lives.

The secret of happiness (and therefore of success) is to be in harmony with existence, to be always calm, always lucid, always willing, 'to be joined to the universe without being more conscious of it than an idiot', to let each wave of life wash us a little farther up the shore. But is it the secret of art? There have been so many Infernos and so few Paradises in European art that the Infernos would seem our true climate. Yet those who have survived Satanism, war, passion and other infernos have cared only for Paradise. In that sense Religion is the sequel to art and the sequel to love, as *Paradise Regained* follows despondently after *Paradise Lost*.

TWO MODERN TAOISTS

'I have never seen a man who had such creative quiet. It radiated from him as from the sun. His face was that of a man who knows about day and night, sky and sea and air. He did not speak about these things. He had no tongue to tell of them . . .'

'I have often seen Klee's window from the street, with his pale oval face, like a large egg, and his open eyes pressed to the window pane.' – J. ADLER.

'The only thing in all my experience I cling to is my coolness and leisurely exhilarated contemplation. If I could influence you to achieve that *je t'aurais rendu un peu de service. J'y tiens TELLEMENT – si tu savais comme j'y tiens.* Let this advice be my perpetual and most solemn legacy to you.' – W. SICKERT (to Nina Hamnett).

'The mind of the sage in repose becomes the mirror of the universe, the speculum of all creation.' – CHUANG TZU.

Whether or not he produces anything, this contemplation is the hall-mark of the artist. He who values it is one, the rest can never be. It is his gelatine, his queen-bee jelly, the compost round his roots: the violent are drawn to such a man by the violence of his serenity.

'Points upon which the Yellow Emperor doubted, how can Confucius know?'*

Palinurus says: 'It is better to be the lichen on a rock than the President's carnation. Only by avoiding the beginning of things can we escape their ending.' Thus every friendship closes in the quarrel which is a conflict of wills, and every love-affair must reach a point where it attains marriage, and is changed, or declines it, and begins to wither.

The friendships which last are those wherein each friend respects the other's dignity to the point of not really wanting anything from him. Therefore a man with a will to power can have no friends. He is like a boy with a chopper. He tries it on flowers, he tries it on sticks, he tries it on furniture, and at last he breaks it on a stone.

There cannot be a personal God without a pessimistic religion. As soon as there is a personal God he is a disappointing God; and Job, Omar Khayyám, Euripides, Palladas, Voltaire and Professor Housman will abuse him. With Buddhism, Taoism, Quietism, and the God of Spinoza there can be no disappointment, because there is no Appointment.

Yet no one can achieve Serenity until the glare of passion is past the meridian. There is no certain way of preserving chastity against the will of the body. Lao-Tsu did. But then he was eighty and he was a librarian.

* A proverb which the Taoists coined to discredit their bustling rival. The Yellow Emperor or Ancestor, revered by the Taoists, flourished *circa* 2700–2600 B.C. 'The close of his long reign was made glorious by the appearance of the Phoenix and the mysterious animal known as the Chi Lin, in token of his wise and humane administration.' – GILES: *Chinese Biographical Dictionary*.

So he inveighed against books and book-learning, and left but one, shorter than the shortest gospel . . . a Kaleidoscope of the Void.

Action is the true end of Western religion, contemplation of Eastern; therefore the West is in need of Buddhism (or Taoism or Yoga) and the East of Communism (or muscular Christianity) – and this is just what each is getting. Undergoing the attraction of opposites, we translate the Tao Tê Ching and the Bhagavad-Gita, they the Communist Manifesto.

The moment a writer puts pen to paper he is of his time; the moment he becomes of his time he ceases to appeal to other periods, and so will be forgotten. He who would write a book that would last for ever must learn to use invisible ink. Yet if an author is of his age, ages similar to his will recur, and he will return to haunt them. He can obsess the minds of living writers, prevent them from sleeping, crowd them out like the *Horla*, and snatch the bread from their mouths.

We come mentally of age when we discover that the great minds of the past, whom we have patronized, are not less intelligent than we are because they happen to be dead.

Fallen leaves on the grass in the November sun bring more happiness than the daffodils. Spring is a call to action, hence to disillusion, therefore April is called 'the cruellest month'. Autumn is the mind's Spring; what is there we have, 'quidquid promiserat annus', and it is more than we expected.

WOMEN

There is no fury like a woman searching for a new lover. When we see a woman meekly chewing the cud beside her second husband, it is hard to imagine how brutally, implacably and pettily she has got rid of the first. There are two great moments in a woman's life: when first she finds herself to be deeply in love with her man, and when she leaves him. Leaving him enables her to be both sadist and masochist, to be stony when he implores her to stay, yet to weep because she has decided to go. Women are different from men, and to break with the past and mangle their mate in the process fulfils a dark need of theirs. Thus a wife's women-friends will derive almost as much satisfaction from her impending departure as she does. Together they prepare the brief against the husband which will strip him of his friends. They love to know the date, to fan the flames, and when the Monster is alone to rush round to inspect him. They can hear the clump of suit-cases a hundred miles away.

Beware of a woman with too many girl-friends, for they will always try to destroy the conjugal WE. One girl-friend is worse, unless we marry her afterwards. In America all the women have their set of girl-friends; some are cousins, the rest are gained at school. These form a permanent committee who sit on each other's affairs, who 'come out' together, marry and divorce together, and who end as those groups of active, healthy, well-informed club-women that govern society. Against them the Couple or Ehepaar is helpless and Man in their eyes but a biological interlude.

In the sex-war thoughtlessness is the weapon of the male, vindictiveness of the female. Both are reciprocally generated, but a woman's desire for revenge outlasts all her other emotions.

> 'And their revenge is as the tiger's spring,
> Deadly, and quick, and crushing; yet as real
> Torture is theirs, what they inflict they feel.'

Yet, when every unkind word about women has been said, we have still to admit, with Byron, that they are nicer than men. They are more devoted, more unselfish, and more emotionally sincere. When their long fuse of cruelty, deceit and revenge is set alight, it is always the thoughtlessness of a man which has fired it.

A woman who will not feign submission can never make a man happy, and so never be happy herself. There has never been a happy suffragette. In a perfect union the man and woman are like a strung bow. Who is to say whether the string bends the bow, or the bow tightens the string? Yet male bow and female string are in harmony with each other, and their arrows can be aimed. Unstrung, the bow hangs aimless; the cord flaps idly.

A man who has nothing to do with women is always incomplete. A puritan is incomplete because he excludes that half of himself of which he is afraid, and so the deeper he imprisons himself in his fastidiousness, the more difficulty he has in finding a woman who is brave enough to simulate the vulgarity by which he can be released.

'Sabba dukkha, sabba anatta, sabba anikka.'*

A stone lies in a river; a piece of wood is jammed against it; dead leaves, drifting logs and branches caked with mud collect around; weeds settle and soon birds have made a nest and are feeding their young among the blossoming water plants. Then the river rises and the earth is washed away. The birds migrate, the flowers wither, the branches are dislodged and drift downward; no trace is left of the floating island but a stone submerged by the water – such is our personality.

If (as Christians, Buddhists, Mystics, Yogis, Platonists, believe), our life is vanity, the world unreal, personality non-existent, the senses deceivers, their perceptions and even reason and imagination false; then how tragic that it is from the Flesh that such deductions are always made! If our mission in life is to evolve spiritually, then why are we provided with bodies which are so refractory that in thousands of years we have not been able to improve them or radically alter them? Not one lust of the flesh, not one single illusion, not even our male nipples have been bred out of us; and still our new-born babies roll about in paroxysms of sensual cupidity and egomaniac wrath.

* 'Sorrow is everywhere
  In man is no abiding entity
  In things no abiding reality.' – BUDDHA ('a dirge that still resounds mournfully in ten thousand monasteries').

Three faults, which are always found together and which infect every activity: laziness, vanity, cowardice. If one is too lazy to think, too vain to do a thing badly, too cowardly to admit it, one will never attain wisdom. Yet it is only the thinking which begins when habit-thinking leaves off, which is ignited by the logic of the train of thought, that is worth pursuing. A comfortable person can seldom follow up an original idea any further than a London pigeon can fly.

Complacent mental laziness is the English disease.

Today our literature is suffering from the decay of poetry and the decline of fiction, yet never have there been so many novelists and poets; this is because neither poet nor novelist will face his difficulties. Irresponsible poets who simulate inspiration trample down the flower of a language as brutally as politician and journalist, with their slovenliness, blunt and enfeeble the common run of words. Many war poets don't try; they are like boys playing about on a billiard table who wonder what the cues and pockets are for. It is no easier for novelists, who can no longer develop character, situation or plot. Flaubert, Henry James, Proust, Joyce and Virginia Woolf have finished off the novel. Now all will have to be re-invented as from the beginning.

Let us consider if there is any living writer whose silence we would consider a literary disaster, who, with three centuries more of art and history to draw from, can sustain a comparison with, for example, Pascal.

Pacal's *Pensées* were written *circa* 1660. Many of them are modern not merely in thought, but in expression and force; they would be of overwhelming importance if they were published now for the first time. Such a genius must invalidate the usual conception of human progress. Particularly modern are his rapidity, detachment and intellectual impatience.

Resemblance. Pascal: Leopardi: Baudelaire.

WISDOM OF PASCAL 1623–1662

'Tout le malheur des hommes vient d'une seule chose, qui est de ne savoir pas demeurer en repose, dans une chambre.'

'Notre nature est dans le mouvement; le repos entier est la mort.'

Ennui: 'Rien n'est si insupportable à l'homme que d'être dans un plein repos, sans passions, sans affaire, sans divertissement, sans application. Il sent alors son néant, son insuffisance, sa dépendance, son impuissance, son vide. Incontinent il sortira du fond de son âme l'ennui, la noirceur, la tristesse, le chagrin, le dépit, le désespoir.'

Misère: 'La seule chose qui nous console de nos misères est le divertissement, et cependant c'est la plus grande de nos misères, car c'est cela qui nous empêche principalement de songer à nous, et qui nous fait perdre insensiblement.'

La Gloire: 'L'admiration gâte tout dès l'enfance: Oh! que cela est bien dit! Oh! qu'il a bien fait! Qu'il est sage, etc. . . .'

'Les enfants de Port-Royal, auxquels on ne donne point cet aiguillon d'envie et de gloire, tombent dans la nonchalance.'

Pascal and Leopardi (both died aged thirty-nine), depress and frighten one because they were ill, almost deformed, and therefore because their deformity renders suspect so much of their pessimism. They are the Grand Inquisitors who break down our alibis of health and happiness. Are they pessimistic because they are ill? Or does their illness act as a short cut to reality – which is intrinsically tragic?* Or did their deformities encourage the herd to treat them thoughtlessly, and so create in them a pejorative impression of human nature? In many of

---

* 'For aught we know to the contrary, 103 or 104 degrees Fahrenheit might be a much more favourable temperature for truths to germinate and sprout in, than the more ordinary blood-heat of 97 or 98 degrees.' – WILLIAM JAMES.

Pascal's reflections one detects not only the scientific accuracy, but the morbidity and peevishness, the *injustice* of Proust.

How was La Rochefoucauld's health?

Pascal's 'moi' is Freud's 'Id'. Thus Pascal writes, 'Le *moi* est haïssable . . . le *moi* a deux qualités: il est injuste en soi, en ce qu'il se fait centre du tout; il est incommode aux autres, en ce qu'il les veut asservir: car chaque *moi* est l'ennemi et voudrait être le tyran de tous les autres'.

This is Freud. But though babies are born *all* 'Id', we do not for that condemn the human race.

We may consider that we are born as 'Id' and that the object of life is to sublimate the 'Id' – the 'Id' is all greed, anger, fear, vanity and lust. Our task is to purge it, shed it gradually as an insect sheds its larval form.

Life is a maze in which we take the wrong turning before we have learnt to walk.

Pascal says: 'Death should infallibly put them [the pleasure-lovers] very soon in the horrible necessity of being eternally unhappy . . .' We forget that he believes in Hell, because we can accept so much else that he believes. Yet believing in Hell must distort every judgement in this life. However much a Christian may say that the central doctrine of the Church is the Incarnation and nothing else, he is led on inevitably to exclusive salvation, to Heaven and Hell, to censorship and the persecution of heresy, till he finds himself among the brothel-owning Jesuits and cannon-blessing bishops of the Spanish war.

Pascal (or Hemingway, Sartre, or Malraux).

'Qu'on s'imagine un nombre d'hommes dans les chaînes, et tous condamnés à la mort, dont les uns étant chaque jour égorgés à la vue des autres, ceux qui restent voient leur propre condition dans celle de leurs semblables, et, se regardant les uns et les autres avec douleur et sans espérance, attendent à leur tour. C'est l'image de la condition des hommes.'

December 12th: Revisit pale Chelsea's nook-shotten Cythera.

Christmas Eve: Dégoûté de tout. Midwinter cafard.

> La Nochebuena se viene
> la Nochebuena se va
> y nosotros nos iremos
> y no volveremos más.

No opinions, no ideas, no real knowledge of anything, no ideals, no inspiration; a fat, slothful, querulous, greedy, impotent carcass; a stump, a decaying belly washed up on the shore. 'Manes Palinuri esse placandos!' Always tired, always bored, always hurt, always hating.

Sacred names: Rue de Chanaleilles. Summer night, limes in flower; old houses, with large gardens enclosed by high walls, silent in the leafy heart of the Faubourg: sensation of what is lost; lost love, lost youth, lost Paris, – remorse and folly. Aïe!

A love affair is a grafting operation. 'What has once been joined, never forgets.' There is a moment when the graft takes; up to then is possible without difficulty the separation which afterwards comes only through breaking off a great hunk of oneself, the ingrown fibre of hours, days, years.

New-year resolution: lose a stone, then all the rest will follow. Obesity is a mental state, a disease brought on by boredom and disappointment; greed, like the love of comfort, is a kind of fear. The one way to get thin is to re-establish a purpose in life.

Thus a good writer must be in training: if he is a stone too heavy then it must be because that fourteen pounds represents for him so much extra indulgence, so much clogging laziness; in fact a coarsening of his sensibility. There are but two ways to be a good writer (and no other kind is worth the being): one way is, like Homer, Shakespeare or Goethe, to accept life completely, the other (Pascal's, Proust's, Leopardi's, Baudelaire's), is to refuse ever to lose sight of its horror. One must be Prospero or Caliban; in between lie vast dissipated areas of weakness and pleasure.

The more I see of life the more I perceive that only through solitary communion with nature can one gain an idea of its richness and meaning. I know that in such contemplation lies my true personality, and yet I live in an age when on all sides I am told exactly the opposite and asked to believe that the social and co-operative activity of humanity is the one way through which life can be developed. Am I an exception, a herd-outcast? There are also solitary bees, and it is not claimed that they are biologically inferior. A planet of contemplators, each sunning himself before his doorstep like the mason-wasp; no one would help another, and no one would need help!

Marriage: 'An experience everyone should go through and then live his own life' *or* 'living one's own life – an experience everyone should go through and then marry'?

The tragedy of modern marriage is that married couples no longer enjoy the support of society, although marriage, difficult enough at any time, requires every social sanction. Thus, in the past, married women censured the unmarried; the constant punished the inconstant; society outlawed the divorced and the dwellers-in-sin. Now it does the contrary. The State harries the human couple and takes both man and wife for its wars, while society waits impatiently for the first excitement of mistress or lover, and lonely neurotic misfits, helpless and envious, make the young ménage their prey.

'In wise love each divines the high secret self of the other, and, refusing to believe in the mere daily self, creates a mirror where the lover or the beloved sees an image to copy in daily life.' – YEATS.

Human life is understandable only as a state of transition, as part of an evolutionary process; we can take it to be a transition between the animal world and some other form which we assume to be spiritual. Anxiety and remorse are the results of failing to advance spiritually. For this reason they follow close on pleasure, which is not necessarily harmful, but which, since it does not bring advancement with it, outrages that part of us which is concerned with growth. Such ways of making time fly past as chess, bridge, drink and motoring accumulate guilt. But what constitutes the spiritual ideal? Is it the Nietzschean Superman, or his opposite, the Buddha? The spiritual trend of human beings would seem to be towards pacifism, vegetarianism, contemplative mysticism, the elimination of violent emotion and even of self-reproduction. But is it impossible to improve animal-man so that instead of being made to renounce his animal nature, he refines it? Can anxiety and remorse be avoided in that way? Imagine a cow or a pig which rejected the body for a 'noble eight-fold way of self-enlightenment'. One would feel that there was a false calculation. If our elaborate and dominating bodies are given us to be denied at every turn, if our nature is always wrong and wicked, how ineffectual we are – like fishes not meant to swim. Have the solitary, the chaste, the ascetic who have been with us now for 3,000 years, ever been proved to be right? Has humanity shown any sign of evolving in their direction? As well as Diogenes or the Stylite, there is always Aristippus or Epicurus as an alternative to the Beast.*

And now we have a new alternative: the Group Man. Man's spiritual evolution, about which I prate, taking the form of a leap from the poorly organized wolf-pack and sheep-flock into an insect society, a community in which the individual is not merely a gregarious unit, but a cell in the body itself. Community and individual are, in fact, indistinguishable. How will you enjoy that, Palinurus?

* The Middle Way.
'Aristippus parlant à des jeunes gens qui rougissaient de la voir entrer chez une courtisane: "Le vice est de n'en pas sortir, non pas d'y entrer." ' – MONTAIGNE (*Essais*, III, v).

A charm against the Group Man

THE MAGIC CIRCLE

Peace-aims: (1) a yellow manor farm inside this magic circle;
               (2) a helicopter to take me to
               (3) an office in London or Paris and
               (4) to my cabin at Almuñecar or Ramatuelle.

Daydream: A golden classical house, three stories high, with *oeil de boeuf* attic windows and a view over water. Outside a magnolia growing up the wall, a terrace for winter, a great tree for summer and a lawn for games; behind it a wooded hill and in front a river, then a sheltered garden, indulgent to fig and nectarine, and in the corner a belvedere, book-lined like that of Montaigne, wizard of the magic circle, with this motto from him: 'La liberté et l'oisiveté qui sont mes maîtresses qualités'.

As I waddle along in thick black overcoat and dark suit with a leather brief-case under my arm, I smile to think how this costume officially disguises the wild and storm-tossed figure of Palinurus; who knows that a poet is masquerading here as a whey-faced bureaucrat? And who should ever know?

The secret of happiness lies in the avoidance of Angst (anxiety, spleen, noia, guilt, fear, remorse, cafard). It is a mistake to consider happiness as a positive state. By removing Angst, the condition of all unhappiness, we are then prepared to receive any blessings to which we are entitled. We know very little about Angst, which may even proceed from the birth trauma, or be a primitive version of the sense of original sin, but we can try to find out what makes it worse.*

Angst may take the form of remorse about the past, guilt about the present, anxiety about the future. Often it is due to our acceptance of conventional habits of living, through an imperfect knowledge of ourselves. Thus to keep someone waiting or to be kept waiting is a cause of Angst which is out of all proportion to the minor fault of unpunctuality. Therefore we may assume that we keep people waiting symbolically because we do not wish to see them and that our anxiety is due not to being late, but to our having to see them at all. A chronically unpunctual person should cancel all engagements for a

---

* Freudians consider anxiety to arise from the repression of anger or love. Kretschmer thinks there is an obscure somatic relation between anxiety and sex. Theologians associate it with the Fall, Behaviorists with undigested food in the stomach, Kierkegaard with the vertigo that precedes sin. Buddha and many philosophers regarded it as concurrent with Desire. Thus Bacon quotes Epicurus: 'Use not that you may not wish, wish not that you may not fear'.

definite period. Similarly, anxiety at being kept waiting is a form of jealousy, a fear that we are not liked.

Fatigue is a cause of Angst, which often disappears if the tired person is able to lie down; bad air is another, or seeing a tube train move out as one reaches the platform.

To sit late in a restaurant (especially when one has to pay the bill) or over a long meal after a cocktail party is particularly productive of Angst, which does not affect us after snacks taken in an armchair with a book. The business lunch is another meal from which we would prefer to be driven away in a coffin. Certainly a frequent cause of Angst is an awareness of the waste of our time and ability, such as we witness among people kept waiting by the hairdresser.

Further considerations on cowardice, sloth and vanity; vices which do small harm to other people, but which prevent us from doing any good and which poison and enfeeble all the virtues. Sloth rots the intelligence, cowardice destroys all power at the source, while vanity inhibits us from facing the facts which might teach us something; it dulls all other sensation.

Home Truth from La Bruyère: 'L'expérience confirme que la mollesse ou l'indulgence pour soi et la dureté pour les autres n'est qu'un seul et même vice'.

I see the world as a kind of Black Hole of Calcutta, where we are milling about in the darkness and slime; now and then the mere being in the world is enough to give me a violent claustrophobia (or is it a physical shortness of breath which creates the sensation of claustrophobia and therefore the image of the Black Hole?) And then I know that it is only by some desperate escape, like Pascal's, that I can breathe; but cowardice and sloth prevent me from escaping.

Who have escaped?

'Those who know don't speak;
Those who speak don't know.'

On the American desert are horses which eat the loco-weed and some are driven mad by it; their vision is affected, they take enormous leaps to cross a tuft of grass or tumble blindly into rivers. The horses which have become thus addicted are shunned by the others and will never rejoin the herd. So it is with human beings; those who are conscious of another world, the world of the spirit, acquire an outlook which distorts the values of ordinary life; they are consumed by the weed of non-attachment. Curiosity is their one excess and therefore they are recognized not by what they do, but by what they refrain from doing, like those Araphants or disciples of Buddha who were pledged to the 'Nine Incapabilities'. Thus they do not take life, they do not compete, they do not boast, they do not join groups of more than six, they do not condemn others; they are 'abandoners of revels, mute, contemplative' who are depressed by gossip, gaiety and equals, who wait to be telephoned to, who neither speak in public, nor keep up with their friends, nor take revenge on their enemies. Self-knowledge has taught them to abandon hate and blame and envy in their lives, and they look sadder than they are. They seldom make positive assertions because they see, outlined against any statement, as a painter sees a complementary colour, the image of its opposite. Most psychological questionnaires are designed to search out these moonlings and to secure their non-employment. They divine each other by a warm indifference for they know that they are not intended to forgather, but, like stumps of phosphorus in the world's wood, each to give forth his misleading radiance.

The two errors: We can have either a spiritual or a materialist view of life. If we believe in the spirit then we make an assumption which permits a whole chain of them, down to a belief in fairies, witches, astrology, black magic, ghosts, and treasure-divining; the point at which we stop believing is dictated by our temperament or by our mood at a given moment. Thus the early Christians believed in the miracles of false prophets, and regarded the pagan gods as devils who had entrenched themselves in secure positions. They were more pagan than I am. On the other hand a completely materialist view leads to its own excesses, such as a belief in Behaviorism, in the economic basis of art, in the social foundation of ethics, and the biological nature of psychology, in fact to the justification of expediency and therefore ultimately to the Ends-Means fallacy of which our civilization is perishing.

If we believe in a supernatural or superhuman intelligence creating the universe, then we end by stocking our library with the prophecies of Nostradamus, and the calculations on the Great Pyramid. If instead we choose to travel viâ Montaigne and Voltaire, then we choke among the brimstone aridities of the Left Book Club.

It is a significant comment on the victory of science over magic that were someone to say 'if I put this pill in your beer it will explode', we might believe them; but were they to cry 'if I pronounce this spell over your beer it will go flat', we should remain incredulous and Paracelsus, the Alchemists, Aleister Crowley and all the Magi have lived in vain. Yet when I read science I turn magical; when I study magic, scientific.

We cannot say that the truth lies in the centre between the spiritual and the material conception, since life must be one thing or the other. But can it be both? Supposing life were created by an act of God willing the accidental combination of chemicals to form a cell; created in fact by deliberate accident. Then, in the confidence of youth when the body seems self-sufficing, it would be natural to emphasize the materialist nature of phenomena, and in old age, when the body begins to betray us, to abandon our sensual outlook for a more spiritual cosmorama – and both times we should be right.

Sunshine streams into the room, the dove grinds her love-song on the roof, in the square the grass turns green, the earth has been cleared round the daffodils as a stage is cleared for the dancers, and under a clean blue sky the streets remember Canaletto; London spring is on its way.

Spring, season of massacre and offensives, of warm days and flowing blood, of flowers and bombs. Out with the hyacinths, on with the slaughter! Glorious weather for tanks and land-mines!

The creative moment of a writer comes with the autumn. The winter is the time for reading, revision, preparation of the soil; the spring for thawing back to life; the summer is for the open air, for satiating the body with health and action, but from October to Christmas for the release of pent-up mental energy, the hard crown of the year.

The duality of man is the heresy of Paul and Plato, heresy because the concept of soul and body is bound to imply a struggle between them which leads on the one hand to asceticism and puritanism, on the other to excess of materialism and sensuality. The greatness of Christ and Buddha lay in their abandonment of asceticism for the Middle Path.

The spiritual life of man is the flowering of his bodily existence: there is a physical life which remains the perfect way of living for natural man, a life in close contact with nature, with the sun and the passage of the seasons, and rich in opportunities for equinoctial migrations and home-comings. This life has now become artificial, out of reach of all but the rich or the obstinately free, yet until we can return to it we are unable to appreciate the potentialities of living. (Whales, branded in the Arctic, are found cruising in Antarctic waters; men, ringed in child-hood, are observed, seventy years later, under the same stone.) We may compare a human being to a fruit-tree whose purpose is its fruit, fruit out of all proportion to the tree's value; yet, unless the tree receives its years of leisure, its requirements of sun and rain, the fruit never ripens. So it is with the spiritual virtues of man, for we have divided man into two kinds: those whose soil is so poor or the climate of whose lives so unsuitable that they can never bear, or those who are forced and cramped under glass, whose lives are so constricted by responsibility that they become all fruit; hasty, artificial and without flavour.

We progress through an intensifying of the power generated from the physical satisfaction of natural man, whose two worst enemies are apathy and delirium; the apathy which spreads outwards from the mechanical life, the delirium which results from the violent methods we use to escape from it.

Happiness lies in the fulfilment of the spirit through the body. Thus humanity has already evolved from an animal life to one more civilized. There can be no complete return to nature, to nudism, desert-islandry: city life is the subtlest ingredient in the human climate. But we have gone wrong over the size of our cities and over the kind of life we lead in them; in the past the clods were the peasants, now the brute mass of ignorance is urban. The village idiot walks in Leicester Square. To live according to nature we should pass a considerable time in cities, for they are the glory of human nature, but they should never contain more than two hundred thousand inhabitants; it is our artificial enslavement to the large city, too sprawling to leave, too enormous for human dignity, which is responsible for half our sickness and misery. Slums may well be breeding-grounds of crime, but middle-class suburbs are incubators of apathy and delirium. No city should be too large for a man to walk out of in a morning.*

Surrealism is a typical city-delirium movement, a violent explosion of urban claustrophobia; one cannot imagine the Surrealists except in vast cities, 'paysans de Paris' and New York. The nihilism of Céline and Miller is another product, and so are those mass-movers Marx with his carbuncles, Hitler with his Beer-Hall. The English masses are lovable: they are kind, decent, tolerant, practical and not stupid. The tragedy is that there are too many of them, and that they are aimless, having out-grown the servile functions for which they were encouraged to multiply. One day these huge crowds will have to seize power because there will be nothing else for them to do, and yet they neither demand power nor

* 'We are not yet ripe for growing up in the streets . . . has any good ever come out of that foul-clustering town-proletariat, beloved of humanitarians? Nothing – never; they are only waiting for a leader, some "inspired idiot" to rend to pieces our poor civilization.' – NORMAN DOUGLAS: *Siren Land*, 1911.

are ready to make use of it; they will learn only to be bored in a new way. Sooner or later the population of England will turn Communist, and then it will take over. Some form of Communism is the only effective religion for the working class; its coming is therefore as inevitable as was that of Christianity. The Liberal Die-hard then comes to occupy historically the same position as the 'good Pagan': he is doomed to extinction.

As we re-live the horrors of the Dark Ages, of absolute States and ideological wars, the old platitudes of liberalism loom up in all their glory, familiar streets as we reel home furious in the dawn.

Wisdom of de Quincey
De Quincey: decadent English essayist who, at the age of seventy-five, was carried off by fifty years of opium-eating.

'Marriage had corrupted itself through the facility of divorce and through the consequences of that facility (viz. levity in choosing and fickleness in adhering to the choice) into so exquisite a traffic of selfishness that it could not yield so much as a phantom model of sanctity.'

'By the law I came to know sin.'

On the first time he took opium in 1804: 'It was Sunday afternoon, wet and cheerless; and a duller spectacle this earth of ours has not to show than a rainy Sunday in London'.

The mystery of drugs: How did savages all over the world, in every climate, discover in frozen tundras or remote jungles the one plant, often similar to countless others of the same species, which could, if only by a very elaborate process, give them fantasies, intoxication, freedom from care? How unless by help from the plants themselves? Opium-smokers in the East become surrounded by cats, dogs, birds and even spiders, which are attracted to the smell. The craving for the drug proceeds from the brain-cells which revolt and overrule the will. The Siberian tribes who eat Agaric say, 'The Agaric orders me to do this or that' – the Hashish smokers feel this too. Horses and cattle which become 'indigo eaters' continue to gorge till they drop dead. Peyotl, one of the rarest and most obscure drugs, yet gave its name to the range of uninhabited mountains where it is found.

The Greeks and Romans looked on alcohol and opium as the lovely twin reconcilers to living and dying presented to man by Dionysus and Morpheus – God-given because of their extraordinary sympathy to us, and because of the mystery of their discovery. If man is part of nature, he may be better understood by his parasites than he knows.

Since there are flowers whose fertilization is impossible except by means of insects, flowers which eat insects and therefore which understand them, since this low and unconscious order has these correspondences with the one above it, may there not be animals and birds who make use of man and study his habits, and if they, why not also insects and vegetables? What grape, to keep its place in the sun, taught our ancestors to make wine?

Everything is a dangerous drug except reality, which is unendurable. Happiness is in the imagination. What we perform is always inferior to what we imagine; yet day-dreaming brings guilt; there is no happiness except through freedom from Angst, and only creative work, communion with nature and helping others are Angst-free.

Fraternity is the State's bribe to the individual; it is the one virtue which can bring courage to members of a materialist society. All State propaganda exalts comradeship, for it is this gregarious herd-sense and herd-smell which keeps people from thinking and so reconciles them to the destruction of their private lives. A problem for government writers, or for the war artists in their war cemeteries: how to convert Fraternity into an aesthetic emotion?

Subversive thought for the year: 'Every man is to be respected as an absolute end in himself; and it is a crime against the dignity that belongs to him to use him as a mere means to some external purpose.' – KANT.

'If I had to choose between betraying my country and betraying my friend, I hope I should have the guts to betray my country.' This statement of E. M. Forster's reminds us how far we have wandered from the ancient conception of friendship, of treating a few hundred souls as ends, not means. 'The Chinese poet recommends himself as a friend, the Western poet as a lover', writes Arthur Waley; but the Western prose-writer also used to recommend himself as a friend; the seventeenth and eighteenth centuries elaborated friendship and made almost a religion of it. In the circle of Johnson, of Walpole and Madame du Deffand, or of the Encyclopaedists nobody could live without his friend. They loved them, and even a misanthropic philosopher like La Bruyère waxed sentimental over the theme. Only the invalid Pascal criticized friendship on the grounds that if we could read each other's thoughts it would disappear.

Now the industrialization of the world, the totalitarian State, and the egotism of materialism have killed friendship; the first through speeding up the tempo of human communications to the point where everyone is replaceable, the second by making such demands on the individual that comradeship can only be practised between workers and colleagues for the period of their co-operation, and the last by emphasizing all that is fundamentally selfish and nasty in people, so that we are unkind about our friends and resentful of their intimacy because of something which is rotting in ourselves. We have developed sympathy at the expense of loyalty.

How many people drop in on us? This is the criterion of friendship. Or tell us our faults? Or do we give presents to? Or remain silent with? The egocentric personality requires, alas, a changing audience, not a constant scrutiny. Romantic love is disloyal, and in making fun of old friends it has discovered one of the most congenial ways of entertaining a new lover.

Voltaire on Friendship: 'C'est un contrat tacite entre deux personnes sensibles et vertueuses. Je dis *sensibles* car un moine, un solitaire peut n'être point méchant et vivre sans connaître l'amitié. Je dis *vertueuses*, car les méchants n'ont que des complices, les voluptueux ont des compagnons de débauche, les intéressés ont des associés, les politiques assemblent des fâcheux, le commun des hommes oisifs a des liaisons, les princes ont des courtisans: les hommes vertueux ont seuls des amis.'

When we see someone living alone, like a beech-tree in a clearing, with no other signs of life around him and displaying his freedom, his possessions and his devotion to his friends, we can be sure that such a person is an ogre and that human bones lie buried under his roots.

MASTERPLAY

Three requisites for a work of art: validity of the myth, vigour of belief, intensity of vocation. Examples of valid myths: The Gods of Olympus in Ancient Greece, the City of Rome and afterwards the Roman Empire, Christianity, the discovery of Man in the Renaissance continued into the Age of Reason, the myths of Romanticism and of Material Progress (how powerful is the myth of bourgeois life in the great works of the Impressionist painters!). The strength of belief in a myth whose validity is diminishing will not produce such great art as the strength of belief in one which is valid, and none is valid today. Yet no myth is ever quite worthless as long as there remains one artist to lend it his faith.

O for the past, when a masterpiece was enough to maintain a reputation for life! All Catullus, Tibullus and Propertius fit into the same volume; Horace or Virgil requires but one tome, so do La Fontaine and La Bruyère. One book for one lifetime and the rest is fame, ease and freedom from Angst. Nature was so indulgent; if we did but write one good book every twelve years we would have done as well as Flaubert. Voltaire wrote *Candide* when he was sixty-five, Peacock wrote *Gryll Grange* at seventy-five, Joinville began his *Life of St Louis* at eighty.

Waste is a law of art as it is of nature. There is always time.

All good writers have to discover the yawning crevasse which separates Man's finite destiny from his infinite potentialities. It is afterwards that they reveal their artistic courage and so register the protest which is their final plea for order, their *Gulliver's Travels*, their *Maxims*, their *Songs of Experience*, their *Saison en Enfer*, their *Fleurs du Mal*. Bad writers either pretend that they have seen nothing, and that all is well, or else howl with self-pity. Optimism and self-pity are the positive and negative poles of modern cowardice.

What makes great writers of the past most vivid to us is the extent of their misery; the despair of Pascal, the bitterness of La Rochefoucauld, the ennui of Flaubert, the noia of Leopardi, the spleen of Baudelaire – none but the truths which have been extracted under mental torture appeal to us. We live in such a desperate age that any happiness which we possess must be hidden like a deformity, for we know that, although all our nature revolts, we can create only through what we suffer.

'We are all conceived in close prison . . . and then all our life is but a going out to the place of execution, to death. Nor was there any man seen to sleep in the cart between Newgate and Tyburn – between prison and the place of execution, does any man sleep? But we sleep all the way; from the womb to the grave we are never thoroughly awake.' – DONNE.

A Modern Rune: 'Pooey on the war!' No one can pronounce these four words and not feel a tremor of earth-shaking dimensions. And when the two thousand and fifty million belligerents can proclaim it in unison, the war will be over.

A Rune for the very bored: When very bored say to yourself: 'It was during the next twenty minutes that there occurred one of those tiny incidents which revolutionize the whole course of our life and alter the face of history. Truly we are the playthings of enormous fates.'

The ten-year torture of two faces. 'The tyranny of the human face.'

When we see a friend in the depth of despair because he has been left by someone whom we know to be insignificant, we must remember that there is a way of leaving and yet of not leaving; of hinting that one loves and is willing to return, yet never coming back, and so preserving a relationship in a lingering decay, and that this technique can be learnt like a hold in jiu-jitsu. The person who has been left is always psychologically groggy; the ego is wounded in its most tender part and is forced back on separation and rejection phobias in infancy. Someone who knows how to prolong this state and to reproduce it at will can be quite insignificant – so is the sand-wasp which stings a grub in the nerve-centre where it will be paralysed, yet remain alive.

Axiom: There is no happiness to be obtained by the destruction of someone else's. To take a wife away from her husband, or a husband from his wife, is a kind of murder; guilt turns lovers into bad accomplices, and the wrecking of homes destroys the wreckers. As we leave others, so shall we be left.

There is sanctuary in reading, sanctuary in formal society, in office routine, in the company of old friends and in the giving of officious help to strangers, but there is no sanctuary in one bed from the memory of another. The past with its anguish and injuries breaks down all the defences of custom and habit; we must sleep and therefore we must dream.

And in our dreams at night, as in the vacant afternoons of London week-ends, enter the excluded, the disinherited, the heartbroken, the heart-breakers, the saboteurs and wrecking crews of our daylight selves. θύραζε κῆρες. Bone-crunching hyenas!

The harbour of Cassis on a bright winter morning; a gull, unable to rise because its wings are fouled with oil, is floating a few yards from the quay. The children pelt it with stones. I drive them away; laughing they run to the farther side and begin again, the stones falling round the bird as it bobs on the water like a painted decoy.

'While under its storm-beaten breast
Cried out the hollows of the sea.'

Causes of Angst: Angst is inherent in the uncoiling of the ego, the *ver solitaire*. It dwells in the *Lacrimae Rerum*, in the contrasting of the Past with the Present. It lurks in old loves, in old letters and in our despair at the complexity of modern life.

Effect: Misery, disgust, tears, guilt.

Temporary cures: (1) Lunch with a new friend, gossip, literary talk, i.e. appeals to vanity; (2) Art (Renoir landscapes), the true escape into *Timelessness*; (3) The office personality (Alibi Ike); (4) Old friends, relationships dating from before the Fall.

Angoisse des Gares: A particularly violent form of Angst. Bad when we meet someone at the station, much worse when we are seeing them off; not present when departing oneself, but unbearable when arriving in London, if only from a day in Brighton. Since all Angst is identical, we may learn something from these station-fears: Arrival-Angst is closely connected with guilt, with the dread of something terrible having happened during our absence. Death of parents. Entry of bailiffs. Flight of loved one. Sensations worse at arriving in the evening than the morning, and much worse at Victoria and Waterloo than at Paddington. Partly this is due to my having gone abroad every vacation and, therefore, to returning to London with guilt-feelings about having spent all my money, or not written to parents, and to endless worry over work and debts.* Going to London as a schoolboy was a jaunt, as an undergraduate an ordeal, a surrender to justice. Later the trips abroad lengthened, and returns were painful because of household worries replacing former debts, and through a particularly strong guilt-feeling about not being at work, or at having been out-distanced by successful stay-at-home friends. But this is not all, for much of our anxiety is caused by the horror of London itself; of its hideous entrails as seen from the southern approaches, its high cost of living, its embodiment of

* But why was I extravagant, why didn't I write to my parents? – A deeper level of anxiety becomes apparent.

ugly and unnatural urban existence. When living in France, I began to feel the same way about Paris, though it has none of the same associations. I deduce, therefore, that though it is wrong for us to live and work in great cities, it is also wrong to live away from them *without working*. Angst begins at Reading (for Paddington), Brookwood, the London Necropolis (for Waterloo), the tunnels through the North Downs (for Victoria), or even in Paris, when we see the grisly English faces homeward bound at the Gare du Nord. First-class or third makes no difference. 'They' will get you, Palinurus, 'they' aren't taken in.

If, instead of Time's notorious and incompetent remedy, there was an operation by which we would be cured of loving, how many of us would rush to have it!

To be laid in a frigidaire for six months or to hibernate in deep narcotic sleep, to be given new drugs, new glands, a new heart, and to wake up with the memory swept clean of farewells and accusations, nevermore to be haunted by the grief-stricken eyes of the assassinated murderers!

But Angst descends; I wake up in anxiety; like a fog it overlays all I do, and my days are muffled with anguish. Somewhere in the mind are crossed the wires of fear and lust and all day long nature's burglar-alarm shrills out in confusion. I dread the bell, the post, the telephone, the sight of an acquaintance. Anguish, anxiety, remorse and guilt: TOUT EST DÉGOÛT ET MISÈRE. When even despair ceases to serve any creative purpose, then surely we are justified in suicide. For what better grounds for suicide can there be than to go on making the same series of false moves which invariably lead to the same disaster and to repeat a pattern without knowing why it is false, or wherein lies the flaw? And yet to perceive that in ourselves revolves a cycle of activity which is certain to end in paralysis of the will, desertion, panic and despair – always to go on loving those who have ceased to love us, and who have quite lost all resemblance to the selves whom once we loved! Suicide is infectious; what if the agonies which suicides endure before they are driven to take their own life, the emotion of 'All is lost' – are infectious too? And if you have caught them, Palinurus, if they have sought you out?

TE PALINURE PETENS, TIBI SOMNIA TRISTIA PORTANS INSONTI?*

Madame du Deffand to Horace Walpole:

'Ennui. C'est une maladie de l'âme dont nous afflige la nature en nous donnant l'existence; c'est le ver solitaire qui absorbe tout . . . "Ah! je le répète sans cesse, il n'y a qu'un malheur, celui d'être né."

Comment est-il possible qu'on craigne la fin d'une vie aussi triste . . . Divertissez-vous, mon ami, le plus que vous pourrez; ne vous affligez point de mon état, nous étions presque perdus l'un pour l'autre; nous ne nous devions jamais revoir; vous me regretterez, parce qu'on est bien aise de se savoir aimé.'

Part Two: Te Palinure Petens

'You are very wise, very understanding and really very kindly. I wonder that you remain the critic. You can go beyond. You must have great fears and doubts, and you have overlaid another personality on the original one, a protective masked being which deals with what you imagine to be a harsh, cruel world.' – HENRY MILLER to Palinurus.

'Had I followed my pleasure and chosen what I plainly have a decided talent for: police spy, I should have been much happier than I afterwards became.' – KIERKEGAARD – *Journals*, 1843.

'Ne cherchez plus mon coeur; les bêtes l'ont mangé.'

* Looking for you, Palinurus, bringing you sad visions which you have not deserved.

APRIL MESSAGE

Pack up. Your situation is untenable, your loss irretrievable *y no hay remedio.* CHANGE YOUR BEDDING!*

ORATE PRO NOBIS

Philip Heseltine, Harry Crosby, René Crevel, Mara Andrews.†

Spring in the Square, when the Nile-green tendrils of the plane trees uncurl against the blue, and the Tree of Heaven prepares its book-plate entry; a soldier and his girl come in to kiss because the gate is open, then lock it behind them and, hours later, are wandering round and round the empty square like insects trying to escape from a pitcher plant. Lying on the fresh grass in the sun and reading about opium as one learns about a new religion. Confessions of an opium-reader! Opium made De Quincey great and Cocteau serious. Would it prove the remedy, the 'Heart-balm'? To take a drug which exploded all the minefields of memory! And afterwards to come out not knowing who one is, not even being able to read, and then to learn to read, and to discover some writers to whom one was strangely attracted – as if one had known them in another life! And then as a fresh start to develop an Adult Personality, to attest that the one way to be happy is to make other people happy; that virtue is social. 'Happiness lies in the approval

---

* Lamas do not die, but on reincarnation, are said to 'change their bedding.'

† Philip Heseltine (Peter Warlock) committed suicide on 17th December 1930, aged thirty-six. The coroner read out part of a letter: 'I would very much rather visit you at some other time than Christmas. It is a season of the year which I dislike more and more as time goes on.'

Harry Crosby (according to Mr Cowley in *Exile's Return*) planned to kill himself on 31st October 1942, at the end of his fortieth year, by flying his plane till it crashed, 'a sun death into sun'. He could not wait, and shot himself in New York in 1929.

René Crevel, surrealist poet, killed himself in Paris in 1935, aged thirty-four. He left a note: 'Je suis dégoûté de tout'.

Mara Andrews, once of the Ile Saint-Louis, committed suicide in New York while this was being written.

of our fellow-men, unhappiness in their disapproval, to earn one is virtue, the other vice.' That is what I should teach, and if sometimes it sounded rather dull, that would mean I was a little constipated.

Civilization is an active deposit which is formed by the combustion of the Present with the Past. Neither in countries without a Present nor in those without a Past is it to be discovered. Proust in Venice, Matisse's birdcages overlooking the flower market of Nice, Gide on the seventeenth-century quais of Toulon, Lorca in Granada, Picasso by Saint-Germain-des-Prés: that is civilization, and for me it can exist only under those liberal regimes in which the Present is alive and therefore capable of combining with the Past. Civilization is maintained by a very few people in a small number of places, and we need only a few bombs and some prisons to blot it out altogether.

The civilized are those who get more out of life than the uncivilized, and for this the uncivilized have not forgiven them. One by one, the Golden Apples of the West are shaken from the tree.

The quince, coing, membrillo, marmelata, pyrus cydonia or portugalensis; emblem of love and happiness to the Ancients, was the golden fruit of the Hesperides, and the love-apple which Greek maidens gave their boys. It was also a symbol of long life and passion. I see it now as the emblem of the civilization of Europe, with its hard tough flesh, bright colour and unearthly savour. The simple flowers, the astringent fruit which ripens only in the south, the mysterious pips full of emulgent oil – all are significant. There are artists like quinces, des vrais coings: their fragrance does not cloy.

Mysteries of nature: The properties of the quince, of the truffle (a truffle placed near a fresh egg will impregnate it with its odour), of the opium poppy and the peyotl bud; the stormy life of wine; the cry of the cicada and the death's-head moth, the flight of the stag-beetle, the philo-parasitism of the ant, the gaze of the mantis*; lemons and the smell of

* 'Elle épouse, elle tue et elle n'est que plus belle.' – (BINET on the Mantis.)

lemon-verbena and lemon-scented magnolias, the colour of gentians, the texture of water-lilies, the vegetable view of man. The smell of cigar-smoke, of coffee being roasted, or of wine-barrels and of herbs in cooking are irresistible, and demonstrate how intense and mutual is our collaboration.

Never would it occur to a child that sheep, pigs, cows or chickens were good to eat, while, like Milton's *Adam*, he would readily make a meal of fruits, nuts, thyme, mint, peas and broad beans, which penetrate further and stimulate not only the appetite but other vague and deep nostalgias. We are closer to the Vegetable Kingdom than we know; it is not for us alone that mint, thyme, sage, and rosemary exhale 'crush me and eat me!' – for us that opium poppy, coffee-berry, tea-plant and vine perfect themselves? Their aim is to be absorbed by man, although they can achieve it only by attaching themselves to roast mutton.

'Les hommes et les insectes font partie de la même nature.' – CAILLOIS.

Why do ants alone have parasites whose intoxicating moistures they drink, and for whom they will even sacrifice their young? Because as they are the most highly socialized of insects, so their lives are the most intolerable.

Protective colouring in insects represents not only their defence against the creatures who prey on them, but their homage to the vegetables by which they are absorbed. The insect resembles a leaf at the wish of a tree. The vast vegetable world governs the tiny animal world by letting itself be assimilated.

Why do soles and turbots borrow the colours and even the contours of the sea-bottom? Out of self-protection? No, out of self-disgust.

The civilization of the nineteenth century was founded on Coal, Electricity, and Central Heating. These brought the northern countries their continuous industrial energy and corresponding increase of population. With air-conditioning the civilization of the twentieth century can move south. Brazil will benefit as once did Canada. This invention, by restoring their dynamic to the Mediterranean countries, may save Europe. We may even abolish the desert and the siesta as far south as Khartoum and Dakar, we may see the Mediterranean become as industrialized as the Great Lakes, with Barcelona as Chicago and Athens as Detroit. England will appeal to these new air-conditioned Carthaginians as a summer resort: a grey little fey little island.

The goal of all cultures is to decay through over-civilization; the factors of decadence – luxury, scepticism, weariness and superstition – are constant. The civilization of one epoch becomes the manure of the next. Everything over-ripens in the same way. The disasters of the world are due to its inhabitants not being able to grow old simultaneously. There is always a raw and intolerant nation eager to destroy the tolerant and mellow. With the Brave New World we may hope to see whole populations on an equal footing, and all the nations wither in unison. We may say with Fontenelle, 'Il faut du temps pour ruiner un monde, mais enfin, il ne faut que du temps'.

There was once a man (reputed to be the wisest in the world) who, although living to an untold age, confined his teaching to the one word of advice: 'Endure!' At length a rival arose and challenged him to a debate which took place before a large assembly. 'You say "Endure",' cried the rival sage, 'but I don't want to endure. I wish to love and to be loved, to conquer and create, I wish to know what is right, then do it and be happy.' There was no reply from his opponent, and, on looking more closely at the old creature, his adversary found him to consist of an odd-shaped rock on which had taken root a battered thorn that presented, by an optical illusion, the impression of hair and a beard. Triumphantly he pointed out the mistake to the authorities, but they were not concerned. 'Man or rock,' they answered, 'what does it matter?' And at that moment the wind, reverberating through the sage's moss-grown orifice, repeated with a hollow sound: 'Endure!'

A love-affair can prosper only when both parties enter it free. If one lover is free and not the other, then in the process of destroying his rival, or the memory of his rival, the one who is free will destroy the illusion of his own virtue. A couple jointly possess so much of their two selves that to hurt one is to wound the other, and, even if they are wounded willingly, resentment is set up. When we want a house we go to the house-agent and inquire what is on the market; we do not pick on the first one we like and force the tenant to leave. The romantic prestige of adultery comes from exaggerating the importance of chastity in the unmarried. If fornication were no sin, then adultery would be condemned, for it is a token form of murder. We do not murder the rival husband or wife, but we murder their image in the eyes of those whom they love and so prepare the cancer of their ego and their slow death by desertion. If opinion allowed promiscuity only to the free, that is to the unmarried, or to those who had both agreed on separation, and if it punished the breaking-up of homes as it punishes robbery-with-violence, then the nervous breakdowns, the resort to alcohol and drugs, would disappear with much of the incurable unhappiness of the betrayed and forsaken.

The greatest charm of marriage, in fact that which renders it irresistible to those who have once tasted it, is the duologue, the permanent conversation between two people which talks over everything and everyone till death breaks the record. It is this which, in the long run, makes a reciprocal equality more intoxicating than any form of servitude or domination. But for the artist it may prove dangerous; he is one of those who must look alone out of the window, and for him to enter into the duologue, the non-stop performance of a lifetime, is a kind of exquisite dissipation which, despite the pleasure of a joint understanding of the human comedy, with its high level of intuition and never-cloying flavour, is likely to deprive him of those much rarer moments which are particularly his own. For this reason the great artists are not always those who repose the most entire confidence in their wives (this is why second wives are sometimes best), and the relation of an artist to his wife is apt to puzzle the spectator.

May 1st: Today we begin a new pincer movement against Angst, Melancholia, and Memory's ever-festering wound: a sleeping pill to pass the night and a Benzedrine to face the day. The sleeping pill produces a thick sleep, rich in dreams that are not so much dreams as tangible experiences, the Benzedrine a kind of gluttonous mental energy through which the sadness persists – O how sad – but very much farther off. Whether they can combine with the mind to produce a new energy, or whether they remain unassimilated, is yet to be seen.

When I take Vitamin B, Metatone or other tonics, they make me calm, coarse and sensual; the voice becomes deeper, the manner more robust. Yet I am aware this is not my real personality, but a toned-up version of it, an escape from the serious ego, and I soon return to my true diffident and dyspeptic self. Confidence does not become me.

Ennui is the condition of not fulfilling our potentialities; remorse of not having fulfilled them; anxiety of not being able to fulfil them – but what are they?

Let us take a simple idea like the desire to improve, to become better. Is it a natural human instinct, or is it the result of early conditioning? Crocodiles, king-crabs, eagles, do not evolve, and yet seem perfectly content with their humble status. And many human beings enjoy a quiet existence without feeling themselves obliged to expand or develop. With the desire to evolve goes the fear of not evolving, or guilt. If there were no parents to make us try to be good, no schoolmasters to persuade us to learn, no one who wished to be proud of us, should not we be happy? Promise is the white child's burden of which the savage, in his pre-mental bliss, has never heard. When we are sick we revert to our childhood pattern. Do we not live according to it to the same degree when we are well? Heard, for example, is the son of a puritan clergyman, Huxley is by birth a public-spirited Victorian; what is their evolutionary zeal but a duty-reflex conditioned by their upbringing? Does Nature care in the least whether we evolve or not? Her instincts are for the gratification of hunger and sex, the destruction of rivals and the protection of offspring. What monster first slipped in the idea of progress? Who destroyed our static conception of happiness with these growing-pains?

MASTERPLAY

The triple decadence: Decadence of the material; of the writer's language. The virgin snow where Shakespeare and Montaigne used to cut their deep furrows, is now but a slope which innumerable tracks have flattened until it is unable to receive an impression. Decadence of the myth, for there is no longer a unifying belief (as in Christianity or in Renaissance Man) to give to a writer a sense of awe, and of awe which he shares with the mass of humanity. And even the last myth of all, the myth of the artist's vocation, of 'l'homme c'est rien, l'oeuvre c'est tout', is destroyed by the times, by the third decadence, that of society. In our lifetime we have seen the arts advance further and further into an obscure and sterile cul-de-sac. Science has done little to help the artist, beyond contributing radio, linotype and the cinema; inventions which enormously extend the artist's scope, but which commit him more than ever to the policy of the State and the demands of the ignorant. Disney is the tenth-rate Shakespeare of our age, forced by his universal audience to elaborate his new-world sentimentality with increasing slickness. There may arise Leonardos of the screen and microphone who will astound us, but not until the other arts have declined into regional or luxury crafts, like book-binding, cabinet-making, thatching or pargetting. Today an artist must expect to write in water and to cast in sand.

Yet to live in a decadence need not make us despair; it is but one technical problem the more which an artist has to solve.

Even in the most socialized community, there must always be a few who best serve it by being kept solitary and isolated. The artist, like the mystic, naturalist, mathematician or 'leader', makes his contribution out of his solitude. This solitude the State is now attempting to destroy, and a time may come when it will no more tolerate private inspiration than the Church once tolerated private worship. State Socialism in politics always goes with social realism in the arts, and eventually the position is reached that whatever the common man does not understand is treason. Yet it is a mistake completely to identify the State with a philistine father-figure and so to react blindly against it. For the State includes those who criticize it, and their criticism may lead to change. Today the State shows a benevolent face to Culture-Diffusion, but to those who create culture no trace of sympathy or indulgence, with the result that we are becoming a nation of commentators, of critics and hack-explainers, most of whom are ex-artists. Everything for the Milk-bar, nothing for the Cow! Patiently and obstinately the artist must convince the State that in the long run it will be judged by its art, and that if the State is to replace the private patron, then it must imitate, and even surpass, that patron's tolerance, humility and liberality. When will the State say, 'Here is a thousand pounds young man; go anywhere you like for six months, and bring me back something beautiful'?

A great artist is like a fig-tree whose roots run a hundred feet underground, in search of tea-leaves, cinders and old boots. Art which is directly produced for the Community can never have the same withdrawn quality as that which is made out of the artist's solitude. For this possesses the integrity and bleak exhilaration that are to be gained only from the absence of an audience and from communion with the primal sources of unconscious life. One cannot serve both beauty and power: 'Le pouvoir est essentiellement stupide.' A public figure can never be an artist, and no artist should ever become one unless his work is done, and he chooses to retire into public life.

An artist grows into a public figure through being always willing to address strangers. 'Pauvre et sans honneurs,' wrote Valéry of Mallarmé, 'la nudité de sa condition avilissait tous les avantages des autres . . . Tout leur semblait naïf et lâche après qu'ils l'avaient lu.'

A Chinese Parallel: Hui Tzu was prime minister in the Liang State. Chuang Tzu went thither to visit him.

Someone remarked: 'Chuang Tzu has come. He wants to be minister in your place.'

Thereupon Hui Tzu was afraid, and searched all over the State for three days and three nights to find him.

Then Chuang Tzu went to see Hui Tzu and said: 'In the south there is a bird. It is a kind of phoenix. Do you know it? It started from the south sea to fly to the north sea. Except on the wu-t'ung tree it would not alight. It would eat nothing but the fruit of the bamboo, drink nothing but the purest spring water. An owl which had got the rotten carcass of a rat looked up as the phoenix flew by, and screeched. Are you not screeching at me over your kingdom of Liang?' (*Musings of a Chinese Mystic.*)

May 4th: Failure of pincer movement. Am unwilling to take sleeping pills which are used up by my friends. Benzedrine has no effect. Apathy, sluggishness and morning tears return, with the sense of 'All-is-lost' and the torture of two faces.

> '. . . et me laissez enfin
> Dans ce petit coin sombre avec mon noir chagrin.'

What is the use of useless suffering? Where is the escape? What can one ever make out of the *nessun maggior dolore*, the stranglehold of the past, the heart broken but never dead? 'Je le répète sans cesse, il n'y a qu'un malheur, celui d'être né.'

Is it possible to love any human being without being torn limb from limb? No one was ever made wretched in a brothel; there need be nothing angst-forming about the sexual act. Yet a face seen in the tube can destroy our peace for the rest of the day, and once a mutual attraction develops it is too late; for when sexual emotion increases to passion, then something starts growing which possesses a life of its own and which, easily though it can be destroyed by ignorance and neglect, will die in agony and go on dying after it is dead.

Like the bee its sting, the promiscuous leave behind them in each encounter something of themselves by which they are made to suffer.

It is the fear of middle-age in the young, of old-age in the middle-aged, which is the prime cause of infidelity, that infallible rejuvenator.

When young we are faithful to individuals, when older we grow more loyal to situations and to types. Confronted by such specimens, we seem to know all about them in an instant (which is true) and thus in spite of our decreasing charms we sweep them off their feet, for young people do not understand themselves, and fortunately for us, can still be hypnotized by those who do.

The mind has its own womb to which, baffled by speculation, it longs to return; the womb of Homer and Herodotus, of the pastoral world where men and gods were ruled by the same passions and where all personal problems seemed easy of solution. Then the womb fills with the Middle Ages, with the Popes, the Crusades and the Renaissance. For some it stretches to include the court of Charles II, or writers of the reign of Anne; it is the Hôtel des Grands Hommes, the Pantheon of mythical or historical figures who were masters of their surroundings, arbiters of their destinies and who went through life bundled together in well-documented cats'-cradles of loving intimacy.

Desire to smoke opium comes back. 'It dulls the moral sense.'

> In blackest noon the shutter falls
> That folds me from the slanting day.
> Before the night a Stranger calls
> Who strikes the fearless and the gay.
>
> There is no love however deep
> Can stay the verdict in his eye,
> There is no laugh however sweet
> Can drown the moment's passing sigh.

'L'obésité a une influence fâcheuse sur les deux sexes, en ce qu'elle nuit à la force et à la beauté . . . L'obésité nuit à la beauté en détruisant l'harmonie de proportion primitivement établie.'

'Proposer à des obèses de se lever le matin, c'est leur percer le coeur.' – BRILLAT-SAVARIN.

Imprisoned in every fat man a thin one is wildly signalling to be let out.

A lazy person, whatever the talents with which he starts forth, will have condemned himself to second-hand thoughts, and to second-rate friends.

Intense emotion, a mixture of relief and despair, at reading Sainte-Beuve's notebook *Mes Poisons*, and discovering 'This is me'. This Elegiac, as he styled himself, who quoted as his my favourite lines of Latin poetry, and who summed up happiness as reading Tibullus in the country 'avec une femme qu'on aime', who called himself 'le dernier des délicats', who loved, suffered and was disillusioned, and yet who recognized love as the true source of happiness, who was sceptical of everyone and everything, a smaller man though a better artist than his romantic contemporaries; who loved the eighteenth century but was never taken in, who hated puritans and prigs and pedants but knew how the wine of remorse is trodden from the grapes of pleasure, and who, with all his scholarship and self-analysis, was a Taoist at heart, respecting the essential mystery ('le vrai c'est le secret de quelques-uns') and what he calls his 'âme pastorale' – how deeply moving to listen to such a voice from the past which in the present becomes an inspiration! I feel like a cringing dog kicked about in a crowd, which, running down an alley, finds there silence, an apprehension of revelation, and then round a corner comes suddenly upon a huge dark doggy statue, a canine colossus from another age; awe-inspiring and faith-restoring, lending him courage and wishing him well.

WISDOM OF SAINTE-BEUVE 1804–69

'L'épicuréisme bien compris est la fin de tout.'

'Que m'importe, pourvu que je fasse *quelque chose* le matin, et que je sois *quelque part* le soir.'

'La saturation, il y a un moment où cela vient dans ce repas qu'on appelle la vie: il ne faut qu'une goutte alors pour faire déborder la coupe du dégoût.'

'Il y a des moments où la vie, le fond de la vie se rouvre au dedans ne nous comme une plaie qui saigne et ne veut pas se fermer.'

'Je suis resté avant tout un Elégiaque et un rêveur. Une grande et solide partie des jours, même aux années réputées graves, s'est passée pour moi dans les regrets stériles, dans les vagues désirs de l'attente, dans les mélancolies et les langueurs qui suivent le plaisir.'

'Je n'ai jamais conçu l'amour sans le mystère, et là où était le mystère, là pour moi déjà était l'amour.'

'Ne me demandez pas ce que j'aime et ce que je crois, n'allez pas au fond de mon âme.'

EPICTETUS: 'When God fails to provide for you, then He is giving the signal of retreat. He has opened the door and says to you, "Come" – "Where?" – "To nothing fearful, but thither whence you were born, to things friendly and akin to you, the Elements".'

Illumination: Tout mon mal vient de Paris. Rue Delambre, Quai d'Anjou, Rue de Vaugirard. Aïe!
　'Ahi tu passasti, eterno sospiro mio.'

The hard black ball of suicidal despair. The door is open.

NERVAL: 'Arrivé sur la Place de la Concorde, ma pensée était de me détruire.'

Bad today; the door is open, Paris 'ma plaie et ma fatalité.'

> 'The wind doth blow today my love
> And a few small drops of rain.'

As the lights in the penitentiary grow dim when the current is switched on for the electric chair, so we quiver in our hearts at a suicide, for there is no suicide for which all society is not responsible.

WISDOM OF CHAMFORT (1741–1794)

'L'indécision, l'anxiété sont à l'esprit et à l'âme ce que la question est au corps.'

'Les passions font *vivre* l'homme; la sagesse le fait seulement *durer*.'

'Quand on a été bien tourmenté, bien fatigué par sa propre sensibilité, on s'aperçoit qu'il faut vivre au jour le jour, oublier beaucoup, enfin *éponger la vie* à mesure qu'elle s'écoule.'

'Otez l'amour-propre de l'amour, il en reste trop peu de chose . . . l'amour, tel qu'il existe dans la société, n'est que l'échange de deux fantaisies et le contact de deux épidermes.'

'Un homme amoureux qui plaint l'homme raisonnable me paraît ressembler à un homme qui lit des contes de fées, et qui raille ceux qui lisent l'histoire.'

'Presque tous les hommes sont esclaves, par la raison que les Spartiates donnaient de la servitude des Perses, faute de savoir prononcer la syllabe *non*. Savoir prononcer ce mot et savoir vivre seul sont les deux seuls moyens de conserver sa liberté et son caractère.'

In the jungles of South America grows a trumpet flower fourteen inches deep, and there also is found a moth with a proboscis of the same length, the only creature able to penetrate to the honey and so procure the plant's fertilization. I, Palinurus, am such an orchid, growing daily more untempting as I await the Visitor who never comes.

> 'On a pour ma personne une aversion grande
> et quelqu'un de ces jours il faut que je me pende.'

Yet there are many who dare not kill themselves for fear of what the neighbours will say.

In the small hours when the acrid stench of existence rises like sewer gas from everything created, the emptiness of life seems more terrible than its misery. 'Inferum deplorata silentia' . . .

Streets of Paris, pray for me; beaches in the sun, pray for me; ghosts of the lemurs, intercede for me; plane-tree and laurel-rose, shade me; summer rain on quays of Toulon, wash me away.

A young man who wished to marry consulted his uncle, an old courtier of the days of Edward P. 'No one will want to marry you as you are,' said his uncle. 'You must get polish, your own particular aroma. Take a house, get to know about furniture and painting, buy the new books, listen to music, know whom to entertain and how to serve food and wine. Then you'll have something to offer, and all the right mothers will snap you up.' The young man did as he was told and some fifteen years later called again on the ancient week-ender of Fort Belvedere, whose old eyes now were seldom far from tears or alcohol.

'My house is perfect,' squeaked the brittle youth, 'the pictures are just right, the bindings of green morocco catch the light of the evening sun; my Louis *Seize* commodes belly out in the alcoves, there are

Malvern water and biscuits by every bed, and in each lavatory the toilet-paper, loosely arranged in scented sheets, is weighted down by a coloured stone. Nobody who dines with me gets quite drunk or goes home quite sober, nobody who comes to luncheon remembers afterwards anything they have said. I am at last perfectly eligible. What shall I do?'

The old Beau laughed and lit his third cigar. 'Just carry on,' he chuckled; 'I think we've got you out of the wood.'

Bournemouth. Branksome Towers Hotel. Steamy tropical atmosphere, avenues of villas hidden in evergreens; the hotel with a long vine-hung veranda and lawn sloping to the sea, which is visible through groups of leaning pine-trees. The pines here with their undergrowth of rhododendron and arbutus form the northernmost tip of the maritime forest which stretches from Hossegor, near Bayonne, by the Landes and Royan, the Ile d'Oleron, La Rochelle, the Vendean coast, La Baule and the Landes of Brittany, to expire at Bournemouth and Le Touquet. Over the sea lies the unspoilt, uninhabited paradise of the Isle of Purbeck, with its sandy beaches and chalk headlands.

Led by chance to discover the hanging foot-bridge over Alum Chine. Walking over the quivering planks I felt rooted, as in a nightmare, to the spot in the centre where the asphalt road lies directly underneath, a leaden water-snake uncurling through pines and giant hemlocks. To drag one's sticky feet across was like plunging through a bog. What a place to make away with oneself, or with some loved one!

L'ennui de la campagne; l'angoisse des villes. Chaque fois que je rentre à Londres, j'assiste à un crime.

I am now forced to admit that anxiety is my true condition, occasionally intruded on by work, pleasure, melancholy or despair.

STEKEL: 'All neurotics are at heart religious. Their ideal is pleasure without guilt. The neurotic is a criminal without the courage to commit

a crime . . . Every neurotic is an actor playing a particular scene. . . .
Anxiety is repressed desire. Every individual who cannot find a form of
sex-satisfaction adequate to himself suffers from an anxiety neurosis.
. . . It is the disease of a bad conscience.'

The mistake which is commonly made about neurotics is to suppose that they are interesting. It is not interesting to be always
unhappy, engrossed with oneself, ungrateful and malignant, and never
quite in touch with reality. Neurotics are heartless: as Baudelaire
wrote 'tout homme qui n'accepte pas les conditions de la vie vend son
âme'.

The true index of a man's character is the health of his wife.

'Aimer et haïr, ce n'est qu'éprouver avec une passion singulière l'être
d'un être.'

'Quand l'univers considère avec indifférence l'être que nous aimons, qui
est dans la vérité?' – JOUHANDEAU.

We think we recognize someone in passing. A moment later we see that
person. This pre-view was our entering on to their wavelength, into
their magnetic orbit.

Like the glow-worm; dowdy, minute, passive, yet full of mystery to the
poet, and passionate significance to its fellows; so everything and everybody eternally radiate their dim light for those who care to seek. The
strawberry hidden under the last leaf cries, 'Pick me'; the forgotten
book, in the forgotten bookshop, screams to be discovered. The old
house hidden in the hollow agitates itself violently at the approach of
its pre-destined admirer. Dead authors cry 'Read me'; dead friends cry
'Remember me'; dead ancestors cry, 'Unearth me'; dead places, 'Revisit
me'; and sympathetic spirits, living and dead, are trying continually
to enter into communion. Physical or intellectual attraction between
two people is a constant communication. Underneath the rational and

voluntary world is the involuntary, impulsive, integrated world, the world of Relation in which everything is one; where sympathy and antipathy are engrossed in their selective tug-of-war.

We learn a new word for the first time. Then we meet it again in a few hours. Why? Because words are living organisms impelled to a crystallizing process, to mysterious agglutinative matings at which the word-fancier is sometimes privileged to assist. The glow-worms light up. . . . The individual also is a moving mirror or screen which reflects in its motion an ever-changing panorama of thoughts, sensations, faces and places, and yet the screen is always being guided to reflect one film rather than another, always seeking a chosen *querencia*. In the warm sea of experience we blob around like plankton, we love-absorb or hate-avoid each other, or are absorbed, devoured and devouring. Yet we are no more free than the cells in a plant or the microbes in a drop of water, but are held firmly in tension by the pull of the future and the stress of the past.

'Du moment que je me fus assuré de ce point que j'étais soumis aux épreuves de l'initiation sacrée, une force invincible entra dans mon esprit. Je me jugeais un héros vivant sous le regard des dieux; tout dans la nature prenait des aspects nouveaux, et des voix secrètes sortaient de la plante, de l'arbre, des animaux, des plus humbles insectes, pour m'avertir et m'encourager. Le langage de mes compagnons avait des tours mystérieux dont je comprenais le sens, les objets sans forme et sans vie se prêtaient eux-mêmes aux calculs de mon esprit; des combinaisons de cailloux, des figures d'angles, de fentes ou d'ouvertures, des découpures de feuilles, des couleurs, des odeurs et des sons, je voyais ressortir des harmonies jusqu'alors inconnues. "Comment", me disais-je, "ai-je pu exister si longtemps hors de la nature et sans m'identifier à elle? Tout vit, tout agit, tout se correspond; les rayons magnétiques émanés de moi-même ou des autres traversent sans obstacle la chaîne infinie des choses créées; c'est un réseau transparent qui couvre le monde, et dont les fils déliés se communiquent de proche en proche aux planètes et aux étoiles." Captif en ce moment sur la terre, je m'entretiens avec le choeur des astres, qui prend part à mes joies et à mes douleurs!' – G. DE NERVAL: *Aurélia.* *

In the break-up of religions and creeds there is but one deity whose worshippers have multiplied without a set-back. The Sun. In a few years there will be such a rush towards this supreme anaesthetic that Scotland will have poured itself into Southern England, Canada into the U.S.A., the U.S.A. have shrunk to Florida, California and New Mexico, while Southern Englanders will have migrated to the Mediterranean, if it still is warm enough. The temperate zone, especially for women, is becoming uninhabitable. Let us leave England to retired Generals and culture-diffusionists, goose-fleshed politicians and bureaucrats, while the rest of us heliotropes cluster nearer to the great bronze disk of church-emptying Apollo, hardener of heart and skin.

July: Once more the bold Dragonfly of pleasure has brushed me with its wing. Divine Sainte-Beuve – 'L'épicuréisme bien compris' – and Hume, the Northern Epicurus. Late June, July and early August – fruit-eating months when the English become callous, pleasure-ridden, amorous and Elizabethan. It is necessary.

After the long suicidal winter Pleasure comes to rescue us from the desert island of the ego, and give us two months' leave. Good-bye sick Pascal and his mouldy troupe; gaunt Kierkegaard, hunch-backed Leopardi, wheezing Proust and limping Epictetus with his Open Door! Midsummer greetings to La Fontaine, Congreve, Aristippus, Horace and Voltaire! Good-bye morning tears, 'All-is-lost', never-again, doubt, despair! Welcome cheese-breathing hang-overs, tipsy mornings for

* This piece, written by Nerval in his madness, resembles a late landscape of Van Gogh. The intense associations of atomical pantheism become what mental doctors call 'Delusions of Reference'. In manic elation communication seems to exist between inanimate objects and the Observer. Flowers signal to him, stones cry out, and all nature approves. In suicidal depression the same phenomenon appears, but in this case nature seems to pass a vote of censure; inanimate objects urge the Observer to finish it properly this time. Are both fatigue and ecstasy poisons which distort our relation to external reality? Or do they liberate deep-buried instinctive perceptions of relationships to which normally we are blind?

gargling poetry, asparagus afternoons, gull's-egg evenings, affection slopping over into gossip, who-was-there's, and ring-a-ling! Taoism at last rewarded! 'Flower o' the Quince', . . . Hour of the Broad Bean.

If all the world loved pleasure as much as Palinurus there would be no wars.

THE PLAY-BOY PERMIT

– I –

'Le plaisir crée une franc-maçonnerie charmante. Ceux qui y sont profès se reconnaissent d'un clin d'oeil, s'entendent sans avoir besoin de paroles, et il se passe là de ces choses imprévues, sans prélude et sans suites, de ces hasards de rencontre et de mystère qui échappent au récit, mais qui remplissent l'imagination et qui sont un des enchantements de la vie. Ceux qui y ont goûté n'en veulent plus d'autres.' – SAINTE BEUVE.

– II –

'Les hommes trouveront toujours que la chose la plus sérieuse de leur existence, c'est jouir.' – FLAUBERT.

Dining-out is a vice, a dissipation of spirit punished by remorse. We eat, drink and talk a bit too much, abuse our friends, belch out our literary preferences, are egged on by accomplices in the audience to acts of mental exhibitionism. Such evenings cannot fail to diminish those who take part in them. They end on Monkey Hill.

Society: A perfect dinner-party for sixteen. Each person as carefully chosen as an instrument in an orchestra – yet how many of the guests would rather be engaged that evening in tête-à-tête? Or be glad to leave early for a brothel?

MESSAGE FROM THE ID

'If you would collect women instead of books, I think I could help you.'

'And there came thunder and lightning and pestilence and famine and the people were sore afraid. And the Lord spake out of the tempest and out of the whirlwind and the earth quaked and all the people trembled with fear, and the Lord cried with a mighty voice: "When thou goest away for weekends thou shalt not stay over Monday; thou shalt not sit long over lunch, nor take taxis, nor buy books; thou shalt travel third class, not first; neither shalt thou drink wine nor giggle nor spoon; thou shalt sorrow and sweat wherever thou goest – for I the Lord thy God am a jealous God, and behold I will crush thee as a slimy worm." And there was silence over the earth and the land lay barren a thousand years.'

Anxiety again, *en grande tenue*. The two faces. Everything connected with them is excruciating: people, places, sounds, smells, habits. Old letters coil up and explode like land-mines, inscriptions in books pronounce life-sentences of betrayal, gramophone records screech from the grave; even the harmless sunbeams and the green surge of summer out of doors are decoys which trap the heart in ambush at some sultry corner. *Da dextram misero!* O, never to have met, or never to have parted! Living in the present (the only escape) has to be contrived by drugs, by injections of work or pleasure, or by the giving 'which plays you least false'. The past is a festering wound; the present the compress vainly applied, painfully torn off. Paris, Chelsea, Cannes – *misère!* We are all serving a life-sentence in the dungeon of self.

Sainte-Beuve's poem, 'Dans l'île Saint-Louis.' He knew.

Imagination = nostalgia for the past, the absent; it is the liquid solution in which art develops the snapshots of reality. The artist secretes nostalgia round life, as worms plaster their tunnels, as caterpillars spin their cocoons or as sea-swallows masticate their nests. Art without imagination is as life without hope.

Egotism sucks us down like the law of gravity. In the small hours the law of gravity is somewhat weakened, we are less subject to it, and even the egotism of the earth, revolving on its axis, seems to fade. As egotism subsides we grow more conscious of the meagre foundations of our lives, the true nature of the Authorities whom we try to please, and by whom we wish to be loved – those who feed our lost selves with their admiration.

For a dark play-girl in a night-club I have pined away, for a dead school boy, for a bright angel-vixen I have wept in vain. If this thoughtless woman were to die there would be nothing to live for, if this faithless girl forgot me there would be no one for whom to write. These two unseen and otherwise occupied figures compose the fragile arch of my being and constitute a Tribunal which they have long ceased to attend.

'The self-torments of melancholiacs, which are without doubt pleasurable, signify a gratification of sadistic tendencies and of hate, both of which relate to an object and in this way have both been turned round upon the self. In the end the sufferers usually succeed in taking revenge, by the circuitous path of self-punishment, on the original object who occasioned the injury and who is usually to be found in their near neighbourhood. No neurotic harbours thoughts of suicide which are not murderous impulses against others redirected upon himself.' – FREUD.

'Damnatae noctes, et vos vada lenta paludes . . .'

The cycle of the hours. 'The Lars and Lemures moan with midnight plaint.' 1 a.m.: Anger turns to Misery. 2 a.m.: Misery to Panic. The low tide and nadir of hope about 2 a.m. to 4. Magical Euphoria always 4 a.m. to 6 – the thalamic 'All Clear'; Peace and Certainty arrive through Despair. All morning the tide of confidence rolls in with its high water of egotism from 2 p.m. to 3. (We are farthest then from the idea of death as in the other small hours we are nearest.) Momentary depression at sunset, though often at my best from 6 o'clock to 10. Then the bilges begin to empty.

Thought can be made to take certain liberties by artificial stimulation of the brain. The cortex is a machine for thinking. It can be revved up, slowed down, choked, fed various types of fuel according to the thought it is required to produce. When the mixture is too rich, as in the small hours, the engine pinks, whence 'Flight of Ideas'.

Thus tea, coffee, alcohol stimulate.

So do heights, wet days, south-west gales, hotel bedrooms in Paris and windows looking over harbours. Also snow, frost, electric bells outside cinemas at night, sex-life and fever.

Cigars, tisanes, long draughts of water or fruit-juice have a clearing, calming effect. They rev down the motor and overcome stoppages. So also do sitting still, relaxing climates, luxury, constipation, music, sunbathing, hang-overs, listening to fountains, waves and waterfalls.

A thorough knowledge of opium, Benzedrine, phosphorus, and other drugs should make it possible for us to feed the brain the right mixture according to the effect desired; whether we contemplate a work of the imagination (putting ideas into our heads) or of the intellect (analysis, memory, reasoning).

When we decide to write, we should first plan the proportions involved. Proportions of heart and head of judgement and imagination. 'A peach of an essay', 'a melon of a poem', 'a quince of a book' – we must let ourselves be impregnated by an archetypal form. Then we should treat the personality with the right mixture till the glaze (style) is suitable – 'for my philosophical novel with a milligramme of nostalgia, I am taking ephedrine twice a week, opium once, with a little mescaline to loosen my imagery, and massaging of the nape of the neck to stimulate the thalamus after the monthly orgy. I am writing two-thirds standing up in the early morning, one third lying down in the afternoon. My supervisor is a Jungian.'

LAST WORDS ON OPIUM-READING

'L'opium est la seule substance végétale qui nous communiqué l'état végétal. Par lui nous avons une idée de cette autre vitesse des plantes.'

'L'opium apprivoisé adoucira le mal des villes.' – COCTEAU.

'Here were the hopes which blossom in the paths of life reconciled with the peace which is in the grave.' – DE QUINCEY.

Others merely live; I vegetate.

O sacred solitary empty mornings, tranquil meditations – fruit of book-case and clock-tick, of note-book and arm-chair; golden and rewarding silence, influence of sun-dappled plane-trees, far-off noises of birds and horses, possession beyond price of a few cubic feet of air and some hours of leisure! This vacuum of peace is the state from which art should proceed, for art is made by the alone for the alone, and now this cerulean atmosphere, which we should be able to take for granted, has become an unattainable end.

The reward of art is not fame or success but intoxication: that is why so many bad artists are unable to live without it. What fathers would I like to vindicate? Who, on reading Palinurus in the Asphodel Club will say, 'I told you so'? Aristippus, Horace, Tibullus, Montaigne, Saint Flaubert and Sainte-Beuve. But Pascal? He frightens me – and Chamfort? I don't think so.

I have much more in common with Chamfort than with Pascal; sometimes I feel that I was Chamfort, for there is nothing of his that I might not with luck have written, yet it is by reading the thoughts of Pascal, which I could never have written, that I change and grow. Literary charm, arising out of the desire to please, excludes those flights of intellectual power which are so much more rewarding than pleasure.

THE PREDICAMENT OF CHAMFORT, 1741–94

His mother was a 'dame de compagnie', his father unknown, and he was christened merely 'Nicolas'. Mother and son came from Auvergne to Paris where Nicolas was a brilliant schoolboy. After dallying with the Church, he plunged into the world of letters. A love-child, Chamfort was swept to success by the favours of women, a success which exhausted him physically and led to serious disorders; however, he obtained well-paid sinecures, literary prizes, and stage successes through his wit, his gallantry, and the love of his friends, and then at forty retired to Boileau's old home at Auteuil; there he fell in love with a 'dame de compagnie' of the Duchesse du Maine, aged forty-eight, who died six months later. After her loss he returned to Paris to become the cynical jester and licensed darling of the Court. 'My sentiments are republican, yet I live with courtiers. I love poverty, my friends are all rich; I believe that illusions are a necessary luxury of life, yet I live without any; I believe that passions are more useful to us than reason, yet I have destroyed my capacity for feeling.' When the Revolution broke out, Chamfort, a genuine republican, sided with his friend and admirer Mirabeau. He spoke at street corners and was one of the first to enter the Bastille. Though he lost all his pensions he plunged with enthusiasm into politics and contributed such slogans as 'Guerre aux châteaux, Paix aux chaumières'! and 'Moi, tout; le reste rien! Voilà le despotisme. Moi, c'est un autre; un autre c'est moi: voilà la démocratie'. In spite of a warning that his sallies would not be tolerated as indulgently as under the old regime, he soon began to mimic and satirize the new personages of the Revolution. In 1793 he sealed his fate with his description of Jacobin ethics: 'Sois mon frère ou je te tue.' 'I am not afraid,' he said, 'Je n'ai pas peur; n'ai-je pas toujours marché au premier rang de la phalange républicaine?' Denounced anonymously, he was taken to prison. He was released, but almost immediately rearrested. Rather than lose his liberty at the hands of the Party to which he knew he belonged, he made an excuse to leave the room, then shot himself. The bullet broke his nose and went into his eye. He next tried to cut his throat with a razor. He partially recovered from his wounds, but died soon afterwards from pneumonia. His last words were: 'Je m'en vais enfin de ce monde, où il faut que le coeur se brise ou se bronze'.

The complexity of Chamfort's character would seem to be due to his temperament as a love-child; he transmuted his passionate love for his mother into a general desire for affection which he concentrated at last on his wife, who resembled his mother. With this need for love went that equally violent feeling, so familiar to bastards, of a grievance against society. The warmth of his affections combined with his sense of injustice and his clear mind to propel him to the crest of the Revolution, but he was one of those observers who cannot blind themselves to the defects of men who logically carry out an ideal in action. Though he himself believed in their cause, he was a philosopher without hope and without pity.* Physically Chamfort was tall and handsome, an Adonis in youth, pale and exhausted in later life; he was a man who lived in spurts, and who seemed kept alive by the fire of his intelligence. Mirabeau called him 'noble et digne' and admired his 'tête électrique', Chateaubriand praised his cold blue eye. His predicament is one with which we are all familiar, and there is every danger that it will soon become only too common; that of the revolutionary whose manners and way of life are attached to the old regime, whose ideals and loyalties belong to the new, and who by a kind of courageous exhibitionism is impelled to tell the truth about both, and to expect from the commissars of King Stork the same admiration for his sallies as they receive from the courtiers of King Log. Most lovable of Chamfort's sayings which, remarkable though they are for their splenetic violence, are apt to be irritating through an excess of point, a somewhat vulgar urbanity, is his final outburst, just after he had attempted his life. He is speaking to a friend in his usual quiet tones of familiar irony: 'Que voulez-vous? Voilà ce que c'est que d'être maladroit de la main: on ne réussit à rien, pas même à se tuer.' He began to explain how, instead of blowing out his brains, he had punctured his eye and the lower part of his forehead, then, instead of cutting his throat, he had gashed his neck and even hacked his chest without succeeding in stabbing his heart. 'Enfin,' he concludes, 'je me suis souvenu de Sénèque, et, en l'honneur de Sénèque, j'ai voulu m'ouvrir les veines;

---

* 'All literature might be ransacked in vain for a more repulsive saying than this (of Chamfort): "A man must swallow a toad every morning if he wishes to be sure of finding nothing still more disgusting before the day is over".' – MORLEY: *Studies of Literature*, p. 95.

mais il était riche, lui; il avait tout à souhait, un bain bien chaud, enfin toutes ses aises; moi, je suis un pauvre diable, je n'ai rien de tout cela. Je me suis fait un mal horrible, et me voilà encore; mais j'ai la balle dans la tête, c'est là le principal. Un peu plus tôt, un peu plus tard, voilà tout.'

WISDOM OF CHAMFORT II

C'est un grand malheur de perdre, par notre caractère, les droits que nos talents nous donnent sur la société.

Il y a une certaine énergie ardente, mère ou compagne nécessaire de telle espèce de talents, laquelle pour l'ordinaire condamne ceux qui les possèdent au malheur. . . . C'est une âpreté dévorante dont ils ne sont pas maîtres et qui les rend très-odieux.

En renonçant au monde et à la fortune, j'ai trouvé le bonheur, le calme, la santé, même la richesse; et, en dépit du proverbe, je m'aperçois que 'qui quitte la partie la gagne'.

La vie contemplative est souvent misérable. Il faut agir davantage, penser moins, et ne pas se regarder vivre.

Il faut recommencer la société humaine.

Les fléaux physiques et les calamités de la nature humaine ont rendu la société nécessaire. La société a ajouté aux malheurs de la nature. Les inconvénients de la société ont amené la nécessité du gouvernement, et le gouvernement ajoute aux malheurs de la société. Voilà l'histoire de la nature humaine.

Les pauvres sont les nègres de l'Europe.

Quand un homme et une femme ont l'un pour l'autre une passion violente, il me semble toujours que . . . les deux amants sont l'un à l'autre *de par la nature*, qu'ils s'appartiennent *de droit divin*.

'Les prétentions sont une source de peines, et l'époque du bonheur de la vie commence au moment où elles finissent.'

'La pensée console de tout.'

Turning to see what Sainte-Beuve thinks of Chamfort, how the old love will greet the new, I find him somewhat severe, the Superego judging the Ego. One would expect him to feel more sympathy for a man as melancholy and disillusioned as he, to whom like himself, people were 'as those insects whose transparent tissue lets us see the veins and all the different shades of the blood'; instead he is over-critical and a little alarmed by him. He admits that Chamfort's aphorisms are like 'des flèches acérées qui arrivent brusquement et sifflent encore', but he reproaches him with being a bachelor, and therefore a recluse on whom Nature took her revenge. With equivocal serenity this other bachelor, the dubious monk of letters of the Rue de Montparnasse, finds fault with Chamfort for two of his maxims – 'Je ne veux point me marier, dans la crainte d'avoir un fils qui me ressemble', and 'Quiconque n'est pas misanthrope à quarante ans n'a jamais aimé les hommes'.

Unwillingly one has to admit the justice of Sainte-Beuve's profound, stern, yet not unsympathetic analysis. Compared to him, Chamfort is a Byronic adolescent. 'J'ai du Tacite dans la tête et du Tibulle dans le coeur,' writes Chamfort. 'Ni le Tibulle ni le Tacite,' adds Sainte-Beuve, 'n'ont pu en sortir pour la postérité'. What makes Sainte-Beuve his superior? He detects Chamfort's tragedy: that he was a moralist whose credentials have never quite been accepted, that there is too much egotism in his judgements (which reflect the guilty self-hatred of those who know that they are neglecting their talent through indolence and hedonism). Chamfort detested humanity, but, unlike Sainte-Beuve, he found no compensation in a love for nature. Chamfort was a classical pagan, Sainte-Beuve a double-minded critic who had passed through the mystical experience and the Romantic Movement to a scepticism infinitely enriched by both.

Another view: 'I believe only in French culture, and I regard everything else in Europe which calls itself culture as a misunderstanding. . . . When one reads Montaigne, La Rochefoucauld, Vauvenargues and Chamfort, one is nearer to antiquity than with any group of authors in any other nation.' – NIETZSCHE.

And with Baudelaire, Flaubert, Sainte-Beuve, nearer to modernity.

Those who are consumed with curiosity about other people but who do not love them should write maxims, for no one can become a novelist who does not love his fellow-men. Being contaminated myself by oriental philosophy, I cannot take people seriously. (Sabba dukka! 'In those countries human life is but a weed.') They all seem replaceable except for the few who carry away sections of our own selves which cannot be replaced. Once we believe that the ego is like a cell which over-asserts itself and causes cancer, the cancer of developing at the expense of society or at the expense of the self's natural harmony with the order of things, a harmony which it drowns by its own din, then we can only dislike the pushing, confident extroverts who, with their petty ambitions, form the backbone of fiction. If we have no use for the idiosyncrasies of minor personalities, then we must fight shy of the novel, which will end by seeming as grotesque to us as the portrait of an alderman to a Tibetan Lama.

> 'When the bells justle in the tower
> The hollow night amid,
> Then on my tongue the taste is sour
> Of all I ever did.'

Vanished symptoms of health: early rising, early shaving, briskness in lavatory and bath, alacrity in crossing streets, care for personal appearance, horror of possessions, indifference to newspapers, kindness to strangers, *Folie des Maures.*

August 7th: the first autumn day. For once I have lived in the present! Walked to the book-shop at closing time. Raining. A girl tried to get into the shop, but the doors were bolted. Went out and followed her past the Zwemmer Gallery and through the streets towards St Giles', only to lose her by the Cambridge Theatre, cursing the upbringing which after all these years has left me unable to address a stranger. Much disturbed by the incident, for this girl, with her high fore-head, her pointed nose, her full lips and fine eyes, her dark hair and her unhappy and sullen expression, personified both beauty and intelli-gence in distress. She was bare-legged, and wore sandals, a green corduroy suit and a linen coat. With an intolerable sense of frustration I watched her out of sight: 'o toi que j'eusse aimée'.

From the violent character of this encounter I understood a little more about the nature of my emotions.

I. To fall immediately in love there has to be what Sainte-Beuve called '*le mystère*'. In my case the mystery must take the form of a rejection of the industrial system and of the twentieth century. It is an aloofness, a suggestion of the primitive that I crave. Hence the appeal of sandals, as they alone permit human beings to hold themselves naturally. This air of aloofness is incompatible with happiness since it springs from a feeling of isolation, a sense of hostility and rebellion against society which cannot in these days make for contentment. Indeed, I think that most of the beauty of women evaporates when they achieve domestic happiness at the price of their independence.

II. This primitive and untamed expression is not enough; it must go with an interest in the arts, especially in modern painting and sur-realism. The gipsy-look must correspond to the chaos of our times, to the spiritual wildness of modern art. This taste is shared, I believe, by others who have made their peace with society. We are captivated by the feminine shadows of the selves we might have been; in my case by that counterpart of the romantic writer who might have had the courage to reject society and to accept poverty for the sake of the development of his true personality. Now when I see such beings I hope that by union with them I can somehow be freed from these short-comings. Hence the recurrent longing to forsake external reality for a dream and to plunge into a ritual flight.

Some fall in love with women who are rich, aristocratic or stupid. I am attracted by those who mysteriously hold out a promise of the integrity which I have lost; unsubdued daughters of Isis, beautiful as night, tumultuous as the moon-stirred Atlantic.*

III. Recognition takes place at the turn of the year and must be followed at once by a ritual flight, and consummation in a cave.

To banish the rainy evening, the dripping plane-trees, the depression of Fitzroy and Charlotte Streets, and the afternoon's disappointment, I asked some friends round to drink a bottle of rum. Since old friends are almost indistinguishable from enemies, we talked about each other's vices. One said the vice of Palinurus was inconstancy. But is it not rather constancy? Fidelity to the experience of abandoning all the world for a new face with its invitation to ecstasy? Or is that but one more autumn ruse for self-destruction?

> 'Shall I believe the *Syren* South again
> And, oft-betray'd, not know the Monster Main?'

* Isis was represented as the moon rising from the sea: 'ista luce feminea collustrans cuncta moenia et udis ignibus nutriens laeta semina'. – APULEIUS. Met. XI.

Part Three: La Clé des Chants

ILLUMINATION: 'La mélancolie elle-même n'est qu'un souvenir qui s'ignore.' – FLAUBERT.

The Sun warms out old memories, the Mist exhumes others, as each brings out the fragrance of trees or the smell of ferns.

First faint impression of urban autumn. There are memories which are brought back into play by certain sounds, smells or changes in temperature; like those tunes which recur on the brain at a given time of year. With the first leaves being swept up in the square, the first misty morning, the first yellowing of the planes, I remember Paris and all the excitement of looking for autumn lodgings in a hotel. Streets round the Rue de l'Université, Rue Jacob, Rue de Bourgogne and Rue de Beaune, with their hotel signs and entrances and their concierges walled in by steamer-trunks. Stuffy salons full of novels by Edith Wharton, purple wall-paper which later we grow to hate as we lie in bed with grippe, chintz screens round the bidets, high grey panelling with cupboards four inches deep. . . .

Hôtel de l'Université for American college girls, Hôtel de Londres with its chestnut tree in the courtyard, Hôtel Jacob for wasting much time; Hôtel de Savoie, Hôtel Delambre, Hôtel de la Louisiane; central-heated Stations of the Cross: names that stir the lees within me.

For an angora pullover, for a red scarf, for a red beret and some brown shoes I am bleeding to death; my heart is dry as a kidney.

Peeling off the kilometres to the tune of 'Blue Skies', sizzling down the long black liquid reaches of Nationale Sept, the plane trees going sha-sha-sha through the open window, the windscreen yellowing with crushed midges, she with the Michelin beside me, a handkerchief binding her hair . . .

'Le coeur a ses raisons' – and so have rheumatism and 'flu. The soles of the feet and nape of the neck remember the embrace of the Mediterranean, pale water streaked with sapphirine sea-shadow, translucent under the Esterel.

Paris afternoons; the quiet of hotel bedroom and of empty lounge; the bed covered with clothes and magazines, the *Chicago Tribune*, the *Semaine à Paris*, programmes of the Pagoda Cinema, The Ursulines, Studio Vingt-huit; faraway cries of 'voici *l'Intran*' answered by the honking of horns . . .

Early morning on the Mediterranean: bright air resinous with Aleppo pine, water spraying over the gleaming tarmac of the Route Nationale and darkly reflecting the spring-summer green of the planes; swifts wheeling round the oleanders, waiters unpiling the wicker chairs and scrubbing the café tables; armfuls of carnations on the flower-stalls, pyramids of aubergines and lemons, *rascasses* on the fishmonger's slab goggling among the wine-dark urchins; smell of brioches from the bakeries, sound of reed curtains jingling in the barber shops, clang of the tin kiosk opening for *Le Petit Var*. Rope-soles warming up on the cobbles by the harbour where the *Jean d'Agrève* prepares for a trip to the Islands and the Annamese boy scrubs her brass. Now cooks from many yachts step ashore with their market-baskets, one-eyed cats scrounge among the fish-heads, while the hot sun refracts the dancing sea-glitter on the café awnings, and the sea becomes a green gin-fizz of stillness in whose depth a quiver of sprats charges and counter-charges in the pleasure of fishes.

Dead leaves, coffee grounds, grenadine, tabac Maryland, mental expectation – perfumes of the Nord-Sud; autumn arrivals at Pigalle, or sorties from Notre-Dame-des-Champs into the lights of Montparnasse, where the chestnuts, glowing red by the métro entrance, live in a warmer climate than other trees. . . .

Our memories are card-indexes consulted, and then put back in disorder by authorities whom we do not control.

Back-streets of Cannes: tuberoses in the window, book-shops over the railway bridge which we comb for old memoirs and detective stories, while the cushions of the car deflate in the afternoon sun. *Petit Marseillais, Eclaireur de Nice*: head-lines about the Spanish war soaked in sun-bathing oil, torn maps, wet bathing-dresses wrapped in towels – and now we bring home memoirs, detective stories, tuberoses, round the dangerous corner of the Rue d'Antibes and down the coast road by the milky evening sea.

The boredom of Sunday afternoons, which drove de Quincey to smoke opium, also gave birth to surrealism: hours propitious for making bombs.

August 15th: Wet Sunday recalling many others. 'Fantômes de Trouville', 'Sea-scape with frieze of girls'.

Beaches of the West: Houlgate. Royan. Saint-Jean-de-Luz. A red digue, colour of porphyry. In the shops are hanging buckets, toy yachts, shrimping-nets and string-bags enclosing rubber balls with a dull bloom, of the same porphyry colour. Children in the shop are choosing sandals and gym-shoes, girls are walking arm-in-arm along the promenade; the west wind from the sea spatters the jetty stones with rain; old bills of casino galas with their faded 'Attractions' roll flapping among the tamarisks. Prowling from the Marquise de Sévigné tea room to the Potinière bar, dark and smelling of gin, we lie in wait for one more glimpse of the sea-side girls in their impregnable adolescence – before the Atlantic sun fades angrily over enormous sands, coloured like the under-belly of soles.

Saint-Jean-de-Luz. Buying a melon in the morning market and eating it for breakfast in a café on the Bidassoa; pursuing macintoshes, berets and strands of wet curl round the sea-wall in the rain. Maize and pimento, light-footed Basques with round lean faces dancing Fandango and Arin-Arin, playing pelota against the church wall while huge green sunsets agonize through plate-glass windows. Angoisse des digues. . . .

The greatness of Hemingway is in that he alone of living writers has saturated his books with the memory of physical pleasure, with sunshine and salt water, with food, wine and making love, and with the remorse which is the shadow of that sun.

August 30th: Morning tears return; spirits at their lowest ebb. Approaching forty, sense of total failure: not a writer but a ham actor whose performance is clotted with egotism; dust and ashes; 'brilliant' – that is, not worth doing. Never have I made that extra effort to live according to reality which alone makes good writing possible: hence the manic-depressiveness of my work – which is either bright, cruel and superficial; or pessimistic; moth-eaten with self-pity.

Whatever I have written always appears dated – except the lines which I have just set down. These seem to be quite different, never subject to the same law, and yet what dates in them does not vary with each period but remains the same: a kind of auto-intoxication which is brought out by the act of writing.

Approaching forty, I am about to heave my carcass of vanity, boredom, guilt and remorse into another decade.

> Lusisti satis, edisti satis, atque bibisti
> Tempus abire tibi est.

Both my happiness and my unhappiness I owe to the love of pleasure; of sex, travel, reading, conversation (hearing myself talk), food, drink, cigars and lying in warm water.

Reality is what remains when these pleasures, together with hope for the future, regret for the past, vanity of the present, and all that composes the aroma of the self are pumped out of the air-bubble in which I live.

When we have ceased to love the stench of the human animal, either in others or in ourselves, then are we condemned to misery, and clear thinking begins. 'La seule réalité, c'est le souci (*sorge*) dans toute l'échelle des êtres. Pour l'homme perdu dans le monde et ses divertissements, ce souci est une peur brève et fuyante. Mais que cette peur prenne conscience d'elle-même et elle devient l'angoisse (*angst*), climat perpetuel de l'homme lucide "dans lequel existence se retrouve." '
— HEIDEGGER.

O, qu'elle est belle l'étoile de mer! The starfish sprawling on Atlantic beaches streaked with shallow pools; ridges of mackerel sand taut under the bare foot; the sun on the spilt water-beads which mark the tide by streamers of bladder-wrack and melting jelly-fish; all these will return and the leisure to enjoy them, to paddle under a razor-shell sky among rocks where transparent prawns lean up against the weed like old men reading in a public library, feathering with their legs and feelers, and rocketing backwards with a flick of the tail. And there will be time to observe the blenny where it lies half out of the water, the hermit-crabs and anemones, the pin-pointed urchins, and sea-slugs on their green sea-salad, the swaying zoster.

> O litus vita mihi dulcius, O mare! felix
> qui licet ad terras ire subinde meas!

Midnight harbours of France, O rain-swept lights on the quay!

Approaching forty, a singular dream in which I almost grasped the meaning and understood the nature of what it is that wastes in wasted time.

Present pleasure kills time, it is like sleep, a harmless anaesthetic: harmless when once we have recognized that our life is so painful as to need what otherwise must distil only guilt and remorse. If, however, we understand that the love of pleasure can be increased or decreased according to need, then as the pleasure fades into the past it will leave behind only a sense of nostalgia, and this nostalgia can be converted into art, and, once so converted, all trace of guilt attaching to the pleasure is washed away.

Art is memory: memory is re-enacted desire.

The body remembers past pleasures and on being made aware of them, floods the mind with sweetness. Thus the smell of sun-warmed pine-needles and the bloom on ripe whortleberries reopen the file marked Kitzbühel and bring back the lake with its warm muddy water, its raft conversations and pink water-lilies; the drives over white Alpine roads through the black fir-woods or the walks over meadows where runnels of water sing in wooden troughs beside the châlets. Remembering all these communicates several varieties of pleasure; those which, like lying in a thick peat-bath on a rainy evening, are purely sensual, which are social like playing bridge in the afternoon, or intellectual like talking to Pierre; pleasures of vanity like flirting in the Tiefenbrünner, or buying local jackets and *lederhosen* – and ever present, as the bald peak of the Kitz-bühlerhorn, the unpunished pleasures of health; of mountain air, good food and natural living. The Wooden Age, where beds and walls and doors and houses are made of pine-logs, where nights are always cold, mornings noisy with rivers and cow-bells, and existence balsam-sharp.

Today my deepest wish is to go to sleep for six months, if not for ever; it is an admission that life has become almost unendurable, and that I must look to pleasure as a waking substitute for sleep. We cannot sleep twenty-four hours a day, but we can at least make sleep and pleasure alternate, if once we admit that, like the deep narcotic treatment for nervous breakdown, they are remedies only for the sick. Reality, union with reality, is the true state of the soul when confident and healthy. Thus when Pope wrote:

> 'So slow the unprofitable Moments roll
> That lock up all the Functions of my soul;
> That keep me from Myself;'

he stated a profound truth. Unreality is what keeps us from ourselves, and most pleasures are unreal.

In the dream of approaching forty I saw myself as about to die and realized that I was no longer myself, but a creature inhabited entirely by parasites, as a caterpillar is occupied by the grubs of the ichneumon fly. Gin, whisky, sloth, fear, guilt, tobacco, had made themselves my inquilines; alcohol sloshed about within, while tendrils of melon and vine grew out of ears and nostrils; my mind was a worn gramophone record, my true self was such a ruin as to seem non-existent, and all this had happened in the last three years.

Approaching forty. A glimpse of wisdom. 'Live in the present, Palinurus; you are too unbalanced to brood upon the past. One day you will remember nothing but its pleasures; now you must force it out of your mind.'

> 'The twelvemonth and a day being up,
>   The dead began to speak:
> "Oh who sits weeping on my grave,
>   And will not let me sleep?" –
>
> ' " 'Tis I, my love, sits on your grave,
>   And will not let you sleep;
> For I crave one kiss of your clay-cold lips,
>   And that is all I seek." –
>
> ' "You crave one kiss of my clay-cold lips;
>   But my breath smells earthy strong;
> If you have one kiss of my clay-cold lips,
>   Your time will not be long.
>
> ' " 'Tis down in yonder garden green,
>   Love, where we used to walk,
> The finest flower that ere was seen
>   Is wither'd to a stalk.

' "The stalk is wither'd dry, my love
So will our hearts decay;
So make yourself content, my love,
Till God calls you away." '*

Paris afternoons: Book-stalls along the quais, with old prints that nobody wants, naughty novels corseted in cellophane; animal shops on the Quai de Gesvres; ferrets, squirming and clucking in the straw, with red eyes and little yawns which reveal their fine white teeth; marmosets chattering over their stump of rotten banana, moulting parrots; the mysterious ailing nocturnal creature that one is always tempted to buy – 'c'est un binturong, monsieur' – and then the walk back over the bridges; poplar leaves eddying in the yellow river; misty black-and-grey streets of the Left Bank; discreet shops full of *bibelots*, bad modern paintings, Empire clocks.

Disorder of the hotel bedroom; books, paintings, clothes and red plush; shadows lengthening, the desirable afternoon sleep with its bewildering nightmare-starts and awakenings, its flash-backs to the past. Then the purple Neon lights shining in at the window and the concierge on the telephone: 'Il y a quelqu'un en bas qui vous demande'. 'Voulez-vous lui dire de monter.'

In youth the animal world obsessed me; I saw life through creatures which were in a state of grace, creatures without remorse, without duties, without a past or a future, which owned nothing but the intense present, and their eternal rhythm of hunger, sleep and play. The ringtailed lemurs and their reverence for the sun, their leaps through the air and howls of loneliness, were dark Immortals of a primitive race; the ferrets with their passionate blood-thirst and their tunnelling mania; the beautiful mute genette, the pine-marten, the racoons, the pitiful coati, the dying ocelot, the slow loris – even the animals which I never had, the beaver, otter, palm-civet and linsang – these bright-fanged, saffron-throated aristocrats held the secret of life for me; they were clues to an

* *Oxford Book of Ballads*: 'The Unquiet Grave'.

existence without thought, guilt or ugliness wherein all was grace, appetite, and immediate sensation: Impressionist masterpieces which Nature flung upon the canvas of a day.

Now I care only for the Vegetable world; my daydreams are no longer of otter-pools and sunny lemurariums, but of slobbering melons, downy quinces and dew-dusted nectarines. I feel that fruit trees are an even stranger form of life, and therefore more rewarding. Nothing is so alien, so unexpected in a tree as its fruit, and yet by the fruit it is known; leaves, height and blossom are sacrificed to it; so by thinking, reading and maintaining an inner calm we too mature and ripen until the life which once flowered in such careless profusion is concentrated into husks, husks which, like pomegranates or tomatoes on our window-sills, continue to mellow long after the leaves have fallen and the plant that bore them has rotted to the ground.

'Good is the passive that obeys reason. Evil is the active springing from energy.' – BLAKE. It is more important, in fact, to be good than to do good because being, rather than doing, is the state which keeps us in tune with the order of things. Hence Pascal's *Pensée* that all the evil of the world comes from men not being able to sit quietly in a room. Good is the retention of energy; evil is the waste of energy, energy which is taken away from growth. Like water, we are truest to our nature in repose.

'Tao is in the emptiness. Emptiness is the fast of the mind.
– CHUANG-TZU.

MASTERPLAY

Three thoughts from Eliot:
'Someone said: "The dead writers are remote from us because we *know* so much more than they did." Precisely, and they are that which we know.'

'What is to be insisted upon is that the poet must develop or procure the consciousness of the past and that he should continue to develop this consciousness throughout his career. What happens is a continual surrender of himself as he is at the moment to some thing which is more valuable. The progress of an artist is a continual self-sacrifice, a continual extinction of personality.'

'The more perfect the artist, the more completely separate in him will be the man who suffers and the mind which creates.'

The supreme liberty is liberty from the body, the last freedom is freedom from time; the true work of art is the one which the seventh wave of genius throws up the beach where the under-tow of time cannot drag it back. When all the motives that lead artists to create have fallen away, and the satisfactions of their vanity and their play-instinct been exhausted, there remains the desire to construct that which has its own order, in a protest against the chaos to which all else appears condemned. While thought exists, words are alive and literature becomes an escape, not from, but into living.

Works of art which survive must all borrow something from the spirit of their age. Thus though Virgil and Horace copied Greek models, they imitated them at a time when the flowering of Roman civilization demanded just such a refinement, a taking over of the trusteeship of the past by the swelling Latin genius. In that sense every writer refashions the literature of the past and produces his tiny commentary, nothing is ever quite new; but there comes a moment when a whole culture ripens and prepares to make its own versions of the great art of its predecessors.

The masterpieces appropriate to our time are in the style of the early Chiricos, the later Rouaults and Picasso's Guernica; sombre, magnificent yet personal statements of our tragedy; works of strong and noble architecture austerely coloured by loneliness and despair.

Flaubert spoke true: a great artist to succeed must have both character and fanaticism and few in this country are willing to pay that price. Our writers have either no personality and therefore no style, or a false personality and therefore a bad style; they mistake prejudice for energy and accept a sense of material well-being as a system of thought.

The English language is like a broad river on whose banks a few patient anglers are sitting, while, higher up, the stream is being polluted by a string of refuse-barges tipping out the muck of Fleet Street and the B.B.C. The English language has, in fact, so contracted to our own littleness that it is no longer possible to make a good book out of words alone. A writer must concentrate on his vocabulary, but he must also depend on the order, the timing and spacing of his words, and try to arrange them into a form which is seemingly artless, yet perfectly proportioned. He must let his omissions suggest that which the language can no longer accomplish. Words today are like the shells and ropes of seaweed which a child brings home glistening from the beach, and which in an hour have lost their lustre.

It is right proportion combined with simplicity of expression and seriousness of thought that enables a book to stand the test of time. To construct from the mind and to colour with the imagination a work which the judgement of unborn arbiters will pronounce almost perfect is the one immortality of which we can be sure. When we read the books of a favourite writer, together with all that has been written about him, then his personality takes shape, and leaves his work to materialize through our own. The page liberates its author; he rises from the dead, and becomes our friend. So it is with Horace, Montaigne, Sainte-Beuve, Flaubert and Henry James: they survive in us, as we increase through them.

But these intimacies can be dangerous. There are some writers who lay siege to our personality, they storm the feeble garrison and occupy the citadel. Thus Flaubert, who appears at first our ally becomes, as we venture further into his work, the terrible Christos Pantocrator of our age, with Sainte-Beuve his John the Baptist and George Sand his Magdalene. We relive his Passion with him, his Temptation, his Agony at Croisset, his Betrayal and Crucifixion by the Bourgeois; his letters become the Sermon on the Mount – 'Tout est là; l'amour de l'Art' – and so we falter and faint and deny him thrice, in the Press, in the Ministry or on the Air – until he rises before us in cold Norman wrath to pronounce 'Justice not mercy!' 'Un homme qui s'est institué artiste n'a plus le droit de vivre comme les autres.'

Flaubert on the Masterpiece
'Je me demande si un livre, indépendamment de ce qu'il dit, ne peut pas produire le même effet? [as the base of the Parthenon]. Dans la précision des assemblages, la rareté des élèments, le poli de la surface, l'harmonie de l'ensemble, n'y a-t-il pas une vertu intrinsèque, une espèce de force divine, quelque chose d'éternel comme un principe? (Je parle en platonicien.) Ainsi pourquoi y a-t-il un rapport nécessaire entre le mot juste et le mot musical? Pourquoi arrive-t-on toujours à faire un vers quand on resserre trop sa pensée? La loi des nombres gouverne donc les sentiments et les images, et ce qui paraît être l'extérieur est tout bonnement le dedans?'

September 10th: Full autumn magnificence; the green and gold streamers of the plane-trees waving transparently against the high sunlit sky. Birthday resolution: From now on specialize; never again make any concession to the ninety-nine per cent of you which is like everybody else at the expense of the one per cent which is unique. Never listen to the False Self talking.
'Le néant d'avoir quarante ans.'

September 15th: Entrée des coings.
Pomifer autumnus fruges effuderit, et mox
Bruma recurrit iners.*

* Horace, Odes, Book IV: 'Autumn, bringer of fruit, has poured out her riches, and soon sluggish winter returns.'

ENEMIES OF ANGST

Houses in the country: the morning awakening of a house, voices of women in a courtyard, the chickens, ducks, geese and dogs being let out; the parrot stropping its beak on the bars of the cage; the smell of breakfast, the gardener bringing in tomatoes and lettuces; Sunday papers, taps running; and the drone of fighter-squadrons overhead. Lunch out of doors.

The afternoon nap, so rich in memory disturbances; the bath in the fading daylight with hot-water pipes rumbling and shrieks of children going to bed, while the cold elmy sunshine westers over liquid fields. The sharp bed-time sortie into the night air.

It is only in the country that we can get to know a person or a book.

The mill where I sometimes stay provides another cure for Angst; the red lane down through the Spanish chestnut wood, the apple trees on the lawn, the bees in the roof, the geese on the pond, the black sun-lit marsh marigolds, the wood-fires crackling in the low bedrooms, the creak of the cellar-door, and the recurrent monotonies of the silver-whispering weir – what could be more womb-like or reassuring? Yet always the anxious owner is flying from it as from the scene of a crime.

Romantic surrealism and classical humanism, however antagonistic, are akin: they breed each other, and the artist of today must contrive from them a synthesis. Blake and Pope or Flaubert and his mad 'Garçon' are complementary. The classical humanist is the parent, the surrealist is the rebellious adolescent. Both are mother-fixed; only 'Social Realism' lies outside the family.

Surrealist and humanist differ as to what proportion of 'strangeness' (*le merveilleux*) is necessary as an ingredient of beauty, and what proportion of violence is best suited to creative emotion.

Surrealism is the last international movement in the arts, but is now in its decadence. Why? Because it borrowed the Communist idea of a small iron-disciplined élite without the appeal to the masses by which

such discipline seeks excuse. An aesthetic movement with a revolutionary dynamism and no popular appeal should proceed quite otherwise
than by a series of public scandals, publicity stunts, noisy expulsions
and excommunications.

For twenty years political mass-movements have absorbed the
creative sap of humanity. Surrealism, like its rival, classical humanism,
is too homesick and too anti-industrial for the times. Our world has no
use for liberal father or rebellious anarchist son. *Le merveilleux*, with
the Sublime of the Humanists, belongs to the nineteenth-century past.
Surrealism is doomed; it is romanticism's last stand.

This is a pity, for as time goes on we see how Surrealism was
revolutionary not only in the sense that all could take it home and
practise it there, but also as the last convulsion necessary to complete
the French artistic cycle, to tie the strands of classicism and romanticism, reason and imagination into a final knot, and so gear once more
the head to the rebel heart.

Classical and romantic: private language of a family quarrel, a dead
quarrel over the distribution of emphasis between man and nature.

Abstract art denies both man and nature, it thrives on the machine
age; Naturalism denies all place to man, while Social Realism places the
entire emphasis on him.

Beware nevertheless of false dualities: classical and romantic, real and
ideal, reason and instinct, mind and matter, male and female – all
should be merged into each other (as the Taoists merged their Yin and
Yang into the Tao), and should be regarded as two aspects of the same
idea. Dualities which are defined at the same moment (stoic and
epicurean, Whig and Tory) are united at last through being contemporary, and they end by having more, not less, in common. In a hundred
years Science and Ethics (power and love), the present day duality, may
seem as dead as the iota controversy, or as good and evil, free will and
determinism, even space and time. Ideas which have for long divided
individuals will become meaningless in the light of the forces that will
separate groups.

Yet ridiculous as may seem the dualities in conflict at any given time, it does not follow that dualism is in itself a worthless process. Truth is a river that is always splitting up into arms that reunite. Islanded between the arms the inhabitants argue for a lifetime as to which is the main river.

EARTH-LOVES OF THE EARTH BOUND: ENNOIA

The three or four people whom I have loved seem utterly set apart from the others in my life; angelic, ageless creatures, more alive than the living, embalmed perpetually in their all-devouring myth.

Ile de Gavrinis: Montagne de la Margeride: Auberge de Peyrebeilhe. 'Mar of murmury mermers in the mind . . .'

Clumps of rushes, brackish water, marram-grass, sea-thistles, *flore des dunes* – Ile de Gavrinis over the green and violet ocean of the Morbihan. The dinghy grounds on white sand printed with the tails of lizards, the ancient lime avenue leads up to the lonely farm where a path winds among gorse and asphodel to the Presence of the Dead. There, in his Tumulus, lies the vast Celtic prince, wrapped in his race's age-long death-wish; his great vault-stones carved with indecipherable warnings; runes of serpents and oak-leaves, of wave-eddies and wind-patterns, finger-prints of giant hands – O powerless to save! And that night in Vannes, the cave-wedding – *Summoque ulularunt vertice Nymphae*. She with sad grave gem-like beauty, and happiness soon to be thrown away.

Leaving Bellac after crossing for two days the plains of the sandy Loire, we enter the Bocage Limousin, traverse a country of tall tree-hedges blueing into the pale spring sky, and reach the first hills, the Blond mountains, and the forest beginnings of the Châtaigneraie. A new strip of maps and the sun always warmer; mountain nights in stone buildings, melted snow in the running water, darker wine in the inns, deeper beds. Rivers tumbling through towns; rain-drenched chestnuts green in the swinging lights of Tulle; Mauriac, Saint-Flour, Saint-Chély-d'Apcher; snow-driven moorlands of the Margeride, pine-forests of Velay and Vivarais; cloud-shadows over the Gerbier de Jonc. There on the edge of the tableland stands the haunted Auberge de Peyrebeilhe, where once so few came out who went in. But now the low room with blackened ceiling has grown less dangerous to lovers than the almond-blossom airs of the warm Ardèche, than the limestone chasm leading down to civilization, where the Furies are awaiting Ennoia and happiness is thrown away.

'Courage is not simply *one* of the virtues but the form of every virtue at the testing point, which means at the point of highest reality.'
– C. S. LEWIS.

Cowardice in living: without health and courage we cannot face the present or the germ of the future in the present, and we take refuge in evasion. Evasion through comfort, through society, through acquisitiveness, through the book-bed-bath defence system, above all through the past, the flight to the romantic womb of history, into primitive myth-making. The refusal to include the great mass-movements of the twentieth century in our art or our myth will drive us to take refuge in the past; in surrealism, magic, primitive religions, or eighteenth-century wonderlands. We fly to Mediterranean womb-pockets and dream-islands, into dead controversies and ancient hermetic bric-à-brac, like a child who sits hugging his toys and who screams with rage when told to put on his boots.

Realities of our time.
  History constructed out of global blocks.
  The Decline of Europe.
  Anglo-American rivalry and imperialism.
  Russian Managerial imperialism.
  Chinese or Japanese imperialism.

English National Suburbanism.
The Great American Vacuum.
Massacres and atrocities, poverties, famines.

'Well, which side are you on? The Corn-Goddess or the Tractor? The Womb or the Bulldozer? Christ, Freud, Buddha, Bakunin, Baudelaire, or Marx, Watson, Pavlov, Stalin, Shaw, Wells and Beveridge? Come clean, moody Palinurus, no synthesis this time and no Magic Circle either! We need men like you in the Group Age. Will you take your turn at the helm as you used to? Remember?

> Princeps gubernator densum Palinurus agebat
> Agmen?*

or do you prefer to daydream in the lavatory, *petit coin sombre* of the Bourgeois Formalist, while a new world is being born?

How do you react to our slogan "Total Everybody Always"? Have you at last understood that your miserable failure as an individual is proof that you pursue a lost cause? Man invents God when he loses his Party Card. He is not an angel, a beast, nor even a vegetable, as you with your mystique of sloth would make him; he is a social unit, a cell, and as such will find fulfilment only through participation in the communal life of an organized group.'

Answer: 'In my beginning is my end.' As the acorn contains the oak or the folded kernel of the Spanish chestnut implies the great split bole and serrated leaf of the full-grown tree, so each human being possesses the form appropriate to him which time will bring out and ripen. 'Tout est dans la semence': the acorns will not make a hedge nor the chestnuts an avenue; we are born with certain shapes ahead of us, certain ideas to fulfil; to seek unity or to bring out diversity; to attack tradition or to perpetuate lost causes; to build the future or to exhume our spiritual

* 'Ahead of all the Master Pilot steer'd.'

226

ancestors and derive hope and inspiration from them; to discover certain places, to love and lose certain faces or to feel immediate antipathy to others. If I had been a true product of the age your question could never have arisen. My rôle is not to belong to the future but, like Eliot's poet, 'to live in what is not merely the present, but the present moment of the past'. I believe that a conscious affinity with Nature forms the shield of Perseus through which man can affront the Gorgon of his fate and that, in the termitaries of the future where humanity cements itself up from the light of the sun, this dragon-slaying mirror will rust and tarnish. So I have nothing to say to the masses or to the machines, to bosses or to bureaucrats, to States or statistics, to Nations or Parties. I am but a link in the chain of individual heretics and failures, a wood-wind solo in the interminable symphony, drowned at once by the brass and percussion, but necessary to the composer's score. An interpreter between intellect and imagination, between reason and the physical world, I tend the graves – *sapientum templa serena* – of Horace and Tibullus, of Pythagoras and Aristippus, of Montaigne and Lao-Tsu; I speak the language of animals and enjoy the confidence of the vegetable powers.

And I answer a seven-fold 'No' to your question: A physiological no, because I am not a cell, but myself. A biological no, because a specialized mutation from the norm indicates the richness and vitality of the species. A sociological no, because those who lack the herd-instinct are generally in advance of the herd, which is always conservative, stupid, intolerant and bourgeois. A psychological no, because those who have been all their lives used to intellectual isolation are those best fitted to remain isolated; they grow adjusted to their maladjustment. A political no, for England will remain the smallest of the great powers, and so must depend for her survival on qualitative standards. An aesthetic no, because the practice of literature is still best carried out through the individual unit. An ethical no, because I do not 'find fulfilment through participation in the communal life of an organized group' – that is tyranny – but in the pursuit of art and knowledge and by communion with the Bourgeois formalism of

Nature. To sum up: I agree with Flaubert, 'A mesure que l'humanité se perfectionne, l'homme se dégrade'.

October. Quince days. Io Lemuria!*

Departure of my tormentors. Philosophic calm, soaring Hope, manic exaltation, mysterious freedom from Angst. Dare I suppose that a cure has been accomplished, the bones of Palinurus buried and his ghost laid? For once it seems that the past has fallen away like the mantle of snow from a creaking fir-tree.

> 'As for the Dog, the Furies and their Snakes
> The gloomy Caverns or the burning Lakes
> And all the vain infernal trumpery
> They neither are, nor were, nor e'er can be.'

There is no hate without fear. Hate is crystallized fear, fear's dividend, fear objectivized. We hate what we fear and so where hate is, fear is lurking. Thus we hate what threatens our person, our liberty, our privacy, our income, popularity, vanity and our dreams and plans for ourselves. If we can isolate this element in what we hate we may learn to cease from hating. Analyse in this way the hatred of ideas, or of the type of person whom one has once loved and whose face is preserved in Spirits of Anger. Hate is the consequence of fear; we fear something before we hate it; a child who fears noises becomes a man who hates noise.

'Whatever you blame, that you have done yourself.' – GRODDECK.

Dark saying of La Rochefoucauld: 'Le seul honnête homme est celui qui ne se pique de rien'.

---

* Roman festival designed to propitiate the Lemures or wandering evil spirits of the dead. Once a year as on our All Souls Eve, they hungrily revisit their loved ones. Broad Beans (a most equivocal vegetable) were thrown to them as an appeasement offering after which they were requested to leave. 'Manes exite Paterni!' Ovid. Fasti, Bk. v.

'Ce serait avoir gagné beaucoup dans la vie que de savoir rester toujours parfaitement naturel et sincère avec soi-même, de ne croire aimer que ce qu'on aime véritablement, et de ne pas prolonger par amour-propre et par émulation vaine des passions déjà expirées.' – SAINTE-BEUVE.

FAREWELL TO SAINTE-BEUVE

'Le souvenir est comme une plante qu'il faut avoir plantée de bonne heure ensemble; sans quoi elle ne s'enracine pas.'

'Les lieux les plus vantés de la terre sont tristes et désenchantés lorsqu'on n'y porte plus ses espérances.'

'Quelle que soit la diversité des point de départ les esprits capables de mûrir arrivent, plus qu'on ne croit, aux mêmes résultats; combien de gens meurent avant d'avoir fait le tour d'eux-mêmes.'

'Je ne suis complètement moi que plume en main et dans le silence du cabinet.'

A child, left to play by itself, says of quite easy things, 'Now I am going to do something very difficult'. Soon, out of vanity, fear and emptiness, he builds up a world of custom, convention and myth, in which everything must be just so; certain doors are one-way streets, certain trees sacred, certain paths taboo. Then comes along a grown-up or other more robust children; they kick over the imaginary walls, climb the forbidden trees, regard the difficult as easy and the private world is destroyed. The instinct to create myths, to colonize reality with the emotions, remains. The myths become tyrannies until they are swept away, then we invent new tyrannies to hide our suddenly perceived nakedness. Like caddis-worms or like those crabs which dress themselves with seaweed, we wear belief and custom.

Taoists believe that devotion to anything except Nature ages them and therefore they live simply on hill-sides or near forests, like the sage whose wants were so few that when he decided to leave his cottage he found that the brambles round it had grown too high for him to pass. But what becomes of loving Nature if Nature does not want us? Let us go for a walk on the moors: at first the high pure air, the solitude under the hot sun, where the burns splash and the grouse shrieks, purge us of our city poisons, until art and civilization seem oppressive and vulgar, rainbow hues on the dying mullet, occupations which cut man off from his primitive vegetation-cult. Then as the day gets hotter and as we stumble on over rufous heather and warm aerated bog there is a change; it would seem that Nature does not share in our communion, and prefers her own backward progeny; grouse's cackle, ravens, falcons, mountain hares, the noisy burn, the whole hill-side in the hot afternoon become ominous and hostile, archaic emblems of Ennui – something we have long grown out of. Once more the craving for architecture, art and the intellect revives. By the evening it is raining and, after the visit to our great, gross, unappreciative Mother, we are glad to get back to our books and fire-side conversation. It is to Civilization, not to Nature that man must return.

The Vegetable Conspiracy: Man is now on his guard against insect parasites; against liver-flukes, termites, Colorado beetles, but has he given thought to the possibility that he has been selected as the target of vegetable attack, marked down by the vine, hop, juniper, the tobacco plant, tea-leaf and coffee-berry for destruction? What converts these Jesuits of the gastric juices make – and how cleverly they retain them! Which smoker considers the menace of the weed spreading in his garden, which drunkard reads the warning of the ivy round the oak? What populations fear the seed-strangling rubber, or have observed the increasing mortality caused by the punctures of the rose? And what of gold, that slow mineral poison?

Money talks through the rich as alcohol swaggers in the drunken, and calls softly to itself to unite into the lava flow which petrifies everything it touches.

No one would start to play a game without knowing the rules. Yet most of us play the interminable game of life without them, because we are unable to find out what they are. But there are only two possible sets of rules, according to whether or not we believe in God. If we believe that the universe is an accident and life an accident contingent on the universe, and man an accident contingent on life; then the rules are made for men to be happy, and it has been found by generations of exponents of these rules that happiness consists in fulfilment of the personality – in former days through the family, now by rendering more and more services to a group – in fact through the happiness of the greatest number. This is the game as played by Epicurus, Holbach, Marx, Mill, Bentham, Comte and William James.

If, however, we believe in God, then our duty is to do His will and not our own, and our conception of the rules varies with our conception of His nature. But whatever this conception is we are united in the belief that the success or failure of our life as such cannot be estimated by any utilitarian standard.

Faced, then, with these completely different sets of rules for this all-important game, can we not find out once and for all whether there is a God; whether He has strewn clues over the universe for man to pick up, or whether we ourselves have invented Him, as a useful three-letter expression for anything which remains outside our knowledge?

The answer seems to rest with three different categories of thinkers; the physicists, who incline to believe in God, but are now all busy making explosives; the biologists and chemists who can produce almost everything except life, and who, if they could create life, would prove that it might have arisen accidentally; and the psychologists and physiologists, who are struggling to discover the relation of mind to brain, the nature of consciousness.

A baby, after an exhibition on the pot, with much anger and howling, stretches out its arms with a little cry, as when its pram is passing under trees, to reveal an immense wonder and love for life – a Soul. I have read that the cuckoo enters life with two advantages over other birds; a special muscle on its back for throwing them from the nest; and a cry which is irresistible to its foster-parents. This sudden cry of recognition and pleasure is what keeps us on the go from cradle to grave. *Volupté!* The eternal cuckoo call.

'O fins d'automne, hivers, printemps trempés de boue,
Endormeuses saisons' . . .

Tout mon mal vient de Paris. There befell the original sin and the original ecstasy; there were the holy places – the Cross-Roads and the Island. Quai Bourbon, Rue de Vaugirard, Quai d'Anjou.

Air: *Transfrétons la Sequane!*

'Nous transfrétons la Sequane au dilicule et crepuscule; nous déambulons par les compites et quadriviers de l'urbe, nous déspumons la verbocination latiale.'

Evening in June: walking down the Rue Vavin, past the shop with ivory canes in the window, away from the polyglot bedlam of Montparnasse into the Luxembourg gardens where children are playing croquet under the black-trunked chestnuts and wool-green catalpas, then out at the corner where the Rue Servandoni's leaning mansards join the sombre Rue de Vaugirard. On by the book-booths of the Odéon, by the shimmering Fontaine de Medicis and the diners in the open air, then through the broad melancholy twilight of the Rue Soufflot to the cold splendour of the Panthéon, past the blistered shutters of the Hôtel des Grands Hommes. There, behind the church, the Rue de la Montagne Sainte-Geneviève, Via Sacra of the Latin Quarter, winds steeply down its Founder's holy hill.

In the doorways sit families on their wooden chairs, while from the Bal Musette where *Fiesta* began the Java fades on the sultry air; then across the Rue des Ecoles with its groaning trams, and so by the stews and noisy wine-shops of the Place Maubert to meet the Seine at the Quai de la Tournelle.

Quai Bourbon. Miserere. The Ile Saint-Louis strains at its moorings, the river eddies round the stone prow where tall poplars stand like masts, and the mist rises round decaying houses which the seventeenth-century nobles raised on their meadows. Yielding asphalt, sliding waters; long windows with iron bars set in damp walls; anguish and fear. Rendez-vous des Mariniers, Hôtel de Lauzun: moment of the night when the saint's blood liquefies, when the leaves shiver and presentiments of loss stir within the dark coil of our fatality.

'Porque sabes que siempre te he querido.'

Quai Bourbon, Quai d'Orléans, Quai d'Anjou.

Then came the days of ferrets with ribs like wish-bones, for whom we bought raw liver from the horse-butcher in the Rue de Seine, while they tunnelled clucking round the octagonal room in the Hôtel de la Louisiane. They pursued oranges and eggs and ping-pong balls, and wore harness with little bells; and from among them there came forth a queen, the tawny, docile Norfolk beauty whom we named the English Rose, who performed her cycle of eating, playing, sleeping and relieving herself, and who saw three continents from a warm sleeve. She hunted the Rue Monge, and the Rue Mouffetard, the courts of the Val de Grâce and the gardens of the Observatoire, the Passage des Princes and the Place de Fürstenberg. She searched the Parc Montsouris and the Buttes-Chaumont, the doss-houses of the Rue Quincampoix and Boulevard de la Chapelle; she visited the tattered buildings in the Rue de la Goutte d'Or, and heard the prostitutes calling to each other from their beds in the Rue de la Charbonnière; she explored the gilt, the plush, the columns and flaking ceilings of the Deuxième Arrondissement, the arcades of the Palais-Royal and the Place des Victoires, the corner-houses, razor-sharp, in the Rue de la Lune. She learnt all the gates of Paris: Porte Saint-Denis, Porte d'Orléans, Porte des Lilas; pocket

gardens of the Gobelin workers along the Bièvre, exposed tendons of
the Nord railway by the Boulevard Barbès, and warehouses on the
Saint-Martin Canal. Yet most she loved, a short walk from her couch
of straw, the stony public garden by Saint-Germain-des-Prés.

And many bars where sad-eyed barmen told the seasons by clipping
chits for 'grogs-américains' and 'champagne-oranges', and many
restaurants, now closed and forgotten, understood her favourite diet of
raw egg. The Moine Gourmet, the Restaurant de la Chaise with its
Burgundy and Lesbians, Montagné's perfection, Foyot's dying autumnal
grandeur, Madame Genot's austere bistro with her home-grown wines,
Rosalie's fresh corn, Lafon's pâté, Marius' pellucid Beaujolais – with all
of these she grew familiar.

And many *boîtes* also made her welcome: the Bateau Ivre in the Place
de l'Odéon, the old Boeuf, Melody's and the Grand Ecart, the trellised
galleries of the Bal Blomet and the Stygian reaches of the Magic River
in Luna-Park. Love came to her in Hampshire and she was covered, and
in Toulon she gave birth to nine fine youngsters in the hotel bath. She
would wash them and clean up their droppings till ambivalence was
engendered, when to escape their demands, she would climb on to a lap,
looking up at us with her pale golden eyes, and yawn to show that
nothing was changed. Then one day, being hungry, she strayed from the
garden and entered a cottage kitchen, where she sat up to beg as she had
been taught, until ignorant peasants kicked her to death, and brought
back to us her limp body; filthy-hearted women; – 'Oui, monsieur, on
a bien vu qu'elle n'a pas voulu mourir.'

It was after the reign of the English Rose that our days were darkened
by the graves of the lemurs; on distant shores they lie – far from
Madagascar, yet never far from those rocks where the flowering cistus
out-blanches the salt-encrusting spray.

'Living for beauty' – October on the Mediterranean; blue skies rinsed
by the mistral, red and golden vine branches, wind-fretted waves
chopping round the empty yachts; plane-trees peeling; palms rearing up

their dingy underclothes; mud in the streets, and from doorways at night the smell of burning oil. On dark evenings I used to bicycle in to fetch our dinner, past the harbour with its bobbing launches and the bright cafés with their signs banging. At the local restaurant there would be one or two 'plats à emporter', to which I would add some wine, sausage and Gruyère cheese, a couple of 'Diplomates' to smoke and a new 'Détective' or a 'Chasseur Français'; then I would bowl back heavy-laden with the mistral behind me, a lemur buttoned up inside my jacket with his head sticking out. Up the steep drive it was easy to be blown off into the rosemary, then dinner would be spoilt. We ate it with our fingers beside the fire – true beauty lovers – then plunged into the advertisements in *Country Life*, dreaming of that Priory at Wareham where we would end our days. 'Living for Beauty' entails a busy life of answering advertisements, writing for prospectuses, for information about cottages in Hampstead, small manors in the West or else for portable canoes, converted Dutch barges 'that could go through the Canals', second-hand yachts, caravans and cars. Homesick, we liked best the detective stories, because they reeked of whisky, beefsteaks, expresses from Paddington, winter landscapes, old inns and Georgian houses that screen large gardens off the main street of country towns. There live the solicitors and doctors and clever spinsters who brew home-made poisons and who come into their own in these exacting tales, there arrives for summer the artist from London or the much-consulted military man. At last we would go to bed, bolting the doors while the lemurs cried in the moonlight, house-ghosts bounding from the mulberries to the palms, from the palms to the tall pines whose cones the dormice nibble, from the pines to the roof and so to our bedroom window where they would press their eager faces to the pane. In the bathroom one of us is washing while the other crams fir-cones in the stove. The stove roars, the water is heated and the room fills with steamy fragrance. The two lemurs are admitted and worm their way down to sleep in the bottom of the bed. In the early morning, while we dream of Wareham, they will creep out round our feet, seize the aromatic tooth-paste in their long black gloves, jump with it through the windows and spring down to the sunny earth by the way they came.

When I think of lemurs depression engulfs me 'à peu que le coeur ne me fend'. As W. H. Hudson says, 'they have angel's eyes' and they die of 'flu.

GRAVES OF THE LEMURS

Whoopee. Gentle and fearless he passed four leafy years in the South of France. He would chase large dogs, advancing backwards on them and glaring through his hind legs, then jump chittering at them and pull their tails. He died through eating a poisoned fig laid down for rats. The children who saw him take the fruit tried to coax him down, but he ran up a tree with it. There they watched him eat and die.

Polyp. Most gifted of lemurs, who hated aeroplanes in the sky, on the screen, and even on the wireless. How he would have hated this war! He could play in the snow or swim in a river or conduct himself in a night-club; he judged human beings by their voices; biting some, purring over others, while for one or two well-seasoned old ladies he would brandish a black prickle-studded penis, shaped like a eucalyptus seed. Using his tail as an aerial, he would lollop through long grass to welcome his owners, embracing them with little cries and offering them a lustration from his purple tongue and currycomb teeth. His manners were those of some spoiled young Maharajah, his intelligence not inferior, his heart all delicacy – women, gin and muscats were his only weaknesses. Alas, he died of pneumonia while we scolded him for coughing, and with him vanished the sea-purple cicada kingdom of calanque and stone-pine and the concept of life as an arrogant private dream shared by two.

As the French solider said of the Chleuhs in Morocco, 'Je les aime et je les tue'. So it is with the lemurs, black and grey bundles of vitality, eocene ancestors from whom we are all descended, whose sun-greeting call some hold to be the origin of the word 'Ra' and thus of the human language – we have treated these kings in exile like Maoris and

Marquesas islanders, or the whistling Guanches of Tenerife, like all those golden island-races, famous for beauty, whom Europe has taken to its shabby heart to exploit and ruin.

To have set foot in Lemuria is to have been close to the mysterious sources of existence, to have known what it is to live wholly in the present, to soar through the green world four yards above the ground, to experience sun, warmth, love and pleasure as intolerably as we glimpse them in waking dreams, and to have heard that heart-rending cry of the lonely or abandoned which goes back to our primaeval dawn. Wild ghost faces from a lost continent who soon will be extinct. . . .

And 'living for beauty': in one lovely place always pining for another; with the perfect woman imagining one more perfect; with a bad book unfinished beginning a second, while the almond tree is in blossom, the grass-hopper fat and the winter nights disquieted by the plock and gurgle of the sea – that too would seem extinct for ever.

'Your time is short, watery Palinurus. What do you believe?'
'I believe in two-faced truth, in the Either, the Or and the Holy Both. I believe that if a statement is true then its opposite must be true.' (Aristotle: 'The knowledge of opposites is one.') Thus now (November the eleventh) I am interested in philosophy, psychology and religion again, and I am reading about Gnosticism, most exquisite and insidious of heresies, and once more I am back among its charms and amulets; its snake-god ABRASAX and the Gnostic theory that Adam in the Garden of Eden was the babe in the womb fed by four rivers (arteries from the navel), and expelled from his mother into the world at the Fall. This time a year ago I was interested in these same ideas, reading Lao-Tsu with as much passion as I now read Epicurus (and now I find that Lao-Tsu was called 'The Chinese Epicurus'), so that it is more true to say that this is the time of year when religions are interested in me. Or is it that in late autumn the season forbids an active existence, and we are forced back on reading and contemplation, on those schemes of thought which imply a corresponding rejection of the world?

To attain two-faced truth we must be able to resolve all our dualities, simultaneously to perceive life as comedy and tragedy, to see the mental side of the physical and the reverse. We must learn to be at the same time objective and subjective – like Flaubert, who enjoyed what Thibaudet called 'la pleine logique artistique de la vision binoculaire', or with that 'double focus' which Auden beautifully describes in *New Year Letter*.

Today the function of the artist is to bring imagination to science and science to imagination, where they meet, in the myth.*

Now that I seem to have attained a temporary calm, I understand how valuable unhappiness can be; melancholy and remorse form the deep leaden keel which enables us to sail into the wind of reality; we run aground sooner than the flat-bottomed pleasure-lovers, but we venture out in weather that would sink them, and we choose our direction. What distinguishes true civilisations from their mass-fabricated substitutes except that tap-root to the Unconscious, the sense of original sin? What artist-philosophers except Voltaire and Goethe have been without it?

'Voilà ce que tous les socialistes du monde n'ont pas voulu voir avec leur éternelle prédication matérialiste, ils ont nié la *douleur*, ils ont blasphémé les trois quarts de la poésie moderne; le sang du Christ qui se remue en nous, rien ne l'extirpera, rien ne le tarira, il ne s'agit pas de le dessécher, mais de lui faire des ruisseaux. Si le sentiment de

---

* Gide gives the perfect two-faced myth-truth about religion (*Attendu que* ... Algiers 1943): 'Il ne peut être question de deux Dieux. Mais je me garde, sous ce nom de Dieu, de confondre deux choses très différentes; différentes jusqu'à s'opposer: D'une part l'ensemble du Cosmos et des lois naturelles qui le régissent; matière et forces, énergies; cela c'est le côté Zeus; et l'on peut bien appeler cela Dieu, mais c'est en enlevant à ce mot toute signification personnelle et morale. D'autre part le faisceau de tous les efforts humains vers le bien, vers le beau, la lente maîtrisation de ces forces brutales et leur mise en service pour réaliser le bien et le beau sur la terre; ceci, c'est le côté Prométhée; et c'est le côté Christ aussi bien; c'est l'épanouissement de l'homme et toutes les vertus y concourent. Mais ce Dieu n'habite nullement la nature; il n'existe que dans l'homme et par l'homme; il est créé par l'homme, ou, si vous préférez, c'est à travers l'homme qu'il se crée; et tout effort reste vain, pour l'extérioriser par la prière.'

l'insuffisance humaine, du néant de la vie, venait à périr (ce qui serait la conséqeunce de leur hypothèse) nous serions plus bêtes que les oiseaux qui au moins perchent sur les arbres.' – FLAUBERT.

If we apply depth-psychology to our own lives we see how enslaved we remain to the womb and the mother. Womb of Mother Church, of Europe, mother of continents, of horseshoe harbours and valleys, of the lap of earth, of the bed, the arm-chair and the bath, or of the Court of Charles II, of Augustan London, or the Rome of Cicero; of the bow-window of the club, of the house by the mill or water-front sacred to Venus; all our lives seeking a womb with a view. Knowing this weakness we can make allowance for it in our thinking, aware that these reassuring womb-symbols have their parallel in certain sets of ideas; particularly in the half-mystical and theological, half-legendary beliefs and prejudices which we derive from the classical world, and which form a kind of old wives' tale, or maternal substitute for the vigour and audacity of constructive thought. Thus I fulfil the childhood pattern of making little expeditions into the world outside my myth-mother, and then running back to her apron. Yet in these days it is important for an artist to grasp that the logical exploratory voyage of reason is the finest process of the mind. Every other activity is a form of regression – 'Penser fait la grandeur de l'homme'. Thus the much vaunted 'night-mind', the subconscious world of myth and nostalgia, of child-imagination and instinctual drives, though richer, stranger and more powerful than the world of reason, as is Isis than Apollo, never-theless owes its strength to our falling back on all that is primitive and infantile; it is an act of cowardice to the God in Man.

Man exudes a sense of reverence like a secretion. He smears it over everything, and so renders places like Stonehenge or the lake of Nemi (Diana's mirror) particularly sacred – yet the one can become a petrol-station, and the other be drained by a megalomaniac; no grove is too holy to be cut down. When we are tired or ill, our capacity for rever-ence, like our capacity for seeing the difficulty of things, increases till it becomes a kind of compulsion-neurosis or superstition; therefore it would seem that the mythoclasts are always right – until we know what these mother-haters, these savagers of the breast, will worship in their turn. Lenin, the father figure mummified, replaces the Byzantine Christ. Reverence and destruction alternate; therefore the wise two-faced man will reverence destructively, like Alaric or Akbar, and like Gibbon, Renan, Gide, reverently destroy.

Example of destructive reverence: *Un Chien Andalou.**

Studio Vingt-Huit – high up a winding street of Montmartre, in the full blasphemy of a freezing Sunday; taxis arriving, friends greeting each other, an excitable afternoon audience of uncowed women and intelligent men. In the hall stands a surrealist book-stall, behind it a bar where a gramophone plays 'Ombres Blanches' and disturbing sardanas, while beyond is a small modern theatre. The lights are lowered and the film begins: 'Prologue'; 'Once upon a time' [I quote from the script], 'a balcony was in the dark. Indoors a man was whetting his razor. He looked up through the window at the sky and saw a fleecy cloud drawing near to the full moon. Then a young girl's head with staring eyes. Now the fleecy cloud passes over the moon. And the razor-blade passes through the girl's eye, slicing it in two. – End of Prologue.' The audience gasp – and there appear the beautiful haunted creatures – Pierre Batchef as the young man, the cyclist, with his intellectual distinction and romantic depravity, then his Spanish-looking heroine. And the lovely girl in the street, who picks up the severed hand with the painted fingers! 'She must at that very moment register an extra-ordinary emotion which completely distracts her. She is as if entranced by echoes of some far-off church music, perhaps it is the music she has heard in earliest childhood . . . She remains rooted to the spot in utter contrition. Motor-cars flash by at break-neck speed. Suddenly she is run over by one and horribly mutilated. Thereupon, with the firmness of one doing what he is fully entitled to do, the cyclist comes up to the other and, having gazed lecherously straight into her eyes, puts his hand

* 'Un Chien Andalou was the film of adolescence and death which I was going to plunge right into the heart of Paris with all the weight of an Iberian dagger.' – DALI: *Autobiography.*

on her jumper over her breasts. Close-up of the eager hands touching the breasts. These themselves appear through the jumper. Thereupon the cyclist's face is seen to take on a look of terrible, almost mortal anguish, and blood dribbles from his mouth on to the girl's bared breast.'

So the film hurries to its end where the woman and her cyclist lover 'lie buried up to their necks in the limitless desert, blind and ragged, roasted by the sun and eaten by a swarm of insects'. This contemptuous private world of jealousy and lust, of passion and aridity, in which its beautiful occupants pattered about like stoats in search of blood, produced an indescribable effect, a tremendous feeling of excitement and liberation. The Id had spoken and – through the obsolete medium of the silent film – the spectators had been treated to their first glimpse of the fires of despair and frenzy which were smouldering beneath the complacent post-war world.

The picture was received with shouts and boos, and when a pale young man tried to make a speech, hats and sticks were flung at the screen. In one corner a woman was chanting, 'Salopes, salopes, salopes!' and soon the audience began to join in. With the impression of having witnessed some infinitely ancient horror, Saturn swallowing his sons, we made our way out into the cold of February 1929, that unique and dazzling cold.*

Why does this strong impression still persist? Because *Un Chien Andalou* brought out the grandeur of the conflict inherent in romantic love, the truth that the heart is made to be broken, and after it has mended, to be broken again. For romantic love, the supreme intoxication of which we are capable, is more than an intensifying of life; it is a defiance of it; it belongs to those evasions of reality through excessive stimulus which Spinoza called 'titivations'. By the law of diminishing returns our desperate century forfeits its chances of being happy and, because it finds happiness insipid, our world is regressing to chaos.

* 'A date in the history of the Cinema, a date marked in blood.' – *Montes* (Dali: *Autobiography*).

Why? Because, as in the days of the Delphic Oracle, happiness consists in temperance and self-knowledge, and now both of these are beyond the reach of ordinary people who, owing to the pursuit of their violent sensations, can no longer distinguish between pleasure and pain.

'Happiness is the only sanction of life; where happiness fails, existence remains a mad and lamentable experiment,' writes Santayana, who but restates Aristotle's definition that happiness, not goodness, is the end of life: 'we choose happiness for itself, and never with a view to anything further; whereas we choose honour, pleasure, intellect, because we believe that through them we shall be made happy.' Yet at once the ring of the words 'mad and lamentable' drowns the definition. A 'mad and lamentable experiment' seems to be more compulsive, more beguiling, and more profound in its appeal to us. Compare Aristotle and Santayana with a mental specialist, Doctor Devine. I quote from his *Recent Advances in Psychiatry*:

'Sometimes the development of a delusion leads to a cessation of tension, and is associated with a feeling of tranquillity and certainty, such as the patient had not hitherto experienced. A study of the past history of these cases sometimes creates the impression that the whole life had been converging to its solution in the psychosis in an inevitable kind of way. It is not unusual for a patient to say that his whole life had been like a dream and that now he feels awake for the first time. The delusion is, as it were, the inspiration for which he had long been waiting. . . . Something altogether unique is created in a psychosis; the mind is invaded by morbid mental growths.'

Thus in opposition to Aristotle's definition of happiness as an intensifying of the life of reason, we can oppose the existence of these illusion-ridden patients, the paraphrenics who have 'achieved a state of permanent bio-psychic equilibrium at the expense of their reason' – and there are also schizophrenes and manic depressives whose lives are rich and crowded above the normal. To quote Dr. Devine: 'The schizophrenic does not suffer from a loss of something, he suffers from a surfeit, psychologically his consciousness is fuller than normal consciousness and the reality which it embraces is more thickly populated than that comprehended by the normal mind. . . . The conscious personality plays a passive role as far as the development of his psychosis is concerned and can do nothing to control what is happening within his organism.'

This moth-and-candle preoccupation with the Morbid Mind is but one of the Approaches to Pain which nowadays seem so rich in glamour. Insanity beckons us to fulfil high destinies, and to recognize our paraphrenic vocations. Milder forms of manic depression withdraw the over-sensitive from circulation to let them off lightly with an anxiety-neurosis or nervous breakdown; tuberculosis offers some a prolonged ecstasy; alcohol clowns others into oblivion; stomach-ulcers, piles and colitis provide us with honourable excuses; impotence or frigidity can always be relied upon to stop the cheque, and every degree of fever is at hand to send up our emotional temperature. And what illness performs for the individual, war accomplishes for the masses, until total war succeeds in plunging the two thousand million inhabitants of the globe into a common nightmare.

Why? 'Because,' say the priests, 'men have forgotten God'; 'wanting the Pilot and Palinure of reason and religion they runne themselves upon the rocks'; 'because,' say the materialists, 'they have neglected economic principles'; 'because,' says a philosopher, 'a madman at Sils Maria once wrote a book which, fifty years later, inspired another in Munich'. Or because we blindly enjoy destruction and can think of nothing better, since for us

'Le printemps adorable a perdu son odeur'?

Why do we like war? Is it that all men would revenge themselves for their betrayal by their mothers and of their mothers, hitting out blindly to efface the memory of the triple expulsion – expulsion from the sovereignty of the womb, from the sanctuary of the breast, from the intoxication of the bed and the lap?

No, it is not so much our weaning which starts us using our teeth on one another, nor even the terrible rebuff which we can still remember, when our mother began to reject our advances and we were packed off to the living death of school, so much as that more subtle conditioning which Freud analyses in *Beyond the Pleasure Principle*. There he argues that certain patterns of childhood unhappiness and separation are re-enacted in later life. 'Thus one knows people with whom every relationship ends in the same way: benefactors whose protégés invariably after a time desert them in ill-will, men with whom every friendship ends in the friend's treachery, lovers whose tender relationships with women each and all run through the same phases and come to the same end . . . in the light of such observations as these, we may venture to make the assumption that there really exists in psychic-life a repetition-compulsion which goes beyond the pleasure principle'. In *Civilization and Its Discontents* Freud considers all prevailing nostrums for happiness and finds them wanting; in our culture Eros and the Death-wish fight it out; in our civilization there is a Superego which makes us all feel guilty, and a repressive and anal element in the bureaucratic tidiness, caution and frugality of the society which we have made.

Yet to blame society or the tyranny of the herd is but in a more general way to distribute the blame on the individual. If we had all enjoyed happy childhoods with happy parents, then prisons, barracks and asylums would be empty. The herd would be kinder, society wiser, the world would be changed. Man, however, is complete not only through being well adjusted to humanity; humanity must also be adjusted to the non-human, to the Nature which it perpetually thwarts and outrages, to the indifferent Universe. In Gide's use of the myth, Prometheus must come to terms with Zeus. If we return to our fortunate madmen, not to the remorse-stricken melancholiacs, but to those who are happier for their renunciation of the external world, we find that they are happy because 'they have achieved permanent bio-psychic equilibrium at the expense of their reason'.

In other words, bio-psychic equilibrium is such an intense and unfailing source of happiness that reason and all personal contact with reality are a small price for these Taoists to pay. Now this bio-psychic equilibrium is but that sensation of harmony with the universe, of accepting life, of being part of nature which we experience in childhood and which we afterwards discover through love, through artistic creation, through the pursuit of wisdom, through mystical elation or luminous calm. 'The greatest good,' wrote Spinoza, 'is the knowledge of the union which the mind has with the whole nature', and those who have found this out, who have opened Nature's Dictionary of Synonyms, do not wish for any other. But we live in a civilization in which so few can experience it, where 'Le vrai, c'est le secret de quelques-uns', where those who have been fortunate are like competitors in a treasure hunt who, while the others are still elbowing each other about and knocking things over, in silence discover the clue, know that they are right, and sit down.

Moreover, even as obscure poisons, foci of infection, septic teeth and germ-crowded colons play a part in the origins of insanity, so do slums, great cities, proletarian poverty and bourgeois boredom, or tyrannies of family and herd contribute to obscure our sense of union with the physical world. 'The misery of mankind is manifold' and breeds everywhere the despair, fear, hate and destruction which ulcerate our peace. Nature is banished from our civilization, the seasons lose their rhythm, the fruits of the earth their savour, the animals, co-heirs of our planet, are wantonly exterminated, the God within us is denied, and the God without. Wisdom and serenity become treasures to be concealed, and happiness a lost art. Resentment triumphs; the frustrated 'Have-nots' massacre the 'Haves'. We are in fact within sight of achieving a world neurosis, a world in which atrophy of the instincts (except that of herd-slaughter), abuse of the intellect, and perversion of the heart will obliterate our knowledge of the purpose of life: humanity will choke in its own bile.

When the present slaughter terminates humanity can survive only through a return to the idea of happiness as the highest good, happiness which lies not in Power or in the exercise of the Will, but in the flowering of the spirit, and which in an unwarped society should coincide with consciousness. The justification for the State therefore will consist in rendering the individuals who compose it happier than they can make themselves by helping them to fulfil their potentialities, to control their Promethean environment and to reverence the Zeus-environment which they cannot master. When once we have discovered how pain and suffering diminish the personality, and how joy alone increases it, then the morbid attraction which is felt for evil, pain and abnormality will have lost its power. Why do we reward our men of genius, our suicides, our madmen, and the generally maladjusted with the melancholy honours of a posthumous curiosity? Because we know that it is our society which has condemned these men to death, and which is guilty because out of its own ignorance and malformation it has persecuted those who were potential saviours; smiters of the rock who might have touched the spring of healing and brought us back into harmony with ourselves.

Somehow, then, and without going mad, we must learn from these madmen to reconcile fanaticism with serenity. Each one, taken alone, is disastrous, yet except through the integration of these two opposites there is no great art and no profound happiness – and what else is worth having? For nothing can be accomplished without fanaticism, and without serenity nothing can be enjoyed. Perfection of form or increase of knowledge, pursuit of fame or service to the community, love of God or god of Love – we must select the Illusion which appeals to our temperament, and embrace it with passion, if we want to be happy. This is the farewell autumn precept with which Palinurus takes leave of his fast-fading nightmare. 'J'ai cueilli ce brin de bruyère.'

And now another year has gone by of knowing nothing: once more the plane trees are bare; the Pleiads are sinking; the bowstring relaxed. Exorcized is the dark face from the island poplars, drowned in the swirl of the moon-tarnished river; dishonoured are the graves of the lemurs; untended the sepulchre of the Prince on Gavrinis, forgotten as an Andalusian dog.

But thou, mimosa-shaded Siagne, flowing clear between the two Saint-Cassiens, receive Palinurus – gently bear him under the scented Tanneron, past Auribeau and Mandelieu, and the shrine on the tufted mount of Venus to his tomb by the shore.*

There, in the harsh sunshine, among the sea-holly and the midday plant, eringo and mesembrianthemum, where the tide prints its colophon of burnt drift-wood and the last susurrus of the wave expires on the sand – naked under his watery sign shall he come to rest; a man too trustful in the calm of sky and sea.

> 'O nimium coelo et pelago confise sereno
> Nudus in ignota, Palinure, jacebis harena.'

---

* Palinurus enters the Siagne by the deserted village of Saint-Cassien des Bois; from there he floats some ten miles down to the wooded mound of Arluc, where stands the chapel of Saint-Cassien, scene of a pilgrimage and other nocturnal festivities on July 23rd. The chapel, which is surrounded by ancient elms and cypresses, overlooks the old delta of the Siagne from the site of a pagan temple dedicated by Roman sailors to Venus. 'Nazarius, vir strenuus et pius, non ferens animas hominum illudi fraude diabolica, delubrum et aram impudicae Veneri dicatam in quodam monticulo qui dicitur Arlucus, quasi *ara-luci*, prope pontem fluminis nunc vulgo nuncupati *Siagnia*, omnino eliminare curavit . . .' – (*Chronol. Lerin.*, II, p. 80.)

(The pious and energetic Nazarius would not permit men's minds to be deceived by a fraud of the Devil, and so he caused the ruined altar, dedicated to licentious Venus, to be utterly destroyed; that 'altar of the grove' on the mound called Arluc, by the bridge over the river now commonly known as the Siagne.)

Palinurus thus completes his periplus among the stone-pines on the beach by La Napoule. This is at variance with Virgil's account in which Æneas names after him Capo Palinuro on the Gulf of Policastro, and marks one more of the discrepancies which lead one to question the author's veracity.

Epilogue: Who was Palinurus?

'The winding shelves do us detain,
Till God, the Palinure returns again.'

FULLER, 1640: Joseph's Coat.

Let us examine him: study the Psychiatrist's confidential report.

REPORT

Diagnosis. Strongly marked palinuroid tendencies.

Prognosis. Grave.

Clinical Picture. The sources for Palinurus are entirely to be found in the third, fifth and sixth books of Virgil's *Aeneid*. The third book forms part of Æneas' relation to Dido of the events that befell him after the fall of Troy, and consequently everything and everyone in it are seen through Æneas' eyes. This may have some psychological importance, where the references in that book are concerned.

Nothing is known of Palinurus' heredity except that, like the physician Iapyx, he was a Trojan and descended from Iasus. Æneas addresses him as 'Iaside Palinure'. There is no evidence of any inherited psychopathic tendencies. The first mention of Palinurus exhibits him in a confusion-state, and suggests that, although usually a well-adjusted and efficient member of society, the pilot was experiencing a temporary 'black-out'. The passage introduces that undulant sea-music which will accompany Palinurus on his all too rare appearances. The translator is Dryden.

> Now from the sight of Land our Gallies move,
> With only Seas around, and Skies above.
> When o'er our Heads, descends a burst of Rain;

And Night, with sable Clouds involves the Main:
The ruffling Winds the foamy Billows raise:
The scatter'd Fleet is forc'd to sev'ral Ways:
The face of Heav'n is ravish'd from our Eyes,
And in redoubl'd Peals the roaring Thunder flies.
Cast from our Course, we wander in the Dark;
No Stars to guide, no point of Land to mark.
Ev'n *Palinurus* no distinction found
Betwixt the Night and Day; such Darkness reign'd around.

('Palinurus in unda' – Note the theme at his first appearance.)

The storm casts the ships on the Strophades, where the Harpies foul and plunder the heroes' open-air buffet. In vain the trumpeter Misenus blows the call to action: the Harpies are attacked but prove invulnerable, and one, Celaeno, curses the leader and his band, prophesying wars and famine. They set sail again, the dactylic sea music reappears, and the pilot Palinurus with it.

'Tendunt vela Noti; fugimus spumantibus undis
qua cursum ventusque gubernatorque vocabat.
jam medio apparet fluctu nemorosa Zacynthos
Dulichiumque Sameque et Neritos ardua saxis.'

'South winds stretch the sails, we run over the bubbling waters where the breezes and the Pilot call the course, now Zacynthos covered with woods appears in the middle of the sea, and Dulichium and Same and Neritus with its steep cliffs' – ('Zante, Zante fiore di Levante'). . . .

At length the pilot's moment approaches –

The Night proceeding on with silent pace,
Stood in her noon; and view'd with equal Face
Her steepy rise, and her declining Race,
Then wakeful *Palinurus* rose, to spie

The face of Heav'n, and the Nocturnal Skie;
And listen'd ev'ry breath of Air to try:
Observes the Stars, and notes their sliding Course:
The *Pleiads, Hyads*, and their wat'ry force;
And both the Bears is careful to behold;
And bright *Orion* arm'd with burnish'd Gold.
Then when he saw no threat'ning Tempest nigh,
But a sure promise of a settled skie;
He gave the Sign to weigh: we break our sleep;
Forsake the pleasing Shore, and plow the Deep.

A situation of considerable strain arises on the passage between Scylla and Charybdis:

First *Palinurus* to the Larboard veer'd;
Then all the Fleet by his Example steer'd.
To Heav'n aloft on ridgy Waves we ride;
Then down to Hell descend, when they divide.
And thrice our Gallies knock'd the stony ground,
And thrice the hollow Rocks return'd the sound,
And thrice we saw the Stars, that stood with dews around.

Harpies, Scylla, Charybdis, the Cyclops, Etna in eruption! The exiled pilot must have undergone trials, each one of which could have occasioned anxiety-neurosis or effort-syndrome in a less well-balanced man. One wonders how he reacted to Æneas' public account of them. Dido, we know, fell disastrously 'in love' with Æneas, and it is when he departs (Æneas abandoning her after their cave-wedding), that Palinurus speaks again. The fleet has stolen out in the early morning and Dido has set alight her funeral pyre, whose glow the sailors see, but only Æneas rightly interprets. At once a storm gets up.

But soon the Heav'ns with shadows were o'erspread;
A swelling Cloud hung hov'ring o'er their Head:
Livid it look'd (the threat'ning of a Storm),
Then Night and Horror Ocean's Face deform.

The Pilot *Palinurus* cry'd aloud,
'What Gusts of Weather from that gath'ring Cloud
My Thoughts presage; e'er yet the Tempest roars.
Stand to your Tackle, Mates, and stretch your Oars;
Contract your swelling Sails, and luff to Wind:'
The frighted Crew perform the Task assign'd,
Then, to his fearless Chief, 'Not Heav'n,' said he,
'Tho' *Jove* hmself shou'd promise *Italy*,
Can stem the Torrent of this raging Sea.
Mark how the shifting Winds from West arise,
And what collected Night involves the Skies!
Nor can our shaken Vessels live at Sea,
Much less against the Tempest force their way;
'Tis Fate diverts our Course; and Fate we must obey.
Not far from hence, if I observ'd aright
The southing of the Stars and Polar Light,
Sicilia lies; whose hospitable Shores
In safety we may reach with struggling oars' . . .
The Course resolv'd, before the Western Wind
They scud amain, and make the Port assign'd.

It seems clear that Palinurus, who had led the fleet between Scylla and Charybdis, recognized that this storm could not be ridden out because he knew it followed on Æneas' betrayal of Dido. He also read the true meaning of the fire which they had seen, and from that moment realized tht Æneas was guilty of hubris and impiety; he was 'not the Messiah'.

In Siciliy Æneas celebrates his arrival with elaborate games. In these – although they include various sailing contests – Palinurus does not join, and he lets other pilots fight them out. One can imagine him brooding over the past while the noisy sports proceed around him. Finally, to prevent their leaving, the women set fire to the ships and four are destroyed. Here occurs an incident for which no scientific explanation is forthcoming, and which, if the narrator were Palinurus and not Virgil, we would be tempted to ascribe to a delusion of reference. Venus begs Neptune to guarantee that her beloved Æneas and all his men will not be subjected to any more disasters and storms at sea by their enemy, Juno. Neptune agrees, but warns her that 'In safety as thou prayest shall he reach the haven of Avernus. Only one shall there be whom, lost in the flood, thou shalt seek in vain; one life shall be given for many.'

> 'Unus erit tantum, amissum quem gurgite quaeres
> unum pro multis dabitur caput.'

Then the fleet sets sail.

> A Head of all the Master Pilot steers,
> And as he leads, the following Navy veers.
> The Steeds of Night had travell'd half the Sky,
> The drowsy Rowers on their Benches lye;
> When the soft God of Sleep, with easie flight,
> Descends, and draws behind a trail of Light.
> Thou *Palinurus* art his destin'd Prey;
> To thee alone he takes his fatal way.
> Dire Dreams to thee, and Iron Sleep he bears;
> And lighting on thy Prow, the Form of *Phorbas* wears.
> Then thus the Traitor God began his Tale:
> 'The Winds, my Friend, inspire a pleasing gale;
> The Ships, without thy Care, securely sail.
> Now Steal an hour of sweet Repose; and I
> Will take the Rudder, and thy room supply.'
> To whom the yauning Pilot, half asleep;
> 'Me dost thou bid to trust the treach'rous Deep!
> The Harlot-smiles of her dissembling Face,
> And to her Faith commit the *Trojan* Race?
> Shall I believe the *Syren* South again,
> And, oft betray'd, not know the Monster Main?'
> He said, his fasten'd hands the Rudder keep,
> And fix'd on Heav'n, his Eyes repel invading Sleep.
> The God was wroth, and at his Temples threw
> A Branch in *Lethe* dip'd, and drunk with *Stygian* Dew:

The Pilot, vanquish'd by the Pow'r Divine,
Soon clos'd his swimming Eyes, and lay supine.
Scarce were his Limbs extended at their length,
The God, insulting with superior Strength,
Fell heavy on him, plung'd him in the Sea,
And, with the Stern, the Rudder tore away.
Headlong he fell, and struggling in the Main,
Cry'd out for helping hands, but cry'd in vain:
The Victor Daemon mounts obscure in Air;
While the Ship sails without the Pilot's care.
On *Neptune*'s Faith the floating Fleet relies;
But what the Man forsook, the God supplies;
And o'er the dang'rous Deep secure the Navy flies.
Glides by the *Syren*'s Cliffs, a shelfy Coast,
Long infamous for Ships, and Sailors lost;
And white with Bones: Th' impetuous Ocean roars;
And Rocks rebellow from the sounding Shores.
The watchful Heroe felt the knocks; and found
The tossing Vessel sail'd on shoaly Ground.
Sure of his Pilot's loss, he takes himself
The Helm, and steers aloof, and shuns the Shelf.
Inly he griev'd; and groaning from the Breast,
Deplor'd his Death; and thus his Pain express'd:
'For Faith repos'd on Seas, and on the flatt'ring Sky,
Thy naked Corps is doom'd, on Shores unknown to lye.'

The account is full of difficulties. 'Te Palinure petens, tibi somnia tristia portans insonti' – 'Looking for *you*, Palinurus, bringing you sad visions, guiltless though you are.' But was Palinurus guiltless? If, as we suggest, he was tired of the fruitless voyage, horrified by the callousness of Æneas, by the disasters which he seemed to attract, by his rowdy games, by the final burning of some of the ships by the angry women – that act unforgivable in the eyes of a man of the sea – then was his disappearance as accidental as Æneas supposed? Sleep first appears disguised as Phorbas. Now Phorbas was already dead – killed in the siege of Troy.

He represents the 'old school' of Trojan. In Virgil's account, the God of Sleep is angry when Palinurus refuses the first temptation. But surely the clue we should notice is that, although the sea is calm, Palinurus when he falls takes with him tiller, rudder and a section of poop. Tillers come off easily, but not part of the stern! Thus he not only provides himself with a raft, but inflicts a kind of castration on Æneas, in removing both his chief pilot and his means of steering, and this within the dangerous orbit of the Sirens! Surely this is a typical example of anti-social hysteroid resentment! And how does Æneas take the helm, when it is there no longer?*

Æneas' last words 'For Faith repos'd on seas . . .':

> 'O nimium coelo et pelago confise sereno
> nudus in ignota, Palinure, jacebis harena.'

are doubly ironical – for Palinurus boasted that he was far too experienced to trust the sea again ('Mene huic confidere monstro?'), and Dido has also prayed for exactly the same fate for Æneas – 'Let him fall before his time' – 'Sed cadat ante diem mediaque inhumatus harena', 'and lie unburied amid the sand'. It would not be fair to the reader to let this subject pass without referring to Mr. W. F. Jackson Knight's fascinating study, *Cumaean Gates* (Basil Blackwell), where he makes the supposition that Palinurus' removal of the stern of the ship was a Virgilian echo of the Babylonian Epic of Gilgamish, in which Gilgamish, bound for the lower regions, loses some essential part of his boat, and has to cut himself a quantity of punt-poles, just as Æneas had to cut the Golden Bough, to ensure his crossing to the underworld.

Palinurus, still clutching the tiller of his improvised raft, tosses on the pallid wastes of the heaving Sicilian. Three times the red sun sinks and the sheen of opal darkens on the cold and ancient gristle of the sea, three times the cloudswept Pleiads glimmer from the rainy South before at

---

* 'What the Man forsook, the God supplies' is an interpolation of Dryden's. Clavus (key, tiller) can also mean penis.

last the creaming and insouciant surf relinquishes its prey. On the
Lucanian shore by Velia he lands and is immediately set upon by the
brutish inhabitants. Not having received burial, he must wait a hundred
years on the banks of the Styx before he can cross. Here Æneas, on his
official visit to the Shades, rejoins him, and Palinurus at once appeals to
him, protesting his innocence in a manner with which those who have
had experience of such patients are familiar.

> Amidst the Spirits *Palinurus* press'd;
> Yet fresh from life; a new admitted Guest.
> Who, while he steering view'd the Stars, and bore
> His Course from *Affrick*, to the *Latian* Shore,
> Fell headlong down. The *Trojan* fix'd his view,
> And scarcely through the gloom the sullen Shadow knew.
> Then thus the Prince. 'What envious Pow'r, O Friend,
> Brought your lov'd Life to this disastrous end?
> For *Phoebus*, ever true in all he said,
> Has, in your fate alone, my Faith betray'd?
> To God foretold you shou'd not die, before
> You reach'd, secure from Seas, th' *Italian* Shore?
> Is this th' unerring Pow'r?' The Ghost reply'd,
> 'Nor *Phoebus* flatter'd, nor his Answers ly'd;
> Nor envious Gods have sent me to the Deep:
> But while the Stars, and course of Heav'n I keep,
> My weary'd Eyes were seiz'd with fatal sleep.*
> I fell; and with my weight, the Helm constrain'd,
> Was drawn along, which yet my gripe retain'd.
> Now by the Winds, and raging Waves, I swear,
> Your Safety, more than mine, was then my Care:
> Lest, of the Guide bereft, the Rudder lost,
> Your Ship shou'd run against the rocky Coast.
> Three blust'ring Nights, born by the Southern blast,
> I floated; and discover'd Land at last:

* In the original, Palinurus makes no mention of being asleep, nor is there any other mention
of Apollo's prophecy, which may be a trap set by Æneas. Notice how Palinurus' reply is
calculated to allay suspicion.

High on a mounting Wave, my head I bore:
Forcing my Strength, and gath'ring to the Shore:
Panting, but past the danger, now I seiz'd
The Craggy Cliffs, and my tir'd Members eas'd:
While, cumber'd with my dropping Cloaths, I lay,
The cruel Nation, covetous of Prey,
Stain'd with my Blood th' unhospitable Coast:
And now, by Winds and Waves, my lifeless Limbs are tost.
Which, O avert, by yon Ethereal Light
Which I have lost, for this eternal Night:
Or, if by dearer ties you may be won,
By your dead Sire, and by your living Son,
Redeem from this Reproach, my wand'ring Ghost;
Or with your Navy seek the *Velin* Coast:
And in a peaceful Grave my Corps compose:
Or, if a nearer way your Mother shows,
Without whose Aid, you durst not undertake
This frightful Passage o'er the *Stygian* Lake;
Lend to this Wretch your Hand, and waft him o'er
To the sweet Banks of yon forbidden Shore.'
Scarce had he said, the Prophetess began;
'What hopes delude thee, miserable Man?
Think'st thou thus unentomb'd to cross the Floods,
To view the Furies, and Infernal Gods;
And visit, without leave, the dark abodes?
Attend the term of long revolving years:
Fate, and the dooming Gods, are deaf to Tears.
This Comfort of thy dire Misfortune take;
The Wrath of Heav'n, inflicted for thy sake,
With Vengeance shall pursue th' inhuman Coast.
Till they propitiate thy offended Ghost,
And raise a Tomb, with Vows, and solemn Pray'r;
And *Palinurus*' name the Place shall bear.'
This calm'd his Cares: sooth'd with his future Fame;
And pleas'd to hear his propagated Name.

It is noteworthy that not Æneas, but the stern Sibyl answers him. Palinurus moreover makes no mention of having fallen asleep, but says 'the helm was violently torn from him'. It is worth remarking that his fate bears a close resemblance to that of Elpenor, in the Eleventh Odyssey. We may contrast Palinurus' appeal 'nunc me fluctus habet . . . da dextram misero' with Elpenor's request for a burial and a proper tombstone, 'memorial of an unhappy man for those who come after'.

His death is very closely paralleled by that of Misenus, the trumpeter of Æneas, who was drowned in the surf at Cumae a few days after Palinurus, while Æneas was consulting the Sibyl, and whose fame is also secured after burial by naming a cape after him. Misenus may have never recovered from the ignominy of his trumpeting to the Harpies. That Æneas should lose two of his most skilled technicians, pilot and trumpeter, and shortly afterwards, his old nurse, Caieta, at this moment when he visits the underworld, and there consecrates himself entirely to his Empire-building mission, may suggest that there was an 'old guard' who had had enough of it, who unconsciously did not wish to enter the promised land or to go through with the fighting necessary to possess it.*

Phrontis, pilot of Menelaus, also died mysteriously while at the helm off Cape Sunium (Od. iii. l. 285).

Virgil in fact makes use of three doubles: Palinurus–Phrontis, the pilot who falls into the sea, Palinurus–Elpenor, the unburied corpse who pleads with the hero in hell, and Palinurus–Misenus, the Cape-christener. Dionysus records an older tradition in which Æneas and his fleet first touched land at Cape Palinuro, in which case Virgil has stolen the honour from him for Cape Miseno and Cumae.

---

* 'Virgil knew the cost of Empire; the cost in suffering, and the cost to conscience and to so many graceful things. That he knew the cost his poem shows so clearly that it has lately been thought to be a savage attack on Augustus and autocracy'. – W. J. KNIGHT, op. cit. p. 168.

The Palinurus passages are so charged with haunting images and golden cadences as to suggest that Virgil has identified himself with his pilot (as did Milton with Orpheus). Both poets reflect their unconscious death-wish. Palinurus: Æneas: :Virgil: Augustus.

Those are all the known facts about Palinurus. Whether he deliberately tried to abandon Æneas, or whether he was the innocent victim of divine vengeance, or a melancholy and resentful character who felt his special nautical gift was henceforth unwanted cannot be deduced from the evidence. His bluff sailor's manner may belie his real state of mind. I am inclined to rule out both suicide (there are no symptoms comparable to those of Dido, when she felt all nature prompting her to the deed), and accident, for the sterns of ships do not fall off in calm seas. We are left, therefore, with design – either a planned act of escape and revenge by Palinurus – or with supernatural intervention, in the shape of a propitiatory sacrifice of the Pilot to Juno, who might otherwise have prevented the safe arrival of Æneas and his whole expedition.

Which of these alternatives we accept is, in the last analysis, a question of the claims of reason versus those of revealed religion.

As a myth, however, and particularly as a myth with a valuable psychological interpretation, Palinurus clearly stands for a certain will-to-failure or repugnance-to-success, a desire to give up at the last moment, an urge towards loneliness, isolation and obscurity. Palinurus, in spite of his great ability and his conspicuous public position, deserted his post in the moment of victory and opted for the unknown shore.

With the sea – age-old symbol of the unconscious – his relations were always close and harmonious, and not until he reaches land is he miserably done to death.

And as with so many of those who resign from the struggle, who quit because they do not want to succeed, because they find something vulgar and even unlucky in success itself – immediately he feels remorse and misery at his abdication, and wishes he had remained where he was. Doing is overrated, and success undesirable, but the bitterness of Failure even more so. Palinurus, in fact, though he despises the emptiness of achievement, the applause of the multitude, and the rewards of fame, comes in his long exile to hate himself for despising them, and so he jumps childishly at the chance to be perpetuated as an obscure cape.*

One last clue: The name Palinurus (παλίνουρος) in Greek, (and we know the importance attached to their names by neurotics), means 'one-who-makes-water-again', and is so used in an epigram of Martial (III. 78) –

'Minxisti currente semel, Pauline, carina.
Meiere vis iterum? Jam Palinurus eris.'

'You have made water once, Paulinus, while your boat was moving fast. Do you want to pumpship again? Then you will be a Palinurus' (i.e. will fall overboard).

These words 'ουρεῖν, mingere, meiere, possess as well a sexual significance, and this opens up possibilities of a deep analysis on Freudian lines, should time permit – and funds be available.

* Cape Palinuro soon acquired a reputation for shipwrecks. The Roman Fleet met with disaster there in 253 B.C., and again in 36 B.C. Horace also had a narrow escape. On the summit of the headland are still visible some ruins which are popularly known as the Tomb of Palinurus. The promontory, through which runs Lat. 40°, retains its ancient name.

Revisiting Greece
(1954)

After examining a clutch of well-made travel books, I have sometimes wondered for how many pages one could keep it up by setting out to tell the truth, not only about places but about the inadequacy of our feelings. (I have known the Acropolis to resemble a set of false teeth in a broken palate.) When at last we take our long-wished-for holiday what really happens?

There is, first, the period of preparation (in a sense the only time we are abroad); guide-books are compared; experts are consulted; a mirage of a brown, lean summer-self descending on an obese island dances before our eyes and we are convincingly importuned by the wrong clothes, the wrong books, the wrong introductions. 'Of course you will need a white dinner-jacket and a cummerbund'; 'you must take the *whole* of Pausanias'; 'an ultra-violet filter'; 'stout walking shoes'; 'the rubber flippers should be made to measure'.

At twenty we travel to discover ourselves, at thirty for love, at forty out of greed and curiosity, at fifty for a revelation. Irresponsible, illiterate, shedding all ties and cares, we await the visitation, the rebirth. Gradually the present dissolves, England becomes totally unreal; we have in fact already left, not yet air-borne but anxiety-cradled; 'if the flippers are not ready, they cannot possibly be sent on'; 'you quite understand that these traveller's cheques are not negotiable on Mount Athos'; 'don't go to the new hotel but the other one'; 'don't go to the old hotel'; 'there are three new hotels'; 'Corfu is the place for you: it has everything'; 'yes, if you like a green island. I prefer Mikonos'; 'it's never too hot on Corfu'; 'you would hate Corfu'.

D-Day. Running in the new dark glasses in the car to the airport.

Livid clouds, infra-red buses, a lurid day-of-judgment air about the hoardings along the clotted avenue. Signs of panic, cleverly concealed, as I board the plane, where I suffer from a private phobia, dispelled only by champagne, that the signal 'Fasten your safety-belts' is staying on for the whole voyage.

Paris: the heat advances across the tarmac, our gaoler for the next six weeks. 'Thick brown overcoat, stout walking shoes, whole of Pausanias,' it mumbles; 'Mr. Connolly? I think we can take care of all that.' Inevitable contrast between London and Paris, the one muffled under its summer cloud-cap, all Wimbledon and roses, the other with a migraine of politics, bleached and persilled in the heat. The bookstall at London Airport for a nation of magazine-readers – if that; at Le Bourget full of expensive works of art and philosophy. The paralysis of suburbia contrasted with the animation of the *banlieue* where a fair is in progress and a horse-drawn dray of children jingles under the catalpas.

How much of a holiday is spent lying gasping on one's back, in planes, trains, cabins, beaches and hotel bedrooms, the guide-book held aloft like an awning? We really travel twice – as a physical object resembling a mummy or small wardrobe-trunk which is shuttled about at considerable expense; and as a mind married to a 'Guide Bleu', always reading about the last place or the next one.

It is suddenly apparent that the heat permits no reading of any kind; whole areas of consciousness must be evacuated, the perimeter of sensation shortened; no past, no future. Only the guidebook survives and the other books we have brought sneak to the bottom of the suitcase. And now the Seven Indispensables perform their ghostly jig from pocket to pocket. The passport, the traveller's cheques, the tickets, the dark glasses, the reading glasses, the pen, the comb. Where are they? I could have sworn I had them a moment ago.

A flying visit to Versailles to see the *petits appartements* rendered famous by the Pompadour, the Dubarry and Madame de Mitford. Intense disappointment; so much redecoration, and everywhere the milling multitudes, locusts of the post-war summer. Illumination: *The human eye deteriorates all it looks at.* Why is the decoration of the

House of the Vettii at Pompeii so much less exciting than the new excavations? Because the human eye has faded the colours, vulgarised the painting. The camera also enfeebles its subject and being photographed too often I believe to cause cancer of the soul.

And now, Venice, city of sore throats, frayed tempers and leaking wallets; alas, never the same for me since I reviewed Hemingway's last novel but one. Much as I disliked the book I remain obsessed by his terrible colonel. I drink Valpolicella and take the fatal stroll to Harry's Bar, stopping on the little bridge where the colonel had a heart-attack on his way from his wine to his martinis. How he would have hated the Biennale! So much painting that should never have come South of the Alps, North of the Po, West of Suez or East of Saint Louis, all maltreated by the heat, the humidity and the merciless light – except the paintings which have some secret poster-quality, Delvaux's clustering cow-like nudes or Bacon's agonising tycoons. Art is bottled sunshine and should never be exposed to it.

And everywhere art-critics, never a painter; symbol of the age of culture-diffusion when publishers and village-explainers travel while authors have to stay at home, when painters in Maida Vale hear from their dealers in Mozambique or Mogador, when Byron would have received a postcard: 'Dear B. London must be very hot. Just off to Ravenna to join the Galignanis and then to meet some Greek publishers at Missolonghi. Hope to be able to do something for you. How goes the Canto? – Yrs., John Murray.'

Revisit the equestrian statue of Colleone in its dingy square. The base is too high. Better in a photograph. Failure to experience any emotion over Tintoretto. Horror of Surrealist masters in Biennale. Moved by nothing later than Pompeii. Great paintings should be kept under lock and key and shown as seldom as wonder-working images. The real connoisseurs of art were the Pharaohs; they took it with them. Intoxication with Venetian gardens, the oleander drooping over the canal at some scabrous corner, the ubiquitous freshwater sea-smell and the best drink in Europe, a tumbler of ice-cold peach-juice in the colonel's bar. More hordes of milling tourists, squeaking *lederhosen*;

Clapham Junction of the mechanised masses in the Piazza. Everybody is somebody. Nobody is anybody. Everyone is everywhere.

At last the boat: survival of an earlier form of travel, obeying the strange psychology of 'on board ship'. Whom we hate on the first day we shall love on the last, whom we greet on the first we shall not bid farewell; boredom will become its own reward and change suddenly to ecstasy. The *Achilleus* is a charmed vessel, trim, white, gay, its inmates friendly and delightful. The islands of the lagoon bob at their moorings as we churn through the warm night and the next blue day past Monte Gargano and Brindisi, with its lemon ices and Roman column, and across to Corfu where we stay for three hours instead of a week, just time to see the famous view at Canoni, so called because the tourist is fired at it like a cannon-ball.

That evening we are streaking through the Corinth Canal like mercury rising in a thermometer. The *Achilleus* has now gone completely Greek. The food is interesting and local, the crew sings, the married couples no longer flash their signals of distress, 'save me, rescue me'. The passengers crane over the rail to where the distant corona of Athens glows above the dark bulk of Salamis. We enter the sooty bustle of Piraeus as the last evening steamers beetle forth to fertilise the expectant islands and are extracted from our carefree cabin like ticks from a dog's ear. Nothing on shore will quite come up to it, even as Nice is never worthy of the Blue Train or New York of the *Queen Mary*. *Arriver, c'est déjà partir un peu.*

~

Great heat, like a smart doctor, begins every sentence 'You'll have to cut out. . . .' With the temperature always around ninety, generalities alone can be appreciated, details and detours must be ignored; we are but fit for the simplest forms of sightseeing.

Air throbs, marble hisses, the sea glistens with malice, the exhausted landscape closes at lunch-time and does not reopen before six o'clock when the sun ceases its daily interrogation. We stagger across the grilled slabs of the Propylaea with only one idea – which is both idea and sensation – the juice of a lemon and an orange in equal proportions poured again and again over cubes of ice. After this post-war duty visit we flee the Parthenon and rush to take the first boat at the Piraeus. It is crowded and unbelievably noisy but there is a cool breeze as we round Sunium.

Bathed in lemon-yellow light like Rabat or Casablanca, Rhodes has some claim to be the perfect island. Neither too large nor too small, too hot nor too cold, fertile, hilly, legendary and exotic, it lives in the present as well as the past. The medieval city of the knights has been so perfectly restored by the Italians as to outdo Carcassonne; it is a golden flypaper for tourists who are led to it like bombers to a dummy target, leaving the real town uninjured. Between the austerity of the medieval fortress and the flamboyant Fascist concrete outside the walls the old Turkish quarter sprawls in exquisite decay.

The few simple elements required by the Moslem conception of beauty, the dome and minaret, fountain, plane-tree and arcaded court-yard are here combined into a dozen similar but never monotonous patterns . . . we are in a tiny Stamboul, a sixteenth- and seventeenth-century quarter of dignified exiles with their Persian tiles and Arabic inscriptions, their memories of fallen grandeur. No farther from the comfortable but hideous Hôtel des Roses than you can spit a pome-granate seed stands the little mosque of Murad-Reïz, its cemetery planted with mulberry and oleander. Few places are more soothing than a Turkish graveyard, where the turbaned tombs are jumbled like spillikins around the boles of cypresses and the cicadas zizz above the silent koubbas.

Here sleeps the commander who captured Tripoli, and probably the administrators who lost it, heroes and footlers together, the generals and admirals, the Beys and Pashas of that cruel, clean, pious, frugal horticultural community. The great admiral's grave is well kept-up and hung with Mecca-green cloth; otherwise the nodding conversation pieces are abandoned to shade and sun, each stone turban proudly proclaiming its owner's status or bearing a verse from the Koran by which we linger in bewilderment – even as one day in some far-flung graveyard a passing Chinese may halt, baffled by the enumeration of our meagre virtues.

Mikonos by contrast is a rude stone altar erected to the stern god of summer. The town is a white African sneer arching brightly round the bay where a row of little restaurants vie with each other in dis-appointments. The heat swaggers through the spotless alleys where bearded Danish painters seal every exit with their easels.

To swim one must bump across the bay to some blinding cove or trudge the iron-hot mountain path, paved with mule-dung and brown thistle. The sun needles the brain cavity, desiccates the lung and obtains a garnishee upon the liver. Doors bang, nerves jangle, little waves bristle and buffet through the afternoon and in our sleep fashionable voices cry 'Mikonos for me', 'il y a toujours du vent à Mikonos'.

After this stony sanatorium its humble neighbour seems to flower with statues, tremendous in its exuberant and irretrievable collapse. Whereas Delphi's mountain womb remains one of the holy places of the human spirit, Delos is complex and baffling, irreverent even in its piety. With its swans and geese and cafeteria, the sacred lake where Apollo was born must have been not unlike the Round Pond in Kensington Gardens; the commercial Roman town survives in better shape than the Greek; the shrines of Isis and the phalloi of Dionysus have stood up better than Apollo's altars. In this centre of the ancient slave trade, this eclectic battener on the world's religions whose moneylending priest-hood were the Rothschilds of antiquity, the god of man's fulfilment in this world, the wielder of the lyre and the bow, is noticeably absent.

Yet Delos is magical. According to the admirable Greek usage, no fence surrounds the ruins nor is there an entrance fee; black with tourists and lizards, prostrate in the sunshine, the ancient stones are part of the world's daily life. Among the Roman pavements is the mysteriously haunting mosaic of anchor and dolphin which was found on the seals of the wine-jars on the Greek ship salvaged outside Marseilles by M. Cousteau, and which aided him to identify his Sextius, owner of the vessel, with the proprietor of this sumptuous villa. By such means are we enabled to creep backwards into time, liberated by significant detail such as the hand, in the museum, from that colossal archaic Apollo which was broken off by the fall of the sculptor Nikias's fabulous bronze palm-tree.

Delphi remains sacred to Apollo while Delos had permission to exploit him; both became enormously rich, both tottered to destruction after Julian's reign in A.D. 363 with full treasuries, gold ceilings and colonnades of marble statues (Delos had 3,000 intact under the opprobrium of the Christians). Abandoned to pirates through the Dark Ages, Delos must still have been one of the wonders of the world, a desert island carpeted with temples and matchless private buildings, a thousand years of sanctity still clinging to the shrines and avenues while Delphi, pillaged by Byzantium, issued its despairing last oracle and the bronze horses of St. Mark's, as I like to think, were reft from the impassive Charioteer.

We may walk across the sacred lake or stand on Apollo's temple at Delphi where the earth-dragon fumed and fretted and the priestess gave out incoherent moans for the priest to polish into the double meanings which answered our desire. But it is difficult to feel aware of the terrible god of youthful strength and intellectual beauty. He exists only in museums. For though Greek architecture has barely survived, and Greek music and painting not at all, we have at last learnt how to display sculpture at its best.

In the new museum at Athens we no longer need to pretend to ourselves; here the chain of masterpieces signal to each other down the ages. This is how Greece was; this is what man can do. Apollo is manifest at last with his smile which seems instantly to annihilate all time and all suffering. Joy is under everything and if we feel pain it is our fault because we are not divine enough. Death has an appropriateness which transcends sorrow; the world belongs to the beautiful; charm is welded to courage, thought to action – even the serpent is a friend.

But humanity could not grow up without a religion of the mother; the world could not always belong to the graceful tactless hearties with red curls, bulging eyeballs, stocky behinds, a try-anything-once look below their waving helmets. Can one think of any archaic sculpture which takes even Zeus beyond early middle age? In this art 'Hippocleides doesn't care' triumphs over the maxims of the seven sages. Irresponsible perfection went out about 475 B.C.; yet is it my imagination or are not the contemporary Greeks one of the happiest as well as the most friendly nations in the world?

Living with Lemurs
(1957)

After twenty years I have a ring-tailed lemur again; my sixth. I still think them the most delightful of all pets; it is their owner, not the breed, who has deteriorated. Yet a singular doubt has grown. Are they clockwork? How do they differ from a machine?

I used to think of them as possessing an unearthly quality – ghosts; *lemures*, like their name – uncanny, primitive, remote; man's one authentic ancestor. Their plaintive cry, their eyes of melting brown under long black lashes, the indescribably forlorn and touching quality of their expression as if dimly aware of their predicament halfway between man and beast, a terrier's head on a fur-lined Pharaoh's body, toenails as well as claws, hands that grip fruit yet cannot peel it. . . .

And now they remind me of Arab musicians. 'How unutterably sad,' I said of such monotonous singing. 'No – the sadness is in you,' my companion replied – and indeed the musicians were shaking with silent laughter. The lemur's typical plaintive cry, for instance, which certainly results from loneliness, from any separation from the herd, is also automatically reproduced in answer to any sound of the same pitch – children's voices or the mew of a cat.

A lemur, in fact, has about six noises each with its corresponding body posture, and runs through them in regular order like the gear changes on a car. They fall into three groups.

1. EMOTION	NOISE	POSTURE
Anxiety, hunger, etc.	= short mew	= skipping with imaginary rope
loneliness, recognition	= plaintive cry sometimes prolonged to a sob	= head lifted, cheeks blown out

2. EMOTION	NOISE	POSTURE
Excitement, irritation, play	= metallic, *bdib, bdib, bdib*	= leaping, bouncing
alarm	= short croak	= stares at suspicious object, jumps to safety
anger	= high squeak	= biting, clawing

3. EMOTION	NOISE	POSTURE
Pleasure	= purring	= licking and cuddling up
sex (males only)	= nasal whinny	= tail held over head and stiffly waggled

Lemurs are inclined to bite when food (or what they consider food – i.e. eyeblack, toothpaste) is taken away from them or when picked up roughly or much against their will, or when sexually rebuffed. If the ribs or armpits are tickled they are compelled to purr, to abandon any other posture and to start licking whatever lies in front of them.

They are, I believe, affectionate and devoted to only one master or mistress whom they will follow or precede closely; yet they appear quite promiscuous, like married couples at a cocktail party. They resent all ties or dependency and have a deep-rooted love of freedom; their temperament is amiable, steadfast, sunny and mischievous. The basic play-form is 'catch me if you can'.

This is how they play together; an impertinent tap or nip is followed by a delirious chase ending in a boxing and wrestling match. They express themselves by their agility and will reserve their longest leaps for the largest audience – they seem to like best children and the very old.

Lemurs regard cats as being germane to themselves and will immediately attempt to groom them; dogs are generally to be teased. They are almost fearless, but all dislike aeroplanes and large birds. They rely on their brilliant timing to get out of the way, will jump on the dog's rump or advance backwards upon it in a manner that even large hounds find completely unnerving.

Their front teeth form a currycomb; the canines grow back like fish-hooks and can give a most painful bite; in addition the males have a blunt claw inside the elbow with which they can rip and tear in moderation; all box cleverly, 'southpaws' who lead at their opponents' eyes.

When a lemur is let loose in a strange room it does not skulk in corners and investigate smells, like a dog or cat, but immediately establishes a four-wall circuit until it can leap round the room at picture level. Each new leap is tested with hilarious *bdib-bdib-bdib-bdib*. In these circuits, pictures, china and even quite large pieces of furniture come rapidly to grief and – since lemurs are beautifully precise and sure-footed – it is clear that they enjoy the crash and jingle of breaking glass or cascading Chelsea. Out of doors they will choose some fragile and elastic shrub and bounce up and down on it, like children on a clump of rushes. They will always answer and come when called yet show the greatest reluctance to being caught, except when feeling tired or cold.

At night they prefer to sleep in a bed, will find their way to the bottom like a hot-water bottle and remain quiet for hours. They rise at dawn. They will not foul their bed but it is impossible to house-train them; any perch above ground is considered a privy.

On the other hand they can be controlled to some extent through the times when they are fed and, being vegetarians, are seldom noxious. They will consume between two and three bananas a day, one or two bits of bread or cake, some grapes or a few leaves of lettuce. They must be protected from alcohol or they become topers.

Lemurs are not greedy and spend very little of their time in eating. Sleep, play and fur-combing come first. Their coat is short, thick and extremely soft with a smell of young kitten. They enjoy travelling and will sit for hours looking out of a railway window.

What are the limits of their intelligence? If tied to a post they immediately become hopelessly entangled and, unlike a monkey, can never unwind themselves. They will not run carrying their leash in one hand, as I have seen a monkey do, but can tug at it if it is bothering them. They altogether lack the imitative impulse of monkeys and their hands are extremely clumsy.

Matches and match-boxes fascinate all lemurs though they have great difficulty in manipulating them; newly cut wood usually sets up the elbow-clawing reaction.* Their sight and hearing are excellent and they perceive everything; in fact, they may well be much more intelligent than anyone has supposed since their reproachful glance or sneer or look of love is subtle almost to the point of imperceptibility.

They never appear as if they are trying to say something – they are too self-satisfied, too much the dandy to give way to emotion. Their parting protest, however, can lacerate one with guilt.

The ring-tailed lemur (*lemur catta*) has a fairly short history. It appears in a Chinese painting of the eighteenth century and in several eighteenth-century pictures, one a charming Stubbs of the Duke of Atholl's family. With the gibbon, Humboldt's woolly monkey, the sea-lion, cheetah, beaver and otter it is in the top flight of pets; it is hardy, diurnal, clever, sensitive and devoted, reasonably clean and very easy to feed as it can be let loose for long stretches in the garden.

Before the war there was a great rush on lemurs and the French Government has now prohibited their export from Madagascar. They are preserved, like the Australian koala, in their dwindling forests. I am not sure that this is the right policy; it would be better to enclose them in various tropical and subtropical zoos where the climate suits (even an English summer day drives them into the shade) to encourage them to breed in captivity.

* Mr. Ivan Sanderson wrote to me that the horny excrescences release a glandular secretion.

But breeding is difficult for human beings seem to exercise a fatal fascination; lemurs will spurn their own image to pursue the huge creatures who, like monkeys and apes, are descended from them, who once possessed a tail with sixteen rings and the lost virtue of irresponsibility.

Confessions of a House-Hunter
(1967)

"Rock of ages cleft for me,
Tell me where to find the key."
"Rawlence and Squarey,"
Said the bells of Saint Mary.
"Cubitt and West,
They know what's best."
"Knight, Frank and Rutley
Would have put it more subtly."
"Messenger, May and Baverstock,
WE have the key that fits the lock."

– From *House-hunting Songs and Shanties*

All my life I have wanted passionately to own a house. Like many of my generation, I belong to the landless gentry with memories of better times. My parents' families had about two thousand acres each in Ireland and the West Country; my father some two and a half acres in the county of Surrey. I have never possessed anything larger than a bookcase. I have been house-hungry now for some forty years without setting eyes on a title deed. It's a man's life; out of doors in all weathers, and one comes across some very interesting people. Should the house-fiend be registered? Is he (or she) a danger to the community? Does house-hunger destroy the moral sense? Or corrupt the young? Is it hereditary? Can it be cured?

A house-fiend is a man who, while signing the contract for his ultimate home, gathers up particulars of all the others, a man who is not quite sane on Wednesday evenings, when he waits up all night for his 'fix' – the new number of *Country Life*. A house-agent lives by actually selling houses, a house-hunter on dreams and curiosity. His whole existence is an order to view. A woman without a home is a snail without a shell; her suffering is biological. But a man without a few particulars in his pocket, a licence to day-dream, is spiritually dead; past hope, past prayer, past analysis (which often exposes a deeper mal-adjustment).

Many house-hunters make delightful companions and some are quite capable of earning their living; we recognise each other instinctively by some secret code, and since most houses for sale are overpriced and once they have failed to reach their reserve at auction remain on the market for several years, we have our stories to tell. 'If only, if only . . .' 'I nearly bought "Greenfingers." ' – 'Why, so did we.' – 'I practically paid a deposit.' 'A little bird whispered "Rising Damp."' 'I even went to the auction.'

The signature of the contract on the auction particulars would have been legally binding: this was a brave man.

I began as a house-hunter in the First World War by tagging along with my mother. These forays in commuting distance of London (my father was working in the War Office) left an indelible impression of oak-beams and lattice-windows among the Surrey pines or the stucco of Worplesdon, or even as far afield as Farnham, Crondall and Odiham. I learned to love the glint of bottled glass, an ingle-nook, a tennis-court under the deodars, a distant view of the Hog's Back.

> *Oak beams and a sagging floor*
> *With a leathern latchet to the door . . .*

My mother taught me the first lesson: always admire everything and leave reservations till afterwards. This was a great help in preparation for the future, for that important moment in the hunt which I shall call the Confrontation. The bell rings, the door opens and the owner awaits us – are we fly to his spider? Or the fox among his chickens? Sometimes one glimpse of the hall with its bull-fighting posters and cocktail bar in imitation red leather makes us want to turn tail. Occasionally I have driven straight up by appointment to some creepered porch, round the gravel sweep, and off again, ringing up the nearest call-box to say that I have been unavoidably detained. Most old houses are sick, most new ones are hideous. There are few exceptions.

The best ones are empty. But perhaps I had better describe the stages of a 'hunt' from the beginning.

1. Mutual Attraction (by advertisement, exploration or hearsay).
2. The Assignation (or 'at the Agents').
3. The Viewing or Confrontation.
4. Crystallisation or Disillusion.
5. The Offer.
6. The Colding of the Feet.
7. The Renunciation (back to Square One).
8. Mutual Attraction (*Country Life* again).

Don't think one can't get hurt. We witness terrible things: the felling of cedars, uprooting of figs, demolition of peach-house and vinery, fireplaces wrenched from their sockets, built-in bookcases carted off to auction. The lamentations of an old gardener can affect one for weeks. There are some houses with which we really do fall in love, and when we lose them, because we keep dithering or can't afford them, the pain may last for several years. But it is almost impossible to distinguish true love from infatuation, especially as it is often directed on houses which are for practical reasons quite unsuitable. An inveterate house-hunter is often a man divided against himself. He wants long eighteenth-century windows, Palladian saloons, lodges, a park and stable clock, and at the same time a penthouse which functions like the latest yacht with press-button efficiency. He sees a house as a frame for his personality when it will turn out only a drain on his income. Whatever its condition when we first see a house – roses dead-headed, clocks ticking – it will end up like all the others we have lived in.

The season for house-hunting lasts from March to October; every house looks beautiful in spring sunshine; few addicts enjoy trudging through dead leaves or examining sodden lawns through rain-swept windows. In winter most gardens seem all cinders and laurel. Then the hunter keeps his eye in with an occasional penthouse or eighteenth-century town mansion or a finca or quinta in the sun. The advertisement pages also shrink, as if owners too were lying low. August is another dowdy time, when only sea and mountain escape the general dullness. Affinities between house-hunting and nest-building make early spring the most dramatic period, with a secondary season in early autumn, connected with hibernation.

Every issue of *Country Life* will contain three or four houses which instantly appeal to the viewer. Some are too big or too far from London, but generally there is a mill or rectory or Georgian farm around which 'mutual attraction' takes place – mutual because such houses imply an affinity with the personality of the owner. Some of these attract us only for romantic or atavistic reasons. In my case Irish country-houses in arrogant disrepair make everything else look vulgar. Manor-houses have all, by now, been shrunk to manageable size by judicious advertising. 'Seven bed and dressing-rooms with staff flat and nursery wing, three reception, study and playroom' means a thirteen-bedroom mansion with billiards. By Thursday we are ringing up or have written for particulars.

These should consist of at least two pages and avoid all whimsy or exaggeration while stressing features dear to the hunter's psyche – streams, lakes, walled gardens, 'extensive' views and gazebos. It can now be assumed that all tennis-lawns and kitchen gardens have long been let go unless there is proof to the contrary. A photograph is essential, although it can be taken so as to conceal arterial roads, pylons, housing developments, even that semi-detachment which, with the division of larger houses into three is becoming increasingly common.

A visit to the agents is one of the pleasures of the chase. Most agents are extremely agreeable, and we take to them like alcoholics to barmen. Always select either an enthusiastic young man who still believes his particulars or an older partner with an air of worldly experience; he is likely to be the only agent who can afford an aesthetic sense. Avoid the oafish type who is invincibly ignorant, or the shark who betrays his eagerness – 'Wheeler speaking – I just rang up to know if you had come to any decision about "Greenfingers," Mr. Hunter: the owner is very anxious to sell.' 'I can well believe it.'

My favourite homefinder – by now a little weary – works in an agency in Folksbourne and has been my companion on innumerable visits when a house or even a flat in that seaside town seemed all that one could desire. Winter afternoons would find him waiting, keys in hand (there is no close season in Folksbourne) by windy maisonettes or sometimes a turreted mansion, usually divided into flats, with soaring gables and overbearing overmantels in rusticated Tudor; bathrooms and lavatories ominous with rails and hand-grips for the arthritic. With unfailing patience and politeness Mr. Oakwood saw me through several courtships all ending in disillusion, culminating in that of a large Edwardian battlecruiser moored on the edge of a state forest, a Forsyte home four hundred feet above sea-level.

There is some part of me that yearns for these houses of around 1900, with stained glass lilies on the landing, glossy overmantels and coved ceilings, shallow stairs haunted by vanished parlour-maids. I yearned: my family did not share the yearning. The straight-backed owner and her agent waited in vain while I pleaded. 'I am sorry that I have led you on so many fruitless errands, Mr. Oakwood,' I burst out one day at an altogether different place. 'The trouble,' he answered, 'is that Folksbourne has such dreadful houses.'

Sundays in Folksbourne, yellow with forsythia, the electric log hissing in the fire-place with its curved plaster surround, 'sun-room' or conservatory ablaze with plastic flowers, an oak porch with my eye to the keyhole, the roast knocking at the hatch, the sea glistening through the macrocarpa . . . Folksbourne will come into its own when the world is tired of Georgian boxes; it will be the last stronghold of the landless gentry who bring their Cotswold saddle stones with them.

William Rufus Hunter, of 'Huntersmoon', 65 Chatsworth Road, Folksbourne. The family of Hunter claim descent from Herne of that Ilk and have long been settled in Chatsworth Road, where a Hunter was summoned for non-payment of rates as far back as 1947. Owns about one-third of an acre. Arms: subject to negotiation. Motto: 'Viewing strictly by appointment.'

Now for the Confrontation.

'I am Mr. Hunter; I have an order to view from Messrs. Wheeler and Dealer.' 'We were expecting you: please come in.' Houses are usually shown by the owners, in which case no chaperone from Wheeler and Dealer is necessary.

Owners fall into three types. (1) Widows; (2) Retired couples; (3) Businessmen. Widows who are recently bereaved make viewing almost impossible. 'This is his' (gulp) and 'This is where he kept his . . .' (gulp). How would you feel if Queen Victoria were showing you round Osborne? The only course is to sympathise and escape. An abandoned or separated wife knows the balm of aggression. 'And this was his so-called study. Really the telephone room.' 'Quite.' 'This used to be the swimming-pool.' 'A swimming-pool can be a very soulless thing.' 'So I found, Mr. Hunter.' Retired couples may prove even more harrowing. 'We'll go round the ground floor together, Mr. Hunter, then my wife will take you upstairs.' 'My husband hasn't been at all well lately.' 'I am sorry to hear it.' This would be the utility room?' 'Yes – in the old days.' 'We hate to leave – we've been very happy here – but our children have grown up and flown and my husband (wife) has not been too well lately. He (she) has Huntington's chorea/cavernous sinus thrombosis/ Madura foot.' 'I am so very sorry.' The businessman makes straight for the central heating installation, 'You can do everything but play a tune on it.'

Family photographs exercise a compelling fascination on viewers, like shoe cupboards and deep freezes. But an empty house for which one picks up the key will provide the deepest satisfaction; an empty house is like a naked woman – just that little bit more ours. I have refrained from saying that houses are like women because it is unclear to me whether a house, in Freudian terms, is masculine or feminine. A room is feminine – but a three-storey five-bay Georgian façade? The house-hunter is a Don Giovanni – he has his list – but what does he really want? An unpunished *voyeur*, he is also a dispossessed exile from Eden. Is his goal coffin or castle? Secluded and, of course, 'with character. . . .'

Alone in an empty house, virgin of decoration, he paces the rooms, peers from the windows, calls 'Come out' up the stairs. Some of my happiest moments have been in a Snowcemmed *fin-de-siècle* retreat in Ashdown Forest by Baillie Scott. It occupies a lost valley under the radar beacons and has an extraordinary atmosphere of architectural felicity and grace. Pine panelling, peacock-tiled fire-places, colophons of stained glass, a Mackmurdo-like staircase of black knitting-needles, an enormous white bath with shower and/or spray, and a handle marked 'WAVES' . . . the whole three acres encircled by a rhododendron tunnel round the estate. I am relieved it has been sold. How painful is the right house in the wrong place.

The Confrontation over, comes the prognostic – infatuation or disappointment? If, after we have admired everything without restriction our objections begin to surface, then nothing remains but to try the next on our list. Should infatuation persist, there follows the second visit, a more serious inspection in which our known and best-loved objects – bookcases, tables, beds – begin to occupy prepared positions and swim into place. By this time a special relationship is established with the owners. 'I thought your husband seemed a little better today.'

After several visits there is still time to withdraw, but infatuation may seize entire hold. Frantic with house-hunger, we constantly write down the name of the new home, add up the digits in the telephone number, consult large-scale maps and local records, pit the dimensions of its room against discarded favourites, balance advantages – position, seclusion, architectural interest, library, drawing-room, gardens, trees, views, water – so as to justify our preferences or give marks for drab realities like central heating, nearness to school or station, rates, condition, upkeep. The deposit rears its ugly head. Now is the time to go round once more with an architect (a brief visit will often save the expense of a survey) or even to make an offer.

This last is a desperate move, equivalent to fixing a date at the registrar's. Buying a house is like getting married; the moment of agreement is a moment of panic. For better or worse, we're hooked. Is this the end to all those sunny afternoons bowling round the countryside, all the interiors, ingle-nooks and breastsummers, the intimate yet formal contacts with other lives? Do all these lead only to 'Greenfingers'? 'Because man goeth to his long home and the mourners go about the streets. . . .'

The offer should be large enough to disarm hostility but not so large as to be accepted. And, of course, 'subject to survey'. I suppose most of us can run to only one survey, just as many confirmed viewers can barely afford the fare if their quarry is outside the Home Counties.

Surveyors are never too encouraging and seem to read our inmost hearts. Watch Mr. Hunter, usually so meek, when with flashing eye he brandishes the explosive document at the agent's 'I have the survey here and it reveals a most unsatisfactory state of affairs at "Greenfingers" – nail-sickness in the potting-shed! Under the circumstances I have no option but to refuse to proceed with the negotiation.' 'I am sure Mrs. O'Meara would be prepared for an adjustment.' 'I am sorry, Mr. Wheeler. I wish to have no further dealings with Mrs. O'Meara.'

To watch poor Hunter at his worst behold him when he is forced to go round a house with a rival party. How pointedly he lags behind or darts ahead, how patronisingly he dismisses the pony prizes and pin-ups in the nursery rooms, the wrought-iron gates before the cocktail bar, the 'small walled hydrangea garden'. His 'have-not' hatred of the householder is exposed. 'I'm afraid I've got to leave now – I am in a great hurry.' 'But Mr. Hunter, you haven't seen the rumpus room.' – 'I'll keep in touch (*snarl*) through Messrs. Wheeler and Dealer.'

No true Hunter has had an offer rejected without a sense of relief, but to be outbid by a rival is a fighting matter. When we lose a house that we really want the remedy is to concentrate on its deficiencies, then find another which has not got them: it will not have the same advantages either, but that is irrelevant. There must be no interregnum. 'The house is gone; let's find a house.' And so we're back to Square One.

But even as we mutter the grim words a thin brown envelope slides under the door or the sophisticated London agent who knows about *cottages ornés* rings up or a house that we have admired from of old is back on the market or a new Belle shows up. 'I rather like the sound of this one, "Old Dripping Manor." . . .' It is a crisp September morning; the copper beech is vituperating through the mauve glass, the penthouse gleams all gin and lime above the esplanade; mill and rectory, oast-house and maisonette put forth their well-worn charms. Auction particulars arrive in colours. 'Only four minutes from the Town Centre, commanding views of the sea and downs, surrounded by its own grounds of well-established trees, flowering shrubs, herbaceous border, lily pond with paved walk and wrought-iron surround, copse, orchard and paddock amounting in all to one-third of an acre. The handsome detached residence dating from the turn of the century, with many gracious period features, including tessellated orangery, known as 'Huntersmoon', 65, Chatsworth Road, Folksbourne, is offered for immediate sale by order of the Executors. Viewing strictly by appointment.'

The Downfall of Jonathan Edax
(1961)

'After all, Jonathan, you can't take it with you.' At lunch, yesterday – Friday – from Brenda, that hoary old cliché again. It set me thinking. Of course, logistically, one couldn't. There's no point in actually being buried with the loot like Tutankhamen though I would enjoy the sight of my coffin being followed to the vault by a procession of packing-cases and tea-chests. Crated rather than cremated. 'For the present, if nobody minds, I'm quite content to stay here.'

But, come to think of it, there *is* a way of taking it with one, and that is to endow the whole thing as a museum. One preserves one's name and it keeps the collection together. More than one dare expect from one's own family. They shall have front seats at the opening – if they can get away from their jobs. I can picture their faces. I'm certainly not going to take *them* with me:

The Edax Foundation: A small closed collection, museum and library open thrice yearly to the general public with microfilm material available to accredited students. Endowed by Mr. Jonathan Edax, this small closed collection contains some of the choicest examples of etc., etc., illustrating the taste and discrimination of its munificent founder. A fitting memorial to the days when it was still possible for a private individual, etc., etc. . . .

'The human eye deteriorates all it looks at' – whoever wrote that should be my first Curator. Museum. Mausoleum. Except on the three annual viewing days the collection should be kept in permanent dark-ness. Pharaoh would have approved. But what about tomb-robbers? Photoscopic devices, the most up to date in existence, will give instant warning of the minutest disturbance, such as the flashing of a light.

But these are morbid thoughts. My collections are incomplete. And I am still here to complete them. I shall go round to little Truslove. He's sure to be away.

Thomas Truslove. My oldest friend. Once a most gifted young poet, he is now completely forgotten and spends all his time on television, editorial boards, P.E.N. Club activities, book of the month clubs and American lecture tours. Last week in Buffalo, this week in Bonn – he only comes to England in his sabbatical year. But – and this is the point – he continues to be deluged with every pamphlet, every privately printed book that comes out. You can find anything at Truslove's. When I go round I always take a second edition of something or a second issue or a defective copy, and substitute it, when his back's turned, for the right one. To him that hath shall be given. He never notices; only likes painting anyway. Sometimes he tries most generously to present me with his own rejections, the ignorant booby. Today I took round a second edition of Hopkins. Virginia Truslove opened the door.

'You've come to see Thomas? He's in Borneo. But he'll be back tomorrow morning. We're lunching with the Clarks.' I gave her the gimlet gaze. 'I've come to see *you*.' Virginia was what some people would consider 'still a beautiful woman'. She looked rather flustered. '*Mille grazie!* Do come in.' I put down my coat in the hall and walked straight into the library. 'Would you like some tea?'

'Nothing better. I'd give my soul for a nice cup of tea – the way you always make it.' 'I'll get it myself.'

It always works! Drinks, no – too often they're on the table. But tea!

'I'd give my soul for it' – and down she goes to the basement. Ten clear minutes and always a warning rattle on the way back!

Sure enough, there was the right Hopkins – 1918. The exchange was the work of a moment and I dived into the pamphlets: 'Poems written in Discouragement', only fifty copies – 'to my young friend Thomas the Rhymer, W. B. Yeats.' 'Prufrock and other observations,' – 'To Thomas from Tom.'

I didn't know where to begin. Even in my inside jacket pocket a slim volume might run a slim risk of being detected. 'Dear Thomas, Even you won't dare to print this, Wystan.' Jiminy cricket! Which shall it be – or why not all three?

Oh!

'Wasn't I quick! That's the electric kettle. I hope you haven't been too bored.'

'Just leafing through a few of Thomas's old circulars.'

'Aren't they a nuisance? As soon as he comes back we're going to have a thorough clean-out. Books are bad enough – but manuscripts, letters – he's kept *everything*.'

'Would you like me to go through them for you?'

'How angelic – but why should you do all this for me?'

'For an excellent reason.' And I looked down at her with my gimlet glance.

'There ought to be a law against it. Look at this one – "With some trepidation, Dylan". Why can't all these poets let poor Thomas alone. Nobody can print anything without inflicting a copy on him. He's like the British Museum.'

'I could start right now.'

'We'd better wait till he comes back. We might throw away a draw-ing by mistake. He won't be long. He's only gone to deliver a message at a conference.'

'In Borneo?'

'He's beamed at the Orient, you know.'

'Fortunate fellow!'

She put the pamphlets back in the glass-fronted bookcase and set the tea-tray on the table. Damned interference.

When I got home with my Hopkins, Brenda was waiting.

'Jonathan – where have you *been*?'

'Went to return a book to old Truslove.'

'Caroline's fallen downstairs.'

'Did she hurt herself?'

'No, thank God. Not this time.'

'Well then, it's not very important.'

'It happens to be important as she fell downstairs because you won't put up a gate, and you won't put up a gate because you're too mean to spend three pounds as all your money goes on teapots and candlesticks and filthy old books and china and glass and furniture and silver and candlesticks and teapots.'

Teapots! It's quite true I had been too busy with that bookcase to have a proper look. The Trusloves were just the kind of people to inherit some Queen Anne. Back to the Trusloves first thing tomorrow!

'Teapots with no tea, decanters with no wine, centrepieces for non-existent dinners – and Caroline could break her neck for all you'd care.'

'Why don't you get the gate yourself?'

'Out of what *you* give me?'

Now I happened to have read that small children have a very good sense of self-preservation even when descending stairs and that if they do fall their little bodies, with so much fat and water content, are extraordinarily resilient. I shut myself into my study and accom-modated Hopkins – 'I am gall, I am heartburn' – among my 'Recent Acquisitions'.

A few minutes later the telephone rang: 'It's me, Virginia. I'm so worried. Thomas has just cabled he's stopping off at Jakarta to judge some Indonesian Abstracts. He'll be late for the Clarks and miss his Lit. Soc. What shall I do?'

'You'd better take me with you.' 'Oh, what a good idea! Jon, you're so thoughtful for me!'

I remembered that I hadn't quite finished my egg at luncheon and retired to the pantry. The Clarks! *Véritable caveau d'Aladdin.* My luck was in. I found the egg and went back to my study. When I stand up before my largest bookcase I call it 'being at the Controls'. I feel like a captain on the bridge or Sandy Macpherson at his Wurlitzer. I quite expect the whole thing to sink down through the floor at the end of my virtuoso performance.

This evening I took out the keys of the plate-chests, then I inspected the green and yellow Sèvres, the Vincennes, the Chelsea and some of the

Meissen and went back to the Controls again. That Yeats, that Eliot, that Auden manuscript perhaps weighed a few ounces between them, occupied the same space as one bad novel, yet were worth several hundred pounds and represented for me the conclusion of years of search and patient effort. Good old Truslove – if he'd only been born a few years earlier and had been given *Mosada* or *A Lume Spento*.

God's most deep decree
Bitter would have me taste. My taste was me.

I couldn't get Hopkins out of my head. 'My taste was me' – what a title for an autobiography! And when one's taste is flawless – near-perfect, and matched by a nose and an eye for a bargain and a bump of curiosity and a righteous ambition to spoil the Philistine, there's no end to what one can pick up. To know what someone else values is to be already on the way to possessing it.

Saturday: Today I woke with a tiny worry. On the landing I heard Brenda and Caroline: 'One two three four, one and two and three and four,' no doubt a charming maternal tableau. Then I remembered. Why hadn't I noticed the teapot? After our lunch we must go back there. And I would take a few old copies of *Horizon* and *Penguin New Writing* to stuff up any gaps I made in the tidying.

With silver and china it's not so easy. One can't 'borrow' somebody's dinner service or pocket a *garniture de cheminée*. One has to learn to carry cash and make unpredictable offers. Carry cash! That hurts. Still, I am a gentleman and a gentleman is someone who can reasonably expect to live in the same style and demand the same treatment as his forefathers in a society which has gone completely haywire. The world owes me a living, says the parasite. No. I owe myself a living, says the gentleman. Let Edax hold what Edax held; and a little bit over for safety.

Telephone! 'It's me, Virginia. Jonathan, I'm so worried. I've rung up the Clarks and they'd rather the lunch was put off till Thomas got back. And now I've no one to lunch with today.' The skinflints. To hell with all of them.

'Well, lunch you know is never very easy for me. But perhaps we can meet afterwards.'

'But if you were free to lunch with the Clarks I thought perhaps you might. . . .'

'And get poisoned in one of those filthy restaurants? I see a man got thrombosis from Scallops Mornay.'

'Well then – you must come and lunch here. I'll have to see what I can do with my own fair fingers. But don't expect the Crown Derby.'

'You have some Crown Derby?'

'Well, I don't know what it is, of course. . . .'

Why do they all say *of course*?

'. . . But I do know it's fearfully old and Granny thought the world of it. It's supposed to be terribly valuable.'

'It sounds like Mason's Ironstone.'

'What's that?'

'I said we'll have to turn it over and look at the marks.'

'No need to be improper.'

'Very well then, one o'clock.'

Silly bitch. The last woman I took out to lunch cost me £12,000 for four words. Well, with her 'Yes' you could say it made five words. I could still hear her in the next room, with her kitchen cough, moving about and making lists of all the things that she and Caroline 'simply had to have' – shoes, shirts, sheets, socks, chocs, each item more perishable than the last – and the Spanish girl with her list, too. Thank God there was the one sane person in this household of crazy women.

The Edax Endowment. A Thought at the Controls; some of my books – some of the rarest – have other people's book-plates, coats of arms, country-house libraries (people with country-house libraries are among the biggest suckers in existence). Should I leave the book-plates in? Or steam them off? Or leave it to the executors? But who are my executors? Do I know a single person who isn't a bloody fool? One might choose an heir by examination. My will would be an examination paper. Or a treasure-hunt. But with all these bibliographies flying around they'd be bound to cheat. But to-day I shall put it aside, I feel sound as a Getty – and all a-tingle for the chase.

'Jonathan – where are you *going*?'

'Out to lunch – for a change.'

'But your egg.'

'Stuff it.'

'And the shopping-money.'

'Borrow from the Spanish girl.'

'Jonathan. Do you realize you haven't paid her wages for three weeks. Caroline's shoes are worn out. Do you expect us to live on air – when do you think I last went to the hairdresser?'

'Oh for God's sake. Get a long-playing record of yourself and send it to the Naggers' Club. Best years of your life. Worn your fingers to the bone. Waiting on me hand and foot. All that jazz.'

The usual screams and yowls in which Caroline joins with automatic mimicry. Thank God somebody keeps his head in this bedlam. Luckily I had chosen my cane and so had no further cause to linger. I blessed the Fermier-Général who had selected the perfectly fitting gold pommel with the reassuring *chinoiserie* and I blessed the country-house croquet set where I had annexed it.

The Spanish girl! Once the Truscloves' proudest possession – nothing she wouldn't do – laundry, mending, no evenings out. I soon got my eye on her. Took a bit of winkling, too – I told her that her employers were atheists who would probably poison her. Brenda is a Catholic, you see. Marriage is a life-sentence with her. So I give – and expect – no quarter. I had to go to church myself, just to convince the *chica*, and listen to the sermon. 'Nor his ox nor his ass nor his manservant nor his maid-servant.' The whole works. Those Spaniards! Eat you out of house and home!

One of my grievances against old Truslove is that he would choose to live halfway between two fare-stages. One either has a goodish walk or has to go on and break into a coin. Luckily it was a fine day.

Virginia opened the door. 'Look at him. Isn't he smart! With the hat and the cane and the Sherlock Holmes profile. Positively satanic.'

Damned impertinence. 'You don't look too bad yourself.' She was what our ancestors called a handsome woman, chivalrously adding 'very fine eyes'. Poor Truslove. Twenty years of marriage, say a pound a week to feed her and another for pin-money – thousands of pounds down the drain. Every woman after forty is a wasting asset.

'I know how you love beautiful things. I've got out all my treasures.' We sat down to a fricassee of chicken and a bottle of rosé. King's Pattern everywhere; all the silver was heavily embossed and the Crown Derby was quite respectable Coalport. 'The place for good china is under lock and key.' I wagged an admonitory finger, 'And now, since you've spoilt me so thoroughly, may I make one more request?'

She gave me a salute of twenty-one gums.

'Granted as soon as asked.'

'Can we have tea instead of coffee?' She looked rather sadly at the Cona machine. 'I'll go and make it myself.' Five minutes to go, with that damned electric kettle. I made a rush at the bookcase. It was locked. It was one of those big mahogany efforts and there, behind the glass, I could see all the presentation copies and the enigmatic untitled backs of the slimmer volumes. It wasn't really locked, I discovered, only jammed, otherwise I should have felt deeply insulted. I gave a good pull and the whole front came away; the hinges had gone. A sheet of glass fell forward and splintered round my head, badly cutting the hand which I raised to protect it. Virginia entered with the tray – 'Oh you poor thing – let me bandage it. You must have a tourniquet. Why, you've bled all over the manuscripts.'

It was true. 'Thomas – even you won't dare to print this' had become completely illegible. She thrust a pamphlet in my pocket – 'Here, have one of these for luck.' And then I spotted the teapot. It was hexagonal, genuine Queen Anne. I even got it up high enough to see the Britannia standard. One would commit murder for such a piece – or worse. What havoc it would wreak among my Georgian urns and melons! It must be worth thousands.

'Jonathan,' said Virginia, 'I've been wanting to talk to you for a very long time. You're not happy, are you?' I gave her the old gimlet. 'Poor old Jon – you can't deceive me. You see I know all about you and Brenda.' 'There's nothing to know.' 'Yes – that's just what I do know – and I know you only married her because she was engaged to Thomas.'

'Virginia—' 'And when you took Brenda – can't you see, Jonathan – there was nothing left for me to do but marry him.' 'Virginia—'

'Stop – and I too know what a marriage with nothing is like because that's what mine is. Married to a poster, a voice on a Dictaphone, an airplane reservation. We can't go on like this, Jonathan. I'm forty now and you must be . . .' 'Virginia!' 'Wait – don't worry – you shall have me. You've been so sweet, so patient, so understanding – coming always to see me when he's out – yet never a word disloyal to him, always his best friend. Don't think I haven't noticed! – Dispelling my loneliness, my emptiness – and you so big, so quiet, so kind.' 'Virginia!' 'Wait – silly. I'm all yours now. Listen. I've cabled: "Don't hurry back. Clark's lunch postponed. All well – Virginia." Now aren't I rather clever!'

'Virginia – the teapot. Whose is it?' 'Mine, you silly-billy. Do you think we would be drinking tea out of it at this moment if it were his. Do you think I wouldn't protect your chivalry. Whither I go, it goes – my dowry – it will be about all I have. There used to be a silly old kettle on a stand as high as myself.' 'Virginia, I feel faint. My wrist. I must see a doctor. No, I can walk, thank you.'

Once in the street I pulled out the pamphlet she had given me. Unbelievable – the ultimate rarity! *The Bourbon Rose and other poems*, by Alberic Chute. Privately printed, Newport Pagnell, 1886. His first book – of which up till now only two copies were known, Hayward's and the Bodleian's. Alberic Chute, that exquisite talent, silenced it was said by some evil tentacle of the Wilde scandal after his third and most remarkable book of poems! He would be nearly ninety now, if this post-Raphaelite pre-Imagist were alive . . .

If he were alive! Why not – and if he is alive then he shall inscribe *The Bourbon Rose* for me and I will possess a better copy than either of the others. I made for a telephone box. There he was! Alberic Chute, Squire's Mount, Hampstead. Should I ring up to make sure? Often the worst of all methods. First they hang up on you and then they won't let you in. Desperate occasions require desperate remedies. I took a taxi. When I rang the bell there was a commotion. The door was opened by an elderly man. 'Can I see Mr. Chute?' 'Mr. Chute is very ill indeed and can see no one.' 'The matter is extremely urgent.' 'I am afraid any question of urgency is now purely relative.' The last word gave me a clue. 'You see, I am his son.' 'Mr. Chute was unmarried.' 'That is my tragedy, not his.' 'Your name.' 'It would mean nothing. Here are my credentials.' I held up the book to him. 'Newport Pagnell – yes – he did live there, for a very considerable time. Well, you had better come in. I am Doctor Prout.'

He led me through to a room on the ground floor. 'I should warn you it may come at any moment. My patient is in uraemia.'

It was a small sitting-room with no good pieces into which a brass bed had recently been moved. On this was lying a tiny old man with closed eyes and a nose like a tin-opener, his hands milking the coverlet. A nurse was standing by. She held a finger to her lips. With my cane in my bandaged hand and *The Bourbon Rose* in the other I tiptoed over.

I have managed to live more years than I care to consider without any close experience of death. There is nothing in such a phenomenon to appeal to the collector. The foot-hills of Death and Love are, however, hunting-grounds for such of us as lay up treasure on earth and pursue enduring artefacts rather than the illusions of common humanity. I have often found a long face at a memorial service lead to substantial pickings.

I was brooding on certain gaps that still needed closing before my serried ranks of Americana could be brought up to combat strength when the nurse disappeared behind a screen. Almost immediately the sick man opened his eyes and seemed to want to sit up. He favoured me with a penetrating stare. I brandished *The Bourbon Rose* before him and reached for my pen; but to do that I had to lean the cane against the bed and a rash movement of his caused it to slip so that the heavy gold knob with its mandarins and pagodas fell with a clatter on the parquet. With glaring eye the old poet tried to heave himself up and thrust forward, his hand jerking at me as the nurse rushed round. 'You—' he gasped and fell backward. I had enough presence of mind as the doctor entered to retrieve my cane and sink my head on my arms. 'My father. . . .'

I was more than relieved to get away on the pretext that I had to telephone and I had run quite a distance from Squire's Mount, my black felt hat in one hand, my cane in the other before I realized that I had left *The Bourbon Rose* behind. Agony! I felt such a stinging sense of loss that I could almost have wept. The greedy old bastard!

By felicitous combinations of the London Transport system I made my way home for I pined to be at the Controls again. My reference library alone is more extensive than all the books to be found in an ordinary household; it starts in my bedroom and spills all over the upper landing. I can trace the mark on a piece of china, the owners of a crest, the rubric of a goldsmith, the succeeding possessors of a book or manuscript, the vicissitudes of some piece in the saleroom, in a matter of minutes. They are the jig-tools of my occupation.

Before letting myself in I sent off three cables to Truslove: care of P.E.N. Club, Jakarta; British Council, Singapore; and Nehru, Delhi. 'Clarks up-fed threaten off-brush. Hurry!' Then I made a dash for the landing. Great God! At the top of the stairs stood a hideous little gate of white metal, stuck on to the wall at each side by suction-pads. For a household of hurdlers!

'Brenda', I shouted. She came out, smiling. 'I thought you'd be surprised. Now our daughter – for you seem to forget that she is yours as well as mine – can grow up without risking her life every few minutes.' 'How did you pay for it?' 'I charged it.' 'You have no account.' 'I put it down on yours.' 'You PUT IT DOWN!' I felt a lump of rage surge up and choke me, like when Caroline tore the book jackets. 'You filthy extravagant slut, I'll sue you.' 'Miserly old madman.' 'I'll put a notice in the papers. I'll hound you out of my house.'

The telephone rang in my bedroom. (I permit no outgoing calls.) 'It's me, Virginia. Darling. He's on his way back. We must leave at once. I'm desperate.' 'Impossible. I can't ever see you again.' 'Then I shall kill myself. Now.' 'Goodbye.' These crazy women! Suddenly I had a vision of the little hexagonal teapot in all its leaden moonglow perfection. Now was my chance. I ran out of my room and took a flying kick at that bloody gate.

'Aaaaaaaahh. . . .'

A verdict of death by misadventure was returned on Mr. Jonathan Edax, the well-known connoisseur and collector who broke his neck by falling down the stairs at his home in Holland Park on Saturday night. The stairs were exceptionally steep and a gate had recently been installed at the top of them by Mrs. Edax; it had presumably been insecurely attached. The deceased had appeared to be in a disturbed frame of mind at the prospect of making his will. Mr. and Mrs. Thomas Truslove were present at the inquest but were not called upon to give evidence. Jonathan Hagan Edax was born in 1895 at Bedford, where his father was a prosperous solicitor. After completing his studies, he had early made his mark in the correspondence columns of learned periodicals and was soon recognized as a formidable opponent in the auction room at a time when it was still possible for a private individual, etc., etc.

Told in Gath
(1936)

(With apologies to Mr. A*d*us H*xl*y)

'Vulgarity is the garlic in the salad of charm.'
ST. BUMPUS.

It was to be a long week-end, thought Giles Pentateuch apprehensively, as the menial staggered up the turret stairs with his luggage – staggered all the more consciously for the knowledge that he was under observation, just as, back in Lexham Gardens, his own tyrannical Amy would snort and groan outside the door to show how steep the back-stairs were, before entering with his simple vegetarian breakfast of stinkwort and boiled pond-weed. A long week-end; but a week-end at Groyne! And he realized, with his instinct for merciless analysis that amounted almost to torture, that in spite, yes, above all, in spite of the apprehension, because of it even, he would enjoy all the more saying afterwards, to his friend Luke Snarthes perhaps, or to little Reggie Ringworm, 'Yes, I was at Groyne last week-end,' or 'Yes, I was there when the whole thing started, down at Groyne.'

The menial had paused and was regarding him. To tip or not to tip? How many times had he not been paralysed by that problem? To tip was to give in, yes, selfishly to give in to his hatred of human contacts, to contribute half a crown as hush-money, to obtain 'protection', protection from other people, so that for a little he could go on with the luxury of being Giles Pentateuch, 'scatologist and eschatologist', as he dubbed himself. Whereas not to tip . . .

For a moment he hesitated. What would Luke Snarthes have done?

Stayed at home, with that splayed ascetic face of his, or consulted his guru, Chandra Nandra? No – no tip! The menial slunk away. He looked round the room. It was comfortable, he had to admit; a few small Longhis round the walls, a Lupanar by Guido Guidi, and over the bed an outsize Stuprum Sabinarum, by Rubens – civilized people, his hosts, evidently.

He glanced at the books on the little table – the *Odes of Horace, Rome* 23 B.C., apparently a first edition, the *Elegancies of Meursius* (Rochester's copy), *The Piccadilly Ambulator, The Sufferings of Saint Rose of Lima, Nostradamus* (the Lérins Press), *Swedenborg, The Old Man's Gita.* 'And cultivated,' he murmured, 'too.' The bathroom, with its sun-lamp and Plombières apparatus, was such as might be found in any sensible therapeutic home. He went down to tea considerably refreshed by his lavage.

The butler announced that Lady Rhomboid was 'serving' on the small west lawn, and he made his way over the secular turf with genuine pleasure. For Minnie Rhomboid was a remarkable woman.

'How splendid of you to come,' she croaked for she had lost her voice in the old suffragette days. 'You know my daughter, Ursula Groyne.'

'Only too well,' laughed Giles, for they had been what his set at Balliol used to call 'lovers'.

'And Mrs. Amp, of course?'

'Of course!'

'And Mary Pippin?'

'Decidedly,' he grimaced.

'And the men,' she went on. 'Giles Pentateuch – this is Luke Snarthes and Reggie Ringworm and Mr. Encolpius and Roland Narthex. Pentateuch writes – let me see? – like a boot, isn't it?' (Her voice was a husky roar.) 'Yes, a boot with a mission! Oh, but I forgot' – and she laughed delightedly – 'you're all writers!'

'Encantado, I'm sure!' responded Giles. 'But we've all met before. I see you have the whole Almanach de Golgotha in fact,' he added.

Mary Pippin, whose arm had been eaten away by termites in

Tehuantepec, was pouring out with her free hand. 'Orange Pekoe or *Chandu*, Giles?' she burbled in her delicious little voice. 'Like a carrier pigeon's,' he thought.

'*Chandu*, please.' And she filled him a pipe of the consoling poppy, so that in a short while he was smoking away like all the others.

'Yes, yes,' continued Mr. Encolpius, in his oily voice which rose and fell beneath the gently moving tip of his nose, 'Man axalotl here below but I ask very little. Some fragments of Pamphylides, a Choctaw blood-mask, the prose of Scaliger the Elder, a painting by Fuseli, an occasional visit to the all-in wrestling, or to my meretrix; a cook who can produce a passable 'poulet à la Khmer,' a Pong vase. Simple tastes, you will agree, and it is my simple habit to indulge them!'

Giles regarded him with fascination. That nose, it was, yes, it was definitely a proboscis. . . .

'But how can you, how can you?' It was Ursula Groyne. 'How *can* you when there are two million unemployed, when Russia has reintro-duced anti-abortionary legislation, when Iceland has banned *Time and Tide*, when the Sedition Bill hangs over us like a rubber truncheon?'

Mary Pippin cooed delightedly; this was intellectual life with a vengeance – definitely haybrow – only it was so difficult to know who was right. Giles, at that moment, found her infinitely desirable.

'Yes, and worse than that.' It was Luke Snarthes, whose strained voice emerged from his tortured face like a cobra from the snake-charmer's basket. 'Oh, decidedly, appallingly worse. The natives of Ceylon take the slender Loris and hold it over the fire till its eyes pop, to release the magic juices. Indicible things are done to geese that you may eat your runions with a sauce of *foie gras*. Caviare is ripped from the living sturgeon, karakul fur torn from the baby lamb inside its mother. The creaking plates of the live dismembered lobster scream to you from the *Homard Newburg*, the oyster winces under the lemon. How would *you* like, Mr. Encolpius, to be torn from your bed, embarrelled, prised open with a knife, seasoned with a few drops of vitriol, shall we say, and sprayed with a tabasco as strong as mustard-gas to give you flavour; then to be swallowed alive and handed over to a giant's digestive juices?'

'I shouldn't like it at all!' said Mr. Encolpius, 'just as I shouldn't, for that matter, like living at the bottom of the sea and changing my sex every three years. Not that it might not' – and he twitched his nose at Mary Pippin – 'have its compensations.'

'S-s-s-s-s-s-s-s-s-s-s-s-s-s-s-s-s-s-s-s-s-s-suppose,' said Reggie Ringworm, who stammered, etc., 'vat vet thilly oyther is weally weady and villing to be ab-s-s-s-orbed, I mean ab-th-th-th-th-th-thorbed, by our fwend, vat vat is in f-f-f-fact exactly ve end for which it was cweated. Vat th-then?'

'What are we to think then,' snarled Snarthes savagely, 'of the Person or Purpose who created creatures for such an end? Awful!' And he took out his notebook and wrote rapidly, 'The end justifies the means! But the end *is* the means! And how rarely, how confoundedly rarely, can we even say the end justifies the end! Like Oxenstierna, like Ximenes, like Waldorf, we must be men of means' – he closed the book with a snap – 'men of golden means.'

'I know what you mean,' cried Mary Pippin from her dovecot. 'That if Cleopatra's nose had been half an inch longer Menelaus would never have run away with her!'

Luke's face softened, and he spread out his splayed fingers almost tenderly. 'And I don't mind wagering, if we can believe Diodorus Siculus, that, the nose unaltered, she bore a remarkable likeness, Mary, to you!'

'Ah, but can we believe old Siculus?' The other nose quested speculative. 'Any more than we can believe old Paterculus, old Appian, Arrian, Ossian, and Orrian? Now a Bolivar Corona or a nicely chambered glass of sparkling Douro – even a pretty tea-gown by Madame Groult, I opine' – and he bowed to Mary – 'these convince me. They have a way with one. Oh, yes, a way, decidedly! And just because they have that way it is necessary for me to combine them, how often, how distressingly often, with my lamentable visits to the Ring at Blackfriars, or to my meretrix in Holland Park. Why is it that we needs must see the highest though we loathe it? That happy in my mud – my hedonistic, radio-active, but never-the-less quite genuine nostalgic *boue*, I should be reminded of the stars, Miss Pippin, and of Cleopatra?' And he snuffled serio-comically, 'Why can't you let Hell alone?'

A gong rang discreetly. The butler removed the pipes and Mrs. Amp and Roland Narthex, who were still in a state of kif, while the others went away to dress. Giles, who found something stimulating in Mr. Encolpius' nose, took out his notebook and wrote:

'Platitudes are eternally fresh, and even the most paradoxical are true; even when we say the days draw in we are literally right – for science has now come largely to the rescue of folk-lore; after the summer and still more after the equinoctial solstice the hours do definitely get shorter. It is this shortness of our northern day that has occasioned the luxuriance of our literature. Retractile weather – erectile poetry. No one has idealized, in our cold climate, more typically than Shakespeare and Dryden the subtropical conditioning. But we can consider Antony and Cleopatra to have been very different from their counterparts in the Elizabethan imagination, for on the Mediterranean they understand summer better and, with summer, sex.

'What were they really like, those prototypes of Aryan passion, of brachycephalic amour? Were Cleopatra's breasts such as "bore through men's eyes" and tormented those early sensualists, Milton, Dante, Coventry Patmore, and St. John of the Cross? We shall never know.

'Professor Pavlov has shown that when salivation has been artificially induced in dogs by the ringing of a dinner bell, if you fire simultaneously into them a few rounds of small shot they exhibit an almost comical bewilderment. Human beings have developed very little. Like dogs we are not capable of absorbing conflicting stimuli; we cannot continue to love Cleopatra after communism and the electro-magnetic field have played Old Harry with our romantic mythology. That characteristic modern thinker, Drage Everyman, remarks, 'Destroy the illusion of love and you destroy love itself,' and that is exactly what the machine age, through attempting to foster it through cinemas and gin-palaces, deo-dorants and depilatories, has succeeded in doing. Glory, glory, halitosis! No wonder we are happier in the present! If we think of the 'Eastern Star', in fact, it is as advertising something. And when we would reconstruct those breasts of hers, again we are faced with the diversity of modern knowledge. What were they like? To a poet twin roes, delectable mountains; to a philanderer like Malthus festering cancers; to a pneumatogogue simply a compound of lacticity and heterogeneous pyrites; to a biologist a sump and a pump. Oh, sweet are the uses, or rather the abuses, of splanchnology! No, for details of the pathological appeal of these forgotten beauties we must consult the poets. The ancients were aware of a good thing when they saw it, and Horace knew, for instance, with almost scatological percipience, exactly what was what.

'There are altitudes, as well as climates, of the mind. Many prefer the water-meadows, but some of us, like Kant and Beethoven, are at home on the heights. There we thermostatically control the rarefied atmosphere and breathe, perforce, the appropriate mental air.'

In another room Luke Snarthes was doing his exercises. Seated in the lotus position, he exhaled deeply till his stomach came against his backbone with a smart crack. After a little he relaxed and breathed carefully up one nostril and down the other and then reversed the process. He took a nail out of the calf of his leg, and after he had reinserted it, it was time to put the studs into his evening shirt. 'I was there,' he murmured, 'when it started, down at Groyne.'

When he had dressed he unlocked his despatch-case and took out a sealed tube. It was marked, 'Anthrax – non-filterable virus, only to be opened by a qualified literary scientist.'

'Jolly little beggars,' he thought, and the hard lines on his face softened. 'I'll take them down to amuse Miss Pippin. She looked the kind of person who'd *understand*.'

'Snuff, peotl buds, hashish, or Indian hemp, sir?' said the butler. Dinner was drawing to an end. It had been an interesting meal. For Giles and Luke (on the 'regime'), grass soup and groundsel omelette, washed down with a bottle of 'pulque'; for Mrs. Amp, whose huge wen, like Saint-Evremond's, made her look more than ever like some heavily wattled turkey, a chicken gumbo; for the rest Risi-bisi Mabel Dodge, bêche de mer, bear steak, and Capri pie.

'There's some *bhang* on the mantelpiece,' said Minnie Rhomboid, 'in poor Rhomboid's college tobacco jar.'

'Delicious.' It was Mr. Encolpius. 'Common are to either sex artifex and opifex,' he continued. 'But, golly, how rare to find them contained in the same person – qualis opifex, Lady Rhomboid! I congratulate you – and this *barask* – perfection!' And he poured himself some more, while the snout wiggled delightedly.

'And you can drink that when Hungary is deliberately making a propaganda war for the recovery and re-enslavement of a hundred-thousand at last sophisticated Slovakians!' It was Ursula Groyne.

Poor Ursula, thought Giles, she carries her separate hell about with her like a snail its carapace! Not all the lost causes, all the lame dogs in the world could console her for the loss of her three husbands, and now she was condemned to the hades of promiscuity – every three or four years a new lover. Poor Ursula!

'And if you knew how the stuff was made!' The phrase was wrung from Luke Snarthes on his tortured cavalry. 'The apricots are trodden by the naked feet of bromidrosis-ridden Kutzo-Vlachs who have for centuries lived in conditions far below the poverty line! The very glass-blowers who spun that Venetian balloon for you are condemned to the agonies of alembic poisoning.'

'Doubtless,' answered Mr. Encolpius urbanely, 'that is why it tastes so good. It all boils down to a question of proteins. You, my dear Ursula, are allergic to human misery; the sufferings of Slovaks and Slovenes affect you as pollen the hay-fever victim, or me (no offence, Minnie) a cat in the room. To ethics, mere questions of good and evil, I am happily immune, like my cara doncella here – am I right, Mary? Let Austin have his swink to him reserved, especially when it is a swink of the Rhomboid order. Go to the slug, thou ant-herd! If you could make up to kings (you remember what Aristippus said to Diogenes, Snarthes), you would not have to live on grass!'

'B-b-b-b-b-b-b-b-b-b-b-b-b-b-b-b-b-but all flesh is gwath, so ve pwoblem is only sh-shelved.' It was Reggie Ringworm!

'Sit down, everybody, it's time for the séance,' commanded Lady

Rhomboid. 'We have persuaded Madame Yoni.'

In darkness they took their seats, Mr. Encolpius and Giles on each side of Mary Pippin, while Snarthes elevated himself to a position of trans-Khyber ecstasy suspended between the table and the laquearia. The *bhang*-sodden bodies of Mrs. Amp and Roland Narthex they left where they were.

The darkness was abysmal, pre-lapsarian. Time flowed stanchlessly, remorselessly, from a wound inenarrable, as with catenary purpose. Madame Yoni moved restlessly, like Bethesda.

In her private dovecot Mary Pippin abandoned herself to the eery. What a thrill, to be here at Groyne, and for a séance! There had been nothing like it since she had joined the Anglican Church, to the consternation of her governess, Miss Heard, because of the deep mystical significance (as of some splendid sinner repenting on the ashes of lust) of the words, 'for Ember Days'. All the same, she was not quite sure if she liked Mr. Encolpius. But what was this? – another thrill, but positive, physical. With moth-like caresses something was running up and down her arm – 1, 2, 3, 4, 5 – spirit fingers, perhaps: the tremulous titivation continued, the moths were relentless, inexorable, 86, 87, 88. Then on her other side, along her cheek, she felt a new set of moth antennae playing. From the chandelier above came the faintest ghostly anticipatory tinkle – someone was on the move as well, up there! 98, 99 . . . Suddenly Madame Yoni screamed – there was a crash, as of three heads bumping together, and the lights went up to reveal Pentateuch and Mr. Encolpius momentarily stunned by the Ixionic impact of the fallen Snarthes. His power had failed him.

'W-w-w-w-w-w-w –' stammered Reggie Ringworm, but he was interrupted by a shout from Luke. 'My God – the anthrax!' He took from his pocket the fragments of the broken tube. 'At the rate of multiplication of these bacilli' – he made a rapid calculation – 'we shall all be by morning, Lady Rhomboid, dead souls.' His splayed face had at last found its justification.

'Death!' said Mr. Encolpius, 'the distinguished visitor! One bids good-bye, one hopes gracefully, to one's hostess, and then, why then I think one degusts the Cannabis Indica. Well, cheerio, kif-kif!' And he picked up the Brasenose jar.

Imperturbable, schizophrene, the portraits of Groynes and Rhomboids by Laurencin and the excise-man Rousseau looked down from the walls. So Miss Heard had been right, thought Mary. The wicked *do* perish. Than this there could have been no other conceivable termination to a week-end of pleasure!

> They say of old in Babylon
> That Harlequin and Pantalon
> Seized that old topiary, Truth,
> And held him by Time's Azimuth. . . .

Why had the nursery jingle recurred to her?

Luke removed a nail or two disconsolately. They would be of little use now. He tried to reassure Minnie Rhomboid. 'After all, what is anthrax? What, for that matter, are yaws, beri-beri, dengue or the Bagdad Boil, but fascinating biochemical changes in the cellular constitution of our bodies, a re-casting of their components to play their new cadaverous roles? Believe me, Lady Rhomboid,' he concluded, 'there are more things in heaven and earth than are dreamt of in the British Pharmacopoeia!'

Giles took out his notebook. 'La Muerte, Der Tod, Thanatos,' he wrote.

'Your C-c-c-Collins perhaps?' stammered Reggie.

Giles began again: 'It was at Groyne, during one of Minnie Rhomboid's most succulent week-ends, that it all happened, happened because it had to happen, because it was in the very nature of Luke Snarthes and Mary Pippin that exactly such things should happen, just as it was character not destiny, character that *was* destiny, that caused Napoleon . . .' He paused and looked up. The menial was regarding him reproachfully.

Where Engels Fears to Tread
(1936/7)

From Oscar to Stalin. A Progress. By Christian de Clavering. (The Clay Press, 12s. 6d.)

Reviewed by CYRIL CONNOLLY

At last the authentic voice of a generation! 'You are all a lost generation,' remarked Gertrude Stein of us post-war age-groups, and now, thanks to Mr. Christian de Clavering, we know who lost us. Let me try and tell you about this book while I am still full of it. First thing you know you have opened it, and there is the dedication:

"TO THE BALD YOUNG PEOPLE"

Then comes a page of fashionable quotations all in German. The middle part by Kafka, the fringes by Rilke and Hölderlin. The rest by Marx. Impeccable! And the introduction.

'Why am I doing this, my dears? Because I happen to be the one person who can do it. My dears, I'm on your side! I've come to get you out of the wretched tangle of individualism that you've made for yourselves and show you just how you can be of some use in the world. Stop worrying whether he loves you or not; stop wondering how you will ever make any money. Never mind whether the trousers of your new suit turn up at the bottom; leave off trying to annoy Pa. We're on to something rather big. The Workers' Revolution for the Classless Society through the Dictatorship of the Proletariat! Yes! It's a bit of a mouthful, isn't it! We're used to words of one syllable, words like Freud, Death, War, Peace, Love, Sex, Glands, and, above all, to Damn,

303

Damn, Damn! Well, all that's going to be changed. Morning's at seven, and you've got a new matron.

'I'm told Mr. Isherwood is writing a book about the 'twenties. Mr. Isherwood is a Cambridge man, and we who made the 'twenties do not wish them looked at through the wrong end of a cocoa-tin. Through either end. My precious 'twenties! He shan't have them! Avaunt. Avanti!'

(And so the autobiography starts. I will quote a few of the dazzling vignettes. For the reasons with which the author concludes, I have refrained from comment.)

Home. Background. Mother.

'Mother, who is that horrible old obesity with the black chin? I believe he's following us.'

'Hush, that's Daddy.'

And so dawned my second birthday.

Home.

'Mother, where is home this time. Heliopolis? Hammamet? Ragusa? Yalta?'

'Guess again.'

'I know. Prinkipo.'

'Warm.'

'Monte Carlo.'

'Very warm.'

'Has it got a clever coastline? I know! Cannes!'

And home for the next two months it was.

'Mother – what does Father do?'

'He has his business, boy o' mine.'

'And what is that?'

'He's a sort of accountant.'

'On 'Change?'

'On the Turf!'

'Poor Mother, poor darling Mother – but we needn't see him, need we?'

'Of course not, precious, but I thought you were old enough to know.'

I pulled the hood down and for a moment it was very stuffy inside the pram. . . .

Children's Party.

'What is your father, Christian?'

'He's interested in racing – my mother is the Honourable. What is *your* father, Edelweiss?'

'A mediatized prince. What sort of racing?'

'Oh, never mind now – let's ask Mother to play some *Rimsky*.'

But I realised I couldn't stay on in Montreux Territet.

My mother an angel. My father a bookie!

'And don't forget, my boy, a tenner for every little nob you bring home with a handle to his name.'

Eton. Henry's holy shade. An impression, above all, of arches, my dears, each with its handsome couple, and study fireplaces always full of stubs of Balkan Sobranie. And the naughtiest elms! While the battle of Waterloo was being fought all around me, I just sat still and watched my eyelashes grow. There were books, of course. Pater, Alma Pater, with his worried paragraphs. His prose reminded me of stale privet – and Petronius, who made me long to know more Latin. (I only learned two words, *curculio* and *vespertilio*, a bat and a weevil, but they got me everywhere, afterwards, on Mount Athos.) And Compton Mackenzie as he then was, and Huxley, before he had acquired his Pope and Bradley manner, and Verlaine of course; Rimbaud, Mallarmé, Baudelaire.

'What is that book, de Clavering?'

'*Les Chansons de Bilitis*, sir.'

'And what is this lesson?'

'You have the advantage, sir.'

'What do you mean, boy?'

'Ah, sir, fair's fair. I told you what my book was. You must tell me what's your lesson.'

'Elementary geometry.'

'But it sounds fascinating! Then this delicious piece of celluloid nonsense is – I know, sir, don't tell me – a set-square?'

'I have been teaching it for twenty years, and never met with such impertinence.'

'Twenty years, and still at Elementary! Oh, sir, what a confession.' And it was a very purple face one glimpsed behind the blackboard. Ah, those Eton masters! I wish I could remember any of their names, for I was really sorry for them. What tragedies went on under their mortarboards! Some of them were quite young, and one often got the impression that they were trying, inarticulately, to communicate; would have liked, in fact, to share in the rich creative life that already was centring round me. They used to teeter round my Baksts, and once I caught my housemaster sniffing at a very special bottle made up for me by Max of Delhez, and gingerly rubbing some on his poor old pate. Worldlings, yet deprived of all worldly grace, of our rich sex-life how pathetically inquisitive! They are all there still, I suppose, and I often wonder, when I motor through Switzerland in summer, if one will not find a bunch of them spawning round some mouldy *arête*, in their Norfolk jackets, like eels in the Sargasso Sea.

The boys of course took up most of my time. I soon found that it was easy to get on with them by giving them presents, and making them laugh. A dozen of claret here, a humidor of Coronas there, a well-timed repartee, and persecution was made impossible. It was easy to find the butts and make rather more skilful fun of them than anybody else. In fact, I give this advice to those of my readers who are still at school. In every group there are boys whom it is the fashion to tease and bully; if you quickly spot them and join in, it will never occur to anyone to tease and bully you. Foxes do not hunt stoats. But always defer to the original teasers, and hand your prey over to them for the *coup de grâce*. And boys like expensive presents, though they are genuinely embarrassed by them. All the same, they were a provincial lot. I never felt very safe unless I had several of them round me, in coloured caps and gaudy blazers, puffing away at my cigarettes and looking for dirty jokes in the *Vie Parisienne*. By cultivating all the Captains of Games in this way I found my afternoons were left free. I would watch them troop away with their shinpads to some mysterious district on the way to Slough, then saunter up to Windsor with a book – on the bridge I would wave to any who seemed to be pushing a particularly big boat underneath it. Happy river of Eton-Windsor! I have always been very vague about its name, but I often pictured it winding away past Reading Gaol and into the great world of somewhere – the world of the Ballet and the Sitwells, of Cocteau and the Café Royal.

'Hello, Faun, what a way to spend your *Après-midi.*'

It was Harold, my most uneasy disciple.

'I was just thinking that summer made a noise like the rubbing together of biscuits.'

'Yes, it is hot,' he replied. 'If it goes on like this I shall have to buy some FLANNELS.'

'And be mistaken for Peter Fleming?'

'Oh, you're cruel. But seriously, what *shall* we do?'

'Well, there's Tull's, and I haven't eaten a lobster patty since this morning – or one might buy a gramophone record – or a very cool Braque of half a dozen ash-blonde oysters – then there's that place one goes to London from.'

'You mean the G.W.R.?'

'Thank you – and by now the school library will probably have heard of William Morris – or one might try the arches and see what one could pick up.'

'Or the Castle.'

'I'm bored with bearskins – but, my dear, that man – he's touched his cap – so familiar.'

'You mean the headmaster?'

It seemed an evil omen.

Then there was the Corps. I quickly joined the signal section. You didn't have to carry rifles. It was there that I first met intellectuals, dowdy fellows mostly, who went in for Medici prints and had never heard of Picasso. I realized for the first time what a gap separated cultured and cosmopolitan art lovers like myself, people who cared equally for music, painting, and literature, from those whose one idea was to pass examinations; literature is a very different thing to a poet and to someone who has to make a living out of it. 'What do you think of Apollinaire?' I asked one of them. 'Good God, we won't get a question on that – he's well outside the period.' 'On the contrary, he's very much of it. His book on Sade is vital.' 'I thought you meant Sidonius Apollinaris.' I could make no contact with them. But signalling was delightful. One sat for hours beside a field-telephone while little figures receded into the distance with the wire. 'Can you hear me?' 'No.' 'Can you hear me now?' 'No.' 'Well, try this.' 'This' was the morse-code machine, and nimbler fingers than mine would fill the air with a drowsy song. Iddy iddy umpty umpty iddy umpty iddy . . . However, all things come to an end, and there were some tiresome scenes – long waits in red-brick classrooms looking at huge sheets of paper – 'write only on one side of the paper.' But which side? and the precious minutes were wasted. Suddenly a lot of people I had always been willing to avoid seemed to have no object in life but to want to meet one. They would cluster round some old cannon outside New Schools, gowns fluttering and tassels wagging. One afternoon, when the place was looking more Raphael Tuck than ever, I went upstairs, and unforgivable things were said. It seemed one was suspected of all the alluvial vices, in fact one was not getting the best out of the curriculum. For the last time I crossed the bridge over the mysterious river, past Tom Browne's, where rather a good pair of 'sponge bags' were being created for me for Ascot, past Hills and Saunders, who had turned out some passable groups of my tea-parties. 'These people are my friends,' I would implore the photographer, 'I want them to look fresh and good-looking and aristocratic and rich.' 'But, sir.' 'Remember, they are not the Shooting Eight, or Mr. Crace's Old Boys, and I don't want to sit in the middle with folded arms and a football. I shall stand rather over to the side and at the back, and the only way you will know I am the host is by this enormous cocktail shaker.'

~

'Oh, my boy, my boy, 'ere am I sweating away on the Turf to edicate you, and just when I 'ope you'll bring the nobs in you go and get sacked. Sacked from Eton!'

'Not sacked, Pater – supered.'

But my father could never appreciate an academic distinction.

∾

Before one can understand Oxford one must have lived in Capri, and it was there that I spent the next few months, cramming. Mother had taken a quiet villa with a view of the funicular. At seventeen it was rather odd to figure fairly recognizably in five novels in three languages. But Monty and Norman were insatiable. 'No one would think it absurd if you sat to five painters,' they remonstrated, and I retorted that I had a jolly good mind to – but I was too busy at that time, sitting for Fersen.*
It was my first introduction to *les paradis artificiels* (not counting Tidworth), and with all a boy's healthy craving for novelty I flung myself down on the Count's couches and sampled poppy after poppy through his amusing collection of Chinese pipes. When the time came for my Oxford vivâ, I was older than the rocks and my eyelids were definitely a little weary. I could not decide. Magdalen and *Sinister Street*, Merton and Max, Balliol and Gumbril? or the House – Peers and Peckwater? Max had praised my eyelashes. Harold said Balliol was perfect for case-histories like mine, but I realized I should find it madly ungay. That Buttery! Finally it was the House I chose, two vast eighteenth-century rooms which I did up in pewter and cinnamon. Harold supplied wax fruit, and antimacassars for the Chinese Chippendale chairs, I added incense, brass trays and Buddhas, and Robert a carpet from the Victoria and Albert (the Yacht, not the Museum.)

My father had become reconciled to me. ' 'Appiest days of your life, my boy, and don't forget, a pony for every youngster you bring 'ome with a 'andle to his name. Good for the business.' I was worried about my father. 'Mother,' I said, 'don't you think Daddy is looking definitely *blafard*?' 'Is he?' she replied. 'You're sitting on the Continental Brad-shaw.'

Most of my Eton friends had also come up to the House, and, as my

---

* The Marsac of *Vestal Fires*.

father had taken a flat in Bicester, 'ponies' and 'monkeys' came rolling in. I spent them on clothes and parties, on entertaining and on looking entertaining. Parties! 'Are you going to de Clavering's to-night?' and woe betide the wretch who had to say no. Nothing much happened at the time, but he soon felt he was living on an icefloe, drifting farther and farther from land, and every moment watching it melt away. De Clavering's to-night! The candles burn in their sconces. The incense glows. Yquem and Avocado pears – a simple meal – but lots and lots of both, with whisky for the hearties and champagne for the dons. 'Have a brick of caviare, Alvanley? More birds' nest, Gleneagles? There's nothing coming, I'm afraid, only Avocado pear and hot-pot.' 'Hot-pot!' 'Christian, you're magnificent!' 'Caviare and hot-pot – Prendy will be blue with envy!' And then dancing, while canons go home across the quad, and David stomps at the piano. I took care at these parties to have a word and piece of advice for everyone.

There was an alert young man in a corner, looking rather shy. 'I know – don't tell me,' I said to him, 'it's your first party.' 'Yes.' I pinched his cheek. 'Si jeunesse savait!' I laughed. It was Evelyn Waugh.

Another merry little fellow asked me if I could suggest a hobby. 'Architecture,' I gave in a flash. 'Thank you.' It was John Betjeman.

'And for me?'

'Afghanistan.'

It was Robert Byron.

'And me?'

'Byron,' I laughed back – it was Peter Quennell.*

And Alvanley, Gleneagles, Prince Harmatviz, Graf Slivovitz, the Ballygalley of Ballygalley, Sarsaparilla, the Duc de Dingy, the Conde de Coca y Cola – for them, my peers, I kept my serious warnings.

'These bedroom slippers, Dingy? I flew them over from my *bottier*.'

'You ought to look a little more like a public school prefect, Alvanley. The front cover of *The Captain*, it's rather more your *genre*. There! Wash out the 'honey and flowers', and try a fringe effect. I want to see a pillar of the second eleven.'

* All of whom, I am told (autumn 1937), still keep afloat.

'Good jazz, Gleneagles, is meant to be played just a little bit too slow.'

'Graf Slivovitz, this isn't the *Herrenclub* in Carpathian Ruthenia, you must take off your hat. Yes – that green growth with the feudal feathers.'

'Sarsaparilla, only the King rouges his knees when he wears a kilt, and then only at a Court ball.'

'Harmatviz, I can smell that Harris a mile away. What on earth is that terrifying harpoon in the lapel?'

'That, de Clavering, is a *Fogas* fly.'*

'More Yquem, Ballygalley?'

'What's that?'

'That – if you mean the thing under your elbow – is how I look to Brancusi; the other is a kind of wine. Stand him up, will you, Ava?'

'Before the war we heard very little of the Sarsaparillas – he would not dare wear that tartan in Madrid.'

'Before the war I hadn't heard of you, Coca y Cola, either; Count, this is a democratic country.'

'I am democrat, we are all democrats. *Vive le roi.*'

'Thank you, Dingy, you must have been reading *Some People*. Now I want all the Guinnesses and Astors to go into the next room and get a charade ready. Alvanley, Gleneagles, Harmatviz, and Slivovitz – you will drive quickly over with me for a few minutes to Bicester to say good-night to father.'

'No I don't think.' – 'My price is ten guineas.' – 'Jolly well not unless we go halves.' – 'Where is my hat and gotha?' – and madcap youth was served.

My crowning moment. The Summerville Grind. Peers and their mothers and sisters in mackintoshes and shooting-sticks. My mount. A huge animal whose teeth need cleaning. For the first time in my life I wear a bowler hat. And my racing colours. White silk shirt with a broad blue stripe – but zigzag! Alvanley and Gleneagles on each side of me – off! I was petrified, my dears; the first fence was enormous and my

* An amusing fish from the Balaton.

animal seemed hours getting over it. There was time for me to get down, and I rolled over. On it thundered, its great ugly stirrups banging together. A man leant over me. 'Not hurt, are you?' he said. And then, *plus fort que lui*, 'Where *did* you get that shirt?' It was on a sigh that I answered, as I lost consciousness, 'Sire, at Charvet's.' It was the Prince.

And there was talk – all kinds – the banter of my friends.

'Ah, de Clavering, if you were only of the nobility. I would ask you to stay at Dingy. What a pity you are not a real goodfellow.'

'Apfelstrüdel! He is coming to Schloss Slivovitz with Pryce-Jones, is not that good enough for you?'

'Slivovitz – how picturesque it must be. But at Dingy we have to consider the *convenances*, my aunt Doudeauville, my Uncle Sagan. . . .'

'She 'appens to be *my* aunt Doudeauville too.* Her mother was of the German branch.'

'I can find no Harmatviz on Madame Sacher's tablecloth.'

'Rosa Lewis says the Claverings are an old Scotch family.'

'Sarsaparilla would know that.'

'Before the war we heard very little of the Sarsaparillas, now it appears . . .'

'Ah, bonjour, Coca y Cola, how is the Alvis?'

'Very well, would you like to look under the bonnet?'

'Haw, haw, haw, what a suggestion.'

'But seriously, de Clavering – you are rich, you are intelligent, why have you no titles? Have you spoken to the King?'

'He may have no title, but I would trust him with my waistcoats.'

'And I shake him by the hand – and say – "Well, what the hell, who cares?"'

'Bravo, Harmatviz, it's a democratic country. *Vive le roi!*'

Then there was a brilliant conversation at Balliol, where the food makes long journeys to the dowdy sitting-rooms, under tins.

'We were discussing, de Clavering, whether it was more correct to say Theophylactus Simocattes or Simocatta –'

* By the marriage of Graf Hubertus Mary von and zu Slivovitz-Slivovitz with Katarina Auburn-Cord.

'You should consider yourself very lucky, Sparrow, to be able to say either.'

'And what the collective noun is for a group of pelicans; there is a gaggle of geese, of course, and pride of lions.'

'A piety of pelicans, I suggest.'

'Thank you – how delightfully Thomas Browne. I shall repeat that.'

'I don't know which I dislike most, people who repeat my epigrams or people who copy my ties – and, by the way, I hope you don't mind. I've brought Raymond Radiguet.'

'Where's he up?'

'He's not up. He lives in Paris.'

'Paris! If I get an All Sogger I am determined to go there. It's right on the way to the British School.'

'I know a very nice little hotel near the *Bibliothèque Mazarine*.'

'I can't see why they don't build an arcade from Brick Top's* to the Ritz.' Nobody laughs. As usual, one can find no contact with them.

My twenty-firster. Fifty people in fancy dress. The orchestra from the *Grand Ecart*. A large silver waste-paper basket. 'To Christian de Clavering, the Great Commoner – Alvanley, Alba, Ava, Abercorn, Andrassy, Aberconway, Argyll, Auersperg' – you can imagine the signatures. As the college barge, which I had taken for the occasion, glided up the Cher, life's goblet seemed full to brimming. But Nemesis pursued me. The dons descended. I suppose they hadn't had enough invitations. It appears that those afternoons which I spent under some hot towels in Germers were full of goings-on, lectures, tutorials, Heaven knows what. Divinity seemed a prominent element in the City of Lost Causes. I went down. Oxford, like Eton, had never really 'given'.

London at last.† The 'twenties. Parties. Parties. Parties. And behind them all an aching feeling. – Was it worth it? What is it all for? Futility. . . .

'Christian – you must dine with me to-night!'

'Gawain – I can't – I've engaged myself to the '*Derries*.'

* Always my favourite nightbox.
† A London then where everybody knew everybody and we all squeezed into one telephone book!

~

'Are you the manager?'

'Yes, sir.'

'My name is de Clavering. I should like to say I have never eaten such a disgusting meal. *Même à la Cour*. But haven't I seen you before?'

'Oui, monsieur, je vous connais depuis l'Eldorado.'

~

'Es usted el cuadro flamenco?'

'Si.'

'Si.'

'Si.'

'Si.'

~

'Beverley, my dear, such a gaffe! I've just gone up to the old Dowager of Buck-and-Chan and mistaken her for the old Dowager of Ham-and-Bran!'

'*Christian!*'

~

'She's got what the Americans call "that".'

'What?'

'What the Americans call "that".'

'What's that?'

' "That" – that's what she's got.'

'But what the Americans call what? I don't even know that.'

'Oh, my dear Duchess!'

For it was sometimes my privilege to give instruction to a very great lady.

~

'M. Picasso – Mr. Hemingway. M. Hemingway – Señor Belmonte. Mr. Nicolson – Mr. Firbank – and now shall we begin without Miss Stein? I'm starving.'

~

'I can't decide whether to stay with Lorenzo in Taos or Crowley in Cefalu – where *does* one go in August?'

~

'Dear Evelyn, *of course*, put me into it!'

~

'Voulez-vous téléphoner à Mr. Proust de venire me trouver dans les bains de la rue de Lappe?'

~

'Herr Reinhardt ist zuschloss?'

~

'You know Diaghilev, of course, Dingy?'

~

'I've found the title for you, Breton – *Surréalisme*.'

~

'And for this rather brusque poem, Osbert, I shall need the "meg".'*

~

Parties. Futility. You can read of most of them in old gossip columns. I still remember my tropical party, when a punkah was heard for the first time in Egerton Crescent. Palms and bananas decorated the rooms. The central heating (it was in July) provided the atmosphere. Some stewards from the P. & O. worked away at the punkahs, or at distributing *reistafel* and planters' punch. The guests wore shorts, sarongs, stingah shifters, or nothing at all.

'But this is *me*,' I remember saying, holding up a slim volume. 'Why haven't I been told about this before, Dadie? Who is this T. S. Eliot?'

'He works in a bank, I believe.'

'Works in a bank – and writes *The Waste Land*! But he should be here, at my Tropical Party! Go and fetch him.'

But there is a new disturbance, and Bolitho, our butler, is at my elbow.

'Some young people, sir.'

'Their names?'

'The *Blackbirds*.'

'Ask them to come up. We shall want some more room. Patrick, help me spread Elizabeth somewhere else. Ronald, come out from under that sofa, you're hunching the springs.† Fallen out of the window, you say, with Brenda? Never mind, for the moment. I want to be alone. I want to read this book.'

And then the blow fell. A summons, next day, to the Royal Automobile Club. 'I'm ruined, my boy. I'm ruined. 'Aven't got a penny left. Those pals of yours, Alvanley and Gleneagles. They've skinned me. You'll 'ave to earn your own living from now on. Oh, your poor mother!' 'It's poor me, you old banana. I've no intention of earning my

---

* A megaphone, and such small ability as I may have acquired with it, now constitute my 'platform manner'.
† Firbank's shyness was proverbial.

own living, thank you.' – 'Ow, wot a boy, wot a boy.' And I flung out. Tears. Consultations.

'I can always sell my Gris.' 'But what will you do then?'

'Oh, write – paint – don't fluster me.'

'And we were to have gone to the Londonderry del Vals!'

'Poor mother.'

One thing stood out with terrible clarity in those dark days. The old life was over. I could never associate any longer with those friends who had been used to look to me for advice, loans, old clothes, and entertainment. They would see to that. The Ritz, the Blue Lantern, must know me no more.

Exile. A few months in Paris – but Montparnasse, now, my dears, *Montparnasse*; a few offers for my memoirs; then Berlin, Munich – and finally, Greece. There, 'in the worst inn's worst room,' I existed, miserably, on fried goat and raki. To write or to paint – to work – but how? Write only on one side of the paper. But which side? It was the old dilemma. A wandering exile, the quays of the Piraeus knew me, the noisy bars of Terreno, the Dôme and the Deux Magots, Bohême and Silhouette, and that place in the Marokaner Gasse. I ate rose-leaf jam with the good monks of Holy Luke and fried locust with the dervishes of Moulay Idris. And one crazy 4th of June, lobster salad with my housemaster! My slim figure lingered, winterbound, in dim cathedrals, and there were beaches where summer licked me with its great rough tongue. Ah, summer! There's a crypto-fascist for you! The spring I never cared for. It held nothing but a promise, and I, too, was promising. The autumns I adored; they smelt of cassia. But poverty was crippling. To whom life once had been a bed of roses – no, of *Strawberry-leaves*, there remained only the 'Welcome' at Villefranche, the old Boeuf in the Boissy D'Anglas, the Pangion. It was not good enough. I came back to live with my mother.

It was then that I saw the light. One day I wandered into a little book-shop near Red Lion Square. It was full of slim volumes by unfamiliar names – who were Stephen, Wystan, Cecil, and Christopher? Madge? Bates? Dutt? These blunt monosyllables spoke a new kind of language to me. I looked at the books. Not at all bad, and some of these young poets, I realized, had even attended my university! One quatrain in particular haunted me.

> M is for Marx
> and Movement of Masses
> and Massing of Arses
> and Clashing of Classes.

It was new. It was vigorous. It was real. It was chic!

> Come on Percy, my pillion-proud, be camber-conscious
> Cleave to the crown of the road

and

> It was late last night when my lord came home
> enquiring for his lady O
> The servants cried on every side
> She's gone with the Left Book
> > Study Circle O!

And everyone was called by their Christian names! So cosy! From that moment I've never looked back. It's been pylons all the way. Of course they didn't want me, at first. The meetings behind the Geisha Café – they suspected me of all sorts of things, I'm afraid – I said quite frankly: 'I realize I shall never understand eclectic materialism but I'm terribly terribly Left!' And I showed them one or two things I'd written for the weekly reviews, all among the waffle-receipts and the guest-house advertisements.* And I called myself Cris Clay. Then – on a drizzling February morning – came my first Procession! It was for me a veritable *Via Crucis*, for we had to march up St. James's Street – past Locks, and Lobbs, and Briggs, and Boodles. All my past was spread out before me. There weren't very many of us, and it was difficult to cheer and shout our slogans.

> One, two, three, four
> Pacifism means War.

* Soon to be published under the title of *I Told You So.*

I raised my eyes to White's bow-window.

Yes, there they were – Alvanley and Gleneagles, with their soiled city faces and little moustaches, their bowlers and rolled umbrellas – and, good heavens, there were Peter, and Robert, and Evelyn! I never felt more ridiculous. When suddenly something made me look round. 'De Clavering, old horse!' 'Well, I'm spifflicated.' 'You old *finocchio!*' '*Spinaten!*' It was too good to be true.

'But, Harmatviz – I see you don't know the first thing about the cut of a corduroy.'

'Not a red shirt, Slivovitz – a red tie if you must.'

'And you, Coca y Cola – you look like a scarecrow.'

'These are good workmen's pants, de Clavering, real dungaree!'

We gave a boo to the bow-window that made the *Tatlers* rattle in their holders.

'But how did you get here?'

'I was expelled for plotting against the Regent in favour of the traitor Otto.'

'I was turned out for lack of enthusiasm for the present regime and communicating with the traitor Wilhelm.'

'I wanted to annoy Sarsaparilla.'

'Anyhow, we're all good anti-Fascists,' cried Comrade Graf Slivovitz.

I wanted to say something more – that I had even been told by the Party that I should be more useful outside it, but I couldn't speak. Old friends had met, travelling a stony road, coming to the same hard conclusions, and together.

≈

And that's about all. There are one or two things I've left out, the war, the slump, the general strike, and my conversion to Catholicism, because I'm so vague about dates. But I think this will remain – A Modern Pilgrimage. And now for the reviewers. I think they'd better be careful. They'd better be very careful indeed. A line is being drawn. I'm going to say it again, and very slowly. A line is being drawn. Quite quietly at present – just a few names jotted down in a notebook – one or two with a question mark after them. They have another chance. And the rest don't. Those lines mean something. Tatatat! Yes, my dears, bullets – real bullets, the kind of bullets they keep for reviewers who step across the party line. One day you're going to see something rather hostile. It will make you feel, perhaps, a little uneasy. It's heavy – and stubby – and rather pointed. Guess? Yes. A machine-gun. POINTED AT YOU. And behind it, with his hand on the trigger, Comrade – no, COMMISSAR – Cris Clay. Did you write such and such an article? Yes (No). It doesn't matter which. Tatatat. It's no good then bleating about how you voted in the last election, or where your sympathies have always been. We don't want your sympathy. We don't want you at all.

You subscribed to the *News Chronicle*, did you? I'm afraid you will be under no necessity to renew that subscription.

You wrote for the *New Statesman*? What did you write about? 'Gramophone records.'

'To sit on the fence is to be on the wrong side of it – line him up, Gollancz.'

'Yes, Commissar.'

'And you – what were you?'

'Turf-Accountant.'

'Your face seems vaguely familiar – but that doesn't make it more pleasant – line him up, Stephen.'

'It was no accident, Pryce-Jones, that you have lived near three royal palaces.'

'But –'

But I am anticipating. There are two ways to review a book like mine, a right and a wrong. The wrong way is to find fault with it, for then you find fault with the book clubs behind it, in fact, with your advertisers. And if I seem too clever it's because you're too stupid. Think it over. The right way is to praise it, and to quote from it in such a way that you can all learn my lesson. I stand no nonsense. Remember, my dears, a line is being drawn. Tatatat. See you at the Mass Observatory.

> Something is going to go, baby,
> And it won't be your stamp-collection.
> Boom!

And that I think could particularly be meditated by the Fascist Connolly.

CRIS CLAY.

Paris – Budapest – Parton St.
1936–1937

Year Nine
(1938)

Augur's Prison – Year IX. I have been treated with great kindness, with a consideration utterly out of keeping with the gravity of my offence, yet typical of the high conception of justice implicit in our state. Justice in sentence, celerity in execution in the words of Our Leader. Excuse my fatal impediment. I call attention to it, as eagerly as in Tintoretto's plague hospital they point to bleeding bubos on the legs and shoulders. Let me tell you how it all happened. With a friend, a young woman, I arranged to spend last Leaderday evening. We met under the clock outside the Youngleaderboys building. Having some minutes to spare before the Commonmeal and because it was raining slightly, we took shelter in the glorious Artshouse. There were the ineffable misterpasses of our glorious culture, the pastermieces of titalitorian tra, the magnificent Leadersequence, the super-statues of Comradeship, Blatherhood, and Botherly Love, the 73 Martyrs of the Defence of the Bourse, the Leader as a simple special constable. There they were, so familiar that my sinful feet were doubly to be blamed for straying – for they strayed not only beyond the radius of divine beauty but beyond the sphere of ever-loving Authority, creeping with their putrid freight down the stairs to the forgotten basement. There, breeding filth in the filth that gravitates around it, glows the stagnant rottenness called Degenerate Art, though only perfect Leadercourtesy could bestow the term Art on such Degeneration! There are the vile pustules of the rotting Demos, on canvases his sores have hideously excoriated. Still Lives – as if life could ever be still! Plates of food, bowls of fruit; under the old regime the last deplorable nightdreams and imaginations of starving millions, the prurient lucubrations of the unsterilized – bathing coves of womblike

322

obscenity, phallic church towers and monoliths, lighthouses and pyramids, trees even painted singly in their stark suggestiveness, instead of
in the official groups; all hideous and perverted symbols of an age of
private love, ignorant of the harmony of our Commonmeals, and the
State administration of Sheepthinkers Groupbegettingday. There were
illicit couples, depicted in *articulo amoris*, women who had never heard
of the three K's, whose so-called clothes were gaudy dishrags, whose
mouths were painted offal. Engrossed in disgust and mental anguish I
thoughtlessly began to mark on my official catalogue the names of the
most detestable fartists. This was partly to hold them up to ridicule at
Commonmeals, partly to use in articles which would refute the pseudo-
criticism of our enemies, but above all unconsciously – a tic expressive
of my odious habit, for I only *chose names that were easily or
interestingly reversible*. That is my only justification. Nacnud Tnarg;
Sutsugua Nhoj; Ossacip. Repip. The filthy anti-Fascists who dared to
oppose our glorious fishynazists! Hurriedly we made for the clean
outdoors, the welcoming statues of the great upstairs, and outside
where the supreme spectacle streams on the filament – the neon
Leaderface. In my haste I dropped my catalogue by the turnstile. The
rest of the evening passed as usual. We attended Commonmeal in seats
7111037 and 7111038 respectively, and after the digestive drill and the
documentaries went to our dormitories. The young woman on
departing blew me a kiss and I called out merrily yet admonishingly:
'None of that stuff, 7111038, otherwise we shall never be allowed to
produce a little 7111037-8. ♂ on Groupbegettingday.'

During the next week nothing happened. But some four days after
that, having occasion to telephone the young woman, and while speaking
to her in a spirit of party badinage, I was astounded to hear a playful
repartee of mine answered by a male eructation. 'Was that you?' I said –
but no answer came. On picking up the receiver again to ask the janitor
for ten minutes' extra light, I heard – above the ringing noise – for he had
not yet answered – an impatient yawn. These two noises made an
enormous impression, for I realized that I was an object of attention
(though unwelcome attention) to a member of a class far above my own,

a superior with the broad chest and masculine virility of a Stoop Trauma!

The next morning my paper bore the dreaded headline, 'Who are the Censors Looking for?' At the office we were lined up at 10.10 and some officials from the censor's department, in their camouflaged uniforms, carrying the white-hot Tongs, symbol of Truth, the Thumb-caps of Enquiry, and the Head on the Dish, emblem of Justice, passed down the line. As the hot breath of the tongs approached, many of us confessed involuntarily to grave peccadilloes. A man on my left screamed that he had stayed too long in the lavatory. But the glorious department disdained force. We were each given three photographs to consider, and told to arrange them in order of aesthetic merit. The first was a reproduction of a steel helmet, the second a sack of potatoes, the third of some couples with their arms around their necks in an attitude of illicit sexual group-activity. I arranged them in that order. One of the inspectors looked for a long time at me. We were then asked to write down the names of any infamous poets or painters we could remember from the old regime. 'Badshaw, Deadwells, Staleworthy, Baldpole,' I wrote. Then, in an emotion, a veritable paroxysm stronger than me, with the eyes of the examiner upon me, my hands bearing the pen downwards as ineluctably as the State diviner bears down on his twig, I added: 'Toilet, Red Neps.' And once more: 'Nacnud Tnarg, Sutsugua Nhoj, Ossacip. *Jewlysses. Winagains Fake.*' The censors this time did not look at me, but passing down the line made an ever more and more perfunctory examination, towards the end simply gathering the papers from the willing outstretched hands of the workers and carelessly tearing them up. They then swept out of the room, escorted by the foreman, the political and industrial commissars of our office, and Mr. Abject, the Ownerslave. We were instructed to continue our duties. As the envelopes came by on the belt I seized them with trembling hand, and vainly tried to perform my task as if nothing had happened. It was my business to lick the top flap of the envelope, whose bottom flap would then be licked by my neighbour, the one beyond him sticking the flaps together – for all sponges and rollers were needed for munitions. At the same time I used my free hand to inscribe on the corner of the envelope my contribution to the address (for all envelopes were addressed to the censor's headquarters) the letters s.w.3. Alas how many illegible s.w.3's that morning betrayed my trepidation, and when I came to licking the outer flap my tongue was either so parched by terror as to be unable to wet the corner at all, or so drowned in nervous salivation as to spread small bubbles of spittle over the whole surface, causing the flap to curl upwards and producing in my near neighbours many a sign of their indignant impatience and true party horror of bad work. Shortly before leader-break the commissars, followed by Mr. Abject, returned down the line. My companions on the belt, now feeling that I manifested emotional abnormality, were doing everything to attract attention to me by causing me to fail in my work, kicking me on the ankles as they received my envelopes, and one of them, seizing a ruler, made a vicious jab upwards with it as I was adding s.w.3, causing acute agony to my public parts. As the commissars came near me they began to joke, smiling across at my neighbours and grunting: 'As long as you can spit, man, the State will have a use for you,' and 'Don't try and find out where the gum you lick comes from, my boyo.' Friendly condescensions which seemed designed to render more pregnant and miserable the silence with which they came to me. At last, with a terrible downward look, the commissar paused before me. The smile had faded from his face, his eyes flashed lightning, his mouth was thin as a backsight, his nose was a hairtrigger. Mr. Abject looked at me with profound commiseration till he received a nudge from the other commissar, and said in a loud voice: 'This is your man.' I was marched out between them while the serried ranks of my old beltmates sang the Leaderchorus and cried: 'Show mercy to us by showing no mercy to him, the dog and the traitor.' Outside the newsboys were screaming: 'Long live the Censor. Gumlicking wrecker discovered.'

Our justice is swift: our trials are fair: hardly was the preliminary bone-breaking over than my case came up. I was tried by the secret censor's tribunal in a pitchdark circular room. My silly old legs were no use to me now and I was allowed the privilege of wheeling myself in on a kind of invalid's chair. In the darkness I could just see the aperture high up in the wall from whence I should be cross-examined, for it is part of our new justice that no prejudicial view is obtained of the personal forces at work between accused and accuser. The charge was read out and I was asked if I had anything to say. I explained the circumstances as I have related them to you, and made my defence. Since an early initiation accident I have never been considered sound of mind, hence my trick of reversing words – quite automatically and without the intention of seeking hidden and antinomian meanings, hence my subordinate position in the Spitshop. My action, I repeated, was purely involuntary. The voice of my chief witness-accuser-judge replied from the orifice:

'Involuntary! But don't you see, that makes it so much worse! For what we voluntarily do, voluntarily we may undo, but what we do not of our own free will, we lack the will to revoke. What sort of person are you, whose feet carry you helplessly to the forbidden basement? Yet not forbidden, for that basement is an open trap. Poor flies walk down it as down the gummy sides of a pitcher plant; a metronome marks the time they spend there, a radioactive plate interprets the pulsations which those works inspire, a pulsemeter projects them on a luminous screen which is perpetually under observation in the censor's office. It was at once known that you were there and what you felt there. But instead of being followed to your Blokery in the normal way you eluded your pursuers by dropping your catalogue. They decided it was their duty to carry it immediately to the cipher department and thus allowed you to escape. Your crime is fivefold:

' "That you of your own impulse visited the basement of degenerate art and were aesthetically stimulated thereby."

' "That you attempted to convince a young woman, 7111038, of the merit of the daubs you found there, thereby being guilty of treason – for Our Leader is a painter too, and thereby being guilty of the far worse sin of inciting to treason a member of the non-rational (and therefore not responsible for her actions) sex."

' "That you made notes on the daubs in question with a view to perverting your fellow-workers."

' "That you caused deliberate inconvenience to the board of censors, attempting to throw them off your trail, thus making improper use of them."

' "That you did not confess before your offence was notified, or even at the time of your examination."

'The penalty, as you know, for all these crimes is death. But there has interceded on your behalf the young woman whose denunciation helped us to find you. To reward her we have commuted your crime to that of coprophagy – for that is what your bestial appreciation of the faeces of so-called democratic art amounts to. Your plea of involuntary compulsion forces me to proclaim the full sentence. For with such a subconscious libido there must surely be a cancerous ego! I therefore proclaim that you will be cut open by a qualified surgeon in the presence of the State Augur. You will be able to observe the operation, and if the Augur decides the entrails are favourable they will be put back. If not, not. You may congratulate yourself on being of more use to your leader in your end than your beginning. For on this augury an important decision on foreign policy will be taken. Annexation or Annihilation? Be worthy of your responsibility. Should the worst befall, you will be sent to the gumfactory, and part of you may even form the flap of an envelope which your successor on the belt, Miss 7111038, may lick! You lucky dog.'

Yes, I have been treated with great kindness.

Bond Strikes Camp
(1962)

Shadows of fog were tailing him through the windows of his Chelsea flat; the blonde had left a broken rosette of lipstick on the best Givan's pillowcase – he would have to consult last night's book-matches to find out where he had grabbed her. It was one bitch of a morning. And, of course, it turned out to be the day! For there was always one breakfast in the month when a very simple operation, the boiling of an egg so that the yolk should remain properly soft and the white precisely hard, seemed to defeat his devoted housekeeper, May. As he decapitated the fifth abort on its Wedgwood launching-pad he was tempted to crown her with the sixteen-inch pepper mill. Three minutes and fifty-five seconds later by his stopwatch and the sixth egg came up with all systems go. As he was about to press the thin finger of wholemeal toast into the prepared cavity the telephone rang. It was probably the blonde: 'Don't tell me: it all comes back – you're the new hat-check from "The Moment of Truth",' he snarled into the receiver. But the voice which cut in was that of his secretary, Miss Ponsonby. 'He wants you now, smart pants, so step on the Pogo.'

Swearing pedantically, Bond pulled away from his uneaten egg and hurried from the flat to the wheel of his souped-up Pierce Arrow, a Thirty-one open tourer with two three-piece windscreens. A sulphurous black rain was falling and he nearly took the seat off a Beatnik as he swerved into Milner. It was that kind of a Christmas. Thirteen minutes later his lean body streaked from the tonneau-cover like a conger from its hole and he stood outside M.'s door with Lolita Ponsonby's great spaniel eyes gazing up at him in dog-like devotion.

'Sorry about the crossed line,' he told her. 'I'll sock you a lunch if they don't need you at Crufts.' Then the green lights showed and he entered.

'Sit down, 007.' That was Grade C welcome indicating the gale warning. There had been several lately. But M. did not continue. He surveyed Bond with a cold, glassy stare, cleared his throat and suddenly lowered his eyes. His pipe rested unlit beside the tobacco in the familiar shell-cap. If such a thing had been possible, Bond would have sworn he was embarrassed. When at length he spoke, the voice was dry and impersonal. 'There are many things I have asked you to do, Bond; they have not always been pleasant but they have been in the course of duty. Supposing I were to ask you to do something which I have no right to demand and which I can justify only by appealing to principles outside your service obligations. I refer to your patriotism. You are patriotic, Bond?'

'Don't know, sir. I never read the small print clauses.'

'Forgive the question, I'll put it another way. Do you think the end justifies the means?'

'I can attach no significance of any kind to such expressions.'

M. seemed to reflect. The mood of crisis deepened.

'Well, we must try again. If there were a particularly arduous task – a most distasteful task – and I called for a volunteer – who must have certain qualifications – and only one person had those qualifications – and I asked him to volunteer. What would you say?'

'I'd say stop beating about the bush, sir.'

'I'm afraid we haven't even started.'

'Sir?'

'Do you play chess, Bond?'

'My salary won't run to it.'

'But you are familiar with the game?'

'Tolerably.' As if aware that he was in the stronger position, Bond was edging towards insolence.

'It has, of course, been thoroughly modernised; all the adventure has been taken out of it; the opening gambits in which a piece used to be sacrificed for the sake of early development proved unsound and therefore abandoned. But it is so long since they have been tried that many players are unfamiliar with the pitfalls and it is sometimes possible to obtain an advantage by taking a risk. In our profession, if it be a profession, we keep a record of these forgotten traps. Ever heard of Mata Hari?'

'The beautiful spy?' Bond's voice held derision. The school prefect sulking before his housemaster.

'She was very successful. It was a long time ago.' M. still sounded meek and deprecating.

'I seem to remember reading the other day that a concealed microphone had replaced the *femme fatale.*'

'Precisely. So there is still a chance for the *femme fatale.*'

'I have yet to meet her.'

'You will. You are aware there is a Russian military mission visiting this country?'

Bond let that one go into the net.

'They have sent over among others an elderly general. He looks like a general, he may well have been a general, he is certainly a very high echelon in their K.G.B. Security is his speciality; rocketry, nerve gases, germ warfare – all the usual hobbies.' M. paused. 'And one rather unusual one.'

Bond waited, like an old pike watching the bait come down.

'Yes. He likes to go to night clubs, get drunk, throw his money about and bring people back to his hotel. All rather old-fashioned.'

'And not very unusual.'

'Ah.' M. looked embarrassed again. 'I'm just coming to that. We happen to know quite a bit about this chap, General Count Apraxin. His family were pretty well known under the old dispensation though his father was one of the first to join the party; we think he may be a bit of a throw-back. Not politically, of course. He's tough as they come. I needn't tell you Section A make a study of the kind of greens the big shots go in for. Sometimes we know more about what these people are like between the sheets than they do themselves; it's a dirty business. Well, the General is mad about drag.'

'Drag, sir?'

M. winced. 'I'm sorry about this part, Bond. He's "so" – "uno di quelli!" – "one of those" – a sodomite.'

Bond detected a glint of distaste in the cold blue eyes.

'In my young days,' M. went on, 'fellows like that shot themselves. Now their names are up for every club. Particularly in London. Do you know what sort of a reputation this city has abroad?' Bond waited. 'Well, it stinks. These foreigners come here, drop notes of assignation into sentries' top-boots, pin fivers on to guardsmen's bearskins. The Tins are livid.'

'And General Apraxin?' Bond decided to cut short the Wolfenden.

'One of the worst. I told you he likes drag. That's – er – men dressed up as women.'

'Well, you tell me he's found the right place. But I don't quite see where we come in.'

M. cleared his throat. 'There's just a possibility, mind, it's only a possibility, that even a top K.G.B. might be taken off guard – if he found the company congenial – perhaps so congenial that it appealed to some secret wish of his imagination – and if he talked at all (mind you, he is generally absolutely silent), well then anything he said might be of the greatest value – anything – it might be a lead on what he's really here for. You will be drawing a bow at a venture. You will be working in the dark.'

'Me, sir?'

M. rapped out the words like a command. '007, I want you to do this thing. I want you to let our people rig you up as a moppet and send you to a special sort of club and I want you to allow yourself to be approached by General Apraxin and sit at his table and if he asks you back to his hotel I want you to accompany him and any suggestion he makes I request you to fall in with to the limit your conscience permits. And may your patriotism be your conscience, as it is mine.'

It was a very odd speech for M. Bond studied his finger-nails. 'And if the pace gets too hot?'

'Then you must pull out – but remember. T. E. Lawrence put up with the final indignity. I knew him well, but knowing even that, I never dared call him by his christian name.'

Bond reflected. It was clear that M. was deeply concerned. Besides, the General might never turn up. 'I'll try anything once, sir.'

'Good man.' M. seemed to grow visibly younger.

'As long as I'm not expected to shake a powder into his drink and run away with his wallet.'

'Oh, I don't think it will come to that. If you don't like the look of things, just plead a headache; he'll be terrified of any publicity. It was all Section A could do to slip him a card for this club.'

'What's its name?'

M. pursed his lips. 'The Kitchener. In Lower Belgrave Mews. Be there about eleven o'clock and just sit around. We've signed you in as "Gerda".'

'And my – disguise?'

'We're sending you off to a specialist in that kind of thing – he thinks you want it for some Christmas "do". Here's the address.'

'One more question, sir. I have no wish to weary you with details of my private life but I can assure you I've never dressed up in "drag" as you call it since I played Katisha in "The Mikado" at my prep. school. I shan't look right, I shan't move right, I shan't talk right; I shall feel about as convincing arsing about as a night-club hostess as Randolph Churchill.'

M. gazed at him blankly and again Bond noticed his expression of weariness, even of repulsion. 'Yes, 007, you will do all of those things and I am afraid that is precisely what will get him.'

Bond turned angrily but M.'s face was already buried in his signals. This man who had sent so many to their deaths was still alive and now the dedicated bachelor who had never looked at a woman except to estimate her security risk was packing him off with the same cold indifference into a den of slimy creatures. He walked out of the room and was striding past Miss Ponsonby when she stopped him. 'No time for that lunch, I'm afraid. You're wanted in Armoury.'

The Armoury in the basement held many happy memories for Bond.

It represented the first moments of a new adventure, the excitement of being back on a job. There were the revolvers and the Tommy guns, the Smith and Wessons, Colts, Lugers, Berettas, killer weapons of every class or nationality; blow-pipes, boomerangs, cyanide fountain-pens, Commando daggers and the familiar heap of aqualungs, now more or less standard equipment. He heard the instructor's caressing voice. 'Grind yer boot down his shin and crush his instep. Wrench off his testicles with yer free hand and with the fingers held stiffly in the V sign gouge out his eye with the other.'

He felt a wave of home-sickness. 'Ah, Bond, we've got some hardware for you. Check it over and sign the receipt,' said the lieutenant of marines.

'Good God, what's this? It looks to me like a child's water-pistol.'

'You're so right – and here's the water.' He was given a small screw-top ink-bottle full of some transparent liquid. 'Don't spill any on your bib and tucker.'

'What'll it stop?'

'Anything on two legs if you aim at the eyes.'

Bond consulted the address of his next 'armourer'. It was a studio off Kinnerton Street. The musical cough of the Pierce Arrow was hardly silent when the door was opened by a calm young man who looked him quickly up and down. Bond was wearing one of his many pheasant's-eye alpacas which exaggerated the new vertical line – single-breasted, narrow lapels, ton-up trousers with no turn-ups, peccary suède shoes. A short covert-coat in cavalry twill, a black sting-ray tail of a tie, an unexpected width of shoulder above the tapering waist and the casual arrogance of his comma of dark hair low over the forehead under his little green piglet of a hat completed the picture of mid-century masculinity. The young man seemed unimpressed. 'Well, well, how butch can you get? You've left it rather late. But we'll see what we can do.'

He turned Bond towards the lighted north window and studied him carefully, then he gave the comma a tweak. 'I like the spit-curl, Gerda, we'll build up round that. Now go in there and strip.'

333

When he came out in his pants, the barracuda scars dark against the tan, a plain girl was waiting in a nurse's uniform. 'Lie down, Gerda, and leave it all to Miss Haslip,' said the young man. She stepped forward and began, expertly, to shave his legs and armpits. 'First a shave, then the depilatory – I'm afraid, what with the fittings, you'll be here most of the day.' It was indeed one bitch of a morning. The only consolation was that the young man (his name was Colin Mount) allowed him to keep the hair on his chest. 'After all, nobody wants you *all* sugar.'

After the manicure, pedicure and plucking of the eyebrows it was time to start rebuilding. Bond was given a jock-strap to contain his genitals; the fitting of an elaborate chestnut wig so as to allow the comma to escape under it was another slow process. And then the artificial eye-lashes. Finally what looked like a box of tennis balls was produced from a drawer. 'Ever seen these before?'

'Good God, what *are* they?'

'The very latest in falsies – foam-rubber, with electronic self-erecting nipples – pink for blondes, brown for brunettes. The things they think of! Which will you be? It's an important decision.'

'What the hell do I care?'

'On the whole I think you'd better be a brunette. It goes with the eyes. And with your height we want them rather large. Round or pear-shaped?'

'Round, for Christ's sake.'

'Sure you're not making a mistake?'

The falsies were attached by a rubber strap, like a brassière, which – in black moiré – was then skilfully fitted over them. 'How does that feel? There should be room for a guy to get his hand up under the bra and have a good riffle.' Then came the slinky black lace panties and finally the black satin evening skirt with crimson silk blouse suspended low on the shoulder, a blue mink scarf over all and the sheerest black stockings and black shoes with red stilettos. Bond surveyed himself in the long glass and experienced an unexpected thrill of excitement; there was no doubt he had a damned good figure.

'Well, you're no Coccinelle,' said the young man, 'but you'll certainly pass. Hip-square! Drag's a lot of fun you'll find. One meets quite a different class of person. Now go and practise walking till you drop. Then get some sleep, and after that, if you're good, we'll make up that pretty face and launch you at the local cinema.'

After practising in high heels for a couple of hours, Bond went back to his couch and lay down exhausted. He dreamed he was swimming under water on a stormy day, the waves breaking angrily above him while, harpoon in hand, he followed a great sea-bass with spaniel eyes that seemed to turn and twist and invite him onward down an ever-narrowing, weed-matted gully.

When he awoke it was dark and he fell avidly on the Blue Mountain coffee and club sandwich Miss Haslip had brought him. 'Now we'll start on the face – and here's your evening bag.' Bond transferred his water-pistol, ink-bottle, Ronson lighter, gun-metal cigarette case and bill-folder and emptied the contents of his wallet; a vintage chart from the Wine and Food Society, an 'Advanced Motorists'' certificate, another from the Subaqua Club, a temporary membership card of the Travellers, Paris, the Caccia, Rome, Puerto de Hierro, Madrid, Brook, Meadowbrook, Knickerbocker and Crazy Horse Saloon, Liguanea, Eagle, Somerset (Boston) and Boston (New Orleans), ending up with a reader's pass for the Black Museum. When he had done, Colin emptied the whole lot into a large envelope, which he told Bond to put in the glove compartment, and handed back the water-pistol and key-ring. 'Try these instead,' and Bond was given a powder-puff, a couple of lipsticks, some Kleenex, a package of cigarettes (Senior Service) with a long cane holder, some costume jewellery and a charm bracelet and a membership card in the name of Miss Gerda Blond for the Kitchener Social Club, Lower Belgrave Mews, S.W.

In a compartment of his evening bag he found a pocket mirror, tortoiseshell comb, enamel compact and a box of eye make-up with a tiny brush. 'When you get mad at someone it's a great relief to take this out and spit on it. The harder you spit, the more of a lady you'll seem.' Mount showed him how to apply the little brush, the mascara and black eye-shadow. 'When you don't know how to answer, just look down for a little – lower those eyelashes, that'll fetch them – and make with the holder. And do be careful in the Loo. That's where nearly all the mistakes are made. Now we're off to the Pictures.'

'What are we going to see?'

'La Dolce Vita.'

In the dark cinema Bond noticed a few interested glances in his direction. A man in the next seat put his hand on his knee. Bond knew the drill; a policewoman in Singapore had shown him. You take the hand tenderly in yours and extend his arm across your knee. Then you bring your other hand down hard and break the fellow's arm at the elbow. He had just got it all set up when the lights went on.

'I wanted you to see that picture, it gives you so many approaches,' said Colin Mount. 'You can try Ekberg – the big child of nature – or one of those sophisticated cats. Now off you go. Better take a taxi, that hearse of yours looks too draughty."

In Lower Belgrave Mews, Bond rang the bell, showed his card and was immediately admitted.

The Kitchener was discreetly decorated in the style of 1914 with a maze of red plush and some old war posters. The familiar, rather forbidding face with pouchy eyes and drooping moustache and the pointing finger, 'Your King and country need you', recruited him wherever he looked. There were two upstair rooms, in one of which people were dancing. The other held a few divans and tables and a little bar. They had once formed a large double drawing-room. On the landing above, the bathrooms were labelled 'Turks' and 'Virgins'.

Bond sat down at a table, ordered 'Eggs Omdurman' washed down by a 'Sirdar Special'. He noticed several couples dancing sedately to the Cobbler's Song from 'Chu Chin Chow' on a pick-up. There were posters of Doris Keane in *Romance* and Violet Loraine in *The Bing Boys* and of Miss Teddy Gerrard. The subdued lighting from pink lampshades, the roomy banquette, the liver-flicking welcome of his 'Eggs Omdurman' and the silken recoil of the 'Sirdar Special' made him feel for the first time content with his preposterous mission. Had he not worn the kilt at Fettes? He was in it now, up to the sporran. All at once a woman's low voice interrupted his reverie. 'Dance?' He lowered his eyes, as he had been told, and thought furiously. To refuse, in fact to tell her to get the hell out, was his first reaction – but that might arouse suspicion. He had better play along. 'Thanks. I'd love to,' he managed in a husky contralto and looked up past a mannish red waistcoat and tweed jacket into a pair of faintly mocking brown eyes. It was Lolita! Speechless with disaster, Bond wondered how long it would be before the story was all over the office. If only his disguise could last a couple of rounds. And then he remembered. Was he not 007 and licensed to kill with his water-pistol? He tensed himself and let the sweat dry on his forehead. In a moment he was hobbling on to the dance floor, where it was much darker, to the strains of 'Japanese Sandman'. His secretary seemed transformed: capably she manoeuvred him into an obscure corner where they rocked up and down as she began to hold him closer, sliding a leg between his and shifting her hand slowly and expertly down his spine. He began to wonder how the jock-strap would hold. Suddenly she drew back a little and looked him in the eyes. 'What's your name?'

'Gerda' – he croaked – 'Gerda Blond.'

'It's your first visit to the Kitch, isn't it? – well, Gerda, I could fall for you in a big way. I bet you could give someone a good butt in the eye with those charleys.' She ran a finger gently up a full, firm breast and gave a start when the nipple shot up trigger-happy as a Sensitive Plant. 'Gerda, I want to ask you a question.'

Bond lowered his eyes. 'Have you ever slept with a woman?'

'Well, no, not exactly.'

'Well, you're going to tonight.'

'But I don't even know your name.'

'Just call me Robin.'

'But I'm not sure that I can tonight.'

'Well, I am. And let me tell you; once you've been to bed with me you won't want anyone else. I know what men are like – I work for one. No girl ever wants a man once she's made it with a dike. It's the difference between a bullfight and an egg-and-spoon race.'

'But I can't imagine what you see in me.'

'Well, you've got a pretty good figure and I like that in-between colour, like a Braque still life, and I adore the wizard tits – and then you're not like the other mice, sort of virginal and standoffish – and I'm crazy about the spit-curl.' She gave it a sharp tug.

'That's not a spit-curl,' pouted Bond. 'That's my comma.'

'Have it your way. And I like your husky voice and those droopy eyes and right now I'm imagining your little black triangle.'

'Oh, belt up, Robin!'

'Come on, Gerda, we're going back to my place.'

Miss Ponsonby began to lug him off the dance floor. Immediately, out of the corner of his eye, Bond caught sight of a stout figure in a dinner-jacket at another table, a bald head and fishy stare and a pair of enormous moustaches, even as a thick forefinger shot up like an obscene grub and began to beckon to him. A deep voice rumbled: 'Would the two little ladies care to accept a glass of champagne?'

'Certainly not,' snapped Miss Ponsonby. 'Father would turn in his vault.'

'Thanks a lot. No objection,' came Bond's husky contralto. His secretary wheeled round. 'Why, you black bitch – you filthy little tart, I suppose you support a basketful of bastards at home all bleating their bloody heads off. Go along and I hope the old Tirpitz gives you a Lulu.' She gave Bond a ringing slap across the eyes and burst into tears. As she left she turned to the new arrival. 'You watch out with that bint. Mark my words. She'll do you in.'

Bond held his smarting cheek. The foreign gentleman patted his arm and pulled him on to the banquette. 'What a headstrong young lady – she gave me quite a turn. But here comes our champagne. I have ordered a magnum of Taittinger Blanc de blancs, '52 – it never departs from a certain "tenu" – independent yet perfectly deferential.' He had a trace of guttural accent but what impressed Bond most were the most magnificent whiskers. He had seen them only once before on a Russian, Marshal Budenny, Stalin's cavalry leader. They gave a raffish Eighth Army-turned-innkeeper look to the big-nosed military man and were perhaps symptomatic of the formidable General's atavism.

Bond collapsed on to the alcove divan and raised the paradisal prickle to his lips, remembering Monsieur Georges, the wine waiter at the Casino Royale who had called his attention to the brand in the first of his annual agonies.

'Perhaps I had better introduce myself,' said the General. 'I am a Yugoslav travelling salesman here to make certain business contacts and tonight is my evening of relaxation. All day I have been in conference and tomorrow I have to go down early in the morning to Salisbury Plain. Vladimir Mishitch. Just call me Vladimir; the accent is on the second syllable.'

Bond noticed he had not inquired his own name and finally volunteered with downcast eye, 'My name is Gerda. I like travelling too but I'm afraid I haven't anything to sell.'

'One never knows. "La plus belle fille du monde, ne peut donner que ce qu'elle a." ' The General stuck his hand into Bond's blouse and ran his fingers through the hair on his chest. 'That's a nice rug you've got there, Gerda.' Bond lowered his eyes again. 'And that – that is pretty too. How do you call it?'

'That's my comma.'

'I see. I'm afraid I make more use of the colon. Ha! ha!' Bond did not know whether to seem amused or bored, and said nothing. 'Tell me, Gerda –' the General's voice took on a warmer colour. 'Have you ever slept with a man?'

'Well no, not exactly.'

'I thought not, Gerda – your little girl friend – the paprikahühn – she would not allow it, hein?'

'Well, it's something we've all got to do sooner or later.'

'And I suggest you do it right now – for when you've been to bed with a real man, a man of age and experience, you won't ever want anyone else. It's like the Salle Privée at the Sporting Club after a tea with your P.E.N.'

He inserted a torpedo-shaped Larranaga such as seldom reaches these shores into an amber holder and poured out the ice-cold champagne until Bond unaccountably found himself sitting on his lap in some disarray, while the General broke into stentorian song:

> How you gonna keep them
> Down on the farm
> After they've seen Paree!

Bond broke away.

'Aren't you going to have a dance with me?'

The General roared with laughter. 'I have never learned to dance except our Yugoslav ones and those we dance only with comrades.'

'I expect I could pick it up.'

'Yes. Like I have picked you up. I will play one to you in my hotel and you will dance like an Ustashi.'

'But they were all fascists, weren't they?'

The General laughed again. 'They danced very well at the end of a rope. Like Homer's handmaidens – with twittering feet.'

Bond found the allusion faintly disturbing. 'It's too hot, let's go.'

The General paid the bill from a bundle of fivers and hurried down the stairs; it was only, Bond noticed, a little after midnight. 'We will take a taxi, Gerda, it is less likely to be followed.'

'But why should anyone want to follow you, Vladimir?'

'Business is business; don't worry your pretty little head.'

The taxi turned off St. James's Street and stopped in a cul-de-sac. 'But this is not a hotel.'

'No, Gerda, furnished service flatlets. Mine is in the basement, so we go down these steps and don't have to face your night porters – so puritanical – and so expensive. Though anyone can see you're not an ordinary lady of the town.' He covered a falsie in his large palm and cupped it hard. 'Pip – pip.'

'Leave me alone. I've got a headache.'

'I have just the thing,' said the General and paid off the taxi, almost flinging Bond in his tight skirt and high heels down the steps into the area. For the first time he felt a twinge of fear. To the taxi-driver he was one of London's many thousand fly-by-nights off to earn their lolly –

yet no one else in the great indifferent city knew his whereabouts nor what manner of man was preparing to have his way with him. At home in Chelsea his black shantung pyjamas would be laid out, the evening papers and the *Book Collector* spread on his night table, the digestive biscuits and Karlsbad plums, a bottle of San Pellegrino, a jigger of Strathisla. Lately he had taken to spinning himself to sleep with a roulette wheel or some Chopi xylophone music from the Transvaal asbestos mines. . . .

Vladimir opened a Yale and then a mortice-lock and let them into a typical furnished basement flat, a beige sitting-room with a sombre bedroom behind. The fog was beginning to probe again, like a second day's grilling by Interpol. 'Here, swallow this for the headache – and have a glass of whisky – Teachers, Cutty Sark, Old Grandad or do you prefer vodka or slivovitz?'

'Old Grandad – and what about you?'

'Oh, I'll help myself to some vodka.' It was a tiny error but a revealing one. But perhaps the General argued that a Yugoslav drank slivovitz enough at home.

Bond put a cigarette in his mouth and just remembered in time to let the General light it. He took the yellow pill which he had been given, palmed it and pretended to follow it with a grimace. 'I hate all these pills and things. I don't believe they're any good AT all.'

The General raised his vodka. 'To Friendship.'

'To Friendship,' chorused Gerda, lifting up her Old-Grandad-on-the-rocks. She was thinking fast. The purpose of the pill she hadn't swallowed must have been to make her sleepy but hardly to put her out. She had better play drowsy.

'Let's have another toast,' said the General. 'Who is your best friend?'

Bond remembered the gambit prawn. 'Guy Burgess.'

The General guffawed. 'I'll tell him. He'll be delighted. He doesn't often get a message from such a pretty girl.'

Bond lowered his eyes. 'He was my lover.'

'One can see that by the way you walk.'

Bond felt a mounting wave of fury. He opened his bag, took out his mascara and spat viciously. The General looked on with approval. Bond produced another cigarette. 'Here, catch.' The General tossed over his lighter. Bond, with the eye-brush in one hand and the pack in the other, brought his legs neatly together as it fell on his lap.

'Where were you at school, Gerda?'

'Westonbirt.'

'And so they teach you to catch like a man – what is a woman's lap for? She widens it to catch, not brings her legs together. And when she drowns she floats upward not downward. Remember that. It may come in useful.'

Bond felt trapped. 'I'm so sleepy,' he muttered. 'I don't understand.'

'Quick, in here.' The General pushed him into the bedroom with its electric fire and dingy satin coverlet. 'Undress and get into bed and then look under the pillow.'

Bond took off his blouse and skirt while the General gallantly turned his back, but kept on his stockings, pants and 'bra', then got out his water-pistol and filled it, dropped the pill behind the bed and finally climbed in and felt under the pillow. The first thing he found was a tube of some oil-looking substance, the next was a shoe-horn with a long cane handle, the last was a piece of paper with 'No one is the worse for a good beating' printed in heavy capitals. 'Ready,' he called and lay quietly until the General in a blue quilted vicuna kimono came simpering in. Bond made a kissy noise and as the General climbed on to the bed and advanced his hairy handlebars reached out with the water-pistol and shot him full in the eye.

The General wiped his face with a silk handkerchief. 'Temper, temper,' he giggled as the liquid ran down his chin. 'What a silly toy for a naughty little girl. Who do you think we are, a black mamba?' He picked up the shoe-horn and dealt Bond a vicious cut across the falsies.

'Help, help, murder,' screamed Bond and once again as the General drew back his mind began to race furiously. Somewhere along the line he had been double-crossed. But when? He lay back drowsily. 'Vladimir – it was only my joke. I'm so sorry. Now let me sleep.'

'Soon you shall sleep – but we have all to earn our sleep. Now shall I beat you first or will you beat me?'

'I will beat you, Vladimir, or I shall certainly drop off before my turn comes. Besides I've never beaten anyone before.'

'Tell that to Guy Burgess.' The General handed over the long shoe-horn and lay down on his stomach. You can kill a man with a short stick, Bond remembered. Get his head forward. Hold the stick in both hands and jab one end up under his Adam's apple. It had all seemed so easy in Armoury. But the General's broad shoulders were in the way. 'How dare you speak to me like that.' Bond jumped up and ran for the bathroom.

As he hoped, the General lumbered after him. 'Come out, you young fool, I can't sit around all night while you play hard to get. I'll miss my train to Porton.'

Porton! The anthrax boys! Bond's nipples stiffened at the name. 'I won't come out till I get my little present.'

'Fifty pounds – if you'll go the limit.'

'I want half now.'

The ends of some five-pound notes protruded under the bathroom door. Bond pulled hard but the General, he guessed, must be standing on them on the other side. That meant he was right by the door which opened inward. Bond would have to fling it open, get Vladimir's head forward and ram his throat in one continuous movement. He was in peak training, his opponent would assume him to be half asleep – it could be done. He counted down from five (the nearest he ever got to a prayer), threw open the door and discovered the smiling General with his hands deep in his kimono pocket and head thrown far back. There was a strong smell of cigar and Floris mouthwash. Still holding the shoe-horn in one hand, Bond lunged forward with the other, got hold of both ends of the handlebars to bring his head down and gave a tremendous tug. There was a screech of rending cardboard and the General gave a yell of pain; a gummy red patch was spreading where the whiskers had been. Bond stared into the cold blue eyes and this time they fell before him.

〜

'I'm sorry, James,' said M. 'It was the only way I could get you.'

Bond drew himself up; his eyes flashed fire, his comma glistened, his breasts firmed, the nipples roused and urgent, his long rangy body flared out above his black silk panties, he looked like Judith carving Holofernes. In two seconds of icy concentration he saw everything that had to be done.

'It's been going on so long. I've been through too much. Don't think I haven't fought against it.'

Bond cut him short. 'I thought fellows like you shot themselves.' M. hung his head. 'Have you got a gun – sir –?' M. nodded. Bond looked at his watch. 'It's a quarter past two. You may employ what means you prefer but if I find out you are still alive by nine o'clock I shall alert every newspaper here, Tass and United Press – Moscow, Washington, Interpol and Scotland Yard, *Izvestia* and the *Kingston Gleaner* with the whole story. If it had been anyone else I might have urged you to leave the country but with modern methods of eliciting information you would be blown in a day.'

'You're quite right, James. I've staked all and I've lost. I hope you'll believe me when I say it would have been the first and last time.'

'I believe you, sir.'

'And now perhaps you'd better leave me, 007; I shall have one or two reports to make.'

Bond flung on his blouse and skirt, worked into his stilettos and snatched up his bag and tippet.

'One last question, James. How did you guess?'

Bond thought of simply confessing that he hadn't guessed, even when the water-pistol had proved a dud. Right down to the Taittinger M.'s arrangement had been perfect. But that might look bad on his file. Then it came back to him. 'You spoke of Homer's handmaidens with "twittering feet" when Ulysses hanged them. That was in Lawrence of Arabia's translation. Robert Graves objected to it. I remembered that you had said Lawrence was your friend. It might have occurred to you that Graves could be mine.'

344

M.'s face brightened and the sickening love-light shone once more. 'Good lad!'

It made Bond want to spit in his mascara. 'Sir.' It was the guardsman's simple dismissal. Without a backward glance he let himself out and stamped up the area steps into the fog. In a few hours the finest Secret Service in the world would be without a head: Miss Ponsonby and Miss Moneypenny would lack an employer. All over the world transmitters would go silent, quiet men grip their cyanide or burn their cyphers, double agents look around for a publisher.

And he would be home in his black pyjamas, snoring up an alibi in his big double bed. There could be only one successor, one person only immediately fitted to take up all the threads, one alone who could both administrate and execute, plan and command. M., as he said, had played and lost. Come egg-time 007 Bond (James) would no longer be a mere blunt weapon in the hands of government. 'M. est mort! Vive le B.!'

And when all the razzamatazz had subsided, he would put on his glad-rags and mosey round to the old Kitch. . . .

'Taxi!' The cab drew up to him in the dim light of St. James's Street. 'King's Road, corner of Milner,' he rasped.

'Jump up in front, lady, and I'll take you for nothing.'

Bond jumped.

Happy Deathbeds
(late 1940s)

The French journalist stuck her face out at him. '*Et maintenant,*' (he knew what was coming) '*M. Brancolee, qui sont les jeunes?*' Green-orange hair: orange eyebrows: imitation tortoise-shell glasses with boot-button eyes behind radish mouth and orange-black face: all of them he took in as he slid down the nursery slopes of his profession.

'Henry Greed, Philip Baldpatch, John Gasper,' he rattled. '*Ils sont très forts.*' The pen-pencil swung across her page.

'*Et qu'est-ce qu'ils font maintenant?*' she heaved. Everything was discreet about her except her expensive scent of tuberose and Cape lobster. Brinkley made a charm-face, his eyes twinkled (how does one manage that?), his mouth budded and so forth into an expression of infantile disloyalty. He was 44.

'*Mais des choses très importantes – Madame Scampi-Lutschberg – les romans, mémoires, livres de guèrre, un peu de tout, enfin – ils sont très jeunes.*'

She took it on the nib. 'Bowldpotch – *et comment ça s'écrit?*'

For ten years now he had been giving this answer to the French, the Belgians, the Dutch, the Americans ('they're very strong') and lately even to Germans and Italians. Greed had been silent ever since he lost his boyfriend: Baldpatch – through excesses – had developed an abscess in the lung: Gasper was now a chicken farmer. They belonged to the glorious days of the war when men in battle dress descending on Normandy really enjoyed the freshness and irony of this lost young generation segregated in the M.O.I. They sent them home camemberts and calvados. And imported their first books in exchange.

The French journalist, whose paper – if they had known it – had perhaps three months longer to live than Brinkley's, sighed ecstatically. He prepared for the next phase. Charles Morgan. Rosamond Lehmann. Her time was nearly up. '*Et que pensez-vous de notre cher . . .*'

Elsa, his secretary entered. 'An urgent call, Mr. Brinkley, on the other line.' He rose and gave the journalist a gluey smile.

'I take up too much of your time,' she rollicked.

'*Mais Rosamond Lehmann,*' he anticipated, '*quelle belle femme.*'

'*Et Stephen Spender,*' they chorused, '*tout de même, il est un très grand poéte.*'

The secretary's smile was ambivalent as usual. 'I rescued you. But you wouldn't do it if you didn't like it.'

The journalist departed with five addresses and a free copy of the current number. '*Et si jamais vous venez à Paris . . .*'

'How would you translate that?' said Brinkley to the secretary.

'I suggest – though it's rather free – "Balls to you, brother."' She handed him a cup of cold black tea. 'You were wonderful, as always,' she lobbed.

'Your timing,' he returned, 'was perfect.' Hate held them exhumed to the spot. The telephone rang: she dared him to pick it up with her forgive-not-forget look. 'Better see who that is,' he surrendered.

Holding the receiver close to her ear, she turned on a fire-hose of sympathy. 'No. How appalling. O but O. Goodness how dreadful. Of course I'll come round. No but now.' Her blue archaic ox-eyes hoovered him out of the room.

At the literary cocktail party two hours later, the French journalist was still in good shape: since leaving she had seen Eliot (it really is only people like her who do see him), Graham Greene, Elizabeth Bowen and several of the angry young not-yet-on-anybody's-list, who had said what they thought of Baldpatch and Brinkley.

'*Découragant et découragé,*' she told him. Now she was mopping up the publishers. Stanways appealed to her especially, he looked so

Georgian-Bloomsbury, with more pens and notebooks falling out of him than any author would presume to carry and his plum-coloured waistcoat with one button missing.

Brinkley's secretary joined the group and was soon giving Madame Lutschberg all the information which he had been unable to contribute. There was no disloyalty: she neither covered up her failure nor exploited it. It was as if the original visit had never been. Brinkley's persecution mania flared up. 'Materials for a complex' he ran over to himself. 'Anxiety in trains, anxiety on planes, anxiety in lifts, anxiety on heights and in depths. Dynamital requests – for money, for names of young writers, for anything which furthered cultural relationship.

Pleasurable: Letters from antique-dealers (if not bills), auction catalogues, wine-lists, the magazines *Connoisseur* and *Apollo*, visits from old friends and new ones with a feeling for objects or connections with Sotheby's or the Wallace Collection, painters, pretty girls with trim behinds.

Painful: letters from authors, editors, bookshops, all manuscripts, visits from literary acquaintances, publishers, middle-aged women. ANYTHING TO DO WITH ELSA.'

Now Elsa and Stanways and Madame Scampi-Lutschberg were deep in the second phase – not '*Qui sont les jeunes?*' but '*Où sont les droits?*' Stanways put down a third edition of *The Castle of Otranto* which he had bought during lunch for two shillings, a roll of galley proofs, an advance copy of Kafka's *The Gallstone*, a sentimental postcard of a Toulon sailor sent him by a don at Cambridge, a tin of mussels for a soup he was going home to cook, a press cutting containing an indecent misprint, a green Morocco commonplace book which had belonged to Harriet Martineau, and a Swiss secondhand bookseller's catalogue in which he had marked against the rarest item 'Almost certainly my grandfather's' and took out a little engagement book with a priority list of telephone numbers. They were joined by two other publishers, the tall grey-headed young Leishmann with his cold blue vulture's eyes and the engaging 'Scottie' Buchanan with his amiable bewildered look like a dog learning to count, which marked an angry contempt for all who were not outstanding in their profession and which disappeared only when he was happiest, that is to say playing squash with young actor-managers. Elsa leading the chorus, they were soon involved in the traditional pastime of trying to get a French publisher to translate Miss Compton Burnett.

Brinkley's face was a mask: or rather, it took on the expression of sulky vacancy which he assumed when the necessity of praising writers whom he couldn't admit in public to disliking so was forced upon him. '*Ah, il faut lire Frères et Soeurs,*' screamed Elsa, '*Non, commencez par Mères et Filles,*' said Leishmann '*et Henry Green – voila un auteur pour vous,*' he added. '*Mais ou sont les droits?*' He beamed. 'You've come to the right man. *Je les ai moi-même.*' Buchanan turned away. Brinkley thought of the apple-green Sèvres in the Wallace Collection and the green and blue, like cornfields by the sea. One day as he drove down a village street he would spot the glint. 'Yes, as a matter of fact they are for sale, sir: fifteen shillings for the lot, glad to have them off my hands. They came from the old lady up at the hall.'

'O but O . . . you must meet her – absolutely my favourite woman. Here's the number. Not in the book of course.'

'And Henry Green you must telephone at his office.'

'*Merci mademoiselle, merci monsieur, merci M. Leishmann.*'

~

Elsa stepped over her morning's breakfast and got into bed. From the bed she took off her sweater, then her brassiere and bunged them across the room on to the armchair. It had been wonderful. Colette Lutschberg was a dear: and if she would really find a publisher for Miss Compton Burnett and Henry Green too of course – it would be just marvellous. O goody goody. And Stanways and Leishmann so cooperative. Poor Brinkley, he was overtired – overtired from underworking as usual. And limited by not having a philosophical mind. But he shouldn't snoop at her telephone conversations. She picked up a book. *The When and the How: Studies in the phenomenological approach,* translated from the

German by — . Then another: *The Metaphysics of Classical Humanism. Six lectures delivered at Lyon University. La Crise de l'homme.* That looked better. And then from underneath the impressive review copies which she had magpied home from the magazine, she dragged her favourite bedside book: *Leadguts: The autobiography of a killer.*

'It was outside Club Sewannée that I noticed her. A real minkie and no ersatz. Blue pelt, long dark hairs down the spine of each skin, shined full cuffs and boy! what lapels – and inside a tall big-eared blonde with airborne breasts and thighs that looked like they'd never faulted. Real class: it made me want to give her a burst right there in the street.'

She dozed off.

Poor Brinkley: it was two years now since he'd been 'creative'. He returned to the house where he lived alone and there, as the door closed behind him, his dead wrapped themselves around him like falling snow – His dead wife, his dead friend, his dead fathers – spiritual and temporal – illumined with their flowing intermittence, the tossing thickets of furniture which the china objects festooned like orchids. For when we die we become what we have loved and those who had loved Brinkley had to put up with this forest of sea-symbols, his brittle weeds and water-babies with a hand off here and a spout broken there, but otherwise – for he was a perfectionist – alarmingly complete. Who was he? The long gilded glasses could not tell him, the mahogany wardrobe with its full length mirror returned only its customary good-night self-portrait: average height, round vacant face, uneasy eyes, receding hair. A prosperous slab of middle-aged jetsam washed up with its trail of murders and griefs almost obliterated. 'Who the hell are you?' he tried again, glaring at his reflection. 'And who the hell cares?' Only the dead could have told him and that night they were not at home. He looked round the bookshelves, lined with fallen favourites, for he seldom read anymore and when a book was taken out it was not returned to its place but laid on its side on the top of the bookcase, or somewhere near to it;

among the little piles which had expired within sight of their cases. China now hung like Spanish moss from many of the bookcases. Sèvres and Vincennes, Worcester, Chelsea and Bow, everything that was softest in soft paste, creamy and coloured and frivolous and cosy: the soul of a great-aunt. After touching one or two, he got into bed and picked up his own well-thumbed feuilleton: Goldprick: the richest man in the world.

'But the best things in life are free?'

'If you've got enough money, everything is free.'

'Do you find that money can buy happiness, Mr. Goldprick?'

'Money buys money unless you're a bloody fool,' he ruminated.

'And how are you spending your money these days, Mr. Goldprick?'

'I don't spend my money: my money spends me.'

'But on what? Our readers would be privileged if you told them.'

'About a hundred thousand pounds ago? – that's what you time-is-money people would call half an hour. I had a brainwave. To give the most expensive dinner ever given in this world – or any other world. I'm just composing the menu. Within the next million dollars my folk will be building a bathysphere and that bathysphere will descend to the greatest known depth of the world's oceans – about a million Swiss francs away from New Guinea I guess to fish up the cheeks of those little neon-lit fishes – just the cheeks mind you. Millions of dollars of young men will be helicopting over Siberia for dinosaur's eggs – and at untold expense an expedition will be fitted out for the main dish. Salad of Mars-and-Venus weed – that's great. Okapi steaks, Tasmanian tiger, Hardwick's civet. They can't make animals extinct fast enough for my menu to catch up on them. I'll end by eating the Great Bear.'

'And for drink?'

'Heavy water.'

'And the guests?'

'No guests.'

'No guests, Mr. Goldprick. Not the Nizam, Mr. Patino, Gulbenkian, the man from Texas, Morgan, Rockefeller, King Farouk?'

'Those guys stink poverty to me, Mr. Brinkley. I guess some of them are so poor they have to tip. I shall dine alone. And now, get yourself a trillion billion platinum piles away from here. I've got a man coming who's going to find me a planet the size of a clove.'

'Good-night Mr. Goldprick.'

'Good-night and God bless.'

~

It was not till three or four in the morning that his father made an uneasy appearance. They drove in a cab up the hill, the horse walked slowly. Brinkley tried to will each moment to last. His aunt sat beside him. 'Well, Sprat, I think you've got everything. Everything that a little gentleman ought to have. He's got – let me see – he's got his woollen pants and his little woollen vests, and he's got his summer pants and his little summer vests, and he's got his shoes and his brushes and his coat and his pillow slip. Most particular about that they were – and he's got his play-box full of grub and if he wants anything more he'll have to ask the matron. You will, won't you, Sprat?' She turned big eyes upon him.

'AND he's got –' his father trumpeted, '– And he's got his cricket bat. No point in getting the best, old boy, because we know you'll soon grow out of this one, but good willow and I hope you'll practise at it. Not that it leads to anything – but I was just good enough to play at a few country houses – and I had an absolutely TOPPING time.'

'Look, there's the Abbey cemetery,' said his aunt. 'That's where your grandfather is buried and your great-grandfather and your great-grandmother and all the funny old uncles and aunts."

'Never left us a penny, damn then,' barked his father.

'Oh, Matt!'

The cab turned up a drive and came to a stop before the school. There was Mrs. T. who seemed always tired and cross and Mr. T. with his violent temper, his B.A. and M.A. and his bushy eyebrows, and there were two other little new boys beside their wooden play-boxes. His father had told the cab to wait: his aunt exchanged lists with Mrs. T.

'He's such a jolly little chap,' he heard her say. 'On Sunday he wears sailor trow-trows.'

The two new boys glared. His father chewed one point of his military moustache. 'Good-bye Major,' said Mr. T. 'We'll look after him.' His aunt said she must give him a great big hug. His father squeezed his hand: 'Work hard and play hard –' they got into the cab which turned round the gravel sweep past the laurestinus shrubbery and creaked down the road. His father sat with his stick between his knees, handsome and military, twiddling the knob. His aunt waved. The tombs in the cemetery stood out against the fading afternoon. Mr. and Mrs. T. pushed the three little boys through the green baize door beyond which stretched a long boarded corridor, gateway to privation. This time yesterday, he thought, he would be in his bath. His father came in to observe the ritual. 'I've come to note the habits of the wild and woolly wombat in its lair.' Jonathan Brinkley roared and splashed. 'I judge the specimen to be about seven years of age, and certainly amphibious.' 'Ho. Ha. Hee.' 'The wild and woolly wombat will now emerge from his lair and be careful to dry between the interstices of his toes.' 'Ho ho ho.' He looked around and burst suddenly into uncontrollable sobbing. The two new boys looked on: one began to cry in silence. The other sat on his play-box and mimicked. 'On Sunday he wears sailor trow-trows.' A gas-jet lit up their drawn faces. The flame burst forth in an interminable metallic sigh.

Forty odd years of not quite growing up snapped together like a telescope. The snow fell thick and fast. The big Rolls from London gave one final discreet rattle and stopped on the hill. The sexton and his men helped the London drivers out with the coffin, the six of them shouldered it, 'A nice bit of elm,' the undertaker had called it. 'You could have pine. But you can't do better than a nice bit of elm.' A hundred pounds for as many miles, the last journey of Brinkley's father had been his only extravagance: a man who, though crippled with arthritis, would not buy an overcoat or stop a taxi which was going the wrong way as turning round added to the fare. Behind the coffin Brinkley and his second wife followed with their flowers and the mimosa for her which his aunt had wired him to buy. The service was soon over: the clergyman had a cockney accent which Brinkley found disconcerting. 'There are three other funerals waiting,' explained the sexton, whose father had been a gardener to Brinkley's grandfather. 'This cold spell knocks 'em off.'

The grave seemed fantastically lonely and deep – the golden local stone showed at the bottom, beside the cross to his father's mother. The February afternoon was appallingly cold. The coffin went down. Some gravel rattled after it. Brinkley flung in some mimosa and narcissus on which the snow was already beginning to fall. Seventy-six years of fear and caution and loneliness and collecting and poverty and vintage port, of fair play and bark worse than bite lay inside it, bitter with arthritis and alcohol. A real gentleman, the sexton said, pocketing a pound with another for the bearers. They walked in the falling dusk down the cemetery path to where the Rolls was stuck and all fell to heaving it out of the drift. 'Hurry up,' said the Rector. 'I want to get on with my job.' Patiently in their wooden caskets the other new boys waited. Through the falling snow Brinkley looked up the hill from the living graveyard to the playing fields and the dark buildings of the dead school. The Rolls was moved, the bearers moved on. The Brinkleys got into the car and began their journey back to London; the memory was so recent and acute that he heaved out of bed, rushed down to the library and looked up the sonnet of Laforgue, which he held to his wound like a barber's styptic.

> *Je songe à tous les morts enterrès d'aujourd'hui.*
> *Et je me figure être au fond du cimetière*
> *et me mets à la place, en entrant dans leur bière,*
> *de ceux qui vont passer là leur première nuit.*

That was only the beginning of his father's death. Weeks later, the afterdeath set in – a vindictive eruption of trunks and boxes full of tram tickets, bus tickets, used envelopes, odd socks, old newspapers and theatre programmes, bundles of receipted bills – everything he had through a long life been too frightened to throw away. Cases of hideous objects resembling fossilised faeces 'not worth twopence of course, old boy, but might come in useful some day' – shrapnel fragments, bits of the Zeppelin that was shot down over Potter's Bar. The invasion nearly succeeded but the basement of the old house proved unexpectedly roomy. Asphyxiation was avoided. The lava flow of junk and rubbish stored harmlessly away.

Christopher Carritt was as much lord of the morning as Brinkley, a 'couche-tard', maggoted by the night. He woke in his distant flat in Kensington as the other fell into uneasy sleep, and then tottered over to inspect his profile. His red hatchet-face leered back at him, sandy eyebrow, cold china-blue eye, goatish nose and chin. Lips like thin elastic bands, skin of porous terra-cotta. They smiled at each other, both having long forgotten what they once looked like. Hangover? Under control. Expense? Dinner: three pounds ten. Drink: five pounds ten. Result of expense? A solemn wink informed the reflection that it had been money well-invested. The sex part had been soon over, then the weekend in rich hard-boiled racing circles clinched in a wedding of engagement books. Bomthorpe Towers . . . it sounded promising. He retched with a sudden twinge of nausea; her hair, black and dead as Indian ink, was certainly dyed – but supposing, even in the dark, her other hair had been grey? How profoundly revolting. He performed an immediate ritual: washed his hands, urinated, washed his hands again, recited a fragment of Greek chorus incorrectly in a high chanting whinny, put on a clean white shirt, dark suit, black shoes, and counted his money. A Dexadrin tablet disappeared, his mouth closing on it like a steel clip.

> 'As I was going to St. Lukes
> I met a man with seven dukes.'

He muttered fearfully. Seven dukes. Devonshire. Met twice at dinner. Very amiable. Wellington. Always most amiable. One, two, three, four. Three more. Leeds. Well, after all, he is a duke. Alba. At the same dinner as the other two. Marlborough. Met in a nightclub. Now for the seventh. Never mind. He might turn up at Bomthorpe. Or on his way to work. He took one more reassuring look at his engagement book. Six dinners at the houses of six ladies aged from fifty-five to eighty, seven free lunches on publishers, editors, Americans and so on, five cocktail parties, three weekends booked up, not a care in the world. He sniffed the air. Unmistakeable. Kidney disease. Incurable. Yours, old boy. Unless you name that seventh duke immediately. The Duke of Windsor. Well, after all, why not?

Quiet on the bus, he undressed a few pretty girls in the advertisements of his newspaper, scanned the other passengers and, descending in Piccadilly, advanced on his favourite chemist's with a kind of strut. His whole appearance by now had a brassy look, as if Byron had survived Missolonghi and gone in for an old age on the boulevards. Hands in pockets of his overcoat (he called it 'great coat' now), black hat wedged over his face, all his hatches battened for action, he bore down on the passers-by with an expression between a leer and a grimace according to general prosperity and beddability of the person he confronted. A smell of cat or a lump of dogshit rocked his whole frame in a paroxysm of nausea, but a flurry of fur and orchid caused the end of his tongue to protrude through his tin mouth, and a smile of roguish complicity to linger there, while he assessed the cost and quality of the skins, jewellery if any, shoes, ankles, arms, neck, behind and tried to guess who owned this lady and whether she could be easily purloined.

In the chemist he drank a hangover medicine, and, more surreptitiously, a golden elixir. 'Has Lord Cramp been in this morning, Gubbins?' he asked in a doggy rattle from the chest which implied that he and Gubbins had a private joke about Lord Cramp together (there's a card for you) but also that he and Cramp were of the upper-draught drinking class, enveloped in the same Regency aura.

'No sir, his lordship hasn't put in so far. I hope he hasn't made a night of it.'

'I hope so too, Gubbins, not too good at his age.'

'I'll tell him you enquired, sir.'

'Well, how much do I owe you for this disgusting stuff? Why do we do it, Gubbins eh?'

'Ah sir, there's many ask me that. Seven and ninepence including yesterday.'

Carritt winced at the thought of the money. Too small for a cheque. Not worth breaking into a pound. It would take up all his silver for cigarettes. Write to your mother today. 'Just put it down then, will you.' His voice had grown cold, off-hand and almost an octave higher, no longer an embattled dandy but a small boy trying it on.

'Very good, sir.'

For a second the play-acting cracked: Gubbins the tradesman glared at his natural enemy, the perpetual bilker; then Carritt reached the door and slid up the street to his office. Here his Mayfair manner came off with his overcoat and he was suddenly the distinguished man of letters, vague, self-deprecating and appearing to depend entirely on his secretary. 'Can you remember if we said there was anything we must do today, Miss Warren?' He counted nine unused matches and three used ones in his box. Seventeen cigarettes. Two and a half hours to lunch. He put out his engagement book and waited for the telephone to ring. 'Lord Chesterfield and his cronies,' he dictated rapidly, 'is not only an entertaining piece of hospitality about that much maligned wit and man of fashion but an excellent birthday present for a young man with his way to make in the world – and *le monde* as well, both 'grand' and 'petit'. Whether we should really have thought the manners of these grandées (one more cigarette and you'll get cancer of the tongue) quite as impeccable and 'rougetalon' (he spelt it out) as did the habitués of Lord Chesterfield and Lady Hervey is open to doubt but I can confidently recommend this half-humorous and excellently illustrated appraisal. New paragraph. Spotlight on murder. Admirers of transatlantic briskness who take their Hammett straight and their O'Hara over bourbon'. There was definitely a small hard button forming at the side of his tongue which he could feel against his teeth. Miss Warren's collar needed brushing. Her breasts. He recoiled from what he imagined

357

them to be but it was too late to stop now: off came her skirt, down went her long woollen pants, he was in bed with her skinny ageing suburban body pressed against him. 'Miss Warren,' he gasped.

'And their O'Hara over bourbon,' she repeated.

He gummed his eyes to the ceiling. 'Who killed Dwight Von Vreeland at the almost maddeningly exclusive Tupelo Club?' he continued. 'It certainly wasn't Luella Dupree.'

～

A midmorning nightmare of exceptional intensity woke Brinkley with a bellow of pain which, though deafening in his dream, emerged like a faint whimper of a sleeping dog. No! His first wife like a dark Greco-Roman ephebe was pointing at her new male genitals. 'Look darling, I've got something you'd like – a surprise.' He moved towards her to reward her devotion and trust – when one of those drunken bitches detained him. She is still waiting, still sadder and sorely dismayed. Her surprise has gone utterly wrong and never can he get her to explain that of all things it is what he most desired. The catfish, its head grotesquely bigger than its body, that he has played for hours like the monster in The Southerner gives up at last and with a great yoick he heaves it to the land. Who is it? 'Daddy!' 'Put me back at once!' his father barks.

Blasphemy intolerable – the noble gills are firmly hooked, the grizzled slime-coated moustache chewed with impotent rage. Brinkley lays impious hands on his only begotten NO NO NO! He woke again, a man to whom unforgivable things had been said. Put it this way. Owing to certain actions, certain lack of actions, since a very early age those who entrusted him with their happiness had been most basely betrayed and been driven to say intolerable things which he could never put out of his mind. 'Every grey hair your mother has, she owes to you.' 'Daddy!' 'You were my rock. For nine years I was faithful. I thought if I knew one man well enough I knew them all.' 'I am offering you the devotion of a lifetime.' 'You have the gift of destroying not only your own happiness but the happiness of all who love you.' How well they expressed themselves! Picked it up from him. It might have been all right if he was Byron and couldn't help it – but he wasn't. He knew he worked really hard to get people to love him to the point at which he could feel sure enough of them to hate them. His betrayals followed a seven-year cycle. He selected his victims and prepared them for sacrifice while pretending that they had selected him. And when he had forced them to desert him he became real to himself. He was like a faulty machine in which some malfunction led to the continual amputation of arms and legs in those who looked after it, because all the time it really was a machine precisely for amputating arms and legs. A safety razor for cutting throats. But the razor was a man and one who wanted above all to be kind. The guillotine had a conscience. Brinkley had never killed anything larger than a fly or a mosquito. He helped wasps and spiders, liked snakes and rats, stroked the milkman's pony: it would be very hard to find a single person on whom he had played a dirty trick. He didn't read letters, make mischief, do down people in their careers or make trouble between husbands and wives, or children and parents: he was generous to friends, mild to his enemies and he paid most of his debts. It was only in his central relationships that he struck through a dense fog of pity, guilt and hate. He had given up all excuses. He was a machine for slowly breaking hearts that people might learn, too late, never to part with them. That was all one could say and even now, the machine was beginning to fall to pieces. Miserable Orpheus who, turning to lose his Eurydice, beholds her for the first time as well as the last. In the dismal and decorative decay of European culture Brinkley and his moribund magazine had a role which obscured his more secret and fatal function, but he could never quite believe in it. Hating blame, he yet found praise all dust and ashes. Helping young writers? But to what did he help them? To jog on for a year or two in the vain hope that they were going to make an income by their writing while the opportunity for earning any other kind of living was inexorably withdrawn from them. J. Brinkley, B.A. Instructor in creative writing. Candidates prepared for the British Council and the administrative departments of the B.B.C.

And pooey on all the wise man braggeth
For pooey is the way the worldë waggeth

Brinkley's Aquitaine. This was the title of that perfect work of art –
travel-book in a sense, evocation of vanished beauty and pristine
freshness which formed a major defense of the guilty editor-publisher
against the horrors of his conscience. It was in a way just a guide book
to a certain part of France, to the provinces of Guyenne and Gascony,
the *département* of the Gironde and the valleys of the Dordogne and the
Garonne, the Tarn and the Lot. This was a book that American and
English publishers had advanced money for: it was for this Jane
Sotheran had taken photographs. It was also a kind of homage to all the
bottles of claret Brinkley had drunk. A vinous and grateful exhalation
for all that had gone down before, and yet it was something greater – a
spiritual wedding of the English genius with the broad provinces of the
South West which had for so long belonged to us – as if the literature
which would have been made had Eleanor of Aquitaine's inheritance
remained in our hands, had Montaigne, Montesquieu, Fenelon, and so
many others been British subjects, humanising us from the Gironde and
keeping the centre of gravity of the combined realm around Winchester
and Southampton. Bristol and Plymouth had flowered into this ultimately civilised experience – Brinkley's Aquitaine. A sigh of blessedness
– and behind it lurked a further circle of perfection: the Roman
province of that name in the great days of the fourth century, the golden
decadence of Ausonius, the shining villas, the broad river, the city with
its temples and fountains, the poetry, the scholarship, the conversation,
the long afternoon of the classical world: Ausonius, Paulinus of Nola,
Sidonius Apollinaris: that was home. Ausonius – a chirpy scholarly
conventional dirty-minded old pedant with yet a strange lyrical gift for
portraying water and the life of the shore: those oysters from
Maveunes, full, fat and white, their succulence enhanced by a subtle
tang of the sea, Saintes, Blaye, Bordeaux and Argen, his three-river
world, his fat friend Theon hunting boars and writing verses among the
pine forests of the Médoc, sailing down to Pauillac under an awning to

swop poems with the scholar sage. The decadence which ennobled all the others because the sun was setting on what had been so incommensurately great, and which yet held nothing of decadence in it because the world was still so young.

Not one word of the book had yet been written, though nearly a hundred thousand had been paid for. It was all in the Guide Bleu anyway, and the escape from guilt had become but another source of guilt as is usual in the course of the disease.

～

Elsa's voice on the telephone was sepulchral. It was her dreaded 'before coffee' voice, hollow as a walled-up toad. Brinkley wavered at the other end of the line but decided it was too late to hang up. 'I just wondered how you were' which meant 'I have been alone for about half an hour and I can't stand it.'

'I can't talk yet. I haven't woken up properly. Lousy I expect.'

'It's half past twelve.'

'Goodness. Well, see you at the office this afternoon.'

'Oh you are coming in. Goody goody.'

He hung up dismally. Of course he was coming in. What about the days she didn't come in? All those hangovers. Worsted as usual.

Her telephone rang again. 'Hello. Oh hello.' Her whole manner changed. It was Paul, proprietor of the magazine and apt to be infinitely gloomier than she.

'How are you dear,' (he pronounced it in the American way to rhyme with 'freer'). 'Had your *café crème*?'

'No, worse luck.'

'Not had your *Wiener mélange*?' He had reached the stage when saying things in French, always as if they were more luxurious than they were, had become a kind of nervous tic.

'No. Do stop it.' A mirthless giggle showed that she had pleased him.

'And how was the publisher's soirée? Très élégante?'

'Hell, of course.'

'You didn't enjoy it,' he purred, '*ce n'était pas à ton hauteur?*'

'No, it was dreadful. All the old faces.' At the other end Paul became quite silent. He could wait like this for several minutes, too polite to terminate a conversation. 'Brinkley was there for a bit.'

'*Il était très brillant?*'

'*Pas tout à fait.*'

'Gracious! I don't know what's eating him.'

'Or what he's eaten.'

'For once he didn't talk about food.' Brinkley's greed was axiomatic, like Elsa's drinking and smoking. 'Pauly darling, could you just wait while I find a cigarette?'

'*Pas possible*,' said Paul. 'I'll say goodbye. See you this afternoon?'

'Yes, of course, will you be coming in?' she said.

'I think so.'

'Oh goody goody. Brinkley said he'd look in.'

'*Quel honneur.*'

'If luncheon permits.'

'And tea at The Dorchester does not encroach.'

'IF.'

They laughed and hung up together. She thought of Paul's thin, sad face, his bath running, the faint backwash from an atonal gramophone record, his money, his distinction, a faun whose summer afternoon had turned into a dark night of thought and horror. A person she could truly love because, being homosexual, he inspired no sexual ambivalence, she could not hate him for desiring her, or for desiring any other woman. In the sex-war, he was a kind of angel of Mons who was on her side. Elsa's intricate character defied analysis and yet certain central traits could be observed. She was a person whose one idea was power and who was quite unconscious of the fact. Art and friendship were her gods, power and the struggle for it, her real ends. What she called 'feminism' in her was a profound and fanatical desire for the domination of the male species which spared only those artists who were feminine and helpless, or those homosexuals who needed her support, whom she therefore despised but did not actively hate. The long battle on behalf of her friend which seemed to her to be all of her existence, was in reality a struggle to make them stick up for their rights, to make wives stand up to their husbands, study unarmed combat and finally strangle them from behind with a piece of cheese-wire. She hated men too much to be a lesbian and hated them the more because she needed them, a commando sergeant fighting behind the enemy lines and disguised as a very pretty girl – at the last moment of the Cold War, before all Anglo-Saxon men and women frankly admit they hate each other.

Elsa's instinctive grading of people:

1. Men.

Men A: Artists (including philosophers). Divided into Genius and Non-Genius. Non-Genius doesn't count. Genius divided into masculine (enemy) and feminine male artists (to be supported). Her lovers were taken from the former and discontinued when transferred to the latter.

Men B: Queers. Necessary allies in the sex-war because they hate husbands but not always to be relied upon.

Men C: Attractive men who are not artists. To be destroyed.

Men D: All other men, businessmen, etc. To be made use of.

2. Women.

Women A: Artists, Doctors etc. To be re-educated for combat, genius not essential.

Women B: Lesbians. Important role as goddess in the new society.

Women C: Friends. This included the three women whom she positively worshipped. Her gods, all unfortunately married.

Women D: Wives and normal women. These she despised. They deserved all they got.

~

In his life, Dick had never been very musical and disembodiment had not improved his ear. The theme song of 'Laurel and Hardy' from Robert le Diable had been his favourite but now he could only introduce himself into Brinkley's unconscious by the first few bars of the Bach voluntary played at his memorial service. It had a certain jollity but even so remained elusive. At last, summoning all the power of his scattered atoms, he mastered it and blew the air into the mind of the dozing Brinkley. Dick! The memory of his dead friend suffused him: the dead take with them their love for us and return it only in dreams until there is no one alive to love us and so we die and dream ourselves back through others. Brinkley recalled first the physical presence: a very tall man and very thin, but without any of a thin man's characteristics. He was what might be called a bad fifty with a large brown open air bald head, too burnt to be attractive, a little greying hair, a long crudely indented face with a projecting upper lip, mark of petulant sensuality and an obstinate cleft chin, the eyes brown and doglike, becoming slightly bloodshot with drink, immensely expressive.

His body was untidy and gangling, a long sway back threw his stomach slightly forward, his legs kept crossing themselves when he walked, his long arms wandered outward. Appallingly dressed, usually in filthy flannel trousers with a Mosleyite black sweater and a ruined mackintosh it was impossible to situate the immense charm which radiated from this uncouth old schoolboy. How can one define it? He had once been incredibly handsome, a Sargent drawing of the 1914 subaltern come to life, a young man superbly gentle with women and horses, with spaniel eyes and otter moustache. Except of course that he hated both. And then this handsome young man of tall athletic build had somehow camouflaged himself into middle age. His nails were always black, his fly buttons undone, his great nose like a blue lump of ice with hairs in it, his teeth yellow and irregular, his chin unshaven, his odour one of tarry anti-scurf preparations. The charm is still hardly adumbrated! In what did it repose? His gait, perhaps, which was somehow shambling and unsuspecting like an elephant wandering into a trap, his voice certainly, which was deep and friendly, a casual English quality, an aristocratic innocence? Eccentricity? Something more than that. The consciousness that he was 'Dick', an actor acting a part but the part was himself and so no acting was necessary. When everyone else acted what they would like to be, he acted what he was. With infinite self-humour. Of his teeth, his baldness, his snoring, he would say that anyone could get women without these disadvantages, his gambling spirit was amused by them, besides, women liked a man who snored. It reassured them when they woke in the night.

He was always accompanied, like a god or a saint, by certain properties. A tin of Egyptian cigarettes, often unopened, for his tobacconist delivered them weekly to a long-standing order with which he could never keep up. A medicine bottle or so containing Valerian and other simple sedatives, an array of broken pencils and fouled biro pens bespeaking the artist and the journalist. A large shabby black notebook full of cryptic half-lines like '2.30 Don't Forget,' 'Blue tie, Toothbrush moustache. Influential,' 'small breasts, tight bottom, free on Wednesdays' sandwiched with lawyers' letters and one or two unsubtle trout-flies – and, heaviest of all, a large silver flask containing some very good whisky with a little water, for a slow and regular flushing of the lively faculties. Matches, string, paints, photographic proofs, negatives of nudes, bazaars and ruined casbahs, a letter, most important, about rents and rates, iodine, Benzedrine, anti-anxiety pills, the address of a negress – it all mounted up but the individual quality is still wanting. Don Giovanni in rags, Don Quixote, as a painter, a schoolboy of 60, Kipling MacTurk as Ancient Pistol, we are getting a little nearer. A face of a Rouault clown with a suspicion of the Western Desert, Secret Service and the Chelsea Arts ball – a battered Bulldog Drummond? Certainly doggy: he looks like a dog, he smiles like a dog, he eats like a dog, pushing a handful of food on to the fork, much of which slops off, pushing too his face down to the plate to meet it, and snap, engulfing as much as he can within the barrier of his yellow false teeth. He eats in fact more like wolf than dog; cutlery must be very strong and fingers kept well out of reach or he will do for them. When the mouthfuls are too large bits hang out of his mouth and plop back on the plate while he glowers about him. A man who must have been in considerable danger of starvation in his period of lactation and spoon-banging infancy, in fact a younger brother. One who never has had enough to eat and so can never get fat, even when he eats his way, as is frequent enough, twice round a thousand franc Burgundian menu. Dear darling irresistible Dick, a man for whom women have taken under-overdoses and jumped at night, fully dressed, into shallow ponds.

Dick is nothing without his home. To know where he lives is to grasp his charm. A lane branches off from a Sussex road and descends steeply through fallen gates. We pass a large wood of Spanish chestnut redolent of bracken and stink fungus, an invisible stream descending through willow and dogwood. Then we are at the door of the Mill. The car, a rakish Railton with seats like hassocks reposing on rusty side-curtains, goes into a wooden garage. In the crisp night air the mill race vibrates with rushing ecstasy. A latch is lifted, the luggage carried along a paved walk, we enter the magic abode. The latticed bedroom windows open to the monotonies of the weir, paintings, the Chirico house, the flowers are as we left them, the usual books are by the bed. Downstairs there are two rooms, a sitting room, small, snug, well-heated, with rather feminine furniture, vellum-bound books damp with mildew, wax-fruit, Victoriana, large paintings stuck with feathers, horse-hair, artificial jewels – across the hall is the dining room with a big open fire and a long oak table where many decanters repose: cut-glass electuaries in which breathe their last the fabulous pre-phylloxeras. Reverentia! The food is always rustic and simple: some potted shrimps and fried sole – or perhaps stewed eel from the pond – washed down with delicious hock or Chablis, then a boiled chicken or a rabbit pie to introduce the vista of clarets, 1924, 1920, 1906, 1899 – Margaux Château d'Issan, Cheval Blanc, Ausone, which a stilton and celery usher out with a fanfare of Bath olivers, and apples, nectarines, nuts with a '21 Yquem till the port is ready.

The logfire crackles, the decanters revolve. The icy sweetness of the Sauternes inflaming the claret-fragrant faces. Arguments begin, the men grow angry, the women diplomatic to the point of panic. A faint wild-boar reddening of the cornea is Dick's danger signal. Brinkley's face appears injected with beetroot, his expression of diffident indecision gives way to that of a Roman bully. Christopher Carritt's voice rises to a screech, Jane Sotheran looks as if she is going to cry with perplexity.

Elsa's eyes grow small and pig-like, her nose points upward, her expression suddenly becomes evil and obstinate. She despises all this cork-sniffing. One because really intellectual men don't do it, two because women don't go in for it at all, three because a drink is a drink anyway and why fuss about it, four because they all taste the same to her. Occasionally she lights up and smokes over the exquisite Tuke Holdsworth and Dick has been known, dropping a chicken bone from his fangs, to take her cigarette out with one hand and give her a fierce slap with the other. Paul, to whom she turned for rescue could only giggle helplessly and murmur, 'Well, well. Gracious.'

For a long time after dinner the little sitting room would spin round and round. Somehow people got to bed, the men going out to urinate on the lawn in the cool night air, the mill-race whispering, the owls hooting in the apple trees, the nightjar chugging in the wood. In the scented double beds the quarrelling couples smacked and copulated, collapsing into country sleep; below in the sitting room Dick and some tusky bachelor, long expelled from the herd, argued over wives and painting, drinking cold beer in china stoops, Dick in his favourite stance, one hand scratching his bottom, the other with his mug as he stood in front of the fire. 'Waal, yaas,' he would drawl, 'if you admit that is wrong, you simply prove my point. She left you to see if you would go after her.'

'Then why did she take the typewriter?'

'Because then you'd have to go after her.'

'I wish I could believe you!'

Breakfast brought surprisingly few hangovers; the mild sweet air and the rusty aperient drinking water (palatable only in whisky or tea) seemed to take care of them. Sausages, fried eggs and Sunday papers. The morning flew by and soon the Captain, as he was locally called, and his guests were out on the croquet lawn. This was a steep little plot punctuated with decaying pomifers. The hoops were set at all angles and the balls always toppled to the bottom of the hill. In fine weather it took more than an hour to complete the nine shot hoops at simple golf-croquet. One was tempted to pick the whole lawn up and shake the balls through as in a pocket puzzle. Dick, the proud inventor of the game, was always the worst at it, his surprise and screams of rage never varied, he regained authority only by enforcing his own rules. At the foot of the tiny sloping lawn was the straggling mill-pond with its willows and water-lilies and the pair of sullen swans that nested there every year. There were geese in the field, moorhens on the stream, mason wasps in the brick terrace, a swarm of wild bees in the red-tiled roof, the croquet balls sometimes cannonaded into the farmer's heifers or rolled down into the lake. The prevailing mood of the place was autumn: morning mist, sunny days, damp evenings, a fire on the hearth, the croquet balls clicking and tocking in the fading daylight, geese honking, Dick's curses sounding like shrieks of agony, the leaves turning on dogwood and balsam poplar, the chestnuts bricking the woodland paths. Wine-hallowed, priapic host, and holy ground.

Younger son of younger son, his elder brother and his elder cousin has been killed in the 1914 war, his uncle had left him a vast inheritance. The getting rid of this had taken him some twenty years while he listened fascinated to the fall of the auctioneer's hammer. Farms, properties, a great country house, Sargent portraits of Edwardian beauties, state papers, rare books, away they went and in came the blondes and the racing cars, the cases of champagne. Rum le tum, rum le tum, tiddely dum, piddely bum! He signed off with his Laurel and Hardy theme and Brinkley jumped suddenly out of bed, ran to the bathroom and turned on the geyser. Five minutes to one: the hooter from a distant factory reminded him of many mornings he had reached the bathroom at precisely that moment, always with a luncheon date at one fifteen which he would reach at one thirty, wondering if it was noticeable that he hadn't shaved. A man of iron routine and clockwork habits. Always punctually twenty minutes late, one could put one's watch back by him. Lying in his bath he considered the plane tree waving through the uncleaned window. A south-west wind pummelled the branch with drifting raindrops. Bordeaux! He went over two valuable pieces of research which had occupied him of late. The main petrol pump at Bazas was outside the Cafe Ausone. The Château Ausone of the St. Emilian vineyard was reputed to stand on the site of the poet's villa. Bordeaux-Bazas, Ausonius, Montaigne, Montesquieu. Three humanists, that is to say, three very rich men.

Humanism is a club with an entrance fee of about a thousand a year. Lying back in the bath, Brinkley considered his prison. What does humanism mean? Deism means believing in God, humanism means believing in man. And what does 'believing' mean? And what, above all, does 'in' signify? Deism does mean believing in God, humanism means believing only in a certain sort of man. A bare-headed pipe-smoking essayist in loafers with an old car, a cottage and a cat. Humanists don't, of course, believe in women, any more than deists believe in goddesses. What went wrong? A humanist was once a person who believed in man rather than God, who accepted man as God, or as a possible God. Then at some time distinction ceases to be made between man and God and is made between one man who is more human than another because he has more scope for self-development.

A humanist is one who believes that humans have a better time than is generally thought. Humanists attract knighthoods and repel advances and science, humanists are reactionary, bitter and vindictive. I, Brinkley, am a humanist. He considered for a moment the group of humanists which formed the nucleus at that time of any literary function. Eliot, the humane deist, Maurice Bowra, David Cecil, Kenneth Clark, Raymond Mortimer, Osbert and Edith Sitwell, Elizabeth Bowen, Rosamond Lehmann, Cecil Day Lewis, Stephen Spender (left flank), John Betjeman, E. Sackville West, Roger Senhouse, Evelyn Waugh, Alan Pryce-Jones, Desmond MacCarthy (right flank). Rose Macaulay. E. M. Forster. Twenty humanists. V.S. Pritchett. William Plomer. Veronica Wedgwood. Graham Greene. Twenty four.

Common factors:

All are kind and tolerant except Evelyn Waugh. Age. Between 40 and 60 (Desmond MacCarthy, E. M. Forster, over sixty, both unlikely to turn up). Young humanists – John Russell, Philip Toynbee. Both perhaps still too young.

Ambition. All of these are ambitious people – they like publicity – and they are responsible people: they have several jobs. Governments have honoured all but the queerest. (One in three is queer.) Rose Macaulay is not ambitious. Of the twenty four humanists then, irrespective of whether they write as well, eight are publishers, others are middle-aged, all but two are ambitious, all have several jobs, nearly all live in London, one in three might be called creative. None are working class – i.e. below a certain income group or educational level. Six (one in four) are indubitably upper-class, five are women (one in five), one in four went to Eton (seven out of twenty four).

The day's research over, Brinkley whizzed out of the bath, dried himself on the wettish towel and ran back to dress. The whole house was in mourning for his second wife. She had left him: he had got her to leave him – he loved her. Nothing more was sent to the laundry, no letters were answered, no china was bought, the bell rung, the telephone tinkled. The milk arrived on the doorstep, the bills for newspapers plopped through the letter-box, a man came with archaic implements to cut off the gas. The house was in mourning because in the game of mutual masochism, each pretending to hurt the other, she had been hurt seriously and by leaving him had given him such offence that he could not ask her to come back. And so now he had put his house into bachelor mourning. Nothing must be removed, the game of cat and mouse must be played with the essential services: the telephone would cut off, mea culpa, mea maxima culpa, to ward off some much more serious, even imaginary danger and guilt.

Poetry – My First and Last Love
(1974)

I have loved poetry and occasionally written it since I was six. I should find it harder to do without than any other branch of literature and be still hard put to it to say whether I preferred it to music or painting.

Of my twelve favourite writers only Petronius, Montaigne, Flaubert and Proust wrote in prose: the rest are all poets. Many people like poetry of one kind or another so I shall not try to explain what I mean by it or why I enjoy it but confine myself to what some poets have meant to me.

Fortunately the procession of poets through my life has been almost chronological; I started my puberty with Homer and ended it with Eliot; since then I have only had to accommodate a few contemporaries like Auden, Lorca and Dylan Thomas and now I'm racing back to Homer again. Without making extravagant claims for the written word one must point out that poetry is the supreme form of communication, that in an ode of Horace or a poem by Po Chii-i we are totally united with the makers, even though every external circumstance connected with their lives and environment be completely unfamiliar. Without Horace and Virgil, Roman Britain would seem absolutely meaningless and so would Rome itself, nor would the Greeks be the 'Greeks' except by our fusion with their minds through Homer, Plato or Sophocles.

I have just been reading Diogenes Laertius's lives of the Greek philosophers. Of Pyrrho, the famous sceptic, he writes "A friend of his used to say he was most fond of Democritos and then of Homer, continually repeating

As leaves on trees, such is the life of man

371

and he would quote these verses as well:

> Come my friend you must die.
> What tears can help your need?
> Patroclus also is dead, a better man far than you.
> See what a man am I, strong of body and fair to view
> A kingly father begot me, I was born of a goddess's womb.
> But over me too stand death and overmastering doom.

That translation is by C. M. Bowra; the words are those which Achilles uses to Lycaon before he kills him. They appealed to Pyrrho (360–270 BC) for their universal application. I learnt the Greek by heart one afternoon at Oxford after catching Bowra's enthusiasm. It seemed a magic talisman when he recited it. So poetry provides a connection with the mind of Pyrrho even as many quotations from the Bible have linked the generations.

When I first began to read poetry, in the latency period, it was the best-known Tennyson and Christina Rossetti that I liked, especially 'Break, break, break' and 'Locksley Hall'. I needed what was melancholy and mysterious – Poe, even Longfellow; the trochaic metre touched some chord. This craving found fulfilment in the poetry of the Celtic revival which used to come at the end of anthologies around 1917.

> Twilight it is and the far woods are dim
> and the rooks cry and call . . .

wrote Masefield, and the Celtic twilight was infinitely richer. Forty years later I met in a Dublin pub an elderly man who had written under the pen-name of Seamas O'Sullivan and surprised him by knowing by heart one of his early poems:

> Softly they pass
> through the grey of the evening
> over the wet road
> a flock of sheep . . .

The Celtic Twilight was soon caught up by 'Georgian Poetry',

O'Sullivan, Colum, James Stephens and Katherine Tynan, by Rupert Brooke and Flecker, while the rhythm of my school's classical teaching embraced Horace, Catullus and Virgil. Horace can be apprehended at many levels; he was essentially a middle-aged melancholy perfectionist whose philosophy was one of controlled self-indulgence with flashes of patriotism, who liked a quiet country life, whose preoccupations were friendship, flirtation and death and who spent nine years on getting his book ready for press.

He is totally unsuited for schoolboy consumption and should be read only by elderly pessimists who enjoy Leopardi, Po Chii-i, Landor and Proust. It is typical that Auden in his later years, after 1960, began to home more and more on this mild domestic beam, which had already attracted Housman and MacNeice (who both translated the same ode), Pound (but not Eliot) and complex Edwardian light-weights like Eddie Marsh and Ronald Storis. Fortunately for schoolboys there is or was a whole tradition of Horace translation in the vein of light verse and it was possible to read Gladstone or Calverley without ever knowing what the poet was really trying to say. The Epistles, which are the quintessence of his sophistication, and have a technical mastery in which he joins company with Pope and Boileau, were hardly taught at all.

Virgil was gospel but I won't linger over him. I don't like most of the Aeneid or those parts of the Georgics which I had to copy out as a punishment; that leaves me with very little, only the Eclogues and some of the sublime set-pieces like the sea-music at the beginning of the Sixth Book of the Aeneid, the Sleep of Palinurus, or the story of Dido. He loses me on land with all those campaigns and combats or directions for pruning; and if there be a smell of opportunism about Horace, the smell of authoritarianism about Virgil is much more pronounced.

On the other hand Virgil probably remains the most gifted writer ever to have existed, for single-handed he produced a great work of art not flawed by unevenness like Shakespeare's or artificiality like Milton's or atrophying theology like Dante.

Virgil has one rival, Lucretius, whose epic, on 'The Nature of

Things,' has been called the greatest single achievement of antiquity; to him all lovers of genius instantly react. While Virgilian codices and commentaries were jealously guarded and survive in abundance, the manuscript of Lucretius nearly perished and he was long the subject of Christian detraction even as Epicurus, his master, was slandered by the Stoics. To deny the existence of the Gods, and in particular the Four Last Things, heaven, hell, death and judgment was extremely unpopular.

> As for the dog, the furies, and their snakes
> The gloomy caverns, and the burning lakes,
> and all the vain infernal trumpery,
> They neither are, nor were, nor e'er can be . . .
> Meantime, when thoughts of death disturb thy head
> Consider, Ancus great and good is dead;
> Ancus, thus better far, was born to die,
> And thou, dost thou bewail mortality? . . .
> The founders of invented arts are lost,
> and wits who made eternity their boast.

The whole passage echoes the words of Achilles to Lycaon which I quoted earlier except that we are more prepared to accept that Patroclus was a better man than ourselves than we are with the shadowy Ancus. And all is forgiven for Dryden's translation. He has to squeeze the longer Latin lines into the shorter English couplets, but the force and brutal simplicity of the original with its unexpectedly delicate imagery are preserved. Lucretius is perhaps too much the exponent of the philosophy of Epicurus to merit a claim to originality; yet his mind, with its grasp of science and poetry, was unique. 'Nothing exists but atoms and the void' taught Democritus, and Epicurus extended this to include an ethical system: life was an accident and happiness was to be enjoyed through freedom from superstition and freedom from the fear of death, through friendship, frugality and peace of mind, the private life reasonably well-disposed to others.

But Democritus, Epicurus and Lucretius were also governed by untiring intellectual curiosity, their prolific output was worthy of the French Encyclopaedists; and their point of view has given birth to a dynasty of writers, one of whom, Philodemus, who wrote Greek love epigrams, was the friend of Maecenas and so of both Virgil and Horace; he lived at Herculaneum, where his charred library was among the first things to be discovered.

Dryden's Juvenal is a lighter companion to his Lucretius and his contemporary Rochester, despite his exemplary death-bed conversion, was also inspired by the same philosophy:

> *Our sphere of action is life's happiness*
> *And he who thinks beyond, thinks like an ass.*
> *After death, nothing is, and nothing death*
> *the utmost limits of a gasp of breath.*

Some poetry appeals to us all through life, but most of it is governed by the laws of familiarity, and goes in and out of favour, as the passions which it illustrates wax and wane. The lover who has battened on Shakespeare or Catullus, on Donne, Byron, or Baudelaire, becomes the elderly cynic or busy tycoon. Finally the heart silts up, until the enjoyment of obituaries and the fear of draughts replace all other emotions.

Poetry, even the best, holds no brevet of immortality and is no more lasting than man's other creations. As civilisations die they become incomprehensible: every language will one day be a dead language and we ourselves wear out like washing machines and lose our zest for our memories. For this reason the poetry of mortality has the edge on the poetry of love; for the sentiment of transience remains with us longer, together with an abiding love of nature – in so far as we have not destroyed that as well:

> *Only thin smoke without flame*
> *from the heaps of couch grass,*
> *Yet this will go onward the same*
> *Though Dynasties pass*
>
> (Hardy)

375

Returning to the days of the Celts and the Georgians, when I first became poetically conscious and absorbed the Greek Anthology through Mackail, I realise that I missed a whole new continent which I was not to discover till ten years later – the poetry of China, which Arthur Waley was introducing from 1916 and 1918 onwards and Ezra Pound in 'Cathay' (1915) with Amy Lowell and the Poems of Li Po. This, like Yeats's Byzantium, is not a country for the young, but possesses one of the finest poets for the old in Po Chii-i (translated by Arthur Waley) as well as the bibulous Li Po, no less gifted, and the wonderful range of the Old Poems and the Book of Songs. Of the 'seventeen old poems' Waley says 'these poems had an enormous influence on all subsequent poetry and many of the habitual clichés of Chinese verse are taken from them.' They date from the first century BC. (In Classical poetry no one is original and nobody cares.)

> *Green rushes with red shoots*
> *Long leaves bending to the wind*
> *You and I in the same boat*
> *Plucking rushes at the Five Lakes*
> *We started at dawn from the orchid island:*
> *We rested under elms till noon.*
> *You and I plucking rushes*
> *had not plucked a handful when night came!*

And then there is the much commoner poetry of separation

> *The jewelled steps are already quite white with dew,*
> *It is so late that the dew soaks my gauze stockings.*
> *And I let down the crystal curtain*
> *And watch the moon through the clear autumn.*

(Li Po translated by Ezra Pound)

Tennyson is a poet for youth, Wordsworth for middle age. Tennyson always carries a hint of adolescence and one likes him best for his lyrics or for 'Maud', that drama of adolescence and revolt with its pulsing love songs, or for poems like 'Tithonus', which is a protest against old

age, or Ulysses, an incitement to further adventures. Wordsworth's
'Prelude' however is a complete great poem, an autobiography of the
mind in verse which towers over the monotonous mood sequences of
'In Memoriam'. Poetry lovers need them both and they lead on to Yeats,
Hardy, Eliot, Pound and Auden.

One of the advantages of reading poetry in later life is that one
rediscovers poems that are framed by early association. If one cannot
react in the same way to a passionate love lyric one can respond to the
memory of the young man who first read it and thought the millions of
words devoted to kissing perfectly natural. 'The moth's kiss first . . . the
bee's kiss now.' 'Full nakedness, all joys are due to thee.'

And then, occasionally, one comes, late in life, on a poem or poet one
had never encountered before and is agreeably surprised. In one or two
anthologies of mediaeval Latin, among the student songs or Carmina
Burana and the well-known drinking songs of the Arch Poet, one finds
the lesser known 'Rumor Letalis' translated by Kenneth Rexroth in
George Steiner's *Penguin Book of Modern Translation*, 'Poem into
Poem,' in which a lover reproaches his lost mistress for her plunge into
promiscuity. The end is magnificent:

> *O the heart-breaking memory*
> *of days like flowers, and your*
> *Eyes that shone like Venus the star*
> *In our brief nights, and the soft bird*
> *Flight of your love about me:*
> *And now your eyes are as bitter*
> *as a rattlesnake's dead eyes,*
> *and your disdain as malignant.*
> *Those who give off the smell of coin*
> *You warm in bed: I who have*
> *Love to bring am not even*
> *Allowed to speak to you now.*
> *You receive charlatans and fools;*
> *I have only the swindling*
> *memory of poisoned honey*

We have all, I fear, been through this experience: but why should another anonymous Latin poem, attributed to Virgil, though more in the vein of Petronius, the 'Copa' (or bar-maid) have such mysterious appeal? It is a hot afternoon; outside her wayside guinguette under its trellis of vine the Syrian bar-maid rattles her castanets – or plays a small bagpipe under her arm (Housman) – inviting the wayfarer to her wine and snacks, with her bed thrown in if he wants it: better enjoy it now, the drinks and the shade and her body – for death comes unexpected and even now may have tweaked your ear. The Latin, metallic in its purity, suggests a fine-quality mosaic: it is neither lyric nor epigram but somehow completely visual, like Rimbaud's 'Cabaret':

> Not one to be scared of a kiss and more,
> Brought the butter and bread with a grin
> And the luke-warm ham on a coloured plate
> Pink ham, white fat, and a sprig of garlic, and a great chope
>   of foamy beer
> Gilt by the sun in that atmosphere.

(translated by Ezra Pound)

One of the side-effects of my love of poetry is that I have been, ever since I can remember, literally taken possession of by stray lines of verse, have harboured them like maggots in the brain. I would write them down repeatedly on scraps of paper, burn them on doors, chant them in lavatories.

Recently two lines of the mediocre early Christian poet Prudentius stuck:

> mundum quem quisquis es coluit
> mens tua perdidit –

– he is reviewing his early life distastefully:

> The world that was yours you have ended by losing
> whoever you are, it was not God's choosing

Lately this has been replaced by two lines from Lorca:

> *aurique sepa los caminos*
> *yo nunca llegare a Cordoba.*

(although I know all the paths, I shall never get to Cordoba)

They are from the poem Cordoba, *lejana y fria* – faraway and cold, in which the gipsy comes nearer to death, which awaits him on the walls, though we are not told what he has done.

To read Lorca is to plunge into the Spanish Civil War, and his intolerable assassination at Viznar. I wondered if we had any English equivalent and found myself re-reading the most moving poem which the Spanish war produced; John Cornford's message to his mistress on his way to his death on the Aragon front. He was only twenty-one.

I omit the first verse:

> *The wind rises in the evening*
> *Reminds that autumn is near.*
> *I am afraid to lose you*
> *I am afraid of my fear*
> *On the last mile to Huesca*
> *the last fence for our pride*
> *Think so kindly, dear, that I*
> *sense you at my side.*
> *And if bad luck should lay my strength*
> *Into the shallow grave,*
> *Remember all the good you can:*
> *Don't forget my love.*

The lines lack the patina of Lorca, they tremble on the verge of banality; it might not have seemed such a good poem had he lived. But it is there, it will do.

The pieces in this volume originally appeared
in the following publications:

Enemies of Promise, part 3: A Georgian Boyhood *Enemies of Promise*
1938; A London Diary *New Statesman* 1937; The Art of Travel *The
New Keepsake* 1931; The Ant-Lion *Horizon* 1939/40; The Unquiet
Grave *The Unquiet Grave* 1944/5; Revisiting Greece: A Critic's
Holiday *Sunday Times* 1954; Living with Lemurs *Sunday Times*
1957; Confessions of a House-Hunter *Sunday Times* 1967; The
Downfall of Jonathan Edax *Sunday Times* 1961; Told in Gath *Parody
Party*, ed. Leonard Russell, Hutchinson 1936; Where Engels Fears to
Tread *Press Gang*, ed. Leonard Russell, Hutchinson 1937; Year Nine
New Statesman 1938; Bond Strikes Camp *London Magazine* 1963;
Happy Deathbeds *Open City* 1996; Poetry – My First and Last Love
Sunday Times 1974